MASTERING THE OLD TESTAMENT

THE COMMUNICATOR'S COMMENTARY SERIES
OLD TESTAMENT

- I *Genesis* by D. Stuart Briscoe
- II *Exodus* by Maxie D. Dunnam
- III *Leviticus* by Gary W. Demarest
- IV *Numbers* by James Philip
- V *Deuteronomy* by John C. Maxwell
- VI *Joshua* by John A. Huffman, Jr.
- VII *Judges, Ruth* by David Jackman
- VIII *1, 2 Samuel* by Kenneth L. Chafin
- IX *1, 2 Kings* by Russell H. Dilday
- X *1, 2 Chronicles* by Leslie C. Allen
- XI *Ezra, Nehemiah, Esther* by Robert M. Norris
- XII *Job* by David L. McKenna
- XIII *Psalms 1–72* by Donald M. Williams
- XIV *Psalms 73–150* by Donald M. Williams
- XV *Proverbs, Ecclesiastes, Song of Solomon* by David A. Hubbard
- XVI *Isaiah* by David L. McKenna
- XVII *Jeremiah, Lamentations* by John Guest
- XVIII *Ezekiel* by Douglas Stuart
- XIX *Daniel* by Sinclair B. Ferguson
- XX *Hosea, Joel, Amos, Obadiah, Jonah, Micah* by Lloyd J. Ogilvie
- XXI *Nahum, Habakkuk, Zephaniah, Haggai, Zechariah, Malachi* by Lloyd J. Ogilvie

MASTERING THE OLD TESTAMENT

NUMBERS

JAMES PHILIP

LLOYD J. OGILVIE, GENERAL EDITOR

WORD PUBLISHING
Dallas • London • Vancouver • Melbourne

[Formerly, *The Communicator's Commentary Series, Old Testament*]

Library of Congress Cataloging in Publication Data
Main entry under title:

Mastering the Old Testament
[The Communicator's commentary.]
Bibliography: p.
Contents: OT4. Numbers/by James Philip
1. Bible. O.T.—Commentaries. I. Ogilvie, Lloyd John. II. Philip, James, 1922–
BS1151.2.C66 1993 221.7′7 93-39330
ISBN 0–8499–3543–1 (v. OT4) [pbk]
ISBN 0–8499–0409–9 (v. OT4) [hd]

Printed in the United States of America

349 AGF 987654321

To
the growing band
of men
in Scotland
dedicated to
the recovery of
expository biblical
ministry

He which hath no stomach to this fight,
Let him depart. . . .
But we in it shall be remembered;
We few, we happy few, we band of brothers;
For he today that sheds his blood with me
Shall be my brother.

Shakespeare. Henry V. IV.iii.35

Contents

Editor's Preface 9
Acknowledgments 15
Introduction 17
An Outline of Numbers 25

1. The Numbering and Arrangement of the Tribes (1:1–2:34) 31
2. The Levites, Their Numbers and Duties (3:1–4:49) 45
3. The Cleansing and Blessing of the Congregation (5:1–6:27) 67
4. The Offerings of the Israelite Princes (7:1–89) 92
5. The Consecration of the Levites (8:1–26) 104
6. The Passover at Sinai (9:1–14) 113
7. The Divine Provision for the March (9:15–10:10) 118
8. From Sinai to Paran (10:11–12:16) 126
9. The Spies at Kadesh Barnea (13:1–14:45) 153
10. Various Laws and Regulations (15:1–41) 175
11. The Rebellion of Korah, Dathan, and Abiram (16:1–17:13) 186
12. The Service of the Priests and Levites (18:1–32) 204
13. The Laws of Purification (19:1–22) 214
14. From Kadesh to Moab (20:1–21:35) 222
15. The "Balaam" Incident (22:1–24:25) 241
16. Various Laws and Incidents (25:1–31:54) 265
17. Miscellaneous Topographical Narratives (32:1–36:13) 321

Epilogue 361
Bibliography 363

Editor's Preface

God has called all of His people to be communicators. Everyone who is in Christ is called into ministry. As ministers of "the manifold grace of God," all of us—clergy and laity—are commissioned with the challenge to communicate our faith to individuals and groups, classes and congregations.

The Bible, God's Word, is the objective basis of the truth of His love and power that we seek to communicate. In response to the urgent, expressed needs of pastors, teachers, Bible study leaders, church school teachers, small group enablers, and individual Christians, the Communicator's Commentary is offered as a penetrating search of the Scriptures of the Old and New Testament to enable vital personal and practical communication of the abundant life.

Many current commentaries and Bible study guides provide only some aspects of a communicator's needs. Some offer in-depth scholarship but no application to daily life. Others are so popular in approach that biblical roots are left unexplained. Few offer impelling illustrations that open windows for the reader to see the exciting application for today's struggles. And most of all, seldom have the expositors given the valuable outlines of passages so needed to help the preacher or teacher in his or her busy life to prepare for communicating the Word to congregations or classes.

This Communicator's Commentary series brings all of these elements together. The authors are scholar-preachers and teachers outstanding in their ability to make the Scriptures come alive for individuals and groups. They are noted for bringing together excellence in biblical scholarship, knowledge of the original Hebrew and Greek, sensitivity to people's needs, vivid illustrative material from biblical, classical, and contemporary sources, and lucid communication by the use of clear outlines of thought. Each has been selected to contribute to this series because of his Spirit-empowered ability to help people live in the skins of biblical characters and provide a "you-are-there" intensity to the drama of events of the Bible which have so much to say about our relationships and responsibilities today.

The design for the Communicator's Commentary gives the reader an overall outline of each book of the Bible. Following the introduction, which reveals the author's approach and salient background on the book, each chapter of the commentary provides the Scripture to be exposited. The New King James Bible has been chosen for the Communicator's Commentary because it combines with integrity the beauty of language, underlying Hebrew and Greek textual basis, and thought-flow of the 1611 King James Version, while replacing obsolete verb forms and other archaisms with their everyday contemporary counterparts for greater readability. Reverence for God is preserved in the capitalization of all pronouns referring to the Father, Son, or Holy Spirit. Readers who are more comfortable with another translation can readily find the parallel passage by means of the chapter and verse reference at the end of each passage being exposited. The paragraphs of exposition combine fresh insights to the Scripture, application, rich illustrative material, and innovative ways of utilizing the vibrant truth for his or her own life and for the challenge of communicating it with vigor and vitality.

It has been gratifying to me as Editor of this series to receive enthusiastic progress reports from each contributor. As they worked, all were gripped with new truths from the Scripture—God-given insights into passages, previously not written in the literature of biblical explanation. A prime objective of this series is for each user to find the same awareness: that God speaks with newness through the Scriptures when we approach them with a ready mind and a willingness to communicate what He has given; that God delights to give communicators of His word "I-never-saw-that-in-that-verse-before" intellectual insights so that our listeners and readers can have "I-never-realized-all-that-was-in-that-verse" spiritual experiences.

The thrust of the commentary series unequivocally affirms that God speaks through the Scriptures today to engender faith, enable adventuresome living of the abundant life, and establish the basis of obedient discipleship. The Bible, the unique word of God, is unlimited as a resource for Christians in communicating our hope to others. It is our weapon in the battle for truth, the guide for ministry, and the irresistible force for introducing others to God.

A biblically rooted communication of the Gospel holds in unity and oneness what divergent movements have wrought asunder. This commentary series courageously presents personal faith, caring for individuals, and social responsibility as essential, inseparable dimensions of biblical Christianity. It seeks to present the quadrilateral Gospel in its fullness which calls us to unreserved commitment to Christ, unrestricted self-esteem in His grace, unqualified love for others in personal evangelism, and undying efforts to work for justice and righteousness in a sick and suffering world.

A growing renaissance in the church today is being led by clergy and laity who are biblically rooted, Christ-centered, and Holy Spirit-empowered. They have dared to listen to people's most urgent questions and deepest needs and then to God as He speaks through the Bible. Biblical preaching is the secret of growing churches. Bible study classes and small groups are equipping the laity for ministry in the world. Dynamic Christians are finding that daily study of God's Word allows the Spirit to do in them what He wishes to communicate through them to others. These days are the most exciting time since Pentecost. The Communicator's Commentary is offered to be a primary resource of new life for this renaissance.

It has been very encouraging to receive the enthusiastic responses of pastors and teachers to the twelve New Testament volumes of the Communicator's Commentary series. The letters from communicators on the firing line in pulpits, classes, study groups, and Bible fellowship clusters across the nation, as well as the reviews of scholars and publication analysts, have indicated that we have been on target in meeting a need for a distinctly different kind of commentary on the Scriptures, a commentary that is primarily aimed at helping interpreters of the Bible to equip the laity for ministry.

This positive response has led the publisher to press on with an additional twenty-one volumes covering the books of the Old Testament. These new volumes rest upon the same goals and guidelines that undergird the New Testament volumes. Scholar-preachers with facility in Hebrew as well as vivid contemporary exposition have been selected as authors. The purpose throughout is to aid the preacher and teacher in the challenge and adventure of Old Testament exposition in communication. In each volume you will meet Yahweh, the "I AM" Lord who is Creator, Sustainer, and Redeemer in the unfolding drama of His call and care of Israel. He is the Lord who acts, intervenes, judges, and presses His people into the immense challenges and privileges of being a chosen people, a holy nation. And in the descriptive exposition of each passage, the implications of the ultimate revelation of Yahweh in Jesus Christ, His Son, our Lord, are carefully spelled out to maintain unity and oneness in the preaching and teaching of the Gospel.

It is a privilege to introduce to you the author of this very outstanding treatment of Numbers. James Philip is the Minister of the Holyrood Abbey Church in Edinburgh, Scotland.

In my search for scholar-preachers around the world to write the volumes of this Communicator's Commentary series, I wanted to include a biblical expositor from the Church of Scotland who is distinguished as a preacher, teacher, and pastor.

During my summer study leaves in Scotland, I visited with church leaders and old classmates from New College where I did my postgraduate studies years ago. I asked for recommendations of a Scots pastor who was making an impact and leading a dynamic church. James Philip's name kept resurfacing. He was held in esteem by fellow clergy. Church leaders expressed admiration for the success of his church. Laity and clergy alike noted his penetrating biblical messages at conferences throughout Great Britain.

My own experience of worship at Holyrood confirmed all of the positive comments I had received from others. I knew I was in for a stimulating time even before I entered the sanctuary. Standing outside of the church building, I watched the steady stream of people coming to the service. I was amazed by the broad spectrum of ages and kinds of people. Young couples, families, mature adults, singles, and a great number of students and faculty from the university made their way into the church with an air of expectancy and intentionality. The remarkable thing was that most of the people came with their Bibles in hand, and many, especially the students, had notebooks tucked next to their Bibles ready to take notes on the sermon.

The worship service in the full sanctuary was all, and more, than I had hoped it would be. Pastor Philip led the traditional order of worship with dignity and power. It was obvious that he knew and loved his congregation. His prayers were filled with a quality of compassion and empathy which drew us all into a fresh experience of the sovereignty and grace of God.

When the Word of God was read, the people followed, intently reading along in their own Bibles. As the sermon began, many opened their notebooks to record the salient steps of the carefully ordered outline of the passage Philip had selected for his exposition. Seldom have I witnessed a more attentive and receptive congregation. And for good reason. The pastor's verse-by-verse exposition was a magnificent blend of inspired teaching and commanding preaching. There was depth of insight and impelling admonition. I knew I was in a biblical church which centered its worship, life, and mission in the study of the Word of God.

In my correspondence and conversations with James Philip about writing one of the volumes of this series, I was delighted to learn that a recent focus of his study, preaching, teaching, and conference ministry had been in the Book of Numbers. I had known that it would be most difficult to find a skilled expositor to interpret with scholarly excellence and contemporary relevance this neglected portion of Scripture. It was encouraging to sense Philip's knowledge of the message of Numbers and his enthusiasm for communicating it to the church today. I was gratified when he agreed to write this volume, his first work to be published in the United States.

Among all of the Old Testament books, Numbers is one that is least understood and appreciated by the contemporary reader—and communicator. Except for gleaning an occasional illustrative story, we tend to overlook Numbers for teaching, preaching, and personal study.

But, in the hands of an able interpreter, Numbers becomes a seedbed for deep theological and practical truths. James Philip is such an interpreter. With his guidance, Numbers speaks relevantly and authoritatively to the church in our time.

James Philip has labored intensively to help us understand the historic intricacies of Numbers. He works carefully and wisely with the text, weeding out obscure interpretations while nurturing those which best reveal the truth of Numbers. Throughout this commentary, Philip interacts with other interpreters of Numbers. In particular, he connects his own reading to the best in Reformed and Evangelical scholarship.

James Philip writes as a pastoral theologian. Always keeping in view the life of modern day Christians, he approaches Numbers from a theological perspective. Philip is not satisfied with superficial applications of Numbers to our situation. Rather, he wrestles deeply with the theological significance of each passage. The commentary is theology at its best—biblical, evangelical, practical.

As Philip writes in his introduction, "The main part of Numbers deals with the experience of divine discipline in the wilderness." Israel's choice at Kadesh Barnea not to enter into the Promised Land stands at the center of Numbers. Therefore, as Philip sagely notes, "Numbers is a book that need not have been!"

But, with Philip, I thank God that Numbers does, indeed, exist today for our edification and growth in discipleship. The contemporary church needs to reckon with Numbers because we stand at our own Kadesh Barnea. We, like the Israelites of old, face the question of whether to move forward in the ministry of God's Kingdom—or to retreat into the security of the past. Perhaps Numbers, the book that need not have been, will help us to become all that God has called us to be. James Philip has labored, with notable success, to this end.

LLOYD OGILVIE

Acknowledgments

Thanks are due to the following writers and publishers for permission to use the undernoted copyright material:

The Lutterworth Press, Cambridge, for quotations from *The Mediator* and *The Christian Doctrine of Creation and Redemption,* Dogmatics, Vol. 2, by Emil Brunner.

The SCM Press Limited, London, and Westminster Press, Philadelphia, for quotations from *Numbers,* Old Testament Library, by Martin Noth.

Thomas Nelson and Sons Limited (Marshall/Pickering), Basingstoke, for a quotation from *Numbers* by N. H. Snaith.

The Cambridge University Press, Cambridge, for a quotation from *Numbers,* Cambridge Bible Commentary Series, 1976, by J. Sturdy.

The Manchester Guardian Weekly (*The Guardian,* Manchester), for a quotation from an article by Cecil Northcott, entitled "America Goes to Church," September 19, 1957.

The Inter-Varsity Press, Leicester, England, and Downers Grove, Illinois, for quotations from *Numbers,* Tyndale Old Testament Commentaries, by Gordon J. Wenham; for quotations from The New Bible Commentary (1953 edition) from *Numbers* by A. A. MacRae, and from The New Bible Commentary (Revised 1970), from *Numbers* by J. A. Thompson; and for a quotation from *An Introduction to the Old Testament,* 1949, by E. J. Young.

Introduction

A passage in Paul's first letter to the Corinthians (1 Cor. 10:1–11) points toward a Christian understanding of the Old Testament:

> 1 Moreover, brethren, I do not want you to be unaware that all our fathers were under the cloud, all passed through the sea,
> 2 all were baptized into Moses in the cloud and in the sea,
> 3 all ate the same spiritual food,
> 4 and all drank the same spiritual drink. For they drank of that spiritual Rock that followed them, and that Rock was Christ.
> 5 But with most of them God was not well pleased, for *their bodies* were scattered in the wilderness.
> 6 Now these things became our examples, to the intent that we should not lust after evil things as they also lusted.
> 7 And do not become idolaters as *were* some of them. As it is written, *"The people sat down to eat and drink, and rose up to play."*
> 8 Nor let us commit sexual immorality, as some of them did, and in one day twenty-three thousand fell;
> 9 nor let us tempt Christ, as some of them also tempted, and were destroyed by serpents;
> 10 nor complain, as some of them also complained, and were destroyed by the destroyer.
> 11 Now all these things happened to them as examples, and they were written for our admonition, upon whom the ends of the ages have come.

These verses crystallize the story of the Book of Numbers for us. The Old Testament story is designed in the providence of God to be an example for us in the Christian life, and the things we read there are so apposite to that life that they can be taken as direct and certain parallels.

The apostle writes in similar vein in Romans 15:4:

> 4 For whatever things were written before were written for our learning, that we through the patience and comfort of the Scriptures might have hope.

This does not mean that the Old Testament is not true or accurate history—that point is not in question. But its purpose is something greater and more important than the recording of the historical process: it is divine revelation, the unfolding of redemptive history in the context of God's dealings with His Old Testament people. As Paul makes plain, Christians may find encouragement and instruction for spiritual life through the reading of the Old Testament Scriptures and, discovering the principles by which God dealt with His people, can apply them in practical ways to their own lives. Looked at in this light, the study of the Old Testament ceases to be a piece of mere historical research having little relevance to daily living and becomes the living Word of God to men in particular situations. It is certain that in our study we shall find all kinds of situations in those far-off days giving forth principles of action, conduct, and thought which are desperately relevant for our time. There would be no point in studying it otherwise. This is the living Word of God, and nothing could be a greater misunderstanding than that we should think of such a study as some abstruse and irrelevant academic exercise. It is not the cloister but the battleground that is the proper environment for the reading of the Old Testament. It is a table prepared for us in the presence of our enemies.

That being said, we must now seek to put the Book of Numbers in its proper setting. The Bible is one book and its theme is one. There is an underlying unity in it, from Genesis through to Revelation, and we do not understand any particular book of the Bible until we see it in relation to the whole. Artists are said to know the right kind of frames to put their pictures in, and only a particular setting will bring out their hidden beauties and suggestions. This is true also in relation to the Scriptures. It is not possible to study the Book of

Numbers *in vacuo;* we need to see where it belongs and how it sits in the general picture.

Christ once said to the Pharisees, "You search the Scriptures, for in them you think you have eternal life; and these are they which testify of Me" (John 5:39). Until we grasp this key we shall never understand the Scriptures aright. The story of Christ starts long before Bethlehem. He is the eternal Son of the Father, the second Person of the Trinity, and belief in the Trinity commits us to the truth that He operated throughout history before His Incarnation. This is the point of Paul's reference to "that spiritual Rock that followed them" (1 Cor. 10:4). Christ was there with the children of Israel in the wilderness, the unseen Presence that guided them and directed them in all their way.

The Old Testament is about Christ. We do not mean by this that He is seen through abstruse and improbable allegorizing of certain passages or texts, but rather in the broad sweep of the story from beginning to end. The Old Testament is the history of the promised Seed, the Seed of the woman (Gen. 3:15), the Seed of Abraham (Gen. 15:5), who was to become the Redeemer of the world. Significantly, Matthew begins his Gospel with the words, "Jesus Christ, the son of David, the son of Abraham." This serves to gather together the whole story of the Scriptures, from Genesis through to the New Testament, into one underlying basic theme, with Jesus Christ at its center. Until we grasp this we will understand neither the Book of Numbers nor any other book of the Old Testament as we are meant to.

Historically, so far as the story of God's people is concerned, Numbers follows the end of Exodus. Indeed, its first verse follows close upon Exodus 40:2ff., with no more than a month elapsing between them. A brief recapitulation of the "story" unfolded up to this point may be useful.

In the beginning God made man in His own image, made him for fellowship with Himself and ordained for him a destiny bright with hope and promise. But sin entered the world, a tragedy overtook the divine creation, and whereas in the beginning all was light, now sin entered and brought darkness. In the opening chapters of the Book of Genesis, it is rather as if one went into a room and switched on the light, which straightway fuses. In that momentary flash from the bulb there is just enough light shed through the room to let one see the position of the furniture in the room, before darkness came down. In the beginning, there was just enough light to show us what was meant to be by God; then the darkness came down. To continue the metaphor (a rough and ready one, but sufficient), God said, "I must bring light again into this darkness." And in the fullness of time there came One who said, "I am the light of the world. He who follows Me shall not walk in darkness, but have the light of life" (John 8:12). That was God bringing the light back again. And the whole of the Old Testament is preparatory to the coming of the One who is the Light of the world. As soon as man fell into sin, God gave the promise of redemption, that the Seed of the woman shall bruise the head of the serpent (cf. Gen. 3:15). That is the primal promise, and from that Seed there comes the growth of the great Tree of life, whose leaves are for the healing of the nations.

By and by, in the story of Genesis, God concentrates His attention on one man. He said, "To put My plan into operation, I need a man." And He laid His hand upon Abraham, making far-reaching and amazing promises to him, "In you all the families of the earth shall be blessed" (Gen. 12:3), and subjecting him to the pressures and disciplines of His grace. It is the story of the clay in the hand of the potter. God takes this lump of clay and begins to shape him into a vessel for His mercy. And the whole Old Testament is concerned with the shaping of that lump of clay. As the story goes on, presently the man of God's choosing becomes a family; miraculously, and contrary to nature, he becomes a family, and that family by a strange concourse of events is brought down into Egypt and begins to multiply there. Brought into bondage and serfdom by the Egyptians, the family is delivered by a man God raises up, Moses. Nor is it surprising that the man He raises up suggests to our minds the One who was to come. The whole record glitters and gleams with suggestions and illustrations and foreshadowings of the real thing that was to come. It is certainly not fancy that we see shadows of Christ in the Old Testament. These are the edges of His ways, just brushing the side of the canvas, so to speak, or the stage of history, before His time.

God brought that providentially constituted and preserved nation out of Egypt and on its way to the Promised Land; and, having first begun to deal with a man, Abraham, He now begins to deal with the seed of Abraham, this great multitude called Israel, according to promise.

The nation begins to be disciplined at Sinai. It receives the law; it receives the whole elaborate system of sacrifices; it receives the cloud and the fire to lead it and guide it. Then, having received the whole institution of the sacrifices and the tabernacle, they were ready to move on, because God's plan for, and promise to, Abraham was to give him the Promised Land, so that, eventually, in the fullness of the time, having been established there, the chosen people might produce the promised Seed, the Savior of the world. The mystery of the Incarnation is the culmination of the drama begun in the call of Abraham. Unless we see that the Christmas story is integrally related in this way to the Book of Numbers, there will be no kind of relevance in our study. But when we do see it, the study of Numbers becomes tremendously important as vital, living truth from beginning to end.

To view the Old Testament history in this way is to see not only that there is a necessary continuity between the Old Testament era and the New, but also an essential unity between the two, and that the experience of the Israelites was, essentially, a spiritual experience: they were inheritors of spiritual, not merely material blessings. It is a serious, not to say fatal, misunderstanding of the Old Testament to suppose that it represents a regime of law and that salvation was then based on law, as opposed to the faith-principle of the New Testament. Israel's deliverance from Egypt was not merely a physical deliverance: they were *redeemed* by blood, and, in being constituted as the people of God by the Passover sacrifice, the Law, as given at Sinai, was to be a pattern of life for the redeemed people to enable them to enjoy and grow in their blood-secured liberty. All this is surely implicit in Paul's words in 1 Corinthians 10, which cannot well be understood except in such an interpretation.

Numbers, then, is the next installment, so to speak, of the story of God's dealing with His people, the continuing discipline of the people of God and the shaping of the vessel by the hand of the Potter.

Some important lessons emerge from all this. The first is that it underlines the glorious fact of the sovereignty of God. God is Lord of history, and this is one of the most comforting and inspiring realities. We are living today in a troubled world, when tensions between East and West become greater rather than less, when moral and spiritual confusion is widespread, and men's hearts fail within them for fear. In such a world we need this message, that God is the Lord of history. It needs to be underlined that the leaders of the superpowers of the world, whether East or West, do not have the last word in the affairs of men, although they may think they have, and would like to have. God is the Lord of history: in all the multifarious concourse of events in the Old Testament, this is the one overriding consideration and reality, and He is ceaselessly working out His purposes, turning even the wrath of man to praise Him.

The history unfolded in Numbers is a far cry from the events recorded in Genesis. But God had promised Abraham that in his seed all families of the earth would be blessed, and that He would make of him a great nation. Since Abraham and Sarah were advanced in years and had no children, it might have been thought impossible that such a promise would be fulfilled. Yet it came to pass, because God had promised. Furthermore, it must have seemed very unlikely that he might ever become a great nation—the Book of Genesis ends with a family of seventy-five people; nevertheless, when the time of the promise drew nigh, God multiplied them (Acts 7:17), and in His time the great nation was an accomplished fact. The opening chapters of Numbers disclose that there were 603,000 men fit for military service at this point in Israel's history. That would bespeak a multitude approaching two million people altogether. The faithfulness of God! What He says He will surely do; heaven, earth, or hell will not prevent Him from fulfilling His faithful promise.

We can learn likewise about the patience of God. People speak of the Old Testament God as a harsh, grim, relentless God. One wonders whether those who say such things ever read the Old Testament. The facts are very different. The God we meet there is a God of unaccountable patience, patient beyond any human capacity and unaccountably long-suffering (Exod. 34:6, Num. 14:18, Ps. 86:15, Jer. 15:15). Again and again when this fractious people rebelled and murmured against Him, He was patient with them, forgiving them (Ps. 78:38ff., 86:5, 99:8, 103:8ff.), leading them on, buffeting them, but never letting them go. And at the end of the story, when they were exiled in Babylon, His hand was upon them, and His grace never left them. Even when they were in the crucible of suffering God was there. Throughout, the love that would not let them go shielded them and led them and guided them right to the end.

Briefly, the story of Numbers is as follows: Israel was preparing to leave Mount Sinai on the road to the Promised Land (10:11ff.). It was a journey of some weeks at the most, if they took a direct route (cf. 10:33, 11:21, 12:15). They proceeded toward the border of the Promised Land to a place called Kadesh Barnea (12:16, 26), where spies were sent in, one man from each tribe. The majority report of the spies was against going forward (13:32) in spite of the known will of God for them to go in and possess the land and in spite of the protests of Caleb and Joshua, two of the spies (14:6ff.) who saw beyond the difficulties and hazards they would undoubtedly have to face to the opportunities set before them by a faithful and enabling God. The pessimistic report won the day, and the people murmured against the Lord (14:10ff.), who turned them back and refused to let them go in! For nearly forty years they were made to wander in the wilderness, until that entire generation died off (14:33). The main part of Numbers deals with the experience of divine discipline in the wilderness, "in the crucible of God." The end of the book shows Israel "not out of the pit" geographically, and not further forward, but a sadder, and a wiser, people. Numbers is a book that need not have been!

Central to the story, then, is this great rebellion of the people at Kadesh Barnea. It was an hour of destiny for the people of God:

> There is a tide in the affairs of men,
> Which, taken at the flood, leads on to fortune;
> Omitted, all the voyage of their life
> Is bound in shallows and in miseries.
> On such a full sea are we now afloat,
> And we must take the current when it serves,
> Or lose our ventures.[1]

One has only to quote these words to realize what a tremendously and urgently critical message this book contains. And it is so relevant—because this is always what God is doing. He presents men with open doors, He opens to men the Kingdom of God in the gospel of Jesus Christ, and He says, "Enter by the narrow gate . . ." (Matt. 7:13). People look in and see the joys and delectable fruits of the Promised Land, but they say, "They cost too much," and they draw back. The rich young ruler is a case in point. He was at the very gate of heaven when Jesus spoke with him, but he could not face the challenge of the cross with which our Lord confronted him, and he went away sorrowful, "for he had great possessions" (Matt. 19:22).

It is possible to miss a tide, tragically, hopelessly. In the history of revival, when whole communities have been offered the riches of grace in the kingdom of God, there have been occasions when those communities have said "no" to Christ. And for generations following, the gospel blessing has passed them by, and they have remained barren and unblessed, almost as if a curse had fallen upon them, while other places have rejoiced in the grace of God. Their hour of opportunity had come and they refused it. And God took them at their word. This is the story of the Book of Numbers.

NOTE

1. William Shakespeare, *Julius Caesar,* act 4, sc. 3, lines 217–23.

An Outline of Numbers

The Book of Numbers derives its English name from the Septuagint, a title given it by the Greek translators because of the accounts of the numbering of the people in chapters 1, 2, and 26. Hebrew tradition generally called the books of the Pentateuch by the first main word of their first sentence, but this "fourth book of Moses" is named by the fourth word of the first verse of the book, *b^{e}midbar,* which means "in the wilderness."

The book falls into three main divisions:

At Sinai (1:1–10:10)
In the Wilderness (10:11–21:35)
In the Plains of Moab (22:1–36:13)

PART ONE: AT SINAI: 1:1–10:10

I. The Numbering and Arrangement of the Tribes: 1:1–2:34
   A. The Census and Its Officers: 1:1–16
   B. The Result of the Census: 1:17–46
   C. The Levites—A Special Case: 1:47–54
   D. Each in His Appointed Place: 2:1–2
   E. The Organization of the Camp and the March: 2:3–34

II. The Levites, Their Numbers and Duties: 3:1–4:49
   A. The Sons of Aaron: 3:1–4
   B. The Levites—Servants to the Priests: 3:5–13
   C. The Numbering of the Levites: 3:14–39
   D. Standing in for the Firstborn: 3:40–51
   E. The Sons of Kohath: 4:1–20
   F. The Sons of Gershon: 4:21–28
   G. The Sons of Merari: 4:29–33
   H. To Each His Appointed Task: 4:34–49

III. The Cleansing and Blessing of the Congregation: 5:1–6:27
   A. The Exclusion of the Unclean: 5:1–4
   B. The Question of Misappropriated Property: 5:5–10
   C. Trial by Ordeal: 5:11–31
   D. The Law of the Nazirite: 6:1–21
   E. The Aaronic Blessing: 6:22–27
IV. The Offerings of the Israelite Princes: 7:1–89
   A. The Spontaneous Giving: 7:1–9
   B. The Offerings of the Chief Men: 7:10–89
V. The Consecration of the Levites: 8:1–26
   A. The Golden Lampstand: 8:1–4
   B. The Purification of the Levites: 8:5–22
   C. The Age Limits for Service: 8:23–26
VI. The Passover at Sinai: 9:1–14
   A. The Passover: 9:1–5
   B. The Problem of Ritual Uncleanness: 9:6–14
VII. The Divine Provision for the March: 9:15–10:10
   A. The Cloud: 9:15–23
   B. The Silver Trumpets: 10:1–10

Part Two: In the Wilderness: 10:11–21:35

VIII. From Sinai to Paran: 10:11–12:16
   A. Departure from Sinai: 10:11–28
   B. Hobab and the Ark: 10:29–32
   C. The Ark in the Vanguard: 10:33–36
   D. Fire in the Camp: 11:1–3
   E. The Spirit of Murmuring: 11:4–10
   F. Moses' Plaint: 11:11–15
   G. The Divine Response: 11:16–24a
   H. The Spirit of the Lord: 11:24b–30
   I. The Quail: 11:31–35
   J. The Vindication of Moses: 12:1–10
   K. Mercy Shown to Miriam: 12:11–16
IX. The Spies at Kadesh Barnea: 13:1–14:45
   A. The Choice of the Spies: 13:1–20

- B. The Journey into Canaan: 13:21–25
- C. The Return of the Spies: 13:26–33
- D. Uproar and Revolt among the People: 14:1–10
- E. The Intercession of Moses: 14:11–25
- F. The Sentence Passed on the People: 14:26–38
- G. The Defeat at Hormah: 14:39–45

X. Various Laws and Regulations: 15:1–41
- A. Instructions on Various Offerings: 15:1–16
- B. The Law of the Heave Offering: 15:17–21
- C. Offering for Unintentional Sin: 15:22–31
- D. Violation of the Sabbath: 15:32–36
- E. The Wearing of Tassels: 15:37–41

XI. The Rebellion of Korah, Dathan, and Abiram: 16:1–17:13
- A. The Issues at Stake: 16:1–7
- B. Moses Rebukes the Levites: 16:8–11
- C. Moses Defied: 16:12–15
- D. The Showdown: 16:16–24
- E. The Punishment of the Rebels: 16:25–35
- F. The Censer Memorial: 16:36–40
- G. The Plague: 16:41–50
- H. Aaron's Rod That Budded: 17:1–13

XII. The Service of the Priests and Levites: 18:1–32
- A. The Duties of Levi: 18:1–7
- B. The Revenues of the Priests: 18:8–20
- C. The Revenues of the Levites: 18:21–24
- D. The Priests' Tithe: 18:25–32

XIII. The Laws of Purification: 19:1–22
- A. The Ashes of the Red Heifer: 19:1–10
- B. General Rules as to Purification: 19:11–13
- C. Special Rules of Purification: 19:14–22

XIV. From Kadesh to Moab: 20:1–21:35
- A. The Incident at Meribah: 20:1–13
- B. Edom's Refusal: 20:14–21
- C. The Death of Aaron: 20:22–29
- D. The Victory at Hormah: 21:1–3
- E. The Bronze Serpent: 21:4–9
- F. The Journey: 21:10–20
- G. The Defeat of Sihon and Og: 21:21–35

Part Three: In the Plains of Moab: 22:1–36:13

XV. The "Balaam" Incident: 22:1–24:25
  A. Invitation and Refusal: 22:1–14
  B. The Warning Voice of God: 22:15–21
  C. The Donkey and the Angel: 22:22–35
  D. Balaam and Balak: 22:36–41
  E. The First Oracle: 23:1–12
  F. The Second Oracle: 23:13–26
  G. The Third Oracle: 23:27–24:13
  H. The Farewell Message: 24:14–25
XVI. Various Laws and Incidents: 25:1–31:54
  A. The Sin of Baal-peor: 25:1–5
  B. The Zeal and Reward of Phinehas: 25:6–15
  C. The Punishment of the Midianites: 25:16–18
  D. The Command to Moses and Eleazar: 26:1–4
  E. The Second Census: 26:5–51
  F. The Faithfulness of God: 26:52–65
  G. The Inheritance of Daughters: 27:1–11
  H. Moses and His Successor: 27:12–23
  I. Daily Offerings: 28:1–8
  J. Offerings for Sabbath and New Moon: 28:9–15
  K. Offerings at Passover: 28:16–25
  L. Offerings at the Feast of Weeks: 28:26–31
  M. The Feast of Trumpets and the Day of Atonement: 29:1–11
  N. The Feast of Tabernacles: 29:12–40
  O. The Law Concerning Vows: 30:1–16
  P. The Defeat of Midian: 31:1–12
  Q. The Return of the Warriors: 31:13–18
  R. The Purification of the Army: 31:19–24
  S. The Division of the Spoil: 31:25–54
XVII. Miscellaneous Topographical Narratives: 32:1–36:13
  A. Request for the Territory of East Jordan: 32:1–15
  B. The Promises Made by Reuben and Gad: 32:16–33
  C. The Conquest of Gilead by Manasseh: 32:34–42
  D. The Journeys of Israel: 33:1–4
  E. From Rameses to Sinai: 33:5–15
  F. From Sinai to Ezion Geber: 33:16–35

G. From Ezion Geber to Moab: 33:36–49
H. Instructions for the Conquest of Canaan: 33:50–56
I. The Appointed Boundaries of Canaan: 34:1–15
J. The Appointment of Supervisors: 34:16–29
K. Cities for the Levites: 35:1–8
L. The Cities of Refuge: 35:9–15
M. Definition of Manslaughter: 35:16–25
N. Various Provisions and Warnings: 35:26–34
O. Daughters' Rights of Inheritance: 36:1–13

Epilogue: "Written for Our Admonition": 1 Cor. 10:1–13

CHAPTER ONE

The Numbering and Arrangement of the Tribes

Numbers 1:1–2:34

THE CENSUS AND ITS OFFICERS

1:1 Now the LORD spoke to Moses in the Wilderness of Sinai, in the tabernacle of meeting, on the
first *day* of the second month, in the second year after they had come out of the land of Egypt, saying:
2 "Take a census of all the congregation of the
children of Israel, by their families, by their fathers'
houses, according to the number of names, every
male individually,
3 "from twenty years old and above—all who *are
able to* go to war in Israel. You and Aaron shall number them by their armies.
4 "And with you there shall be a man from every
tribe, each one the head of his father's house.
5 "These are the names of the men who shall stand
with you: from Reuben, Elizur the son of Shedeur;
6 "from Simeon, Shelumiel the son of Zurishaddai;
7 "from Judah, Nahshon the son of Amminadab;
8 "from Issachar, Nethanel the son of Zuar;
9 "from Zebulun, Eliab the son of Helon;
10 "from the sons of Joseph: from Ephraim, Elishama
the son of Ammihud; from Manasseh, Gamaliel the
son of Pedahzur;
11 "from Benjamin, Abidan the son of Gideoni;
12 "from Dan, Ahiezer the son of Ammishaddai;
13 "from Asher, Pagiel the son of Ocran;
14 "from Gad, Eliasaph the son of Deuel;

15 "from Naphtali, Ahira the son of Enan."
16 These *were* chosen from the congregation, leaders of their fathers' tribes, heads of the divisions in Israel.

Num. 1:1–16

The conception of God's character which underlines the opening chapters of Numbers is "one which would emphasize His love of order and His hatred of confusion, divine attributes which are sometimes forgotten or ignored."[1] This is to put the emphasis in the proper place, since it underlines the fact of revelation at the outset. The book is about *God's* dealings with His people, not primarily an account of their experiences, although it is this also. Still more important, the opening words of the chapter, *"The Lord spoke to Moses in the Wilderness of Sinai,"* are designed to remind us that that revelation is an authoritative one. The Book of Numbers is a word from God. It is as such, therefore, that the Christian must study it. It is written, as Paul says, for our learning (cf. Introduction, page 18).

The book begins with the Lord's command to Moses to number the people, an operation which, as we see from a comparison of 1:1 with 10:11, took nineteen days. The object of this exercise was to list the numbers of men twenty years of age and above who were *"able to go to war"* (v. 3). This indicates its military purpose. The God of Israel was mustering His people for advance into the Promised Land and into the fulfillment of His sovereign purposes for them.

The list of those summoned to help Moses and Aaron in making the census is given in verses 5–16 (for similar lists see 2:3ff., 7:12ff., 10:14ff.). These were all tribal princes (vv. 4, 16).

The Result of the Census

1:17 Then Moses and Aaron took these men who had been mentioned by name,
18 and they assembled all the congregation together on the first *day* of the second month; and they recited their ancestry by families, by their fathers' houses, according to the number of names, from twenty years old and above, each one individually.

19 As the LORD commanded Moses, so he numbered them in the Wilderness of Sinai.

20 Now the children of Reuben, Israel's oldest son, their genealogies by their families, by their fathers' house, according to the number of names, every male individually, from twenty years old and above, all who *were able to* go to war:

21 those who were numbered of the tribe of Reuben *were* forty-six thousand five hundred.

22 From the children of Simeon, their genealogies by their families, by their fathers' house, of those who were numbered, according to the number of names, every male individually, from twenty years old and above, all who *were able to* go to war:

23 those who were numbered of the tribe of Simeon *were* fifty-nine thousand three hundred.

24 From the children of Gad, their genealogies by their families, by their fathers' house, according to the number of names, from twenty years old and above, all who *were able to* go to war:

25 those who were numbered of the tribe of Gad *were* forty-five thousand six hundred and fifty.

26 From the children of Judah, their genealogies by their families, by their fathers' house, according to the number of names, from twenty years old and above, all who *were able to* go to war:

27 those who were numbered of the tribe of Judah *were* seventy-four thousand six hundred.

28 From the children of Issachar, their genealogies by their families, by their fathers' house, according to the number of names, from twenty years old and above, all who *were able to* go to war:

29 those who were numbered of the tribe of Issachar *were* fifty-four thousand four hundred.

30 From the children of Zebulun, their genealogies by their families, by their fathers' house, according to the number of names, from twenty years old and above, all who *were able to* go to war:

31 those who were numbered of the tribe of Zebulun *were* fifty-seven thousand four hundred.

32 From the sons of Joseph, the children of Ephraim, their genealogies by their families, by their fathers'

house, according to the number of names, from twenty years old and above, all who *were able to* go to war:

33 those who were numbered of the tribe of Ephraim *were* forty thousand five hundred.

34 From the children of Manasseh, their genealogies by their families, by their fathers' house, according to the number of names, from twenty years old and above, all who *were able to* go to war:

35 those who were numbered of the tribe of Manasseh *were* thirty-two thousand two hundred.

36 From the children of Benjamin, their genealogies by their families, by their fathers' house, according to the number of names, from twenty years old and above, all who *were able to* go to war:

37 those who were numbered of the tribe of Benjamin *were* thirty-five thousand four hundred.

38 From the children of Dan, their genealogies by their families, by their fathers' house, according to the number of names, from twenty years old and above, all who *were able to* go to war:

39 those who were numbered of the tribe of Dan *were* sixty-two thousand seven hundred.

40 From the children of Asher, their genealogies by their families, by their fathers' house, according to the number of names, from twenty years old and above, all who *were able to* go to war:

41 those who were numbered of the tribe of Asher *were* forty-one thousand five hundred.

42 From the children of Naphtali, their genealogies by their families, by their fathers' house, according to the number of names, from twenty years old and above, all who *were able to* go to war:

43 those who were numbered of the tribe of Naphtali *were* fifty-three thousand four hundred.

44 These are the ones who were numbered, whom Moses and Aaron numbered, with the leaders of Israel, twelve men, each one representing his father's house.

45 So all who were numbered of the children of Israel, by their fathers' houses, from all who *were able to* go to war in Israel—

46 all who were numbered were six hundred and
three thousand five hundred and fifty.

Num. 1:17–46

The census was carried out on the same day that it was commanded (vv. 17–19). The result of it was as follows (v. 20ff.):

Reuben	46,500	Ephraim	40,500
Simeon	59,300	Manasseh	32,200
Gad	45,650	Benjamin	35,400
Judah	74,600	Dan	62,700
Issachar	54,400	Asher	41,500
Zebulun	57,400	Naphtali	53,400

In all, the tribes numbered 603,550 men under arms. One obvious point to note is the unequal strength of the various tribes. Numbers are not insignificant from the human point of view, and it needs to be asked whether there is a significance in this particular disposition of the tribes. The remarkable passage in Genesis 49, where the dying Jacob gives his blessing to his sons and makes some very penetrating and shrewd comments on them, may be a key to understanding the significance of these figures. The tribe of Reuben, for example (46,500), is one of the smaller tribes; yet Reuben was Jacob's firstborn. In Genesis 49:4, Jacob's comment on him is: "Unstable as water, you shall not excel." The reference is probably to the birthright which Reuben forfeited and lost to the sons of Joseph (1 Chron. 5:1) because of his sin against his father (Gen. 35:22). It is more than probable that there is a connection between Reuben's sorry history and the subsequent insignificance of his tribe. It is a matter of history that no king, judge, or prophet is ever recorded as having sprung from the tribe of Reuben.

Furthermore, it is worthy of note that the great, outstanding figures of Old Testament history, as also in the New Testament, belong in the main to a few tribes such as Judah, Benjamin, Ephraim, rather than to the others. Moses was of the tribe of Levi, Joshua was of the tribe of Ephraim, Caleb of the tribe of Judah, Gideon of the tribe of Manasseh, Samuel of the tribe of Ephraim, David of the tribe of Judah, Saul of Tarsus of the tribe of Benjamin. It is impressive to realize that the tribes that stemmed from men who sinned grievously seldom raised up any great figures, or men of renown. There is such a thing as the entail of sin, just as there is an entail of grace, and influence for good and evil can spread to the third and fourth generations, and often far beyond. No man lives unto himself. We are making our future now, and, it may be, the future of our families also. (cf. Isa. 58:12, "You shall raise up the foundations of many generations.")

The Levites—A Special Case

1:47 But the Levites were not numbered among them
by their fathers' tribe;
48 for the LORD had spoken to Moses, saying:
49 "Only the tribe of Levi you shall not number, nor
take a census of them among the children of Israel;
50 "but you shall appoint the Levites over the
tabernacle of the Testimony, over all its furnishings,
and over all things that belong to it; they shall carry
the tabernacle and all its furnishings; they shall attend to it and camp around the tabernacle.
51 "And when the tabernacle is to go forward, the
Levites shall take it down; and when the tabernacle
is to be set up, the Levites shall set it up. The outsider who comes near shall be put to death.
52 "The children of Israel shall pitch their tents,
everyone by his own camp, everyone by his own
standard, according to their armies;
53 "but the Levites shall camp around the tabernacle of the Testimony, that there may be no wrath
on the congregation of the children of Israel; and
the Levites shall keep charge of the tabernacle of the
Testimony."
54 Thus the children of Israel did; according to all
that the LORD commanded Moses, so they did.

Num. 1:47–54

In the census of the twelve tribes (vv. 17–46), Levi is not numbered, the tribe of Joseph being divided into two, Ephraim and Manasseh, to make up the twelve (the numbering of the tribe of Levi in chapter 3 was not for military purposes but in order that the firstborn of the other tribes might be matched one by one with the numbers of the tribe of Levi). In these verses the omission of Levi from the census is now explained. The Levites were set apart for the spiritual service of the sanctuary.

Two points of considerable spiritual importance arise from the peculiar position of Levi in the divine economy. First of all, Paul, as has been observed in the Introduction, invites us, in his attitude toward the Old Testament Scriptures, to look for spiritual lessons relating to the church in the history of Israel. This much, then, can be said at the outset: In any company of God's people, He sets some apart for the work of the sanctuary. This is the unquestionable benchmark of an authentic congregation or people of God. Furthermore, it is clear that this "setting apart" was an integral part of the life and experience of Israel—there was nothing "special" about it; on the contrary, there is almost a "matter-of-factness" about it, even an inevitability.

The apostle Paul has a good deal to say about this in the New Testament, in his teaching about the church as the body of Christ, with members in particular exercising different gifts. In Ephesians 4:8ff., Paul says of Christ, "When He ascended on high, / He led captivity captive, / And gave gifts to men. . . . And He Himself gave some to be apostles, some prophets, some evangelists, and some pastors and teachers, for the equipping of the saints for the work of ministry. . . ." This is precisely the principle seen here, God setting apart some in the fellowship for specific spiritual service. In any company of God's people, if they are an authentic people of God, this will happen in their midst.

If then, in the church, people are not being set apart for divine service, this will give some indication as to where to look for the reasons: (a) either God is not in the midst, calling people apart; or (b) God's people are not responsive to His voice. As to (a), if we ask how to "bring" God into the midst, this can be said: At the head of this people of old, there stood Moses, man of God. Israel had a leader who had died a thousand deaths in the lonely discipline of obedience to the divine will, and it was to him that God once said, "My Presence will go with you" (Exod. 33:14). There is a sense in which, from the human point of view, it was Moses who made the people into a living congregation where God was, and where God was seen to be.

This is a lesson that needs to be learned in the church today: it is spiritual values in a congregation that alone can create the possibility of people being set apart for service. Only where the presence of God is seen to be real in a church do people hear His voice. In the story of Isaiah's call to service (Isa. 6:1ff.), we should recall that it was after his experience of cleansing, that is to say when he entered into a new obedience to God, that he heard the voice of God saying, "Whom shall I send, and who will go for Us?" (Isa. 6:8). It is when the spiritual life and vitality of the church are conserved and promoted that God the Lord is heard to call to people to serve Him.

The second point of importance to be underlined is that the service the Levites were to render to God owed little to their numbers. It is impressive to realize that when they were counted for the purpose of matching them one by one with the firstborn of the other tribes (3:12ff.), their number amounted to only 22,000—less than half most of the other tribes, even the smallest. Quality, not quantity, was to be the criterion. Their strength lay not in numbers, but in their being separated unto God in purity of life. Given this, one with God is always a majority. One recalls the story of Gideon and his men in Judges 7, when God deliberately cut down a great army of over thirty thousand men to a mere three hundred, through whom the hosts of Midian were defeated. "'Not by might nor by power, but by My Spirit,' says the Lord of hosts" (Zech. 4:6). God chooses the weak things of the world to confound the mighty (1 Cor. 1:27). There were only twelve apostles, but they turned the world upside down.

Each in His Appointed Place

> 2:1 And the LORD spoke to Moses and Aaron, saying:
> 2 "Everyone of the children of Israel shall camp by his own standard, beside the emblems of his father's house; they shall camp some distance from the tabernacle of meeting.
>
> *Num. 2:1, 2*

This chapter delineates the organization of the camp of the Israelites and the order of their forward march. The purpose of God in having numbered the people and arranged them in this way has been variously assessed, in military, utilitarian, or religious terms. It is clear that the mode of Israel's advancement in their journey to the Promised Land was laid down by God: this is how they were to journey, and this was the order of the pilgrimage. But it is just as clear that they were drawn up in battle array, because they were to be God's instruments of judgment against the heathen nations of Canaan, who had filled up their cup of wrath to the brim, having lived lives of such degradation that they were fit for nothing but judgment. This is the real meaning of the wars of Israel in the Promised Land. They were wars of judgment: Israel was the rod of God's anger against the wickedness of the Canaanite civilization just as, much later, He raised up the Assyrian hosts, and Nebuchadnezzar and Cyrus, to be the instruments of His chastisement against His own sinning people.

The Old Testament scholar Martin Noth makes the observation that "the idea of the organization of a camp can be based either on the concept of a military camp or else on the concept of a pilgrim camp on the occasion of some cultic festival. In the present chapter elements of both concepts are present. The catchword 'host,' which occurs with each tribe and which, from time to time, includes 'those who are mustered,' is reminiscent of a military camp."[2]

The double emphasis upon pilgrimage and warfare is borne out by the interesting reference to the sons of Gershon of the tribe of the Levites, where the phrase "to perform the service" is translated in the KJV margin "to war the warfare."[3] There is a real sense in which even the Levites who were set apart for the service of the sanctuary were involved in a holy warfare; and this is one of the reasons why this particular arrangement of the tribes can be spoken of both in military and in religious terms, and why by analogy we may speak of the Christian life as both a pilgrimage to the Promised Land and as a warfare for the kingdom of God. Both are true, and both are foreshadowed here.

In this connection it may serve to illumine our understanding of a seemingly prosaic and rather mundane record of tribal dispositions to think of the modern analogy of troop movements during wartime. Many who served in the armed forces during World War II were frequently tempted to feel that there was neither rhyme nor reason in the way in which they were moved hither and thither across the face of the earth. There seemed to be no discernible pattern evident to them. But at the top, at General Staff headquarters, such movements were not only plain but purposeful: they were making a disposition of troops for battle, and they needed particular troops at particular points at particular times for the overall strategy of victory.

We should look at the arrangements set forth in this chapter in relation to the underlying and unifying purpose of God in the unfolding of the Old Testament history. The Book of Numbers is but one episode in the great overall conception of divine initiative. Thus viewed, every individual movement takes on a completely new significance.

The Organization of the Camp and the March

2:3 "On the east side, toward the rising of the sun, those of the standard of the forces with Judah shall camp according to their armies; and Nahshon the son of Amminadab *shall be* the leader of the children of Judah."

4 And his army was numbered at seventy-four thousand six hundred.

5 "Those who camp next to him *shall be* the tribe of Issachar, and Nethanel the son of Zuar *shall be* the leader of the children of Issachar."

6 And his army was numbered at fifty-four thousand four hundred.

7 "Then *comes* the tribe of Zebulun, and Eliab the son of Helon *shall be* the leader of the children of Zebulun."

8 And his army was numbered at fifty-seven thousand four hundred.

9 "All who were numbered according to their armies of the forces with Judah, one hundred and eighty-six thousand four hundred—these shall break camp first.

10 "On the south side *shall be* the standard of the forces with Reuben according to their armies, and the leader of the children of Reuben *shall be* Elizur the son of Shedeur."

11 And his army was numbered at forty-six thousand five hundred.

12 "Those who camp next to him *shall be* the tribe
of Simeon, and the leader of the children of Simeon
shall be Shelumiel the son of Zurishaddai."
13 And his army was numbered at fifty-nine thousand three hundred.
14 "Then *comes* the tribe of Gad, and the leader
of the children of Gad *shall be* Eliasaph the son of
Reuel."
15 And his army was numbered at forty-five thousand six hundred and fifty.
16 "All who were numbered according to their
armies of the forces with Reuben, one hundred and
fifty-one thousand four hundred and fifty—they
shall be the second to break camp.
17 "And the tabernacle of meeting shall move out
with the camp of the Levites in the middle of the
camps; as they camp, so they shall move out, everyone in his place, by their standards.
18 "On the west side *shall be* the standard of the
forces with Ephraim according to their armies, and the
leader of the children of Ephraim *shall be* Elishama the
son of Ammihud."
19 And his army was numbered at forty thousand
five hundred.
20 "Next to him *comes* the tribe of Manasseh, and
the leader of the children of Manasseh *shall be*
Gamaliel the son of Pedahzur."
21 And his army was numbered at thirty-two
thousand two hundred.
22 "Then *comes* the tribe of Benjamin, and the
leader of the children of Benjamin *shall be* Abidan
the son of Gideoni."
23 And his army was numbered at thirty-five
thousand four hundred.
24 "All who were numbered according to their
armies of the forces with Ephraim, one hundred and
eight thousand one hundred—they shall be the third
to break camp.
25 "The standard of the forces with Dan *shall be*
the north side according to their armies, and the
leader of the children of Dan *shall be* Ahiezer the son
of Ammishaddai."

26 And his army was numbered at sixty-two thousand seven hundred.
27 "Those who camp next to him *shall be* the tribe
of Asher, and the leader of the children of Asher
shall be Pagiel the son of Ocran."
28 And his army was numbered at forty-one thousand five hundred.
29 "Then *comes* the tribe of Naphtali, and the leader
of the children of Naphtali *shall be* Ahira the son of
Enan."
30 And his army was numbered at fifty-three
thousand four hundred.
31 "All who were numbered of the forces with Dan,
one hundred and fifty-seven thousand six hundred—
they shall break camp last, with their standards."
32 These *are* the ones who were numbered of the
children of Israel by their fathers' houses. All who
were numbered according to their armies of the forces
were six hundred and three thousand five hundred
and fifty.
33 But the Levites were not numbered among the
children of Israel, just as the LORD commanded Moses.
34 Thus the children of Israel did according to all
that the LORD commanded Moses; so they camped by
their standards and so they broke camp, each one
by his family, according to their fathers' houses.

Num. 2:3–34

As to the specific arrangement and disposition of the tribes, they were set out as follows: on the east side, Judah, Issachar, and Zebulun, totalling 186,400 men; on the south, Reuben, Simeon, and Gad, numbering 151,450 men; on the west, Ephraim, Manasseh, and Benjamin, numbering 108,100 men; on the north, Dan, Asher, and Naphtali totaling 157,600. Within this rectangle there was the tabernacle at the center, with the three subdivisions of the Levites positioned on three sides (v. 17), the Gershonites on the west (3:23), the Kohathites on the south (3:29), and the Merarites on the north (3:35); and on the fourth side of the tabernacle were Moses, Aaron, and his sons (3:38). Such was the disposition of the tribes in encampment. On the march, they were to be in the following order: leading the host came the tribe of Judah, accompanied by Issachar and Zebulun (vv. 3–9); following Judah was the tribe of Reuben, accompanied by Simeon and Gad (vv. 10–16); next came the tabernacle in the midst of the Levites (v. 17); following the tabernacle was Ephraim, accompanied by Manasseh and Benjamin (vv. 18–24); and bringing up the rear was Dan, accompanied by Asher and Naphtali (vv. 25–31).

It will be seen from this arrangement that the vanguard and rearguard of the host had the strongest forces—186,400 and 157,600 respectively—with the smaller tribal groupings within them and the tabernacle in the center.

To each tribe, then, there was given a specific place and function, and each was to be in his divinely appointed place. It is not difficult to see shadows of New Testament patterns here. The apostle Paul says, "Let each one remain in the same calling in which he was called" (1 Cor. 7:20), and "You are the body of Christ, and members individually" (1 Cor. 12:27). The words in verse 17, *"everyone in his place,"* provide the direct link with these New Testament references. The Danites, for example, were behind the others in most of the march; yet they were good fighting men, and therefore particularly fit for that position. They were needed there to ward off surprise attacks from the rear.

The whole pattern presents a vital picture: here are the people of God on the move, with the ark of the covenant in their midst, the Word of the living God at the heart of everything, as it were, directing all the operations and sending forth its influence in grace and power. And a church with the Word of God at the heart of its life is a church that will advance purposefully, because it is one that has life and influence. It is certainly no accident that, later in the ongoing story of Israel (Josh. 2:10, 11), when the Canaanite tribes heard of the advancing host of Israel, their strength was turned to water within them because they knew that in the midst of these Israelites was a real and living God, a mighty God who did exploits for His people.

The concept of a church advancing with a living power at its heart is one that is sorely needed today. It can hardly be doubted, from all available evidence, that it is the presence of the living Word among the people of God that gives meaning, direction, and purpose to their corporate life. If there is anything calculated to encourage and hearten in the church situation of our time, it is the steady recovery of the Word in power and authority in more and more churches and gatherings. It is a familiar biblical pattern: at a later stage than the history of Numbers, with the raising up of Samuel the prophet (1 Sam. 3)—after a long time of drought, barrenness, and dearth, in which the Word of the Lord was a scarce commodity, and there was no open vision in the land—at that moment, when the lamp of God was flickering in the temple, God laid His hand on the young man Samuel. And presently it began to be noised abroad that the Word of the Lord was with him. In a quarter of a century—it took all of that time—the whole national situation was transformed.

This is the message of the chapter. It is when God and His Word are in the midst of the church that it moves forward like a mighty army. Plant the Word of God in the heart of the church's life, and once again it will move forward to some purpose. Life for Israel was to be related to the ark and submissive to its principles. Not only so: the ark was to be protected and reverence shown it. The divine institutions were to be honored and the divine order maintained, according to the pattern shown in the mount. God's warfare was to be fought in God's way. It was because Israel later became disobedient that she failed to go forward. The lesson for today's Christian church is surely clear and plain.

NOTES

1. L. Elliott Binns, introductory note to *The Book of Numbers* (London: Methuen & Co., Ltd., 1927).

2. Martin Noth, *Numbers: A Commentary,* Old Testament Library (London: SCM Press, 1968), p. 23. Noth adds, however, "The organization of the tribes around the central sanctuary, which is not at all suitable for a serious war, conjures up the picture of a pilgrimage festival at a great sanctuary at which the vast crowds of pilgrims set up their tents round the central cultic point. It is highly likely that such festival camps existed in ancient Israel at the period of the conquest and, indeed, there are examples of such a practice from the most recent Palestinian past."

3. Binns, *Numbers,* p. 10. Binns maintains that "The idea which is expressed by the camp so arranged is 'that of the sanctifying presence of God in Israel's midst' (cf. v. 3; Lev xv. 31); in other words its significance is not military or utilitarian but religious."

CHAPTER TWO

The Levites, Their Numbers and Duties

Numbers 3:1–4:49

This section deals with the special position of the Levites. In 3:1–51 is described the nature of their calling and the purpose of their being set apart, while 4:1–49 delineates the service that the various branches of the tribe were to perform.

The Sons of Aaron

3:1 Now these *are* the records of Aaron and Moses when the LORD spoke with Moses on Mount Sinai.
2 And these *are* the names of the sons of Aaron: Nadab, the firstborn, and Abihu, Eleazar, and Ithamar.
3 These *are* the names of the sons of Aaron, the anointed priests, whom he consecrated to minister as priests.
4 Nadab and Abihu had died before the LORD when they offered profane fire before the LORD in the Wilderness of Sinai; and they had no children. So Eleazar and Ithamar ministered as priests in the presence of Aaron their father.

Num. 3:1–4

These introductory verses about the sons of Aaron serve to explain why Eleazar and Ithamar, Aaron's younger sons, figure in the narrative of Numbers rather than Nadab, his firstborn, and Abihu, his second son. Nadab and Abihu, we are told in verse 4, *"died before the Lord when they offered profane fire before the Lord in the Wilderness of Sinai."* For the details of this solemn and remarkable incident, see Leviticus 10:1–7. The sin of Nadab and Abihu was a manifold one, as one scholar points out: (a) they each took his own censer and not the sacred utensil of the sanctuary; (b) they both offered it together, whereas incense was only to be offered by one; (c) they presumptuously encroached upon the functions of the high priest; for according to the Law the high priest alone burnt incense in a censer (cf. Lev. 16:12, 13; Num. 17:11); (d) they offered the incense at an unauthorized time, since it was apart from the morning and evening sacrifice.[1]

All this is true. But the operative phrase in the incident is *"profane fire"* ("profane" here has the force of "unlawful" or "common"). The presumptuous priests committed sacrilege by filling their vessels with common fire instead of taking it from the holy fire of the altar, which was always to be used in the burning of incense (cf. Lev. 16:12, 13).

We have already seen in the previous section the emphasis on the importance of a proper order of proceedings. This is a theme which runs throughout not only the Pentateuch, but indeed throughout the Old Testament as a whole (Exod. 25:40; Num. 8:4; 1 Chron. 15:13, 16:40, 28:11, 12, 19; Heb. 8:5). It is this that explains the severity of the judgment that came upon them. Their infringement was conscious and deliberate and, doubtless, accentuated by the fact that Nadab and Abihu were among those who ascended the mount of God with Moses (Exod. 24:1, 9).

The lesson of the incident underlines the seriousness of departing from God's way and God's command in His service. It is a lesson of timeless and perennial significance. There is a service of the sanctuary and a service of the Lord that He is not prepared to own, which owes its inspiration not to the holy fire of the altar of the gospel but to other sources and other fires, and, be it never so sincere, never so earnest, never so dedicated, it is bound to come to grief. To serve God acceptably, we must light our flame at His altar. This must be our only inspiration and dynamic.

This is a word of considerable relevance today, when the need for new, modern methods in "getting out the gospel" to our generation is repeatedly emphasized. We need to beware lest a question of methodology become one of theology. It is easy to stray from the divine order through a desire for innovation, for innovation's sake, and thereby lose contact with the divine fire which alone can give true inspiration. It is relevant also, indeed, in the realm of worship, as Calvin points out very forcibly in his comments on Matthew 15:1 ff., where he speaks of "the extraordinary insolence that is displayed by men as to the form and manner of worshipping God; for they are perpetually contriving new modes of worship, and when any one wishes to be thought wiser than others, he displays his ingenuity on this subject. . . . God has laid down the manner in which he wishes that we should worship him."[2]

James Denney has a notable passage in a sermon on the temptation of Jesus, entitled "Wrong Roads to the Kingdom," which underlines this lesson very graphically:

> There is always a tendency in the Church to trust to methods which appeal rather to the senses than to the soul, or which are believed to be reaching the soul though they never get past the senses. . . . How tempting it is to trust to such impressions, as though the coming of the kingdom were really secured by them. . . . No doubt such things make an impression and have an influence; but they are not the influence and the impression through which that kingdom of God can come for which Jesus lived and died. How little He had of all that the Churches are tempted to trust in now! How little there is in the gospels about methods and apparatus! . . . The trust of the Church in other things is really a distrust of the truth, an unwillingness to believe that its power lies in itself, a desire to have something more irresistible than truth to plead truth's cause; and all these are modes of atheism. Sometimes our yielding to this temptation is shown in the apathy which falls upon us when we cannot have the apparatus we crave, sometimes in the complacency in which we clothe ourselves when we get it and it draws a crowd. This is precisely the kind of crowd which Jesus refused to draw. The kingdom of God is not there, nor is it to be brought by such appeals. It is not only a mistake, but a sin, to trust to attractions for the ear and the eye, and to draw people to the church by the same methods by which they are drawn to places of entertainment. What the evangelist calls "the word"—the spiritual truth, the message of the Father and of His kingdom—spoken in the Spirit and enforced by the Spirit, told by faith and heard by faith—is our only real resource, and we must not be ashamed of its simplicity.[3]

THE LEVITES—SERVANTS TO THE PRIESTS

3:5 And the LORD spoke to Moses, saying:
6 "Bring the tribe of Levi near, and present them
before Aaron the priest, that they may serve him.
7 "And they shall attend to his needs and the
needs of the whole congregation before the tabernacle of meeting, to do the work of the tabernacle.
8 "Also they shall attend to all the furnishings of
the tabernacle of meeting, and to the needs of the
children of Israel, to do the work of the tabernacle.
9 "And you shall give the Levites to Aaron and
his sons; they *are* given entirely to him from among
the children of Israel.
10 "So you shall appoint Aaron and his sons, and
they shall attend to their priesthood; but the outsider
who comes near shall be put to death."
11 Then the LORD spoke to Moses, saying:
12 "Now behold, I Myself have taken the Levites
from among the children of Israel instead of every
firstborn who opens the womb among the children of
Israel. Therefore the Levites shall be Mine,
13 "because all the firstborn *are* Mine. On the day
that I struck all the firstborn in the land of Egypt, I
sanctified to Myself all the firstborn in Israel, both
man and beast. They shall be Mine: I *am* the LORD."

Num. 3:5–13

The significance of the Lord's claim on the firstborn of Israel, and His choice of the Levites instead of them, is somewhat complex, and the substitution of the one for the other must be examined before we can draw out the lesson that it undoubtedly contains.

In Exodus 13 we read how the Lord claimed the firstborn of Israel for Himself, following the Passover in Egypt, when all the firstborn of Egypt were slain by the angel of death. This much is clear and without complication. But now (vv. 11–13, 44ff.) the Lord announces that instead of the firstborn He will take the tribe of Levi for Himself. In verses 40ff., we are told how this substitution and changeover took place.

The questions that arise here are: Why this change? And why Levi? The selection of one tribe rather than a heterogeneous mixture of the firstborn from all twelve tribes may in fact have been purely a matter of practical expediency: they would be more easily identifiable and more easily managed than a selection from all twelve tribes could possibly have been. With the Levites, God had a unit ready-made and able to work harmoniously together.

The firstborn were, in the most direct sense, the beneficiaries of the death of the (Passover) lamb, and thus in a special way the Lord's possession. They must be given to Him. In the case of animals, this was done by death; and in the case of human firstborn, it was done by the substitution of the Levites on a one-for-one basis. For those who could not be accounted for in this way (cf. 46—the 273 who were in excess of the number of the Levites) it was done by purchase (vv. 47ff.), in that they were redeemed by silver, the price being paid in ransom to Aaron and his sons.[4]

But why Levi, rather than another tribe? One possible reason may be found in a consideration of the incident recorded in Exodus 32:26–29. Levi had been most zealous for the honor of the Lord at the time of the worship of the golden calf. When Moses stood in the gate of the camp and uttered his famous challenge, "Whoever is on the Lord's side, let him come to me," it is recorded that all the sons of Levi gathered themselves together to Moses. Here, at a critical point in the history of the people of God, and at the point of challenge and destiny, the sons of Levi rose magnificently to the challenge and came out decisively on the Lord's side. Surely this must be the special reason why God chose them. They had been put to the test, and proved, in much the same way as Caleb and Joshua were later to be tried and proved by the way they reacted on their return with the spies from the foray into the Promised Land, (Num. 13–14), when they said, "We are well able to overcome it" (13:30). In both cases, they "made their future" in terms of qualifying themselves for the assumption of responsibility in the work of God in days that were to come.

The Numbering of the Levites

3:14 Then the LORD spoke to Moses in the Wilderness of Sinai, saying:
15 "Number the children of Levi by their fathers'

houses, by their families; you shall number every
male from a month old and above."
16 So Moses numbered them according to the word
of the LORD, as he was commanded.
17 These were the sons of Levi by their names:
Gershon, Kohath, and Merari.
18 And these *are* the names of the sons of Gershon
by their families: Libni and Shimei.
19 And the sons of Kohath by their families: Amram,
Izehar, Hebron, and Uzziel.
20 And the sons of Merari by their families: Mahli
and Mushi. These *are* the families of the Levites by
their fathers' houses.
21 From Gershon *came* the family of the Libnites
and the family of the Shimites; these *were* the families
of the Gershonites.
22 Those who were numbered, according to the
number of all the males from a month old and above—
of those who were numbered *there were* seven thousand five hundred.
23 The families of the Gershonites were to camp
behind the tabernacle westward.
24 And the leader of the father's house of the Gershonites *was* Eliasaph the son of Lael.
25 The duties of the children of Gershon in the
tabernacle of meeting *included* the tabernacle, the tent
with its covering, the screen for the door of the tabernacle of meeting,
26 the screen for the door of the court, the hangings of the court which *are* around the tabernacle
and the altar, and their cords, according to all the
work relating to them.
27 From Kohath *came* the family of the Amramites,
the family of the Izharites, the family of the Hebronites, and the family of the Uzzielites; these *were*
the families of the Kohathites.
28 According to the number of all the males, from
a month old and above, *there were* eight thousand six
hundred keeping charge of the sanctuary.
29 The families of the children of Kohath were to
camp on the south side of the tabernacle.
30 And the leader of the fathers' house of the

families of the Kohathites *was* Elizaphan the son of Uzziel.

31 Their duty *included* the ark, the table, the lampstand, the altars, the utensils of the sanctuary with which they ministered, the screen, and all the work relating to them.

32 And Eleazar the son of Aaron the priest *was to be* chief over the leaders of the Levites, *with* oversight of those who kept charge of the sanctuary.

33 From Merari *came* the family of the Mahlites and the family of the Mushites; these *were* the families of Merari.

34 And those who were numbered, according to the number of all the males from a month old and above, *were* six thousand two hundred.

35 The leader of the fathers' house of the families of Merari *was* Zuriel the son of Abihail. These *were* to camp on the north side of the tabernacle.

36 And the appointed duty of the children of Merari *included* the boards of the tabernacle, its bars, its pillars, its sockets, its utensils, all the work relating to them,

37 and the pillars of the court all around, with their sockets, their pegs, and their cords.

38 Moreover those who were to camp before the tabernacle on the east, before the tabernacle of meeting, *were* Moses, Aaron, and his sons, keeping charge of the sanctuary, to meet the needs of the children of Israel; but the outsider who came near was to be put to death.

39 All who were numbered of the Levites, whom Moses and Aaron numbered at the commandment of the LORD, by their families, all the males from a month old and above, *were* twenty-two thousand.

Num. 3:14–39

The substance of this central section of the chapter concerns the numbering of the tribe of Levi and the apportionment of tasks to the individual groups within it, represented by the families of Gershon, Kohath, and Merari. These families formed an inner circle around the tabernacle, with Gershon on the west side, Kohath on the south, and Merari on the north. Moses, Aaron, and his sons encamped on the east side.

To the Gershonites (vv. 21–26) there was given the care of the whole of the tabernacle fabric (its actual structure was the responsibility of the Merarites, v. 36). The original account of the arrangements for the construction of the tabernacle in Exodus 25ff. may be usefully consulted, particularly Exodus 26:1–6 (cf. also Num. 4:21–28 and 1 Chron. 15).

In verses 27–32 the responsibilities of the Kohathites are said to be the care of the sacred contents of the tabernacle, the ark, the table, the lampstand, and the vessels of the sanctuary. The Kohathites were therefore entrusted with the most important and valuable items of the sanctuary. Why they, the family of the second son of Levi, should be given this preference is unknown, although in the next chapter (4:2ff.) they are placed first, as they are in Numbers 4:4–15 and 1 Chronicles 15:5.

To the Merarites (vv. 33–37) was given the custody and charge of *"the boards of the tabernacle, its bars, its pillars, its sockets, its utensils, all the work relating to them, and the pillars of the court all around, with their sockets, their pegs, and their cords"* (cf. also Num. 4:29–33).

Standing in for the Firstborn

3:40 Then the LORD said to Moses: "Number all the firstborn males of the children of Israel from a month old and above, and take the number of their names.

41 "And you shall take the Levites for Me—I *am* the LORD—instead of all the firstborn among the children of Israel, and the livestock of the Levites instead of all the firstborn among the livestock of the children of Israel."

42 So Moses numbered all the firstborn among the children of Israel, as the LORD commanded him.

43 And all the firstborn males, according to the number of names from a month old and above, of those who were numbered of them, were twenty-two thousand two hundred and seventy-three.

44 Then the LORD spoke to Moses, saying:

45 "Take the Levites instead of all the firstborn

among the children of Israel, and the livestock of the
Levites instead of their livestock. The Levites shall be
Mine: I *am* the LORD.
46 "And for the redemption of the two hundred
and seventy-three of the firstborn of the children of
Israel, who are more than the number of the Levites,
47 "you shall take five shekels for each one individually; you shall take *them* in the currency of the
shekel of the sanctuary, the shekel of twenty gerahs.
48 "And you shall give the money, with which the
excess number of them is redeemed, to Aaron and his
sons."
49 So Moses took the redemption money from
those who were over and above those who were redeemed by the Levites.
50 From the firstborn of the children of Israel he took
the money, one thousand three hundred and sixty-five
shekels, according to the shekel of the sanctuary.
51 And Moses gave their redemption money to
Aaron and his sons, according to the word of the LORD,
as the LORD commanded Moses.

Num. 3:40–51

These verses record the interesting transaction by which the Levites were substituted for the firstborn of Israel and to which reference has already been made. On the basis of a one-for-one exchange or substitution of Levites for firstborn, 273 firstborn remained unaccounted for. These, as has already been said, could not be simply left, but were to be redeemed with silver and the price paid in ransom for them to Aaron's sons.[5]

This use of the idea of ransom or redemption well illustrates what the same words signify when they are used in connection with the idea of atonement in the New Testament, and it may underlie Peter's words in his first epistle (1:18ff.), "Knowing that you were not redeemed with corruptible things, like silver or gold, from your aimless conduct received by tradition from your fathers, but with the precious blood of Christ, as of a lamb without blemish and without spot. He indeed was foreordained before the foundation of the world but was manifest in these last times for you who through Him believe in God." Central to all is the notion of a substitutionary payment, assessed as an exact equivalent to whatever specific need was being met. It is this that is carried over into the New Testament doctrine of atonement. It is true, as Emil Brunner points out in his book *The Mediator,* that although the idea of an "equivalent" has exercised a widespread and dominant influence in the history of the doctrine of atonement, signifying that behind it there lies a deep truth, there can in fact be no human equivalent, and that "every sacrificial cult, as an attempt to buy oneself off, only offers a 'cheap' solution. *But the search for an equivalent is not false.* For it expresses the idea that only on this presupposition is it possible to live on at all, the feeling that we simply cannot go on any longer 'without something.'"[6]

The most important thing in this transaction was the Lord's claim upon the firstborn, which was a symbol of His claim upon all the redeemed people. He had redeemed them all out of Egypt, so that they all belonged to Him by right of redemption; but He claimed the firstborn for Himself as a symbol of this fact. This is analogous to the claim He made upon the tithe, or tenth, of His people's goods and possessions, which was a symbol of the fact that everything they had was His and that what they retained could not be regarded, as of right, their own.

The firstborn (and by analogy the Levites) belonged to God by virtue of substitutionary atonement having been made for them in the Passover lamb, as we see from Exodus 13. The firstborn of Israel had been spared the visitation of death through the sheltering blood of the lamb that had been slain: The blood marks on the doors of Israel indicated that death had already knocked upon them. The Lord's claim upon them, therefore, is meant to signify that they really "died" in the Passover judgment, so that they were "not their own," but "bought with a price," that, in this sense, they had no real right to be alive at all. Life for them was purely in the grace of God. This is the significance of the claim on the firstborn.

It is the fact that Israel is repeatedly spoken of in the Old Testament as Jehovah's firstborn that underlies the New Testament's use of the symbol of belonging to the Lord. It is there that it comes into its own and enlarges to embrace the whole redeemed community. The body of believers is called "the general assembly and church of the firstborn" (Heb. 12:23); that is to say, every believer, incorporated into the body of Christ, is in the position of the firstborn, claimed by God, given to God, and sealed unto God, in being redeemed with the precious blood of Christ. We are no longer our own, but the Lord's, "a holy priesthood" to offer up spiritual sacrifices "acceptable to God through Jesus Christ" (1 Pet. 2:5).

The apostle Paul sums up the situation perfectly in 2 Corinthians 5:14ff.: "We judge thus: that if One died for all, then all died; and He died for all, that those who live should live no longer for themselves, but for Him who died for them and rose again."

The Sons of Kohath

4:1 Then the LORD spoke to Moses and Aaron, saying:

2 "Take a census of the sons of Kohath from among the children of Levi, by their families, by their fathers' house,

3 "from thirty years old and above, even to fifty years old, all who enter the service to do the work in the tabernacle of meeting.

4 "This *is* the service of the sons of Kohath in the tabernacle of meeting, *relating to* the most holy things:

5 "When the camp prepares to journey, Aaron and his sons shall come, and they shall take down the covering veil and cover the ark of the Testimony with it.

6 "Then they shall put on it a covering of badger skins, and spread over *that* a cloth entirely of blue; and they shall insert its poles.

7 "On the table of showbread they shall spread a blue cloth, and put on it the dishes, the pans, the bowls, and the pitchers for pouring; and the showbread shall be on it.

8 "They shall spread over them a scarlet cloth, and cover the same with a covering of badger skins; and they shall insert its poles.

9 "And they shall take a blue cloth and cover the lampstand of the light, with its lamps, its wick-trimmers, its trays, and all its oil vessels, with which they service it.

10 "Then they shall put it with all its utensils in a

covering of badger skins, and put *it* on a carrying beam.

11 "Over the golden altar they shall spread a blue cloth, and cover it with a covering of badger skins; and they shall insert its poles.

12 "Then they shall take all the utensils of service with which they minister in the sanctuary, put *them* in a blue cloth, cover them with a covering of badger skins, and put *them* on a carrying beam.

13 "Also they shall take away the ashes from the altar, and spread a purple cloth over it.

14 "They shall put on it all its implements with which they minister there—the firepans, the forks, the shovels, the basins, and all the utensils of the altar—and they shall spread on it a covering of badger skins, and insert its poles.

15 "And when Aaron and his sons have finished covering the sanctuary and all the furnishings of the sanctuary, when the camp is set to go, then the sons of Kohath shall come to carry *them;* but they shall not touch any holy thing, lest they die. These *are* the things in the tabernacle of meeting which the sons of Kohath are to carry.

16 "The appointed duty of Eleazar the son of Aaron the priest *is* the oil for the light, the sweet incense, the daily grain offering, the anointing oil, the oversight of all the tabernacle, of all that *is* in it, with the sanctuary and its furnishings."

17 Then the LORD spoke to Moses and Aaron, saying:

18 "Do not cut off the tribe of the families of the Kohathites from among the Levites;

19 "but do this in regard to them, that they may live and not die when they approach the most holy things: Aaron and his sons shall go in and appoint each of them to his service and his task.

20 "But they shall not go in to watch while the holy things are being covered, lest they die."

Num. 4:1–20

We come now to the delineation of the services that the various branches of the tribe of Levi were to perform. That the separated life of the Levites was a full and rich one (God Himself was their inheritance) may be seen from the reference to their function in Deuteronomy 10:8, 9, "At that time the Lord separated the tribe of Levi to bear the ark of the covenant of the Lord, to stand before the Lord to minister to Him and to bless in His name, to this day. Therefore Levi has no portion nor inheritance with his brethren; the Lord is his inheritance, just as the Lord your God promised him." They were to "bless in His name" and could very aptly be described, in the apostle Paul's words in 2 Corinthians 6:10, "as poor, yet making many rich; as having nothing, and yet possessing all things." It is within this context of a rich, full life, which is both life-giving and fruit-bearing, that we are to set the lessons of this section. Just how rich and how life-giving and fruit-bearing that life was in the providence of God becomes plain in the sections which follow, simple and uncomplicated as they are in terms of exegesis. The sons of Kohath, Gershon, and Merari each had particular work appointed to them, and within each family special tasks were apportioned to individuals. The precedence of the Kohathites has already been commented upon (see note on 3:27–32). Perhaps pride of place was given to them (although Kohath was but the second son of Levi) because Aaron and Moses belonged to this branch of the family of Levi (see Exod. 6:16–20, 1 Chron. 6:1–3). This may also serve to explain the disproportionate number of verses allocated to the sons of Kohath (vv. 1–20), compared with those describing the Gershonites (vv. 21–28) and the Merarites (vv. 29–33). The description of the various duties follows the uniform pattern throughout, in spite of the larger section devoted to Kohath, beginning in each case with the divine command to make a census (vv. 2, 22, 29), and followed by a delimitation of the period of levitical service (vv. 3, 23, 30).

An interesting point arises from a consideration of the period of service for the Levites, here represented as being a twenty-year period, from the thirtieth to the fiftieth year. This is, however, differently represented elsewhere. In 8:23–26 the span is from the twenty-fifth year to the fiftieth; while in 1 Chronicles 23:3, 24, two different figures are given, thirty years and twenty years respectively. Different constructions have been placed on these variations. Some have attributed them to scribal errors. The Septuagint assimilates verse 3 to 8:23ff. by reading twenty-five in both places. It is hardly a satisfactory explanation, however, to suggest that the variant readings represent a combination of different traditions. A redactor could hardly be so obtuse as to include the two different numbers together in the same chapter without noticing it. The most satisfactory explanation would seem to be that differing conditions required a change of age limits as time went on. If, for example, David (in 1 Chron. 23) discovered that the elaborate arrangements that he made under the guidance of the Spirit required more men than the narrower age range would provide, he would naturally lower the age limit to include a larger number. Or, for example, if the duties proved to be less onerous than he had originally anticipated, perhaps younger and less experienced men could be employed to perform them.[7]

With regard to the upper age limit there is unanimity. Retirement was at the age of fifty. Nowadays, when life expectancy is so much more than it was even a hundred years ago, this age limit seems needlessly low, although in fact the wheel seems to have come around full circle in our highly sophisticated industrial age, when men are regarded as too old even at forty for new employment.

There is a principle of some importance at work, however, in the variation in the age of entry into the work of the Levites, and it is this: There is no question of any legalism at work, or any question of standing by the letter of the law as if it were unchangeable. Rather, there is evidence of adaptation of the letter of the law, to observe the principle enshrined in it. It is true that ancient usage does give a sanctity to old custom, but ancient usage ought not to make old customs inviolable. What was good enough for one age may not necessarily be best for another, and the principle is surely more important than the letter of the law. The important thing to realize is that the service performed by the Levites was responsible service, requiring responsible people to fulfill it worthily. This consideration may in fact underlie Paul's injunction to Timothy, "Not a novice, lest being puffed up with pride he fall into the same condemnation as the devil" (1 Tim. 3:6). Whatever the age for the service of the kingdom, this consideration should always be important.

What this teaches us does not lie in any literal approximation of age for service, and this is not the lesson that the Holy Spirit means us to learn. Rather, what this bears witness to is that there is a need in Christian service for people who are mature, and who are prepared to be trained and equipped for that service. This is a needful reminder in a day in which it becomes increasingly common for people to suppose that, given willingness, anyone can work the work of God, without training, without equipment, and even without a particular aptitude. Good will in itself is not enough for the work of the kingdom of God, and no one who is not prepared to submit himself to the disciplines of spiritual training, with all that this involves, will be able to fulfill that service. It is not by accident that the apostle Paul uses metaphors and imagery from the athletic field and the field of battle to describe Christian service, nor is it without significance that the word in verse 3, translated here as "service," has as its root meaning "warfare."[8]

The Sons of Gershon

4:21 Then the LORD spoke to Moses, saying:
22 "Also take a census of the sons of Gershon, by
their fathers' house, by their families.
23 "From thirty years old and above, even to fifty
years old, you shall number them, all who enter to
perform the service, to do the work in the tabernacle
of meeting.
24 "This *is* the service of the families of the Gershonites, in serving and carrying:
25 "They shall carry the curtains of the tabernacle
and the tabernacle of meeting *with* its covering, the
covering of badger skins that *is* on it, the screen for
the door of the tabernacle of meeting,
26 "the screen for the door of the gate of the court,
the hangings of the court which *are* around the
tabernacle and altar, and their cords, all the furnishings for their service and all that is made for these
things: so shall they serve.
27 "Aaron and his sons shall assign all the service
of the sons of the Gershonites, all their tasks and all
their service. And you shall appoint to them all their
tasks as their duty.
28 "This *is* the service of the families of the sons of
Gershon in the tabernacle of meeting. And their duties *shall be* under the authority of Ithamar the son of
Aaron the priest.

Num. 4:21–28

There is little to comment upon in these verses that has not already been covered in the comments on verses 1–20. The task of the Gershonites was simpler and probably regarded as less important and honorable than that of the sons of Kohath. Nevertheless, the terminology is the same as in the description of the latter's task. The phrase in verse 23, "*perform the service,*" again has the force of "wage warfare." Interestingly, the charge of both the Gershonites and the Merarites is committed to Ithamar (vv. 28, 33), who as a son of Aaron was a Kohathite. This again argues the precedence of the Kohathites over the others, but it also serves to indicate a measure of interdependence among the three families.

The Sons of Merari

4:29 "*As for* the sons of Merari, you shall number them by their families and by their fathers' house.
30 "From thirty years old and above, even to fifty years old, you shall number them, everyone who enters the service to do the work of the tabernacle of meeting.
31 "And this *is* what they must carry as all their service for the tabernacle of meeting: the boards of the tabernacle, its bars, its pillars, its sockets,
32 "and the pillars around the court with their sockets, pegs, and cords, with all their furnishings and all their service; and you shall assign *to each man* by name the items he must carry.
33 "This *is* the service of the families of the sons of Merari, as all their service for the tabernacle of meeting, under the authority of Ithamar the son of Aaron the priest."

Num. 4:29–33

The duty of the Merarites was to attend to the transport of the boards, bars, pillars, and sockets of the tabernacle with all their accompanying furnishings, that is to say, the basic framework of its structure. For this task, carts and oxen were provided for them, as were also provided for the Gershonites (cf. 7:7, 8).

To Each His Appointed Task

4:34 And Moses, Aaron, and the leaders of the congregation numbered the sons of the Kohathites by their families and by their fathers' house,
35 from thirty years old and above, even to fifty years old, everyone who entered the service for work in the tabernacle of meeting;
36 and those who were numbered by their families were two thousand seven hundred and fifty.
37 These *were* the ones who were numbered of the families of the Kohathites, all who might serve in the tabernacle of meeting, whom Moses and Aaron numbered according to the commandment of the LORD by the hand of Moses.
38 And those who were numbered of the sons of Gershon, by their families and by their fathers' house,
39 from thirty years old and above, even to fifty years old, everyone who entered the service for work in the tabernacle of meeting—
40 those who were numbered by their families, by their fathers' house, were two thousand six hundred and thirty.
41 These *are* the ones who were numbered of the families of the sons of Gershon, of all who might serve in the tabernacle of meeting, whom Moses and Aaron numbered according to the commandment of the LORD.
42 Those of the families of the sons of Merari who were numbered, by their families, by their fathers' house,
43 from thirty years old and above, even to fifty years old, everyone who entered the service for work in the tabernacle of meeting—
44 those who were numbered by their families were three thousand two hundred.
45 These *are* the ones who were numbered of the families of the sons of Merari, whom Moses and Aaron numbered according to the word of the LORD by the hand of Moses.
46 All who were numbered of the Levites, whom

> Moses, Aaron, and the leaders of Israel numbered, by
> their families and by their fathers' houses,
> 47 from thirty years old and above, even to fifty
> years old, everyone who came to do the work of ser-
> vice and the work of bearing burdens in the taberna-
> cle of meeting—
> 48 those who were numbered were eight thousand
> five hundred and eighty.
> 49 According to the commandment of the LORD they
> were numbered by the hand of Moses, each according
> to his service and according to his task; thus were they
> numbered by him, as the LORD commanded Moses.
>
> *Num. 4:34–49*

These verses record the results of the numbering of the Levites according to their separate families, in fulfillment of the divine command given to Moses in verses 2–3. The number of the Kohathites was 2,750; of the Gershonites 2,630; and of the Merarites 3,200; the total being 8,580.

The apportionment of the various tasks to the three families foreshadows a principle that comes into its own in the teaching of the New Testament doctrine of the church as the body of Christ. It is undoubtedly true that a superficial reading of this section might seem to indicate that the service of the Kohathites was more important than that of the Gershonites and that of the Gershonites, in turn, more important than that of the Merarites. Although this is in one sense true, in another and still more important sense no such distinction can be made, for in fact the work is one, and each family simply makes its contribution with equal force and importance. The one could not exist without the other. This is seen clearly in the New Testament parallel, in Paul's teaching in 1 Corinthians 12:14–25, in the wonderful analogy of the body. The contrast between the various members of the body reveals differentiation of function, not inferiority. Indeed, Paul stresses that when certain members seem to be more feeble than others they are in fact more necessary, just as those thought to be less honorable are all the more necessary. The contrast is seen not so much as between two members of the body which are both visible as between, say, the head and the heart, the one seen, the other unseen. In a building, which is more important—the tower, the frontage, or the foundation?

There are vital lessons here. For one thing, we are reminded that there is spiritual work to be done that is unseen, as foundations are unseen; and spiritual people will not object to not being in the limelight. They are not like Diotrephes, who "loves to have the preeminence" (3 John 9). It is, alas, possible to want to do God's work so as to be seen of men; it is possible, almost unconsciously, to covet the showy, demonstrative place in Christian service. The unostentatious tasks are sometimes not very attractive to the Christian.

In this connection there is a significant statement in verse 32. The words "by name" are referred by some translations (KJV and RSV) to the objects which the sons of Merari were to carry, but the NKJV rendering here (supported by the NEB), "assign to each man by name the items he must carry," indicates that in the so-called lowest grade of service, individuals are appointed and taken notice of *by name.* This is the importance which God attaches to what seems to us to be more humble and menial work. The truth is that all work in the kingdom of God is royal service, however unostentatious and, from the human standpoint, lowly and insignificant.

The distinction between differentiation and inferiority is one that is borne out clearly in the contrast presented by two of our Lord's parables, that of the talents (Matt. 25:14ff.) and that of the pounds (Luke 19:11ff.). The former reminds us that gifts may differ from one person to another, with one having five talents, another two, another one; but the latter refers not to gifts but to equal responsibility in face of an equal stewardship in the gospel. Here, to each believer is given the same sacred deposit (cf. 1 Tim. 6:20, "O Timothy! Guard what was committed to your trust"). We each may have different tasks, and for these, different gifts and enduements are given. But to each is given the solemn responsibility of doing his appointed task with all his heart and with all his might. In the apostle Paul's list of the gifts of the Spirit in 1 Corinthians 12:28, all alike are responsible equally to God for honorable work, and all need the same enduement of the Spirit to make them faithful. Bezaleel the artisan (Exod. 31:2ff.) was anointed by the same Spirit for the carving of the vessels of the tabernacle as Moses was for the leadership of the people of God.

A similar distribution of gifts and responsibilities is seen in the Acts of the Apostles, where we have not only the mighty preaching of Peter and Paul, but also the associated caring and pastoral ministries of people like Barnabas, Aquila, Priscilla, Dorcas, and Phoebe. It can hardly be said that these faithful servants of God were prominent and in the limelight as Peter and Paul were; nor, indeed, did they covet aimlessly and uselessly the latters' gifts. Rather, they were content to fulfill their own gifts. The words of Anna Laetitia Waring's lovely hymn readily come to mind in this connection. After warning against the danger of:

> the restless will
> That hurries to and fro,
> Seeking for some great thing to do,
> Or secret thing to know

the hymn ends with the significant couplet:

> Content to fill a little space,
> If Thou be glorified.
> (Consecration and Discipleship, 1848)

This is the mark of the wise and discerning Christian. It is a question of finding one's place and one's task, and staying in it and doing it with all one's might. There is no other way of contributing one's proper share to the well-being of the body.

This seems to be the force of the injunction given to Moses in verses 18–20. He was to see to it that they all kept their various places and did not trespass on those of others. This is not merely a preventive role. It is also, by implication, a positive one, namely, that of seeking to direct people into their proper spheres, where they will "find themselves" in the service of the Lord, that thus hidden aptitudes and beauties may be brought out in them, so contributing to the well-being, and therefore to the spiritual vitality, of the whole people of God. In this remarkable Old Testament picture, the work of each was necessary and essential before the tabernacle could function at all as it was meant to do in the economy of God.

And it is so also in the Christian church. When believers spend fruitless time coveting others' place and work, failing to do their own, not having found their own proper sphere, the whole work of the church is stultified and hindered. The outreach of any Christian fellowship will depend on whether its individual members are fulfilling their God-given stewardship in the power of the Spirit, a stewardship that may at times seem quite unrelated to the business of winning men to Christ, but necessary nevertheless. If we are the body of Christ and members individually, we must find our God-appointed place and task and be and do what He wants us to be and do. Happy is the man who has found his true place and who fulfills with a glad and faithful heart the work that God has given him!

NOTES

1. C. J. Ellicott, *Leviticus,* An Old Testament Commentary for English Readers (London: Cassell & Co., Ltd., 1897), p. 371.
2. John Calvin, *Commentary on Harmony of Matthew, Mark and Luke,* vol. 2 (London: Calvin Translation Society, 1845).
3. James Denney, *The Way Everlasting* (London: Hodder and Stoughton, 1911), pp. 196–98.
4. L. Elliott Binns, *The Book of Numbers* (London: Methuen & Co., Ltd., 1927). Binns in an interesting footnote suggests that the substitution of the Levites was a compensation for the loss of the services of the eldest sons as natural priests, for as such they were apparently regarded by some ancient peoples. This suggestion is favored by some commentators but opposed by Wellhausen, who points out that there is not in the Old Testament "a single trace of the priesthood of the firstborn" (Hist. of Isr., p. 121). Binns, remarking that difficulty is found in the fact that the firstborn are elsewhere said to be redeemed by a money payment (18:15 ff.), adds: "It is possible to reconcile the two conceptions by supposing that the taking of the Levites is a substitution for all the firstborn then existing, and that the redemption by payment was intended to refer to those born subsequently."
5. In v. 39, the number of the Levites is stated as being 22,000. This total does not agree with the figures of 7,500 (v. 22), 8,600 (v. 28), and 6,200 (v. 34), amounting to 22,300. The total of 22,000, however, is the right one, as may be seen from v. 46, which indicates that the firstborn, numbering 22,273 (v. 43) exceeded the number of Levites by 273. Different suggestions are made to explain this discrepancy. One is that the figure in verse 28 should be 300 instead of 600, Binns pointing out (op. cit., p. 18, note on v. 28), "The omission of a Hebrew letter has caused this reading (600) instead of the correct number 300." Ellicott mentions the possibility that the 300 were themselves firstborn sons who had been born since the command to sanctify the firstborn, and that it is on this account that they were not included in the census.

6. Emil Brunner, *The Mediator* (London: Lutterworth Press, 1934), p. 481.

7. Ellicott, *Leviticus*, p. 506. Ellicott has an interesting comment on the figure of twenty-five years old (8:24): "This regulation may be understood as referring to the age at which the Levites were to enter upon their duties after the people had taken possession of the land of Canaan, and it appears to have remained in force until the time of David, who substituted the age of twenty for that of twenty-five, because the necessity of carrying the Tabernacle and its furniture from place to place, which arose but seldom after the entrance into Canaan, finally ceased after the removal of the ark to Mount Zion. The time of service during the wanderings in the wilderness was from thirty to fifty (4:3, 23, 30), during which time the constant removal of the Tabernacle required the services of men in the full vigor of life. The chronological order of events is not always observed in this book, and the directions contained in 23–26 may have been given at a later period, but inserted here in connection with the account of the appointment of the Levites to their office. On the other hand, it is quite possible that from the first the Levites entered upon the lighter parts of their office at the age of twenty-five years, but were not employed before they were thirty years of age in the more onerous duties of removing the Tabernacle, or in bearing on their shoulders the sacred vessels, as in the case of the Kohathites."

8. Binns, *Numbers*, p. 22. The note on Numbers 4:3 remarks, "In our own day, and indeed since the time of St. Paul, the conception of the service of God as a warfare is perfectly familiar. A famous preacher of the last generation went so far as to say that 'work for God, of whatever kind it be, which Christian people are bound to do, and which is mainly service for men for God's sake, will never be rightly done until we understand that it is *warfare* as well as work.'" Alexander Maclaren, *Exodus*. Exposition of Holy Scripture, 11 vols. (London: Hodder and Stoughton, 1907), 2:297.

CHAPTER THREE

The Cleansing and Blessing of the Congregation

Numbers 5:1–6:27

A number of laws and ordinances relating to the general theme of separation are next unfolded in this section. They are probably best understood in the context both of the military and the spiritual situation of the Israelites. The camp is placed on a war footing, not only so far as possible enemies are concerned, but also in relation to Israel's calling as a separate people. In fact, these two aspects belong inseparably together.

The Exclusion of the Unclean

5:1 And the LORD spoke to Moses, saying:
2 "Command the children of Israel that they put out of the camp every leper, everyone who has a discharge, and whoever becomes defiled by a corpse.
3 "You shall put out both male and female; you shall put them outside the camp, that they may not defile their camps in the midst of which I dwell."
4 And the children of Israel did so, and put them outside the camp; as the LORD spoke to Moses, so the children of Israel did.

Num. 5:1–4

It should be noted that not only leprosy but every form of ritual uncleanness is included in this injunction, whereas in Leviticus 13–15 the regulation applies only to lepers, and those suffering from discharges of whatever kind, or from contact with the dead, are not put out of the camp. It has been suggested that the greater severity of the regulations in this passage is to be accounted for by supposing that they apply to a military camp. But the commentator L. Elliott Binns points out that although special regulations were imposed on Hebrews during military service (cf. Deut. 20:1 ff., 23:9 ff.), the inclusion of women here (v. 3) seems to rule out such an interpretation. The important consideration, however, is that the exclusion of all ritual uncleanness from the camp was imperative because God dwelt in it (v. 3). No possible source of defilement could be tolerated if His presence was to remain with them.

These regulations need to be viewed in their proper context because of the possibility of misunderstanding them, missing the point they are making and the lessons they hold. It would be easy, for example, to set these stringent requirements about leprosy in contrast with passages in the New Testament which tell of our Lord's compassionate cleansing of lepers, and say, "How different is the New Testament attitude to that of the Old, and how harsh and unchristian the spirit that this passage breathes compared with the Gospels." At first glance, this seems plausible and unanswerable, but in fact the attitude that it represents is false and open to fatal objection. Indeed, it would be just as easy to take isolated passages of Scripture and set them in contrast in such a way as to reach the opposite conclusion—namely that the Old Testament is more compassionate and Christian than the New. One thinks, for example, of the story of Ananias and Sapphira in Acts 5:1–11, in which summary and well-deserved punishment was meted out for an admittedly serious offense. Or one might think of the offending moral leper in 1 Corinthians 5:1–5 who received correspondingly stringent treatment, in contrast with the story in 2 Kings 5:1–19 of Naaman the leper, an outcast and alien from the commonwealth of Israel, who was nevertheless cleansed by the compassion of God.

This is a measure of how misleading it can be to take the Scriptures in isolation and out of context. We cannot say, in the light of this passage, "Does the God of the Old Testament have no care or compassion for lepers?" any more than we can say, in the light of Acts 5, or 1 Corinthians 5, "Is the God of the New Testament harsh and severe?" The truth is, this passage and that in the Gospels deal with different matters, just as the story of Ananias and Sapphira and that of Naaman do.

The compassion shown in the Old Testament and in the New alike reveals the attitude of God in His love and grace to the poor and needy—and this is the same in all ages and dispensations, Old and New. The firmness, however, and indeed the severity shown, whether in this passage or in Acts 5 and 1 Corinthians 5, refer to the discipline of God among His people. The question at issue is not whether God has a care for the afflicted or not; it is that of keeping the people of God pure and undefiled. This has already been foreshadowed in previous sections, in the idea of the separate character of the people, called to be distinct, in spiritual nonconfirmity with the world. The great concern of God was to preserve the identity of His people as a peculiar people, and the image of purity was to be preserved at any cost in their corporate life. This was the point behind the ceremonial enactments of the levitical legislation. One can also see the force of this regulation as a purely hygienic measure. If leprosy had spread throughout the camp, there soon would not have been much of a people for God to use as the instrument of His grace for the furtherance of His purposes of redemption. Everything depended on a true relationship with God, and this in turn depended on removing everything that was unclean and impure and maintaining a holy, separate character. Only thus could Israel fulfill her calling to be a light to the Gentiles.

This is seen all the more clearly in the New Testament passages already mentioned (Acts 5, 1 Cor. 5), in both of which matters of discipline are involved. There is a sense in which the word "harsh" could be used of both episodes, on a certain superficial interpretation. But we must remember that discipline is harsh, as is divine censure. As the apostle says in Hebrews 10:31, "It is a fearful thing to fall into the hands of the living God." The truth is, summary judgment had to fall on Ananias and Sapphira at that particular juncture. The young church was newly born, and this evidence of ugly, deadly hypocrisy and double-dealing constituted a threat to its very life, a virus that would undoubtedly, if left unchecked, have done untold and permanent harm, possibly paralyzing the church's witness and forever preventing it from becoming what it finally became in the ancient world.

Is it impossible, or difficult, to see the same pattern in the Old Testament, in God's dealings with His people, in His desire and concern to have a pure instrument of His purposes, especially since having such a pure instrument would in the end lead not to the exclusion of the lepers, but to their cleansing and blessing? For this disciplinary exclusion was a means to an end, the end being seen in its fullness in the ministry of Christ and the word of the gospel.

This is a principle embedded in the divine revelation itself. We read, for example, in Genesis 10 that God set aside the nations of men when the world was young and chose the Hebrews as His peculiar people. The nations were excluded, not because God did not care for them, but because He did, and because this was the only way that ultimate blessing could be ensured for them. By their exclusion, and the choice of the Hebrews, all nations were finally included in the blessings of the gospel. One writer perceptively observes, "The tenth chapter of Genesis is a very remarkable chapter. Before God leaves, as it were, the nations to themselves and begins to deal with Israel, His chosen people from Abraham downward, He takes a loving farewell of all the nations of the earth, as much as to say, 'I am going to leave you for a while, but I love you. I have created you: I have ordered all your future'; and their different genealogies are traced."[1]

This does much to explain to us God's seemingly arbitrary choice of one people rather than another. We sometimes ask, "Is it fair of God to set aside all the other nations and concentrate on one only?" But surely we see here that it is the underlying purpose that explains all. This was the way—the only way—for God to deal with the problem of sin. He could not help but set aside the others to take up the one. It is through the emphasis on the one rather than all that eventually all would be given the opportunity of blessing. This is borne out in the wonderful picture in the Book of Revelation (7:9) of "all nations, tribes, peoples, and tongues" gathered around the throne of God worshiping the Lamb that was slain for their redemption. Thus, the "narrowing-down" in Genesis 10 was but a stage in the whole divine plan of the ages. Well might we say, with Paul, "How unsearchable are His judgments and His ways past finding out!"

Such is the basic, underlying principle that made the exclusion of the lepers and others who were defiled from the camp of Israel necessary and inevitable.

Significantly, in Acts 5 we are explicitly told that there was a new accession of power in the early church following the divine disciplinary visitation. It is significant, too, that in the period of Israel's history when she was most faithful to her calling to be separate (notably in the Book of Joshua, e.g., 2:9–11), she was most powerful and effective as an instrument in the hand of God. This is the ultimate justification for striving for a church that is purged and cleansed from the leprosy of "other things" that rob it of its influence in the world (cf. 2 Cor. 6:14–18). The church has never had a greater influence in the world than when she has been most separate from it.

The Question of Misappropriated Property

5:5 Then the LORD spoke to Moses, saying,
6 "Speak to the children of Israel: 'When a man or
woman commits any sin that men commit in unfaith-
fulness against the LORD, and that person is guilty,
7 'then he shall confess the sin which he has
committed. He shall make restitution for his trespass
in full, plus one-fifth of it, and give *it* to the one he
has wronged.
8 'But if the man has no relative to whom restitution may be made for the wrong, the restitution for
the wrong *must go* to the LORD for the priest, in addition to the ram of the atonement with which atonement is made for him.
9 'Every offering of all the holy things of the children of Israel, which they bring to the priest, shall be
his.
10 'And every man's holy things shall be his; whatever any man gives the priest shall be his.'"

Num. 5:5–10

These verses deal with the question of guilt and restitution, and the regulations laid down here supplement Leviticus 6:1–7. In both passages what is in view is the damage done and loss sustained through wrong dealing between man and man; in both, such wrong acts against a fellow man are regarded as sins or "breaches of faith" against the Lord; in both, the demand for restitution to be made includes the addition of a fifth part of the original principle. What is new here is the additional provision that if the wronged person has no kinsman (v. 8) the restitution must not nevertheless be left unpaid, but should go to the priest who, as the Lord's representative, stands in the place of the injured party, in much the same way as the state does in modern law. Only thus would the act of atonement be completed. This is in fact the law of the trespass offering. *"Trespass"* differs from *"sin"* in that trespass involves injury to another, whether man or God. All trespass is sin; but all sin is not trespass.

This ordinance provides another illustration of the way in which the Lord's people were to be kept pure and their character maintained, if the divine Presence was to continue among them. This purging and purifying of the fellowship is reflected in various ways in the Old Testament itself. One example is the story of the sin of Achan in Joshua 7 and the paralyzing effect it had on the forward march of Israel. The lesson is the same as in verses 1–4: the people of God cannot prevail in the work of the kingdom as long as there is sin in the camp. It must be dealt with.

We should also note the twofold emphasis on confession and restitution. Confession is putting things right with God; restitution is putting things right with one's fellows. Both are necessary for a wrong situation to be rectified, that is, if atonement is to be made. As to confession, we need to be clear about what it implies and involves. It is more than the mere admission of wrongdoing, for admission need not accept responsibility for the offense. When God confronted Adam and Eve in the Garden with their sin, each in turn admitted what he or she had done, but neither accepted responsibility: Adam blamed "the woman whom You gave to be with me," and Eve blamed the serpent. Both fell short of true confession, which by derivation means "to say the same thing" about it as God does, that is "to call it by its proper name," and accept full responsibility for it. There must be no "passing the buck" in this realm. We must say, without reserve, "I have done this terrible thing, and I have no excuse for having done so."

As to restitution, we may observe that the Mosaic law is considerably in advance of our own. Restitution has hardly figured at all in our criminal law until comparatively recently. If one's house is burgled, and valuables stolen, the thief when caught will receive a prison sentence, but we may never recover our lost property, and our courts have been very slow to help with any compensation. It is of course open to us to take the criminal to the civil court and sue him for damages, but the process is so cumbersome that it could take years for the case even to be heard.

It may be appropriate at this point to venture some general guidelines in the matter of confession. The Bible does not encourage indiscriminate confession (which can sometimes be unhealthy and morbid). Sins committed against God should be confessed to God, sins committed against one's fellow confessed to him, and sins committed against the fellowship confessed to the fellowship. Any marked crossing of these general boundaries is to be deprecated, since it is quite possible to become overly preoccupied with sins, especially other people's, as considerable evidence in the history of the church in experience-oriented situations serves to indicate. It is sadly true that even in the context of genuine spiritual awakening the "confession syndrome" has from time to time become almost a fetish, amounting to a sometimes gross distortion of biblical teaching.

We should also remember, however, that the peace of God will not come with mere confession, if it lies within a man's power to make restitution for his sin, and he does not do so. Sometimes, alas, restitution to those we sin against can no longer be made, and when repentance comes, this can be a matter of lifelong regret. If I steal another man's goods, I can pay him back; but if I steal his good name, and vilify him to others, this is something I may never be able to rectify. I will have done him permanent harm and hurt; I may have broken his heart and may bring him to a premature grave. And I can never make restitution there—a frightening thought, indeed. Well may Wesley sing,

> Ah! give me, Lord, the tender heart
> That trembles at the approach of sin;
> A godly fear of sin impart,
> Implant, and root it deep within,
> That I may dread Thy gracious power,
> And never dare offend Thee more.

The last word on this theme must come from the New Testament. The apostle John says in his first epistle (1 John 1:9), "If we confess our sins, He is faithful and just to forgive us our sins and to cleanse us from all unrighteousness." This is the promise of God, and when we come to Him with hearts opened, confessing and forsaking all that would grieve Him, putting it away in penitence and contrition, allowing the white light of His Holy Spirit to search and probe into the deepest places of our hearts until we walk in the light as He is in the light, so shall we have fellowship with Him, and so shall the blood of Jesus Christ His Son cleanse us from all sin.

Trial by Ordeal

5:11 And the LORD spoke to Moses, saying,
12 "Speak to the children of Israel, and say to them: 'If any man's wife goes astray and behaves unfaithfully toward him,
13 'and a man lies with her carnally, and it is hidden from the eyes of her husband, and it is concealed that she has defiled herself, and *there was* no witness against her, nor was she caught—
14 'if the spirit of jealousy comes upon him and he becomes jealous of his wife, who has defiled herself; or if the spirit of jealousy comes upon him and he becomes jealous of his wife, although she has not defiled herself—
15 'then the man shall bring his wife to the priest. He shall bring the offering required for her, one-tenth of an ephah of barley meal; he shall pour no oil on it and put no frankincense on it, because it *is* a grain offering of jealousy, an offering for remembering, for bringing iniquity to remembrance.
16 'And the priest shall bring her near, and set her before the LORD.
17 'The priest shall take holy water in an earthen vessel, and take some of the dust that is on the floor of the tabernacle and put *it* into the water.
18 'Then the priest shall stand the woman before the LORD, uncover the woman's head, and put the offering for remembering in her hands, which *is* the grain offering of jealousy. And the priest shall have in his hand the bitter water that brings a curse.
19 'And the priest shall put her under oath, and say to the woman, "If no man has lain with you, and

if you have not gone astray to uncleanness *while* under your husband's *authority,* be free from this bitter water that brings a curse.

20 "But if you have gone astray *while* under your husband's *authority,* and if you have defiled yourself and some man other than your husband has lain with you"—

21 'then the priest shall put the woman under the oath of the curse, and he shall say to the woman—"the LORD make you a curse and an oath among your people, when the LORD makes your thigh rot and your belly swell;

22 "and may this water that causes the curse go into your stomach, and make *your* belly swell and *your* thigh rot." Then the woman shall say, "Amen, so be it."

23 'Then the priest shall write these curses in a book, and he shall scrape *them* off into the bitter water.

24 'And he shall make the woman drink the bitter water that brings a curse, and the water that brings the curse shall enter her *to become* bitter.

25 'Then the priest shall take the grain offering of jealousy from the woman's hand, shall wave the offering before the LORD, and bring it to the altar;

26 'and the priest shall take a handful of the offering, as its memorial portion, burn *it* on the altar, and afterward make the woman drink the water.

27 'When he has made her drink the water, then it shall be, if she has defiled herself and behaved unfaithfully toward her husband, that the water that brings a curse will enter her *and become* bitter, and her belly will swell, her thigh will rot, and the woman will become a curse among her people.

28 'But if the woman has not defiled herself, and is clean, then she shall be free and may conceive children.

29 'This *is* the law of jealousy, when a wife, *while* under her husband's *authority,* goes astray and defiles herself,

30 'or when the spirit of jealousy comes upon a man, and he becomes jealous of his wife; then he shall

stand the woman before the LORD, and the priest shall execute all this law upon her.
31 'Then the man shall be free from iniquity, but that woman shall bear her guilt.'"

Num. 5:11–31

The full and detailed account given in this passage of the procedure to be carried out in determining the guilt or innocence of a woman suspected of adultery, through what may be called "trial by ordeal," is some indication of its importance in the life of the people of God. The subject relates to a particular type of defilement that constituted a threat to the peace and well-being of the congregation of Israel within the camp. Two possibilities are envisaged: either, a woman has been unfaithful to her husband, but the sin has been hidden and secret, and there are no witnesses (the husband suspects but does not have proof, vv. 12–14a); or, the woman is innocent, and the husband is jealous and suspicious without cause (v. 14b). Clearly, it is a matter which cannot be determined by conclusive evidence. In such a situation, it is God who must judge between them; and the ritual is laid down for the priest, as the representative of God, to perform: to determine whether the woman is guilty or not. The husband must bring to the priest *"a grain offering of jealousy, an offering for remembering,"* to bring guilt to remembrance; the woman must take an oath of purgation, and drink a potion described as *"the bitter water that brings a curse"* (v. 18). If innocent, she would come to no harm from drinking it; but if guilty it would have dire consequences for her (vv. 21, 27).

This is ordeal indeed, and it must surely raise questions in our minds today. One's first, instinctive reaction to such a ritual, grim as it reads, is to think of it in terms of its belonging to some ancient, primitive custom that can surely have no place in our thinking today. It is sometimes said that the practice was common to Israel's heathen neighbors, and was of animistic origin, and therefore to be dismissed as such. But commitment to a belief in the inspiration of Scripture really forbids us any escape route by such an interpretation, and we need to hold to the view that it is an enactment given by God to His people, however difficult its interpretation may be. One commentator points out that the ordeal was not much resorted to in Israel and that with the probable exception of Exodus 22:8ff.

this is the only example of it in the law. Another points out it is nowhere stated that this test was intended to be used after the people settled in the Promised Land (nor is there any evidence that it was ever so used). In view of this, it may be reasonable to suppose it to have been a provision intended only for the wilderness journey—and therefore invested with divine power only for the particular circumstances of that time. It may help us to appreciate this more if we think of another divine institution of those days which we would not employ now, namely the casting of lots. As the Book of Proverbs says (16:33), "The lot is cast into the lap, but its every decision is from the Lord." It would be easy to dismiss the casting of lots as the operation of mere chance or luck (and a case could certainly be made for saying this if it were employed regularly today!), but this would be to ignore the divine dispensation involved, making it *for that time* one of the appointed means for discerning the Lord's will. In the same way, this trial by ordeal was designed to make known the divine verdict on a situation which could not otherwise be determined.

The exact nature of the punishment that was to befall the guilty woman is uncertain (vv. 27, 28). The British Old Testament scholar Gordon J. Wenham says:

> Josephus suggested dropsy. More recent suggestions include a miscarriage (NEB), thrombophlebitis, or a false pregnancy. Exact diagnosis is unimportant; as the contrast with the innocent wife makes clear (28), the adulteress will be childless and therefore an *execration among her people* (21, 27). Genesis 20:17 mentions that Abimelech's wives became sterile as a result of his intention to commit adultery with Sarah. Leviticus 20:20 ff. predict that the same penalty will befall couples guilty of incestuous relationships.[2]

The lesson this ritual teaches us, apart altogether from its relevance or otherwise for today, is that of the sanctity of the marriage bond and the fateful consequences of any act or attitude by which it might be endangered or put at risk. It is not a light thing that something so sacred in God's sight should be assailed, and we should learn from this passage just how seriously He regards any departure from total faithfulness within the marriage relationship and chastity outside it. What is clear is that the health, well-being, and indeed safety of the whole nation was held to be imperiled by such an act—hence the full and detailed account of the procedure to deal with it.

This is the realism of Scripture: it sees, although our careless, modern age does not, that the erosion of the sanctities of marriage and of deep and intimate personal relationships cannot but undermine the foundation of society, simply because marriage and the family have such a fundamental place in the structure of human existence as created by God.

There is much need for a thorough-going rehabilitation of the biblical doctrine of marriage in our time. Today increasing numbers even of Christian people seem to take these sanctities lightly. They seem to have adopted an attitude to the marriage bond which regards it as little more than a civil contract, to be broken at will by mutual agreement, forgetting that the marriage service contains the words "till death us do part" and not "till we no longer are in love with each other." And what are we to say about the attitude underlying the words spoken by the mother of a bride who whispered to her daughter as she was about to leave on her honeymoon, "If it doesn't work out you can always get a divorce"?

If, as Scripture teaches, two people when they are married are made "one flesh," it means that a new person has been brought into being by God, and it is therefore impossible to think of marriage as a mere association of two individuals which can be broken at will and by consent. To break up a marriage is to tear themselves in pieces; as Calvin puts it: "He who divorces his wife tears, as it were, the half of himself. But nature does not allow any man to tear in pieces his own body."

And what are we to say of the man or the woman who destroys a marriage? They call it love; they may be desperately, hopelessly, passionately in love, and they imagine that that is the justification for so doing. But there is a higher consideration than desperate, hopeless, passionate love, and that is the thing that God has done in marriage, in making two people one flesh. He has created something unique and will always in that situation say, "It is not lawful for you to have her" (Matt. 14:4).

The passage before us closes on a dark and grim note, with the guilty woman bearing her guilt (v. 31), and we need another note to offset what would otherwise be a message of despair. Thank God, there is forgiveness with Him—the whole system of sacrifices unfolded in Leviticus proclaims this—and even in this somber and tragic area there can be reconciliation, healing, and new hope, as the beautiful story in John 8:1–12 makes plain. But it is well that the seriousness of the sin spoken of here should be shown in all its ugliness and horror.

The Law of the Nazirite

6:1 Then the LORD spoke to Moses, saying,
2 "Speak to the children of Israel, and say to them: 'When either a man or woman consecrates an offering to take the vow of a Nazirite, to separate himself to the LORD,
3 'he shall separate himself from wine and *similar* drink; he shall drink neither vinegar made from wine nor vinegar made from *similar* drink; neither shall he drink any grape juice, nor eat fresh grapes or raisins.
4 'All the days of his separation he shall eat nothing that is produced by the grapevine, from seed to skin.
5 'All the days of the vow of his separation no razor shall come upon his head; until the days are fulfilled for which he separated himself to the LORD, he shall be holy. *Then* he shall let the locks of the hair of his head grow.
6 'All the days that he separates himself to the LORD he shall not go near a dead body.
7 'He shall not make himself unclean even for his father or his mother, for his brother or his sister, when they die, because his separation to God *is* on his head.
8 'All the days of his separation he shall be holy to the LORD.
9 'And if anyone dies very suddenly beside him, and he defiles his consecrated head, then he shall shave his head on the day of his cleansing; on the seventh day he shall shave it.
10 'Then on the eighth day he shall bring two turtledoves or two young pigeons to the priest, to the door of the tabernacle of meeting;

11 'and the priest shall offer one as a sin offering
and *the* other as a burnt offering, and make atonement for him, because he sinned in regard to the
corpse; and he shall sanctify his head that same day.
12 'He shall consecrate to the LORD the days of his
separation, and bring a male lamb in its first year as
a trespass offering; but the former days shall be lost,
because his separation was defiled.
13 'Now this *is* the law of the Nazirite: When the
days of his separation are fulfilled, he shall be brought
to the door of the tabernacle of meeting.
14 'And he shall present his offering to the LORD:
one male lamb in its first year without blemish as a
burnt offering, one ewe lamb in its first year without
blemish as a sin offering, one ram without blemish
as a peace offering,
15 'a basket of unleavened bread, cakes of fine flour
mixed with oil, unleavened wafers anointed with oil,
and their grain offering with their drink offerings.
16 'Then the priest shall bring *them* before the LORD
and offer his sin offering and his burnt offering;
17 'and he shall offer the ram as a sacrifice of a
peace offering to the LORD, with the basket of unleavened bread; the priest shall also offer its grain
offering and its drink offering.
18 'Then the Nazirite shall shave his consecrated
head *at* the door of the tabernacle of meeting, and
shall take the hair from his consecrated head and put
it on the fire which is under the sacrifice of the peace
offering.
19 'And the priest shall take the boiled shoulder of
the ram, one unleavened cake from the basket, and
one unleavened wafer, and put *them* upon the hands of
the Nazirite after he has shaved his consecrated *hair,*
20 'and the priest shall wave them as a wave offering before the LORD; they *are* holy for the priest, together with the breast of the wave offering and the
thigh of the heave offering. After that the Nazirite
may drink wine.'
21 "This is the law of the Nazirite who vows to the
LORD the offering for his separation, and besides
that, whatever else his hand is able to provide;

according to the vow which he takes, so he must do
according to the law of his separation."

Num. 6:1–21

The repeated insistence and emphasis on the idea of separation, seen already in the instruction about the service of the Levites in the tabernacle (3:5 ff.) and in the legislation about the lepers in the camp (5:1 ff.), is underlined even more impressively and forcibly in the laws concerning the Nazirite vows. The Nazirite vow was a vow of separation. The word derives from *nāzîr,* meaning "to separate." It was a vow that could be taken for a specific period (e.g., for thirty days, as here), perhaps as an act of consecration, perhaps following repentance, or, as has been said "to reassure himself that underlying the routine of daily life he was devoted to God." But that there were also lifelong Nazirites is equally clear in Scripture, as is evident for example in the case of Samson (Judg. 13–16), who was chosen and appointed by God as consecrated to Him, and regarded as the divine gift to Israel in time of particular need (cf. Amos 2:11). The latter does not, however, seem to be in view in these verses.

The relation between the temporary vow and the lifelong commitment is an uncertain one,[3] and commentators find the subject perplexing. It is obvious that Samson's case presents some peculiar features when compared with the regulations set out here, only one of which—that of the long, unshorn hair—seems to have been important for him.

The temporary vow, envisaged in these verses, principally involved three conditions: abstinence from intoxicating liquor (vv. 3, 4), abstinence from the cutting of the hair (v. 5), and abstinence from contact with any dead body, involving ritual defilement and uncleanness.

The first condition to be observed during the period of the vow, abstinence from wine and intoxicating drink,[4] had probably a twofold purpose. On the one hand, the abstinence would ensure full clarity of the mind when engaged in the service of the Lord. On the other hand, the extension of the prohibition to include the eating of grapes, whether fresh or dried, or from partaking of anything connected with the vine, seems to indicate that these were regarded as symbolizing all sensual enjoyments by which holiness could be impaired. One commentator quotes a phrase from Hosea 3:1 which speaks of "the raisin cakes of the pagans" as referring to "dainties sought after by epicures and debauchees" and cited by the prophet "as a symbol of the sensual attractions of idolatry, a luxurious kind of food, that was not in harmony with the solemnity of the worship of Jehovah."[5]

The second regulation, that no razor was to come upon the Nazirite, is thought to have been originally the most important of the prohibitions, "and a feature common to the different types of Nazirite vows recorded in the Old Testament."[6] The free growth of the hair is called in verse 7 *"his separation to God . . . on his head,"* rendered by a commentator as "the diadem of his God upon his head, like the golden diadem upon the turban of the high priest (Exod. 29:6), and the anointing oil upon the high priest's head (Lev. 21:12)." He maintains therefore that the growing of the hair was neither a sign of separation nor the profession of a renunciation of the world, nor a sign of abstinence from self-gratification or of self-denial, but rather the symbol of strength and abundant vitality (cf. 2 Sam. 14:25, 26). It signified that all the natural gifts and growth of the body were the Lord's.[7] Calvin is content with the explanation that "God would constantly exercise them in the faithful performance of their vow by this visible sign."

The third prohibition (6:6ff.) is dealt with in greater detail than the others. The strictness of the enactment is seen in that not only contact with a dead body is forbidden but even, it would seem (cf. Lev. 21:11), entering a room in which a dead body lay. So strict, indeed, is the prohibition that even unintentional or accidental contact with the dead (v. 9) was regarded to have nullified the consecration, and a new beginning had to be made (v. 12). Calvin distinguishes two points in the prohibition. As to why contact with a dead body was a pollution, he concludes that "because by death is represented God's curse, the wages of sin, the Israelites were thus admonished to beware of dead works." As to the question of mourning he adds that "those who profess the special service of God should set an example to others of magnanimity and submission." As the first regulation of the vow (vv. 3–4) restrained the Nazirite from indulgence of the senses, so now a remedy is applied in the realm of sorrow. Calvin adds, "Although all ought to seek to indulge it moderately, yet something more is prescribed to the Nazirites, that, as if disentangled and stripped from earthly affections, they should go further than the rest of the people." One wonders whether this may be what lies behind our Lord's seemingly stern and forbidding answer to the disciple who said, "Lord, let me first to go and bury my father," in the words "Follow Me, and let the dead bury their own dead." This is a challenge to discipleship indeed, but it can hardly be controverted that our Lord's words breathe the spirit of the Nazirite vow, whether He had them in mind or not.

On the expiration of the time of the vow (vv. 13–21), the Nazirite was to offer a burnt offering, a sin offering, and a peace offering, with the customary meal, or cereal offerings (cf. Lev. 2:4). The significance of the peace offering and the burnt offering are, Calvin thinks, obvious, in terms of thanksgiving on the one hand, and the discharge of pious duty on the other. As to the sin offering he adds, "Here we clearly perceive, that however cheerfully and earnestly men endeavour to offer themselves altogether to God, yet they never attain to the goal of perfection nor arrive at what they desire, but are always exposed to God's judgment, unless He should pardon their sins." This point is made more specifically by the scholar Delitzsch who speaks of the sin offering as "an expiation for the sins committed involuntarily during the period of consecration (cf. 6:9 ff.)."

After the offerings were presented by the priest, the Nazirite shaved off his hair at the door of the tabernacle and burned it on the sacred fire (v. 18). This was the completion of the surrender to God symbolized in the vow. Finally, the priest made a wave offering of a portion of the peace offering and the meal offering, which thereby became holy and the perquisite of the priest. Thereupon, the Nazirite returned to normal living and to the drinking of wine. The following comments on the significance of the vow are helpful and illuminating, as being expressive of "a condition of life consecrated to the Lord, resembling the sanctified relation in which the priests stood to Jehovah, and differing from the priesthood solely in the fact that it involved no official service at the sanctuary, and was not based upon a divine calling and institution, but was undertaken spontaneously for a certain time and through a special vow."[8]

It is not difficult to see the Christian application of the Nazirite vow, for the matters it speaks of are integral to the Christian life as a whole, all the time, and witness to a vigilance that must never be slackened. The message is one of consecration and separation—not only from wine as such, but from anything and all that panders to the senses and desires of the flesh. Not only hair as such, but all natural gifts and energies must be baptized into the death of Christ, and sanctified and hallowed for His service; not only separation from dead bodies as such, but from all that partakes of the life of sin, so that we may live unto God. Nor are we left in doubt in the New Testament as to the things that pander to the flesh in us, as Galatians 5:19–21 makes clear. The apostolic injunction in Romans 12:2, "Do not be conformed to this world," stands in direct descent from the Nazirite vow in this regard.

As to the need for all natural gifts to be baptized into the death of Christ, we need to remember, with Milton, that God does not need man's gifts. Some natural gifts are of no use to God in spiritual work, and they need to be given over to Him, that He might put them "in cold storage" indefinitely. Christians occasionally speak of laying their gifts on the altar for the service of the Lord, and God is sometimes pleased to use these gifts. But is laying the gifts on the altar on our part conditional on God being prepared to use them? Some gifts tend to pander to the flesh in spiritual life and become a snare in spiritual service and must therefore simply be set aside. The point about laying something on the altar is surely that it is placed there *beyond recall.* If God gives it back, well and good; if not, we can have no complaint.

The Nazirite "spirit" is well exemplified in an entry in the private diary of James Elliot, one of the Auca Indian martyrs, particularly in relation to the "dead things" that can touch Christians' lives—questionable habits or unhallowed relationships—and act like a canker on spiritual vitality: "He makes His ministers *a flame of fire.* Am I ignitible? God deliver me from the dread 'asbestos' of 'other things.' Saturate me with the oil of the Spirit that I may be a flame. But flame is transient, often short-lived. Canst thou bear this, my soul—short life? In me there dwells the Spirit of the Great Short-lived, whose zeal for God's house consumed Him. 'Make me Thy fuel, flame of God.'"[9]

The question of whether there is a place in the Christian life for a temporary vow is an important one. Paul himself seems to have taken such vows on occasion (cf. Acts 18:18; 21:18–26), and we should bear in mind that echoes of the Nazirite vow seem to ring in Paul's teaching also, as for example in 1 Corinthians 6:13, "the body is . . . for the Lord, and the Lord for the body," and 1 Corinthians 10:31, "eat or drink . . . to the glory of God."

The apostle's teaching about "the good things of life" is a good starting point here: "I will not be brought under the power of any," he says about the things that are lawful (1 Cor. 6:12), and in the next chapter he speaks of those "who use this world as not misusing it" (1 Cor. 7:31). These statements, and others in similar vein, are an indication of Paul's detachment from "things." But how is the believer to be sure that this obtains in his case at any given time? How other, than by applying a temporary discipline to his life, and *doing without them* for a time, can he reassure himself that underlying the daily routine of life he is, after all, really devoted to God? We must be careful, of course, not to fall into legalism here, but it would do us all a great deal of good if this kind of discipline figured in our lives from time to time, to keep us on our spiritual toes. We can so easily deceive ourselves.

We need to ask ourselves questions for example with regard to the good, legitimate pleasures and joys which God gives us to gladden our hearts. Do they take undue prominence in our lives? Have they come to mean more to us than they ought? Would it not be good to test ourselves here, to make sure that we are not in fact displacing God from His rightful place?

The apostle Paul was able to write from his own prison, "I know how to be abased, and I know how to abound. Everywhere and in all things I have learned both to be full and to be hungry, both to abound and to suffer need" (Phil. 4:12). A true detachment was the distinctive mark of his life. It is here that we see the point of the Nazirite going back to ordinary life after the fulfillment of the vow. It is possible for the believer to have the full enjoyment of the legitimate gifts of God without being worldly or preoccupied with them, because they mean precisely nothing to him in the deepest sense (he is "in the world" but not "of the world"—John 17:11, 16), just as it is possible to be physically cut off from them all and still be worldly at heart. This is an area of life in which Christians are required to think more honestly than they are often prepared to do. David speaks in Psalm 131 of behaving and quieting himself as a child who is weaned of his mother, and adds, "Like a weaned child is my soul within me." This is the point. The question the Nazirite vow poses for us is: "Are we weaned from our dependence on things, or do they hold us, whether we have them or do not have them?" A man can be outwardly separate from the world, and yet have the world in his heart, just as a man of the world may be fully weaned in spirit from all these things.

The most important lesson, however, to be learned about this vow lies in its being a symbol of lifelong separation unto God. This, in fact, is the challenge and summons of the gospel. Consecration is not an optional extra; it is the only logical response we can make to the mercies of God in Christ (Rom. 12:1–2).

This kind of separation, however, even when taken in the strictest and most literal fashion, is never to be thought of in terms of a monastic seclusion, even though the Nazirites may legitimately be described as "the monks and nuns of ancient Israel."[10] It is worth noting that in the few instances in Scripture where men are specifically referred to as having been separated unto God all their lives, there is no trace of such seclusion. Joseph is spoken of (Gen. 49:26) as "separate from his brothers," that is, set apart (the word used is *nāzîr*). In this sense he was a Nazirite, and set apart for God, but he was assuredly not a recluse, but fulfilled a tremendous purpose in the will of God. Samson (Judg. 13:7) is described as "a Nazirite to God from the womb to the day of his death," but was nevertheless a most active servant of the divine purposes, involved in the Lord's battles, and indeed most successfully involved when he was most separate unto Him. Samuel, of whom it was said that he was "lent to the Lord" (1 Sam. 1:28) as long as he lived, and therefore a Nazirite (1 Sam. 1:11), nevertheless traversed the land tirelessly, bearing the burden of a nation's spiritual renewal on his own shoulders, a far-seeing, far-sighted statesman and spiritual prophet all his days, immersed in the things of the world of his time and yet separate unto God, and indeed because separate, making a mighty impact on the nation.

John the Baptist was likewise a Nazirite (Luke 1:15), being filled with the Holy Spirit from his mother's womb. It is true that he was in the deserts till the day of his manifestation to Israel (Luke 1:80), but God launched him into the maelstrom of Judean history as a mighty prophet whose words scorched and blistered the conscience of a nation. There was nothing impractical and secluded about him.

It can hardly be denied that there is a desperate need in the church today for such leadership, for men utterly given over to God for His purposes—not men of fanatical zeal (which can very often be fleshy and even devilish), but men of controlled fire, men who can truly say, "One thing I do" (Phil. 3:13), men of whom it can be said that the love of Christ constrains them, giving their lives depth, drive, and direction in the service of God. The Nazirite vow calls us as Christians to a separation unto the living God that will make our lives and our ministries immensely significant in the divine economy. There was another Nazirite, and He once said, "For their sakes I sanctify Myself." Looking on a lost world, He separated Himself unto God, unto the sacrifice of the Cross.

The Aaronic Blessing

6:22 And the LORD spoke to Moses, saying:
23 "Speak to Aaron and his sons, saying, 'This is
the way you shall bless the children of Israel. Say to
them:
24 "The LORD bless you and keep you;
25 The LORD make His face shine upon you,
And be gracious to you;
26 The LORD lift up His countenance upon you,
And give you peace."'
27 "So they shall put My name on the children of
Israel, and I will bless them."

Num. 6:22–27

In the light of all that has been said, the last verses of the section assume an enormous significance. The priestly, or Aaronic, blessing "gives terse and beautiful expression to the thought that Israel owes all to Yahweh, who shields His people from all harm, and grants them all things necessary for their welfare."[11] That it should be found at this point in Numbers has excited controversy among scholars,[12] who question whether this is its original position; but its spiritual significance is surely that it is the man who is wholly separated unto God who can bless others in His name. In the spiritual realm it is always such lives that tell for Him. It was because Joseph, Samuel, and John the Baptist were set apart for God that they were made a blessing to their day and generation. Just as it is by one Man's obedience many are made righteous (Rom. 5:19), so also it is by the separation of the few that the many are blessed, and the face of the Lord made to shine upon them, and the light of His countenance lifted up upon them. Jesus' separation unto the work God gave Him to do and His obedience to the point of death (Phil. 2:8) has meant that this wonderful priestly benediction and blessing has been poured upon a lost world.[13]

The blessing itself is a beautiful and moving utterance, but familiarity with it should not be allowed to blind us to the richness of its content and meaning. We should note first of all that Aaron and his sons were commanded to bless the children of Israel. This blessing is not the mere expression of pious hope; and it is a measure of how far our thinking has departed from biblical ideas that we should consider it as no more than that. The priests were anointed with authority to bestow blessing, to mediate it from God, just as the patriarchs of old were, by virtue of their being priests within their families. This may be seen from the fact that the blessing bestowed by the aged Isaac upon his son Jacob, even though procured by guile and dishonesty, was something which, once bestowed, could not be recalled (Gen. 27:27 ff.), and was recognized as such by the tragically deceived old man. A New Testament parallel to this is the authority delegated to the apostles by our Lord (Matt. 16:19, 18:18 ff.) to "bind" and "loose," and exercised by them (cf. Acts 15:19 ff.) in the early church.

The nature of the blessing is threefold. It speaks first of all in terms of an invocation of divine protection (v. 24), surely an apposite assurance at that particular moment in Israel's history, faced as they were with all the hazards of the wilderness before them, and one echoed on many occasions and in many forms in succeeding generations, both in the prayers of God's people and in His prophetic Word (cf. Pss. 67:1, 121:7, 8; Isa. 26:3, 41:10, 14, 42:6; Jer. 31:10; cf. also 2 Tim. 1:12).

The second part of the blessing speaks, in vivid metaphor, of the Lord's face shining upon His people (v. 25). This spells out and amplifies the meaning of the first part, defining it in terms of the favor and grace of God. One readily thinks in this connection of the words of the Benedictus (Luke 1:68 ff., "He has visited and redeemed His people"), where "visited" has the meaning of "turned His face upon" His people. The glorious message of Christmas (which fulfills the Aaronic benediction) is that God, whose face had been turned from mankind because of sin, has now once for all turned toward men in love and pity. The final part of the blessing (v. 26) continues this thought. When the Lord looks thus upon His people, all the resources of the Godhead are made available to them (cf. Pss. 33:18, 19; 34:15, 16). Such is the measure of the peace He bestows!

NOTES

1. Adolph Saphir, *The Divine Unity of Scripture,* quoted by W. H. Griffith Thomas in *Genesis, A Devotional Commentary* (London: Religious Tract Society, 1913), p. 126.

2. Gordon J. Wenham, *Numbers,* Tyndale Old Testament Commentaries (Leicester: Inter-Varsity Press, 1981), p. 84ff.

3. That there is a distinction between the Nazirite spoken of in this law and the concept of a lifelong Nazirite is surely clear, but what the relationship between the two was is uncertain. G. B. Gray in *A Critical and Exegetical Commentary on Numbers,* International Critical Commentary (Edinburgh: T. & T. Clark, 1903), p. 58, comments, "Whether lifelong devotees and persons who had taken a particular form of temporary vow were in one and the same period alike termed Nazirite, or whether it was only after lifelong Nazirites had died out that the name was passed on to persons under a vow and distinguished by certain features that had marked the lifelong Nazirites, the evidence does not allow us to determine for certain. But in any case there is a marked difference between the two classes."

L. Elliott Binns in *The Book of Numbers* (London: Methuen & Co., Ltd., 1927), p. 36f. comments as follows: "The subject of the Nazirite in Israel is a very puzzling one, as apparently the term Nazirite was used at different times with various connotations. The institution seems to have existed from very early days (see Jud xiii–xvi; Am ii.11 f), and survived into the days of our Lord (1 Macc iii.49 f; Joseph Ant. xix. vi. 1, and of the description of St. James by Hegesippus in Eusebius Hist. Eccles. II.xxiii.4), and even later.

"The case of Samson presents peculiar features when compared with the regulations here set out. In the first place, his dedication was no temporary measure enforced by a vow, but a lifelong service, undertaken in response to a divine command which preceded his own birth. The most important regulation concerning him was that by which no razor came upon him (Jud xvi. 17); whether he himself had to avoid the use of intoxicants does not appear, though his mother was to abstain from such before his birth (Jud xiii. 4); in regard to the third of the prohibitions here laid down Samson seems to have been quite unconcerned (Jud xiv. 8)."

4. Binns, *Numbers,* p. 37, cites the description in Jer. 35 "of a whole family who, in obedience to an ancestral command practised the same self-denial; in their case and probably in that of the Nazirite the avoidance of wine and allied products was not a temperance measure, but a protest against the use of fruits which were the gift of the Baalim." A. Motyer points out that the Rechabites abstained from the vine because of

its association with settled occupation (as distinct from a nomadic lifestyle), just as they abstained from stone-built houses.

5. Carl L. Keil and Franz Delitzsch, *Numbers,* Commentary on the Old Testament, vol. 3 (Grand Rapids: Wm. B. Eerdmans, repr. 1971), p. 38.

6. Binns, *Numbers.*

7. Keil and Delitzsch, *Numbers.*

8. Ibid., p. 38 adds: "The object was simply the realization of the idea of a priestly life, with its purity and freedom from all contamination from everything connected with death and corruption, a self-surrender to God stretching beyond the deepest earthly ties, 'a spontaneous appropriation of what was imposed upon the priest by virtue of the calling connected with his descent, namely, the obligation to conduct himself as a person betrothed to God, and therefore to avoid everything that would be opposed to such surrender' (Ochler). In this respect the Nazarite's sanctification of life was a step towards the realization of the priestly character, which had been set before the whole nation as its goal at the time of its first calling (Ex. xix.5); and although it was simply the performance of a vow, and therefore a work of perfect spontaneity, it was also a work of the Spirit of God which dwelt in the congregation of Israel, so that Amos could describe the raising up of Nazarites along with prophets as a special manifestation of divine grace."

9. Elisabeth Elliot, *The Shadow of the Almighty* (London: STL Publications).

10. Wenham, *Numbers,* p. 85.

11. Gray, *Numbers,* p. 71.

12. Binns, *Numbers,* p. 41, maintains that "this fragment is quite obviously out of its context, and the suggestion that it originally came after Lev. ix. 22 has much to recommend it on grounds of fitness, though there is no actual evidence in support of it." Gray, *Numbers,* p. 72, speaks of the passage as a liturgical poem which "would have been a natural product of the period of the Josianic Reformation. The centralisation of worship must have strengthened the sense of the religious unity of the people as well as that of the unity of Yahweh. The blessing may, of course, be considerably earlier; but the positive reasons adduced for holding it to be such are not cogent." He quotes Ewald, however, as referring it to the Mosaic period on account of its antique simplicity, and this viewpoint is taken also by Martin Noth, *Numbers: A Commentary,* Old Testament Library (London: SCM Press, 1968), p. 58, who says "It may well belong to the traditions handed down from the earlier period and its simplicity of expression would even argue for great antiquity."

13. Keil and Delitzsch, *Numbers,* p. 42, refers in a footnote to Luther's Exposition of the blessing: "Luther refers the first blessing to 'bodily life

and good'. The blessing, he says, desired for the people 'that God would give them prosperity and every good, and also guard and preserve them.' This is carried out still further, in a manner corresponding to his exposition of the first article. The second blessing he refers to 'the spiritual nature and the soul,' and observes, 'Just as the sun, when it rises and diffuses its rich glory and soft light over all the world, merely lifts up its face upon all the world; . . . so when God gives His word, He causes His face to shine clearly and joyously upon all minds, and makes them joyful and light, and as it were new hearts and new men. For it brings forgiveness of sins, and shows God as a gracious and merciful Father, who pities and sympathizes with our grief and sorrow. The third also relates to the spiritual nature and the soul, and is a desire for consolation and final victory over the cross, death, the devil, and all the gates of hell, together with the world and all the evil desires of the flesh. The desire of this blessing is, that the Lord God will lift up the light of His word upon us, and so keep it over us, that it may shine in our hearts with strength enough to overcome all the opposition of the devil, death, and sin, and all adversity, terror, or despair.'"

CHAPTER FOUR

The Offerings of the Israelite Princes

Numbers 7:1–89

The offering of gifts by the princes of Israel recorded in this section took place on the completion by Moses of the erection of the tabernacle at Sinai and was one of the last events prior to the departure of the people of Israel from Sinai. It is an extremely long section, falling into two unequal parts, 1–9 and 10–88, with a final sentence (v. 89) describing Moses' fellowship and concourse with the Lord within the tabernacle. The events recorded in it do not follow chronologically upon the previous chapters. The setting up of the tabernacle took place on the first day of the first month of the second year (Exod. 40:17), and this date is already past, in Numbers 1:18. Historically, it should follow Leviticus 8:10, 11. It is placed here, according to one commentator, "at the head of the events which immediately preceded the departure of the people from Sinai, because these gifts consisted in part of materials that were indispensably necessary for the transport of the Tabernacle during the march through the desert."[1]

The princes, who are mentioned in the same order as in 2:3–29, make a sacred offering, each identical to the other, consisting of six covered wagons and twelve oxen (v. 3). These are received from them by Moses, who gives them to the Gershonites and Merarites for use in connection with the services of the tabernacle, and particularly for its imminent departure on its wilderness journeyings (vv. 4–9). The composition of the offerings in each case is a silver platter and a silver bowl, both filled with fine flour mingled with oil for a grain offering; a golden spoon full of incense; a bullock, a ram, a lamb for a burnt offering; a kid for a sin offering; and two oxen, five rams, five he-goats, five lambs for a peace offering. The offerings are formally presented by the princes on twelve successive days (vv. 12–83). The total amount offered by them is finally recorded in verses 84–88.

The Spontaneous Giving

7:1 Now it came to pass, when Moses had finished setting up the tabernacle, that he anointed it and consecrated it and all its furnishings, and the altar and all its utensils; so he anointed them and consecrated them.

2 Then the leaders of Israel, the heads of their fathers' houses, who *were* the leaders of the tribes and over those who were numbered, made an offering.

3 And they brought their offering before the LORD, six covered carts and twelve oxen, a cart for *every* two of the leaders, and for each one an ox; and they presented them before the tabernacle.

4 Then the LORD spoke to Moses, saying,

5 "Accept *these* from them, that they may be used in doing the work of the tabernacle of meeting; and you shall give them to the Levites, *to* every man according to his service."

6 So Moses took the carts and the oxen, and gave them to the Levites.

7 Two carts and four oxen he gave to the sons of Gershon, according to their service;

8 and four carts and eight oxen he gave to the sons of Merari, according to their service, under the authority of Ithamar the son of Aaron the priest.

9 But to the sons of Kohath he gave none, because theirs *was* the service of the holy things, *which* they carried on their shoulders.

Num. 7:1–9

The offerings by the princes seem to have been a spontaneous act following the completion and anointing of the tabernacle. It almost seems to be implied, from what is said in verses 4–5, that Moses awaited some indication as to whether their offerings were in order (they had already been very generous in their offerings for the construction of the tabernacle, Exod. 35:27). On learning that their generosity had in fact been prompted by God, Moses received the gifts, to be applied to the purposes of the tabernacle, and delivered them over to the Levites in accordance with their respective duties. The distribution was not an equal one, but it was in line with their particular offices. The Gershonites received one-third of the wagons for their duties (cf. 4:25, 26), whereas the Merarites, who had much heavier burdens to bear (cf. 4:31, 32), received two-thirds. The Kohathites received none, since their duties did not require them (cf. 4:1–15). Their place was to attend to the sanctuary, which was to be borne on their shoulders—for which task they were provided with poles. That the offerings of the princes were generous to a degree is evident; that they were sufficient for the divine purposes is just as clear, and this is some indication of how much the princes were under the inspiration and control of the Spirit of God in their large-hearted giving. With such an attitude, the work of God could not but prosper!

The Offerings of the Chief Men

7:10 Now the leaders offered the dedication *offering* for the altar when it was anointed; so the leaders offered their offering before the altar.

11 For the LORD said to Moses, "They shall offer their offering, one leader each day, for the dedication of the altar."

12 And the one who offered his offering on the first day *was* Nahshon the son of Amminadab, from the tribe of Judah.

13 His offering *was* one silver platter, the weight of which *was* one hundred and thirty *shekels,* and one silver bowl of seventy shekels, according to the shekel of the sanctuary, both of them full of fine flour mixed with oil as a grain offering;

14 one gold pan of ten *shekels,* full of incense;

15 one young bull, one ram, and one male lamb in its first year, as a burnt offering;

16 one kid of the goats as a sin offering;

17 and for the sacrifice of peace offerings: two oxen, five rams, five male goats, and five male lambs in their first year. This *was* the offering of Nahshon the son of Amminadab.

18 On the second day Nethanel the son of Zuar, leader of Issachar, presented *an offering.*

19 *For* his offering he offered one silver platter, the weight of which *was* one hundred and thirty *shekels,* and one silver bowl of seventy shekels, according to the shekel of the sanctuary, both of them full of fine flour mixed with oil as a grain offering;

20 one gold pan of ten *shekels,* full of incense;

21 one young bull, one ram, and one male lamb in its first year, as a burnt offering;

22 one kid of the goats as a sin offering;

23 and as the sacrifice of peace offerings: two oxen, five rams, five male goats, and five male lambs in their first year. This *was* the offering of Nethanel the son of Zuar.

24 On the third day Eliab the son of Helon, leader of the children of Zebulun, *presented an offering.*

25 His offering *was* one silver platter, the weight of which *was* one hundred and thirty *shekels,* and one silver bowl of seventy shekels, according to the shekel of the sanctuary, both of them full of fine flour mixed with oil as a grain offering;

26 one gold pan of ten *shekels,* full of incense;

27 one young bull, one ram, and one male lamb in its first year, as a burnt offering;

28 one kid of the goats as a sin offering;

29 and for the sacrifice of peace offerings: two oxen, five rams, five male goats, and five male lambs in their first year. This *was* the offering of Eliab the son of Helon.

30 On the fourth day Elizur the son of Shedeur, leader of the children of Reuben, *presented an offering.*

31 His offering *was* one silver platter, the weight of which *was* one hundred and thirty *shekels,* and one silver bowl of seventy shekels, according to the shekel of the sanctuary, both of them full of fine flour mixed with oil as a grain offering;

32 one gold pan of ten *shekels,* full of incense;

33 one young bull, one ram, and one male lamb in its first year, as a burnt offering;

34 one kid of the goats as a sin offering;

35 and as the sacrifice of peace offerings: two oxen, five rams, five male goats, and five male lambs in their first year. This *was* the offering of Elizur the son of Shedeur.

36 On the fifth day Shelumiel the son of Zurishaddai, leader of the children of Simeon, *presented an offering.*

37 His offering *was* one silver platter, the weight of which *was* one hundred and thirty *shekels,* and one silver bowl of seventy shekels, according to the shekel of the sanctuary, both of them full of fine flour mixed with oil as a grain offering;

38 one gold pan of ten *shekels,* full of incense;

39 one young bull, one ram, and one male lamb in its first year, as a burnt offering;

40 one kid of the goats as a sin offering;

41 and as the sacrifice of peace offerings: two oxen, five rams, five male goats, and five male lambs in their first year. This *was* the offering of Shelumiel the son of Zurishaddai.

42 On the sixth day Eliasaph the son of Deuel, leader of the children of Gad, *presented an offering.*

43 His offering *was* one silver platter, the weight of which *was* one hundred and thirty *shekels,* and one silver bowl of seventy shekels, according to the shekel of the sanctuary, both of them full of fine flour mixed with oil as a grain offering;

44 one gold pan of ten *shekels,* full of incense;

45 one young bull, one ram, and one male lamb in its first year, as a burnt offering;

46 one kid of the goats as a sin offering;

47 and as the sacrifice of peace offerings: two oxen, five rams, five male goats, and five male lambs in their first year. This *was* the offering of Eliasaph the son of Deuel.

48 On the seventh day Elishama the son of Ammihud, leader of the children of Ephraim, *presented an offering.*

49 His offering *was* one silver platter, the weight of

which *was* one hundred and thirty *shekels,* and one
silver bowl of seventy shekels, according to the shekel
of the sanctuary, both of them full of fine flour mixed
with oil as a grain offering;
50 one gold pan of ten *shekels,* full of incense;
51 one young bull, one ram, and one male lamb in
its first year, as a burnt offering;
52 one kid of the goats as a sin offering;
53 and as the sacrifice of peace offerings: two
oxen, five rams, five male goats, and five male lambs
in their first year. This *was* the offering of Elishama
the son of Ammihud.
54 On the eighth day Gamaliel the son of Pedahzur,
leader of the children of Manasseh, *presented an
offering.*
55 His offering *was* one silver platter, the weight of
which *was* one hundred and thirty *shekels,* and one
silver bowl of seventy shekels, according to the shekel
of the sanctuary, both of them full of fine flour mixed
with oil as a grain offering;
56 one gold pan of ten *shekels,* full of incense;
57 one young bull, one ram, and one male lamb in
its first year, as a burnt offering;
58 one kid of the goats as a sin offering;
59 and as the sacrifice of peace offerings: two
oxen, five rams, five male goats, and five male lambs
in their first year. This *was* the offering of Gamaliel
the son of Pedahzur.
60 On the ninth day Abidan the son of Gideoni,
leader of the children of Benjamin, *presented an offering.*
61 His offering *was* one silver platter, the weight of
which *was* one hundred and thirty *shekels,* and one
silver bowl of seventy shekels, according to the shekel
of the sanctuary, both of them full of fine flour mixed
with oil as a grain offering;
62 one gold pan of ten *shekels,* full of incense;
63 one young bull, one ram, and one male lamb in
its first year, as a burnt offering;
64 one kid of the goats as a sin offering;
65 and as the sacrifice of peace offerings: two
oxen, five rams, five male goats, and five male lambs

in their first year. This *was* the offering of Abidan the son of Gideoni.

66 On the tenth day Ahiezer the son of Ammishaddai, leader of the children of Dan, *presented an offering.*

67 His offering *was* one silver platter, the weight of which *was* one hundred and thirty *shekels,* and one silver bowl of seventy shekels, according to the shekel of the sanctuary, both of them full of fine flour mixed with oil as a grain offering;

68 one gold pan of ten *shekels,* full of incense;

69 one young bull, one ram, and one male lamb in its first year, as a burnt offering;

70 one kid of the goats as a sin offering;

71 and as the sacrifice of peace offerings: two oxen, five rams, five male goats, and five male lambs in their first year. This *was* the offering of Ahiezer the son of Ammishaddai.

72 On the eleventh day Pagiel the son of Ocran, leader of the children of Asher, *presented an offering.*

73 His offering *was* one silver platter, the weight of which *was* one hundred and thirty *shekels,* and one silver bowl of seventy shekels, according to the shekel of the sanctuary, both of them full of fine flour mixed with oil as a grain offering;

74 one gold pan of ten *shekels,* full of incense;

75 one young bull, one ram, and one male lamb in its first year, as a burnt offering;

76 one kid of the goats as a sin offering;

77 and as the sacrifice of peace offerings: two oxen, five rams, five male goats, and five male lambs in their first year. This *was* the offering of Pagiel the son of Ocran.

78 On the twelfth day Ahira the son of Enan, leader of the children of Naphtali, *presented an offering.*

79 His offering *was* one silver platter, the weight of which *was* one hundred and thirty *shekels,* and one silver bowl of seventy shekels, according to the shekel of the sanctuary, both of them full of fine flour mixed with oil as a grain offering;

80 one gold pan of ten *shekels,* full of incense;

81 one young bull, one ram, and one male lamb in
its first year, as a burnt offering;
82 one kid of the goats as a sin offering;
83 and as the sacrifice of peace offerings: two
oxen, five rams, five male goats, and five male lambs
in their first year. This *was* the offering of Ahira the
son of Enan.
84 This *was* the dedication *offering* for the altar
from the leaders of Israel, when it was anointed:
twelve silver platters, twelve silver bowls, and twelve
gold pans.
85 Each silver platter *weighed* one hundred and
thirty *shekels* and each bowl seventy *shekels.* All
the silver of the vessels *weighed* two thousand four
hundred *shekels,* according to the shekel of the sanctuary.
86 The twelve gold pans full of incense *weighed*
ten *shekels* apiece, according to the shekel of the
sanctuary; all the gold of the pans *weighed* one hundred and twenty *shekels.*
87 All the oxen for the burnt offering *were* twelve
young bulls, the rams twelve, the male lambs in their
first year twelve, with their grain offering, and the
kids of the goats as a sin offering twelve.
88 And all the oxen for the sacrifice of peace offerings were twenty-four bulls, the rams sixty, the male
goats sixty, and the lambs in their first year sixty.
This *was* the dedication *offering* for the altar after it
was anointed.
89 Now when Moses went into the tabernacle of
meeting to speak with Him, he heard the voice
of One speaking to him from above the mercy seat
that *was* on the ark of the Testimony, from between
the two cherubim; thus He spoke to him.

Num. 7:10–89

There is some question as to how precisely the offerings were carried out, but it would seem that all the various gifts were presented by the princes at the same time as the wagons and oxen (v. 10); after this, a more formal presentation and acceptance of the gifts was made by each prince on successive days. The order in which the offerings were made follows the order of the tribes in chapter 2, as they were set out on all sides of the ark of the covenant. This, as we saw, was to be their marching order, and indeed their battle order. The association of service, worship, and battle is an interesting one, and may be intentional on the part of the writer.

It will be remembered that the place where these offerings were made was Mount Sinai, which is so often associated with the severity of the law. But here is an act that is full of grace, the response of grateful hearts to God for His giving of the law and for His establishing of the tabernacle. Indeed, rightly understood, grace is just as evident as law in this context. It is a false antithesis to suppose that the Old Testament signifies law, while the New Testament signifies grace. In fact, law and grace go hand in hand, and are side by side, in both the Old Testament and the New; and the real picture that comes through from a true reading of the Old Testament is that of a God full of grace and compassion, rich in mercy and tender in His love toward His people. The facile assumption made by many (who do not appear to have read the Old Testament at all) that it is a sub-Christian God we meet there is wide of the mark.

The offering of the princes, then, was the spontaneous response of grateful hearts to the goodness and grace of God. This sets the question of Christian liberality in its true perspective, and the scriptural principle is not difficult to see. Where people are conscious of the blessing of God in their lives, they will give spontaneously—and keep on giving. Finance in the church is directly related to faith and consecration. An attitude of glad-hearted consecration on the part of the people of God will always provide a sufficiency, and indeed an abundance. One thinks of the similar spirit of generosity shown in the giving for the construction of the tabernacle in Exodus 35ff., when the people's response was so great that Moses was obliged to appeal to them to stay their hand (Exod. 36:6). It could hardly be said to be usual in our day for people to be restrained from giving! It is what the apostle Paul would call "abounding more and more" (1 Thess. 4:1, 10; cf. 2 Cor. 8:1–5).

Another point of importance to note is that although the offerings from each of the princes, and therefore from each of the tribes, were identical, each one is recorded separately and in detail. This is done not merely to draw attention to the identity of the offerings but—far more important—to show that each one was noted individually by God. There is surely the love of a Father revealed in this. When an earthly father receives gifts from his children he does not lump them together in a heap and say, "Thank you all very much." Rather, he acknowledges them individually, one by one, expressing his personal pleasure and gratitude in personal terms. This is what God is doing here with the gifts of the princes.

This should be an enormous encouragement in spiritual life, for it means that in God's book on high, what we do in love for Him is recorded precisely and individually. This is another—and a necessary "other"—side of the idea of the recording angel. All the expressions in Scripture about "writing down" and "entering in a book" tend to make us think in terms of sin and guilt; and this is solemnly true—all that we have ever done is written down (cf. Col. 2:14). But there is a blessed counterpart to this, as is evidenced here (cf. Mal. 3:16, 17). God is not unjust to forget our work and labor of love which we show toward His name (Heb. 6:10).

The possibility of giving pleasure to God by our glad thanks-offerings and worship may be a somewhat remote thought in the minds of Christians, but if so it is a measure of how much the church has lost sight of the real heart of the Christian experience, which is fellowship with the Father and the Son through the Spirit (1 John 1:3). How should we suppose, if this fellowship is real, that God is indifferent to it from His side? If our chief end is "to enjoy Him," should it be thought strange or improbable that He takes pleasure in His people (Ps. 149:4)?

We should note that no mention is made of any trespass offering being made by the princes. The distinction between confessing sin and confessing themselves sinners is a real one, for on this occasion the princes were not coming to God in contrition, but in worship. This serves to remind us that there may be occasions in our relationship with God when contrition is out of place. One of the impressive things in the New Testament, and particularly in Paul's epistles, is to see how very little place there is, comparatively speaking, for contrition. Paul does not grieve about his sins to the Lord; he is "up higher." Perhaps we should recognize that there is a grieving about sin, and a preoccupation about it, that is frankly dishonoring to Christ, and calls in question the perfection of His sacrifice for us. It is not that we forget we are sinners, still less that we underestimate the heinousness and the ugliness and the affront of sin in the sight of a holy God, but rather that preoccupation with it is displaced by the outgoing of the heart in glad adoration and worship. If God is able to say, "Their sins and their lawless deeds I will remember no more" (Heb. 10:17), ought not we also to be able to be delivered from undue preoccupation with them? Is this one of the things that the writer to the Hebrews means by the words, "Therefore, leaving the discussion of the elementary principles of Christ, let us go on to perfection, not laying again the foundation of repentance from dead works and of faith toward God . . ." (Heb. 6:1)?

The supreme point in this whole section comes in its final verse (v. 89), following the catalogue of the totals of the offerings, massive and munificent as they were. When Moses went into the tabernacle to speak with God, the divine voice spoke to him from above the mercy seat on the ark of the testimony. Scholars are not certain whether what follows in the next section gives the substance of what the Lord spoke to him, or whether verse 89 is intended "as an independent statement and not simply as an introduction to a divine address."[2] What is important, however, from a spiritual point of view, is the fact that God spoke with Moses when the tabernacle was completed and the altar consecrated and dedicated. In other words, when the *ground* of fellowship was properly established according to the pattern shown in the mount, then God met with Moses, and through Moses with the people. This speaks to us of the only way in which fellowship with God is really possible—on the ground of a God-appointed system of atonement and approach to Him. It is only through Christ the Mediator that we can have fellowship with God and that God can speak with us.

Furthermore, and from a spiritual point of view even more important, the possibility of God speaking with His people is linked here directly with the dedication of the princes and their gifts to the Lord. In this connection we may recall what we are told in 1 Samuel 3, about the days following the period of the Judges when the word of the Lord was a rare commodity and there was no open vision. The reason for this is not hard to find. It was because God had been grieved away by the sin of His people that He did not speak.

When this is the situation, the need is twofold. Firstly, God's people must recover a biblical pattern for life and a biblical doctrine of "approach"—in Christian terms, the recovery of the theology of the cross. One compelling reason why the church of God has made so little headway in modern society is that it has so substantially departed from biblical foundations and thinking. Secondly, there must be a recovery of the spirit of glad abandonment to God in His gospel. The spirit of dedicated stewardship was followed by the coming of the word of the Lord to Moses and to the people. The prophet Malachi sums it up: "'Bring all the tithes into the storehouse, that there may be food in My house, and prove Me now in this,' says the Lord of hosts, 'If I will not open for you the windows of heaven and pour out for you such a blessing that there will not be room enough to receive it'" (Mal. 3:10). This is the glad reward of true and faithful stewardship; and this is the message of the section.

NOTES

1. Carl L. Keil and Franz Delitzsch, *Numbers,* Commentary on the Old Testament, vol. 3 (Grand Rapids: Wm. B. Eerdmans, repr. 1971), pp. 42–43.
2. Martin Noth, *Numbers: A Commentary,* Old Testament Library (London: SCM Press, 1968), p. 65.

CHAPTER FIVE

The Consecration of the Levites

Numbers 8:1–26

The Golden Lampstand

> 8:1 And the LORD spoke to Moses, saying:
> 2 "Speak to Aaron, and say to him, 'When you arrange the lamps, the seven lamps shall give light in front of the lampstand.'"
> 3 And Aaron did so; he arranged the lamps to face toward the front of the lampstand, as the LORD commanded Moses.
> 4 Now this workmanship of the lampstand *was* hammered gold; from its shaft to its flowers it *was* hammered work. According to the pattern which the LORD had shown Moses, so he made the lampstand.
>
> *Num. 8:1–4*

The account of the consecration of the Levites is prefaced by a brief section dealing with the setting up of the lamps on the golden lampstand, or candlestick (cf. Exod. 25:31–40). According to the instructions given in Exodus 30:7 and Leviticus 24:1–4, the lamps were to burn during the night only.[1] The following comment on the placement of the lamps is helpful: "Their being placed in the connection in which we find them may be explained from the signification of the seven lamps in relation to the dwelling of God, viz. as indicating that Israel was thereby to be represented perpetually before the Lord as a people causing its light to shine in the darkness of this world."[2]

The pattern in verse 4 is ever that revealed to Moses in the mount. In this connection Calvin makes the comment that "God is the father of lights, who illuminates His Church, by His Spirit, that it may not wander in darkness; and so, whilst darkness covers the whole earth, He is as an everlasting light to believers instead of the sun and moon, as says Isaiah (60:19)."

The spiritual significance of this brief paragraph becomes clearer when we consider it alongside 7:89. In the comment on that verse we made reference to the story in 1 Samuel 3 as an example of how the word of the Lord came among God's people after a long dearth. It was "before the lamp of God went out in the tabernacle of the Lord where the Ark of God was" (1 Sam. 3:3) that the Lord called Samuel. There is a certain symbolism in these words, in that it was at the darkest hour of the night and just before the dawn of a new day that the Lord called Samuel. And in the coming of the word of the Lord to Samuel, and through him to the people, light also came into the darkness of that time. Word and light went together in that situation, and word and light go together here also. For any forward movement—and the children of Israel were about to move forward from Sinai toward the Promised Land—the need is both for the Word of the Lord and the light of the Lord shining in the midst.

This, then, shows us the desire and concern of God for His house—it is to be a place where His voice is heard speaking and where His light shines into the darkness of men's hearts, bringing illumination upon the dark places of their experience. As the psalmist puts it, "Your word is a lamp to my feet and a light to my path" (Ps. 119:105). Nor can the two ever be separated: Word without light cannot be of divine origin, and is inconceivable; light without word, on the other hand, can cause error and heresy.

Furthermore, the position of this passage has its significance. On the Israelites' onward march to the Promised Land, word and light were to be the content of the pillar of cloud and fire that was to lead them. It is in relation to this that we can best understand the passage that follows, dealing with the consecration of the Levites (vv. 5–22), because their consecration was in spiritual terms the lighting of innumerable lamps among the people of God giving them light from Him. The twofold emphasis in Jesus' words, "I am the light of the world" (John 8:12) and "You are the light of the world" (Matt. 5:14) is illustrated clearly in this. In the absolute sense it is He alone who gives light. When He comes, by His Word, light comes to men. But when consecration takes place, light is shed abroad in the church (and this is as true of preachers as of other people).

The Purification of the Levites

8:5 Then the LORD spoke to Moses, saying:

6 "Take the Levites from among the children of
Israel and cleanse them *ceremonially*.

7 "Thus you shall do to them to cleanse them:
Sprinkle water of purification on them, and let them
shave all their body, and let them wash their clothes,
and *so* make themselves clean.

8 "Then let them take a young bull with its grain
offering of fine flour mixed with oil, and you shall
take another young bull as a sin offering.

9 "And you shall bring the Levites before the
tabernacle of meeting, and you shall gather together
the whole congregation of the children of Israel.

10 "So you shall bring the Levites before the LORD,
and the children of Israel shall lay their hands on the
Levites;

11 "and Aaron shall offer the Levites before the
LORD *like* a wave offering from the children of Israel,
that they may perform the work of the LORD.

12 "Then the Levites shall lay their hands on the
heads of the young bulls, and you shall offer one as a
sin offering and the other as a burnt offering to the
LORD, to make atonement for the Levites.

13 "And you shall stand the Levites before Aaron
and his sons, and then offer them *like* a wave offering to the LORD.

14 "Thus you shall separate the Levites from
among the children of Israel, and the Levites shall
be Mine.

15 "After that the Levites shall go in to service the
tabernacle of meeting. So you shall cleanse them and
offer them *like* a wave offering.

16 "For they *are* wholly given to Me from among
the children of Israel; I have taken them for Myself
instead of all who open the womb, the firstborn of
all the children of Israel.

17 "For all the firstborn among the children of
Israel *are* Mine, *both* man and beast; on the day that
I struck all the firstborn in the land of Egypt I sancti-
fied them to Myself.

18 "I have taken the Levites instead of all the firstborn of the children of Israel.
19 "And I have given the Levites as a gift to Aaron
and his sons from among the children of Israel, to
do the work for the children of Israel in the tabernacle of meeting, and to make atonement for the children of Israel, that there be no plague among the
children of Israel when the children of Israel come
near the sanctuary."
20 Thus Moses and Aaron and all the congregation
of the children of Israel did to the Levites; according
to all that the LORD commanded Moses concerning
the Levites, so the children of Israel did to them.
21 And the Levites purified themselves and washed
their clothes; then Aaron presented them *like* a wave
offering before the LORD, and Aaron made atonement
for them to cleanse them.
22 After that the Levites went in to do their work
in the tabernacle of meeting before Aaron and his
sons; as the LORD commanded Moses concerning the
Levites, so they did to them.

Num. 8:5–22

The substance of this section is parallel to what we have already seen in chapters 3 and 4. It deals with the choice of the Levites for service in the sanctuary, in place of the firstborn of the people, and the duties binding upon them. It is not a matter of repetition, however, for as the Old Testament scholar Martin Noth remarks, "The Levites are conceived of as an offering brought by the Israelites at God's command. This is a novel idea, going beyond anything in chapters 3 and 4. This is not a reason for the peculiar position of the Levites, rather is that position presupposed and interpreted in the sense of their specially belonging to Yahweh, an idea which, for its part, is now based on a dedication on the analogy of a sacrifice."[3] Furthermore, in the earlier chapters, what was given was a description of the consecration to which the Levites were destined by God. Here what we have is their actual committal to this consecration. The particular value of the passage is that it shows the Levites entering into their true destiny in the service of God. And that must always be a moving experience, in much the same way as an admission of members into full communion in the church ought to be for us, and usually is.

The regulations for the Levites are less stringent than for those of the priests: this is not to "play down" their office, but rather to distinguish them from the priesthood. The sprinkling is with *"water of purification"* (v. 7) (or "water for expiation," RSV), which one scholar takes as referring to "the water in the laver of the sanctuary, which was provided for the purpose of cleansing of the priests for the performance of their duties (cf. Exod. 30:18ff.)."[4] Thus cleansed, they were designated as the offering of the whole people (vv. 9, 10) by the symbolic ritual of the laying on of hands. This offering was to be made by Aaron (v. 11—although in v. 13 it seems to be Moses who offers them; but all this may mean is that Moses received the command to do so, while Aaron acted as his executive). Calvin suggests that Aaron's involvement in the dedication rather than Moses was designed to prevent the "danger of their being puffed up with pride against all others," and to remind them (the Levites) that their degree of honor was not similar to or the same as that of the priests.

By whomsoever the offering was made, however, it completed the symbolic act of the laying on of hands (v. 10) and signified the "transfer to the Levites of the obligation resting upon the whole nation to serve the Lord in the persons of its first-born sons, and present them to the Lord as representatives of the first-born of Israel, to serve Him as living sacrifices."[5] The Levites in turn were to complete the transfer of themselves to the Lord with a sin offering and a burnt offering, laying their hands on the animals in the same way as hands were laid on them by the Israelites.

This "double" identification, the people with the Levites and the Levites in turn with the sacrificial animals, is explained in verses 13–19. The Levites belonged to the Lord and were given by the people to Him for His own, and they were taken thus to be His own in place of all the firstborn of the people. The execution of the command is recorded in verses 20–22.

The principle implicit in the idea of the laying on of hands is, of course, that of identification. The Levites were representing the people of Israel, who were thereby identifying themselves, and being identified, with the Levites in their consecration (just as the Levites in turn identified themselves with the sacrificial animals). They recognized the Lord's claim on the firstborn as being a claim on all His redeemed people. It is this that constitutes the challenge of the passage for us who read it today. God shows in it a pattern, as He showed Moses and Israel a pattern in the mount, to which He calls His people to conform. He has chosen us in Christ for a destiny not only of salvation but also of service, and His ringing summons to us is to throw in our lot with His work, identifying ourselves with it and committing ourselves irrevocably to it.

The symbol of "belonging" to the Lord comes into its own in the New Testament and is fulfilled for the whole Christian community. The church is called "the general assembly and church of the firstborn" (Heb. 12:23); that is, every believer incorporated into the body of Christ is set apart to be the Lord's. Even in the Old Testament, however, the idea of separation for the whole congregation of the Lord's people is decisive, as may be seen in the incident recorded in 1 Samuel 8:5, 19, 20, which tells of Israel's insistence on having a king "that we also may be like all the nations," an insistence that was to cost them dearly. The whole point of their calling to be God's people was that they should not be like the other nations, but rather be God's peculiar people, separated unto Himself, with *different* standards, ideals, and patterns from those of the peoples around them.

It is significant that it was in those times when Israel most approximated to this separated character that they most fully realized their true destiny. The tragedy was that so often, particularly in the period of the kings, separation was so substantially at a discount. If there is one general message for the Christian church written large on the pages of the Old Testament, it is that the people of God must take their call to spiritual nonconformity with the utmost seriousness. Only thus can they fulfill their destiny as lights in the world.

Nor is this separated existence to be regarded as cramping or restricting. Indeed, it was the opposite for the Levites, for God said to them that He was their inheritance (cf. Deut. 10:9), just as He had said earlier to Abraham, "I am your shield, and your exceedingly great reward" (Gen. 15:1). God is no man's debtor. Those who, called to a one-track life, respond with wholehearted devotion live life most fully, and most interestingly, too. One of the lessons to be learned from some of the seemingly boring genealogies in the Old Testament (these long lists of people of whom little or nothing is said apart from the recording of their names) is that there is in fact little to record about lives that are outside the covenant purposes of God. They are dull and lifeless, even boring, figures, lacking in substance and vitality. It is the life committed to the divine purposes that is really full and meaningful. Not only so: the separated life is also life-giving, and fruit-bearing. This is implicit in the idea of the Lord being their inheritance and it finds its best and fullest expression in the Pauline statement in 2 Corinthians 6:10, "As poor, yet making many rich."

A moving statement of the principle of identification underlined in this section is given in the following words from a meditation entitled "The Way of the Cross," which exercised a profound influence in the early formative years of my Christian life:

> If we are called to the fellowship of His suffering, as well as to partnership in His service, the essential features of motive and work must be the same in us as in Him. What does that mean in practical life? It means that the man who takes up the cross and follows Christ lives in the will of God for the service of man. As the Son of God placed all the resources of His glory at the disposal of man's need, so every disciple abandons all to God for the blessing of man. He is God's steward, and the sphere of his stewardship is in the sin and sorrow of the world. He becomes a co-worker with God in Christ Jesus. The experience of salvation leads to co-operation in the work of salvation. Acceptance of the cross is a proclamation that its bearer stands in the midst of a sinful and burdened world in Christ's stead. The cross calls to itself the weary and heavy laden, and pledges its bearer to lift their burdens and lead them into the way of rest. The Christian undertakes to be as Christ in the world, to do His work, to minister in His Spirit, and for this he lays all at the feet of his Lord.
>
> This is bearing the cross; sorrowing over the world's sin, bearing the world's burden, carrying the world's shame, ministering to the world's need, laying down our life for the world's salvation. This is the badge and test of discipleship. Have we taken up the cross? Have we dared to come out from the world, antagonised ourselves to it, and borne its reproach? Are we

surrendered in all things to the will of God? Has all been placed at His disposal and consecrated to His saving purpose among men? Have we returned to the world as Christ came to it? Do we weep over it, pray for it, live for it, die for it? It is for these the cross stands, and without the cross we cannot be Christ's disciples.[6]

THE AGE LIMITS FOR SERVICE

8:23 Then the LORD spoke to Moses, saying,
24 "This *is* what *pertains* to the Levites: From twenty-five years old and above one may enter to perform service in the work of the tabernacle of meeting;
25 "and at the age of fifty years they must cease performing this work, and shall work no more.
26 "They may minister with their brethren in the tabernacle of meeting, to attend to needs, but they *themselves* shall do no work. Thus you shall do to the Levites regarding their duties."

Num. 8:23–26

The concluding paragraph of this section deals with the question of the age at which the Levites were to commence and conclude their service of the sanctuary. The variation in the lower age limit as compared with 4:2ff. (cf. also 1 Chron. 23:3) has already been referred to.[7] Both this passage and the earlier one are indicative of the divine concern for His servants' welfare. There is always a special love and care that God expends on those faithful to Him in His service. He was intent upon seeing that they were not overburdened and set limits to their service. It was as if He said, "I do not expect you to go on beyond your strength." "Those who honor Me, He says, I will honor" (1 Sam. 2:30)—and care for too. This may be taken as part of the "hundredfold now in this time" (Mark 10:30) our Lord promises to those who are faithful to Him in discipleship. We need have no fears or misgivings in serving Him. He is a generous and faithful Master. It is surely not difficult for overburdened, hard-pressed, and discouraged servants of God to take this as a word of encouragement and assurance that the future is in His hands, and that He will provide.

NOTES

1. L. Elliott Binns, *The Book of Numbers* (London: Methuen & Co., Ltd., 1927), p. 49 points out that in later times some of the lamps were kept burning continuously (Tamid III.9, vi.1; Joseph. Ant. III. viii.3). He cannot be right, however, in suggesting that in the days of Samuel (1 Sam. 3:3) the lamps would seem to have gone out at night, and to have burned during the day. A more likely explanation of the reference there must surely be that it was late in the night, possibly some little time before dawn, when the Lord spoke to Samuel, before the Temple light went out.

2. Carl L. Keil and Franz Delitzsch, *Numbers,* Commentary on the Old Testament, vol. 3 (Grand Rapids: Wm. B. Eerdmans, repr. 1971), p. 46.

3. Martin Noth, *Numbers, a Commentary,* Old Testament Library (London: SCM Press, 1968), p. 67.

4. Delitzsch, *Numbers,* p. 47.

5. Delitzsch, *Numbers,* p. 48.

6. From the chapter entitled "The Way of the Cross," in *Humanity and God* by Samuel Chadwick, The Expositor's Library (London: Hodder and Stoughton, n. d.).

7. C. J. Ellicott, *Leviticus,* An Old Testament Commentary for English Readers (London: Cassell & Co., Ltd., 1897), p. 506. See note 7 on page 66 of this volume.

CHAPTER SIX

The Passover at Sinai

Numbers 9:1–14

THE PASSOVER

9:1 Now the LORD spoke to Moses in the Wilderness of Sinai, in the first month of the second year after they had come out of the land of Egypt, saying:
2 "Let the children of Israel keep the Passover at its appointed time.
3 "On the fourteenth day of this month, at twilight, you shall keep it at its appointed time. According to all its rites and ceremonies you shall keep it."
4 So Moses told the children of Israel that they should keep the Passover.
5 And they kept the Passover on the fourteenth day of the first month, at twilight, in the Wilderness of Sinai; according to all that the LORD commanded Moses, so the children of Israel did.

Num. 9:1–5

At the outset of their forward march to the Promised Land, the children of Israel were enjoined to keep the Passover on the appointed day (i.e. the fourteenth day of the first month). Calvin suggests that it was carelessness, even ingratitude, that made this reminder necessary, and that "if they had been voluntarily assiduous in their duty, it would have been unnecessary to repeat what had been so severely enjoined even with threats" (cf. Exod. 12:14, 24, 25).[1] One distinguished commentator, however, more charitably thinks that the purpose of the command was to underline the necessity for the observance rather than "to postpone it, that is, according to an interpretation that might possibly have been put upon Exodus

12:24, 25, until they came to Canaan, but to keep it there at Sinai."[2] The significant point is, it was kept (v. 5) entirely in accordance with the instructions they had received through Moses a year earlier. There was no corruption of "the pure institution with any strange leaven," to use Calvin's words. The Reformer is surely right in reading into verse 5 the implication that their obedience was praised "because they had neither added anything to, nor diminished anything from, God's command."[3] There is a certain impressiveness in the way in which the statement in verse 5 follows the divine command of verses 1–4.

From a spiritual point of view, the command to keep the Passover was a significant reminder that everything in Israel's experience, as a people of God called to pilgrimage, depended and rested upon the mighty act of God on their behalf when He made bare His holy arm and plucked them out of the land of Egypt and the house of bondage. Indeed, their very existence as the people of God depended on what He had done in delivering them. The Passover pointed them to the blood of the slain lamb and to the divine substitution that had rescued them from death. "When I see the blood, I will pass over you" (Exod. 12:13)—their entrance on pilgrimage was made on this ground alone. The New Testament parallel is complete—the mighty intervention of God in Christ for the salvation of men, the great reconciliation and propitiation wrought in His blood whereby the barriers are broken down and the way opened up for men to return, in penitence and faith, to God. This is the gospel, and it is on this basis that the invitation to pilgrimage is made. Christ is the Way, as He is also the Door, and here is the blood-sprinkled door of the new covenant by which if any man enter in he shall be saved.

Furthermore, the Passover was something Israel was commanded to eat as well as to observe, and this bears witness to the fact that the mighty act of God was for them not only the basis and foundation of their pilgrimage, but also a source of sustenance and nourishment for them on their journey. It was, so to speak, a sacrament for the Old Testament people of God and was repeated again and again as a source of spiritual nourishment to them. Not only so. It pointed to the spiritual reality behind it, namely that meditation on the mighty act of God, and dependence upon it day by day, is what affords spiritual sustenance and help in the pilgrim's life.

So it is also in the Christian way. The cross is our source of supply as well as being the place where we begin the Christian life. This is what Christ meant when He spoke of eating His flesh and drinking His blood. A life rightly related to the message of the cross is one that will always be well nourished and sustained. There is always a sufficiency of supply, and no one who embarks on the Christian life will ever fail of food and provision on the way.

Furthermore, keeping the Passover was a reminder to Israel of the standard under which they were to advance, and the principle by which they were to walk. Their lives were to be rightly related to the redemption that God had wrought. In the New Testament antitype, this speaks to us in the language of Christ: "If anyone desires to come after Me, let him deny himself, and take up his cross, and follow Me" (Matt. 16:24). For the Christian this is the order of the march, and there is no other way.

The Problem of Ritual Uncleanness

9:6 Now there were *certain* men who were defiled by a human corpse, so that they could not keep the Passover on that day; and they came before Moses and Aaron that day.

7 And those men said to him, "We *became* defiled by a human corpse. Why are we kept from presenting the offering of the LORD at its appointed time among the children of Israel?"

8 And Moses said to them, "Stand still, that I may hear what the LORD will command concerning you."

9 Then the LORD spoke to Moses, saying,

10 "Speak to the children of Israel, saying: 'If anyone of you or your posterity is unclean because of a corpse, or *is* far away on a journey, he may still keep the LORD's Passover.

11 'On the fourteenth day of the second month, at twilight, they may keep it. They shall eat it with unleavened bread and bitter herbs.

12 'They shall leave none of it until morning, nor break one of its bones. According to all the ordinances of the Passover they shall keep it.

13 'But the man who *is* clean and is not on a journey, and ceases to keep the Passover, that same

> person shall be cut off from among his people, because he did not bring the offering of the LORD at its appointed time; that man shall bear his sin.
>
> 14 'And if a stranger dwells among you, and would keep the LORD's Passover, he must do so according to the rite of the Passover and according to its ceremony; you shall have one ordinance, both for the stranger and the native of the land.'"
>
> *Num. 9:6–14*

Supplementary regulations were next added to cater for cases where the celebration of the Passover at the normal time was prevented for one reason or another. Their formulation arose through an incident occurring at the observation of this second Passover. There were certain men who were ceremonially defiled (v. 6) and could not therefore keep the feast on the day appointed. On inquiring for a ruling on this (v. 8), Moses was given it (vv. 9 ff.) and pronounced accordingly, enunciating a general principle covering all like situations.[4] The feast was to be kept exactly a month later, and with all due observance of the regulations. Gray suggests that the meaning of the question put by the men in verse 7 is virtually a petition for a modification of the law which, on this occasion, had prevented them from keeping the Passover, since they did not need to ask why they were prevented; they knew that the reason lay in their uncleanness.[5]

Whether the later celebration of the Passover was obligatory or voluntary for those who had been unable to observe the main feast is uncertain. What is clear, however, is that there was to be no misuse of this supplementary legislation. Failure to observe the Passover at the appointed time either through indifference or carelessness, when neither uncleanness nor being on a journey was involved, was to be regarded as a punishable offense. The sentence referred to in verse 13 could mean either death or excommunication. If, however, we bear in mind the rigor of the New Testament interpretation of excommunication (cf. 1 Cor. 5:5, 11:30; 1 Tim. 1:20), the distinction between death and excommunication in this context may for practical purposes be an artificial one.[6]

The stranger in verse 14 who is allowed to participate in the Passover feast is one who, though not born an Israelite, becomes one by acceptance of circumcision and who has given himself to the service of the God of Israel. As such, he enjoys the same rights, and is bound by the same laws, as the true Israelite.

NOTES

1. John Calvin, *Harmony of the Pentateuch,* 1:475.
2. Carl L. Keil and Franz Delitzsch, *Numbers,* Commentary on the Old Testament, vol. 3 (Grand Rapids: Wm. B. Eerdmans, repr. 1971), p. 50.
3. Calvin, *Harmony,* 1:475.
4. Martin Noth, *Numbers: A Commentary,* Old Testament Library (London: SCM Press, 1968), p. 71 (footnote) calls this a "charismatic judgment" and refers to a similar passage in Lev. 24:10–23, where out of a specific instance a general ruling is given.
5. G. B. Gray, *A Critical and Exegetical Commentary on Numbers,* International Critical Commentary (Edinburgh: T. & T. Clark, 1903), p. 84. L. Elliott Binns agrees with this view and comments (op. cit. p. 52), "this second passover is interesting as exhibiting a spirit of accommodation in the law, such as is often supposed to be lacking in it."
6. Ibid. Gray quotes Gunkel, "On the much debated question whether this is a threat of death or excommunication, Gunkel (Genesis, p. 246) seems to hit the mark: 'Doubtless men like P desired the death of such a sinner . . . . and when the heathen government permitted it, certainly also inflicted it; in Lev 17:9 ff, 20:3,6 we can read between the lines that such capital punishment of the religious transgressor was not permitted by the government, and that it was necessary to rest content with the belief in the destruction of such a sinner *by God.*' "

CHAPTER SEVEN

The Divine Provision for the March

Numbers 9:15–10:10

The Cloud

9:15 Now on the day that the tabernacle was raised
up, the cloud covered the tabernacle, the tent of the
Testimony; from evening until morning it was above
the tabernacle like the appearance of fire.
16 So it was always: the cloud covered it *by day,*
and the appearance of fire by night.
17 Whenever the cloud was taken up from above
the tabernacle, after that the children of Israel would
journey; and in the place where the cloud settled,
there the children of Israel would pitch their tents.
18 At the command of the LORD the children of
Israel would journey, and at the command of the
LORD they would camp; as long as the cloud stayed
above the tabernacle they remained encamped.
19 Even when the cloud continued long, many
days above the tabernacle, the children of Israel kept
the charge of the LORD and did not journey.
20 So it was, when the cloud was above the tabernacle a few days: according to the command of the
LORD they would remain encamped, and according
to the command of the LORD they would journey.
21 So it was, when the cloud remained only from
evening until morning: when the cloud was taken up
in the morning, then they would journey; whether
by day or by night, whenever the cloud was taken
up, they would journey.

22 *Whether it was* two days, a month, or a year that
the cloud remained above the tabernacle, the children of Israel would remain encamped and not journey; but when it was taken up, they would journey.
23 At the command of the LORD they remained
encamped, and at the command of the LORD they journeyed; they kept the charge of the LORD, at the command of the LORD by the hand of Moses.

Num. 9:15–23

This passage marks the beginning of Israel's departure from Sinai on the way to the Promised Land, and it is fitting that the divine leading and direction of the people should first be described. The date mentioned in verse 15 links the passage with Exodus 40 (vv. 2ff., 34–38). The pillar of cloud and fire has already been mentioned in the story of Israel (Exod. 13: 21ff., 14:19–24, 24:1ff., 33:9, 10, 40:34ff.). Sometimes the emphasis is upon the pillar going before the people, sometimes the cloud stands over or upon the tabernacle, and sometimes its nighttime appearance as a pillar of fire is stressed. The Exodus references show that Israel was already used to being led of God by the pillar, in their journey from Egypt to Sinai, and this pattern is described again here, in detail. Calvin observes that the additional fact recorded here is that the cloud now rested on the tabernacle, that is, as its characteristic and specific locus:

> The people were indeed previously directed by the sight of the cloud, as we have seen; but that here a new fact is related, viz. that since the tabernacle was set up, the cloud, which hitherto was suspended in the air and went before the camp, now settled on the sanctuary: for a fresh acquisition of grace is here proclaimed by the more certain and conspicuous sign, as if God shewed Himself more closely and familiarly as the leader of the people. Although, therefore, the cloud had been the director of their march from its very commencement, yet it more fully illustrated the glory of the tabernacle when it proceeded from thence.[1]

It remains an open question whether the Israelites experienced two kinds of guidance on their journeys, one by the direct voice of the Lord speaking to or through Moses and the other by the manifestation of the pillar of cloud and fire. This uncertainty is seen in verse 18, where *"at the command of the Lord"* is, literally, "at the mouth of the Lord," which seems to indicate an oral command (although one scholar suggests that the word "mouth" had probably lost its original force), yet verses 18b and 19 imply that the divine "word" came through the cloud.

Either way, however, the picture of Israel's dependence on the divine guidance is a beautiful one; but it has been well said that "the children of Israel in the wilderness, surrounded by miracle, had nothing which we do not possess. . . . Their guidance came by the supernatural pillar; ours comes by the reality of which that pillar was nothing but a picture."[2] This statement is a pointer to the kind of spiritual lessons that flow from the symbol of the pillar. They are many and rich. For one thing, it was the token of God's abiding presence with the people. He went before them (Exod. 13:21, 40:38) until the day they entered the land. This is an eloquent reminder, in New Testament terms, that the Christian life is not the acceptance of a system, but the entrance into a fellowship, into a relationship of companionship with Christ.

Not only so; when one thinks of the fractious nature of the Israelites, their murmurings and backslidings, their turning aside and falling away from God, it becomes an even greater marvel to realize that throughout all, His presence was unchangeably with them. He had to rebuke them and chastise them. Many times He was angry with them, but He never left them. What could speak more forcefully than this of a God whose grace is greater than our sin? This is the assurance that the invitation to pilgrimage brings with it, and it comprehends every other consideration, every other possible blessing. If God is for us, says the apostle—and, we may add, with us—who can be against us (Rom. 8:31)?

The pillar was also the guarantee to Israel of God's shelter and protection. As the psalmist puts it, "He spread a cloud for a covering" (Ps. 105:39). One recalls the marvelous story of the deliverance from Egypt, when the pillar moved around and stood between Israel and the oncoming Egyptians: "The Lord looked down upon the army of the Egyptians through the pillar of fire and cloud, and He troubled the army of the Egyptians" (Exod. 14:24). This is what God does for His people. David expresses it beautifully, and accurately, in the immortal words of Psalm 121. The protecting love of God is fierce and tender, rugged and gentle. Blessed are all they who put their trust in Him.

All this, in addition to the assurance of the divine guidance: the Lord led them unerringly *where* they were to go, and *when* (in spiritual life the "when" is quite as important as the "where"; to move before God's time always leads to trouble). Commenting on Israel's wilderness journeyings, the psalmist says, "He led them forth by the right way" (Ps. 107:7)—not always the expected way, or even the shortest way (cf. Exod. 13:17–19), but with God in the lead, the longest way round is the shortest way home. There is plan and purpose in all He does, and all He does is for the best. He guides! This is the overruling consideration. We are not left to walk alone. He knows the way through the wilderness. "How can we know the way?" asked doubting Thomas, perplexed and troubled as he was at that point about many things (as the best of Christians are, from time to time). But our Lord's assurance, "I am the way," reminded him, and us, that in fellowship with Him there is a sure way through even impossible situations. It does not matter that we may not be able to see our way through them: He sees the way through, and He is all powerful. Human difficulties, however great and intractable, are not difficulties to Him. "I will instruct you and teach you in the way you should go; I will guide you with My eye" (Ps. 32:8).

There are two further thoughts implicit in the idea of the pillar. One is that of *revelation.* God revealed Himself to Moses and to Israel in the cloud: "The Lord descended in the cloud and stood with him there, and proclaimed the name of the Lord" (Exod. 34:5). And in the New Testament, God has revealed Himself finally to men in Christ, as the God of love and grace—and in such a complete way that Jesus could say, "He who has seen Me has seen the Father" (John 14:9).

The other is that of *communion* (Exod. 33:9–11): when the cloudy pillar descended and stood at the door of the tabernacle, "the Lord spoke to Moses face to face, as a man speaks to his friend." This is the ultimate possibility of the cloud. It points to this personal communion that all who trust in Christ may have with the Father and the Son. It is not merely forgiveness that the gospel proclaims, though that were a gospel all in itself; nor is it merely a gospel of new life, or of the restoration of the divine image in man; best of all, it is fellowship with Him. Jesus said, "You are My friends" (John 15:14). We know the power of friendship even on the human level to exercise a decisive and definitive influence in our lives; how much more must this be true of the friendship of Christ. His is *the* transforming friendship; it is the fellowship of the burning heart (Luke 24:32). We become our true selves when we walk with Him.

The Silver Trumpets

10:1 And the LORD spoke to Moses, saying:
2 "Make two silver trumpets for yourself; you shall make them of hammered work; you shall use them for calling the congregation and for directing the movement of the camps.
3 "When they blow both of them, all the congregation shall gather before you at the door of the tabernacle of meeting.
4 "But if they blow *only* one, then the leaders, the heads of the divisions of Israel, shall gather to you.
5 "When you sound the advance, the camps that lie on the east side shall then begin their journey.
6 "When you sound the advance the second time, then the camps that lie on the south side shall begin their journey; they shall sound the call for them to begin their journeys.
7 "And when the assembly is to be gathered together, you shall blow, but not sound the advance.
8 "The sons of Aaron, the priests, shall blow the trumpets; and these shall be to you as an ordinance forever throughout your generations.
9 "When you go to war in your land against the enemy who oppresses you, then you shall sound an alarm with the trumpets, and you will be remembered before the LORD your God, and you will be saved from your enemies.
10 "Also in the day of your gladness, in your appointed feasts, and at the beginning of your months, you shall blow the trumpets over your burnt offerings and over the sacrifices of your peace offerings; and they shall be a memorial for you before your God: I *am* the LORD your God."

Num. 10:1–10

The connection between this passage and what immediately precedes it is clear: the forward march of Israel was to be determined by the movement of the cloud (9:15–23), and announced by the sounding of the trumpets (10:1 ff.). The institution of the trumpets is the final instruction given to Israel prior to their setting out on their journey.[3] Five different uses of the trumpets are mentioned: (a) the calling together of the whole congregation (v. 3) when both the trumpets were blown; (b) the calling together of the princes alone (v. 4) when only one was blown; (c) the blowing of an alarm as a signal for marching (vv. 5 ff.); (d) the trumpets were to be blown when they reached Canaan for a memorial before God to bring them to His remembrance, and enlist His help (v. 9); (e) they were to be sounded also in days of festival and sacrifice to secure God's attention (v. 10).

From this we see that the sounding of the trumpets for the summoning of the people and the princes was different from that which indicated the forward march, although it is not certain in what this difference consisted. "Blowing" in verse 7 is distinguished from "sounding an alarm." Delitzsch distinguishes the two by saying that the one signifies blowing in short, sharp tones and the other blowing in a continued peal;[4] but Calvin seems to take the opposite view, suggesting that the alarm was a "louder and more protracted sound, but blown with intervals."[5] Either way, however, it is clear that the sound of the trumpets had a twofold reference. It spoke to the people, gathering them together in assembly and directing them on their way; it spoke also to God, and brought His people in remembrance before Him in time of need, and recorded their glad thankfulness to Him for His goodness to them.

Calvin's comment on the symbolism of the trumpets is a pertinent one:

> We must, however, observe the promise, which is inserted, that the Israelites "should be remembered before the Lord," that He should put their enemies to flight; not as if the safety or deliverance of the people was attached to the trumpets, but because they did not go to the battle except in reliance on God's aid. For the reality itself is conjoined with the external symbol, viz. that they should fight under God, should follow Him as their Leader, and should account all their strength to be in His grace (cf. Psalm 20:7, 33:16–18).[6]

A good deal can be made of all this, in relation to prayer, for example; for more important than the fact that the trumpets spoke to the people, they also spoke, as has been already indicated, to God. When they sounded, God held His people in remembrance in their time of need. They were, so to speak, a signal to God for help, and God heard and remembered, and delivered them from their foes. There is never any battle in which we fight, in which we need be without divine remembrance. This is the provision of God, that in every situation of pressure, hazard, or danger, prayer can be made to, and heard by, God; nor should there be any victory won by the believer or by the church, which does not issue in glad praise to God, in worshipful prayer and thanksgiving. Many of the psalms echo and exemplify this, both in the answers given to cries of distress and in the praise and thanksgiving that followed (cf. Pss. 18:6ff.; 28:1, 6, 7; 107:6, 13, 19, 31ff.; 118:5ff.); and what better illustration could be found than the thrilling and dramatic account in Acts 12:5ff. of the deliverance and release of the apostle Peter from prison in answer to the prayers of the saints? The message is surely clear: with a praying church, anything can happen. This is perhaps the greatest lesson the church has to relearn in our time. Until it does, our problems will remain—and multiply.

NOTES

1. John Calvin, *Harmony of the Pentateuch,* 4:7.

Delitzsch in Carl L. Keil and Franz Delitzsch, *Numbers,* Commentary on the Old Testament, vol. 3 (Grand Rapids: Wm. B. Eerdmans, repr. 1971), p. 53 adds: "The settling down of the cloud upon the Tabernacle we can only understand in the following manner, as the Tabernacle was all taken to pieces during the march: namely that the cloud visibly descended from the height at which it ordinarily soared above the Ark of the Covenant, as it was carried in front of the army, for a signal that the Tabernacle was to be set up there; and when this had been done it settled down upon it."

2. Alexander Maclaren, *Exodus,* Expositions of Holy Scripture, 11 vols. (London: Hodder and Stoughton, 1907), p. 305.

3. G. B. Gray, *A Critical and Exegetical Commentary on Numbers,* International Critical Commentary (Edinburgh: T. & T. Clark, 1903), p. 88, points

out that there is no reference to the trumpet (hazozerah) in any preceding part of the narrative of the Exodus, but that the horn ("yobel" translated "trumpet" in both NKJV and RSV, as also "shophar") is mentioned in Exodus 19:13, 16, 19; 20:18. The words "yobel" and "shophar" are derived, L. Elliott Binns points out, from roots which have some connection with "ram," and adds, "it is probable that 'yobel' remained always an actual 'horn,' whilst 'shaphar' retained its curved, horn-like shape even when made in metal. In contrast, 'Hazozerah' was 'a long straight, slender metal tube, with flaring end.'"

4. Keil and Delitzsch, *Numbers,* p. 55.
5. Calvin, *Pentateuch,* 2:104.
6. Ibid., 2:104–5.

CHAPTER EIGHT

From Sinai to Paran

Numbers 10:11–12:16

DEPARTURE FROM SINAI

10:11 Now it came to pass on the twentieth *day* of the
second month, in the second year, that the cloud was
taken up from above the tabernacle of the Testimony.
12 And the children of Israel set out from the
Wilderness of Sinai on their journeys; then the cloud
settled down in the Wilderness of Paran.
13 So they started out for the first time according
to the command of the LORD by the hand of Moses.
14 The standard of the camp of the children of
Judah set out first according to their armies; over
their army was Nahshon the son of Amminadab.
15 Over the army of the tribe of the children of
Issachar *was* Nethanel the son of Zuar.
16 And over the army of the tribe of the children
of Zebulun *was* Eliab the son of Helon.
17 Then the tabernacle was taken down; and the
sons of Gershon and the sons of Merari set out, carrying the tabernacle.
18 And the standard of the camp of Reuben set out
according to their armies; over their army *was* Elizur
the son of Shedeur.
19 Over the army of the tribe of the children of
Simeon *was* Shelumiel the son of Zurishaddai.
20 And over the army of the tribe of the children
of Gad *was* Eliasaph the son of Deuel.
21 Then the Kohathites set out, carrying the holy
things. (The tabernacle would be prepared for their
arrival.)

22 And the standard of the camp of the children of
Ephraim set out according to their armies; over their
army *was* Elishama the son of Ammihud.
23 Over the army of the tribe of the children of
Manasseh *was* Gamaliel the son of Pedahzur.
24 And over the army of the tribe of the children
of Benjamin *was* Abidan the son of Gideoni.
25 Then the standard of the camp of the children
of Dan (the rear guard of all the camps) set out according to their armies; over their army *was* Ahiezer
the son of Ammishaddai.
26 Over the army of the tribe of the children of
Asher *was* Pagiel the son of Ocran.
27 And over the army of the tribe of the children
of Naphtali *was* Ahira the son of Enan.
28 Thus *was* the order of march of the children of
Israel, according to their armies, when they began
their journey.

Num. 10:11–28

At this point the account of the journeyings of Israel from Sinai to the borders of the Promised Land begins. The whole journey, from Sinai to Kadesh in the desert of Paran, is given summarily in verses 11 and 12, and what follows in 10:13–12:16 is an expansion and elaboration of this.[1] From Sinai to Kadesh was in point of fact a journey of only eleven days (cf. Deut. 1:2). Thus speedily did the people of God reach the borders of their future inheritance. Clearly, therefore, the long and protracted period of some thirty-eight years of wandering in the wilderness (to which a considerable part of the remaining chapters of Numbers is devoted to describing) calls for some explanation. This is given in the present section and particularly in the story of the spies' expedition and its tragic sequel in the section that follows (chapters 13–14).

In verses 13 through 28 the order of Israel's march is more fully described, in terms of the detailed layout of the camp given in 2:1–31 (the only difference being the additional note in vv. 17 and 21 about the order in which the different houses of the Levites bore the ark and its furniture). The Gershonites and Merarites followed the tribes of Judah, Issachar, and Zebulun, and were followed by Reuben, Simeon, and Gad. They would thus be in a position to set up the framework of the tabernacle at the chosen place for the next encampment, and have it ready for the Kohathites, who bore the holy things. Behind the holy things came the banners of Ephraim, with Manasseh and Benjamin (see 2:18–24), and Dan with Asher and Naphtali (cf. 2:25–31). These last formed the rearguard of the host, "that division of the army which kept the hosts together" (Delitzsch). This arrangement, as Ellicott observes, serves to throw light on the statement in Psalm 80:2, "Before Ephraim, Benjamin, and Manasseh, stir up Your strength, and come and save us!"

The sight of such an army on the march must have been an impressive, even awesome one. It is hardly surprising that the surrounding tribes and peoples through whom they were to pass should have felt threatened and been filled with disquiet (cf. Josh. 2:9–11). It was not merely the size of the Israelite host, but the fact that the Lord Himself was in their midst that gave them an air of purpose that must have marked them out as a force to be reckoned with. The tragedy is that by their repeated murmurings and rebellion they so substantially lost that character.

Hobab and the Ark

> 10:29 Now Moses said to Hobab the son of Reuel the Midianite, Moses' father-in-law, "We are setting out for the place of which the Lord said, 'I will give it to you.' Come with us, and we will treat you well; for the Lord has promised good things to Israel."
>
> 30 And he said to him, "I will not go, but I will depart to my *own* land and to my relatives."
>
> 31 So *Moses* said, "Please do not leave, inasmuch as you know how we are to camp in the wilderness, and you can be our eyes.
>
> 32 "And it shall be, if you go with us—indeed it shall be—that whatever good the Lord will do to us, the same we will do to you."
>
> *Num. 10:29–32*

The incident recorded in these verses is full of interest. The identity of Hobab is somewhat uncertain, and has been the subject of considerable discussion and difference of opinion. In the text of verse 29 the wording is ambiguous, and it leaves open to question whether Moses' father-in-law was Hobab or Reuel (Raguel in Septuagint and KJV). The reference to Hobab in Judges 4:11 explicitly calls him the father-in-law of Moses, but Ellicott points out that "according to the ordinary rules of Hebrew syntax, Hobab . . . is here spoken of as the 'Hothen' of Moses . . . and inasmuch as the cognate noun 'hathan' is used to designate any near relation by marriage—as, e.g., the son-in-law of Lot (Gen 19:14)—the word 'hothen' may here and in Judg 4:11 be rendered 'brother-in-law.'"[2] Gray in International Critical Commentary thinks that Hobab is a member of the clan Reuel, and that his name has fallen out before the word "Reuel" in Exodus 2:18. This, however, to say the least, creates more problems than it solves. For one thing, it would make Zipporah, Moses' wife, the daughter of Hobab and since at this point in Numbers Moses was upwards of eighty years old, it is hardly likely that he would be seeking the help of a man of a considerably greater age than that as a guide through the wilderness. It is better to accept Ellicott's interpretation of "Hothen" and identify Hobab as the son of Reuel (or Jethro, Exod. 2:18, 3:1).[3]

Moses' invitation to Hobab to accompany Israel on their journeyings was extended on the ground of his familiarity with the terrain through which they were to pass. His initial unwillingness to go with them called forth a repeated and more urgent invitation from Moses which, although it is not explicitly stated, seems to have prevailed upon him. That this was the likely outcome is supported by the fact that otherwise there would be little point in the incident having been recorded. This seems to be confirmed by the reference in Judges 4:11 which indicates a presence of the descendants of Hobab in the Promised Land among the tribes of Israel.

Some think Moses was in error in thus inviting Hobab to act as a guide, and that he showed lack of faith in doing so when he had the pillar of cloud and fire to lead. Thus verse 33b contains an implied rebuke; but this may be reading more into the text than is really there. God does not disdain using human instruments in helping His people, and there is nothing necessarily contradictory in the thought of Hobab being used as a guide—any more than it was wrong or lacking in faith to send spies in to spy out the land from Kadesh, when they had God to guide and assure them. It is hardly likely that Moses would so insensitively default in this way;

besides, if he had made a mistake, the Lord must surely have corrected him.

The incident affords us a useful and important illustration, in Christian terms, of the invitation to pilgrimage. It is hardly possible that Hobab, as the son of the priest of Midian, should have been unaware of the history of Israel from the time of their departure from Egypt up to this point. It is likely that right from the outset he had been aware of the mighty acts of God in bringing Israel out of bondage and constituting them His people. For all practical purposes, what is said of Jethro in Exodus 18:1 ff. could be said with equal force of Hobab—when he "heard of all that God had done for Moses and for Israel his people" he praised the God of Israel. It is the *general impression* that must have been created in Hobab's mind that is important—for it was the impression of a living God in the midst, who worked wonders, and was all-sufficient, all-powerful, and all-loving.

It is against this background that we must seek to interpret the significance of Moses' invitation to him to cast in his lot with the people of God. This is always the proper setting of the gospel invitation—it is in view of the mercies of God manifested in the redemption in Christ Jesus that the appeal is made to men to receive the reconciliation, become children of God and enter into pilgrimage.

This is ever the pattern unfolded in New Testament preaching: the apostles proclaimed the birth, anointing, life and ministry, sufferings and death of Christ, and His rising again. On the basis of this they preached forgiveness through His name, inviting men: "Come thou with us, and we will do thee good: for the Lord hath spoken good concerning Israel." And where men know Him, and are persuaded of the good He has promised in the gospel, they will be so gripped and mastered by it that their lips will be touched with holy fire. Thus they will speak persuasively to others concerning Christ and, like Moses, refuse to take no for an answer.

The Ark in the Vanguard

10:33 So they departed from the mountain of the LORD
on a journey of three days; and the ark of the covenant

of the LORD went before them for the three days' journey, to search out a resting place for them.
34 And the cloud of the LORD *was* above them by
day when they went out from the camp.
35 So it was, whenever the ark set out, that Moses
said:

"Rise up, O LORD!
Let Your enemies be scattered,
And let those who hate You flee before You."

36 And when it rested, he said:

"Return, O LORD,
To the many thousands of Israel."

Num. 10:33–36

There has been much discussion and confusion about the precise interpretation of these verses. Critics have taken verse 33b to mean that the ark of the covenant went ahead of the people by three days, in order to search out a resting place—a position, as one writer points out, "useless to those who came after and dangerous to the advance party."[4] Gray thinks the ark "is conceived of as moving by itself,"[5] surely an absurd literalism. It is idle to compare this with the moving of the cloud, since the cloud was a supernatural manifestation, the ark man-made. Another scholar[6] maintains that there is no grammatical necessity of interpreting the phrase *"three days' journey"* in this way, and stands by the KJV rendering "in the three days' journey" which, while involving a measure of interpretation, is consistent with the context, and entirely possible grammatically.

The difficulties, however, remain: there is an apparent contradiction between the position of the ark before the people in verse 33, and what is said in verses 17 and 21, where the ark is clearly in the midst of the host, not in front. Two possible interpretations may be made: one, that on this particular occasion the position of the ark was different than at any other time, (a) because the first three days of the march "were through rough wilderness country, devoid of human enemies, but presenting unusual difficulties in finding suitable camping spots";[7] and (b) to typify the divine leadership of the people in symbolic form. The rabbinic interpretation suggests this view. The other interpretation is that the phrase "before them" (v. 33) may have the force of "in their presence" as in Deuteronomy 3:28, 10:11, 31:3, where "Joshua or Moses is said to go before the people under circumstances which clearly indicate that they were not physically in front of them, but before them in the sense of being visible to them and in authority over them."[8]

The following comment on verses 33 and 34 is worthy of notice:

> (They) have a poetical character, answering to the elevated nature of their subject, and are to be interpreted as follows according to the laws of a poetical *parallelism:* The one thought that the ark of the covenant, with the cloud soaring above it, led the way and sheltered those who were marching, is divided into two clauses; in ver. 33b only the ark of the covenant is mentioned as going in front of the Israelites, and in ver. 34 only the cloud as a shelter over them: whereas the carrying of the ark in front of the army could only accomplish the end proposed, viz. to search out a resting-place for them, by Jehovah going above them in the cloud, and showing the bearers of the ark both the way they were to take, and the place where they were to rest.[9]

In verses 35 and 36 the going forth of the ark seems to be represented as the Lord going forth to battle, rather than in guiding His people. As Noth puts it, "It is a question not of leadership along unknown ways, but of enemies and war."[10] But this is not necessarily incompatible or inconsistent with the emphasis in the previous verses. It is a statement, in summary form, of Moses' usual practice throughout the journeyings; and since in these journeyings they would be quite likely to meet with unknown enemies on the way, it would be a natural attitude to adopt day by day. To be forewarned is to be forearmed.

It is also, however, an expression of the spirit of faith and confidence with which Moses addressed himself to the task of leading the people of God and a recognition of the nature of their journeying as being both pilgrimage and warfare. It was surely failure to appreciate the sense of high destiny into which they had been called, both as to the spiritual implications of their pilgrimage and as to the nature of the encounters with their enemies, that led to the tragedy of what followed, in the events leading up to Kadesh Barnea.

This surely has important lessons for us. To live with a conscious sense of destiny is a high way to live, and the temptation to take lower ground is very real, and often yielded to; when it is, spiritual life degenerates at best into a chilling mediocrity and at worst into all sorts of turning aside, backsliding, and even tragedy. The high hopes and the eager confidence with which Moses uttered these words proved to be sadly misplaced, but it need not have been so; nor is it ever hazardous or foolhardy to give such expression to spiritual aspiration. Indeed, without such an attitude, expressed so challengingly in William Carey's words, "Expect great things from God, attempt great things for God," spiritual advancement either in personal life or in the work of the kingdom is likely to be negligible and short-lived. It was said of Mallory and Irving, the climbers lost on Mount Everest in the early years of this century, that "when last seen, they were still climbing." This is the spirit that motivated the patriarch Moses when he uttered these words; without such a spirit the work of the gospel and of the kingdom is certain to go by default.

FIRE IN THE CAMP

> 11:1 Now *when* the people complained, it displeased the LORD; for the LORD heard *it,* and His anger was aroused. So the fire of the LORD burned among them, and consumed *some* in the outskirts of the camp.
> 2 Then the people cried out to Moses, and when Moses prayed to the LORD, the fire was quenched.
> 3 So he called the name of the place Taberah, because the fire of the LORD had burned among them.
> *Num. 11:1–3*

The section of the book beginning with these verses and continuing into chapter 14 recounts the development of a spirit of discontentment among the people, and their consequent murmuring against Moses and against the Lord. This murmuring, we are meant to understand, became a continuing characteristic and had a cumulative effect. It was not merely that the people murmured once or twice. They developed a murmuring, complaining spirit, and it was this that came to a climax at Kadesh Barnea, when they failed at a critical time of opportunity. They were turned back by God into the wilderness, and kept there for forty years. Israel finally entered into the Promised Land, but *that generation* of Israel did not, and were not allowed to enter by God. The lesson is not that they were finally lost, but that they were disqualified in the purposes of God—a grim and solemn reality. This murmuring, complaining, critical spirit, it is clear, got into them, and did something to them, rendering them progressively incapable of rising to their divine calling until, at a moment of crisis, they crashed. Such is the context in which the series of incidents recorded in these verses and in those which follow must be studied.

The absence of any specific reason being given in these verses for the people's complaint seems to indicate a general spirit of discontentment, and we are left to assume that the normal hardships of such a desert march were the occasion of it. Calvin lists a number of alternative interpretations but opts for the idea of fainting.[11] Whatever the nature of the complaint, however, it incurred the severe displeasure of the Lord, and fire came from on high upon the outlying parts of the camp. It seems clear that the whole camp did not suffer, but that it might well have done so, but for the intercession of Moses (v. 2) which extinguished the fire very quickly. One commentator suggests that "in this judgment the Lord merely manifested His power to destroy the murmurers, that He might infuse into the whole nation a wholesome dread of His holy majesty."[12]

What we need to recognize here is this: the divine reaction is that of the overshadowing purpose of God who is determined to have His way with His people. He is working to a plan, He is involved in nothing less than the redemption of the world, and all that He does, with His people of old or with us, must be interpreted in that light. He must correct and chastise from that overruling standpoint. He sees best what is good, and must discipline His people toward this, however grimly. It is possible to take these verses as a brief summary of the whole ongoing spiritual breakdown, with verses 4 ff. describing and elaborating the details of it; alternatively the events in these verses could be taken as preceding those that follow. Either way, it is clear that verses 4 ff. give the substance of the problem that faced Moses. What it amounts to is this: God had bestowed on Israel the dignity and privilege of a spiritual calling and destiny; He had made bare His holy arm on their behalf, shown them the bright and glorious prospect that faced them if they were prepared to walk in His ways—and they sneered at it, reacted against it, lightly esteemed it, and turned their backs on their destiny, in sheer carnal worldliness. Discontent with a spiritual calling—this is the theme, and its relevance and importance are surely obvious for us, in relation to how He dealt with them for their sins.

THE SPIRIT OF MURMURING

> 11:4 Now the mixed multitude who were among them yielded to intense craving; so the children of Israel also wept again and said: "Who will give us meat to eat?
>
> 5 "We remember the fish which we ate freely in Egypt, the cucumbers, the melons, the leeks, the onions, and the garlic;
>
> 6 "but now our whole being *is* dried up; *there is* nothing at all except this manna *before* our eyes!"
>
> 7 Now the manna *was* like coriander seed, and its color like the color of bdellium.
>
> 8 The people went about and gathered *it*, ground *it* on millstones or beat *it* in the mortar, cooked *it* in pans, and made cakes of it; and its taste was like the taste of pastry prepared with oil.
>
> 9 And when the dew fell on the camp in the night, the manna fell on it.
>
> 10 Then Moses heard the people weeping throughout their families, everyone at the door of his tent; and the anger of the LORD was greatly aroused; Moses also was displeased.
>
> *Num. 11:4–10*

The fact that this next instance of murmuring follows immediately after the incident recorded in verses 1–3 may suggest, that "the unbelieving and discontented mass did not discern the chastising hand of God at all in the conflagration which broke out at the end of the camp, because it was not declared to be a punishment, and was not preceded by a previous announcement."[13] This seems quite likely; otherwise it would be necessary to interpret the murmuring in this chapter as having reached such an extreme pitch that divine judgment was swift and general; whereas the pattern unfolded in this and following chapters indicates rather that it had a cumulative effect, leading to the grim pronouncement at Kadesh Barnea (14:1ff.).

The spirit of murmuring becomes specific in these verses, and its cause attributed to the rabble among the people (this seems to be the force of the phrase "mixed multitude," which one commentator renders as "riff-raff"). This rabble-rousing element among the people certainly spread a major disaffection throughout the camp. As Calvin comments, the contagion of vice easily spreads. But the responsibility for this disaffection fell upon Israel, and as the following verses show it was Israel, not merely the "rabble," who were punished. The weariness they expressed with what they felt to be a monotonous diet of manna, and their disparagement of it, as they longed for the Egyptian fare they had known—fish in plenty and a variety of vegetables—kindled the divine anger.

One would have thought that Israel would never have forgotten the terrible conditions of their slavery in Egypt and the horrors, privations, and tortures that had made life such a misery for them, and would have been content with any change from that, let alone the dignity of a high calling and destiny and the provision of a faithful and bounteous God. But no; they were actually looking back to these Egyptian experiences as if they had been a paradise for them (v. 5).

From this we may learn that looking back on "the good old days" is always a matter of wearing rose-colored glasses. The one word to describe the attitude of those who do so is hum-bug! It was, of course, the existence of the false among the true in Israel that caused the trouble, for this is always a fruitful source of infection. The truth is, the spiritual destiny is intolerable for a worldly people to contemplate—hence the telltale phrase in verse 6, *"nothing at all except this manna,"* even when what follows (vv. 7–9) describes that manna as a pleasant, God-given food sent with the dew of heaven, and described in Psalm 78:24ff. as "the bread of heaven" and "angels' food." There are those for whom "nothing except manna" is heaven itself, and every kind of joy, and others for whom it is sheer hell and unbearable; for manna is a heavenly food, and to appreciate heavenly food one needs a heavenly taste. It is this that serves to explain why in the same congregation one man may fret and fidget when the sermon goes beyond ten minutes, while another will go out with the comment, "we did not know how hungry we were."

MOSES' PLAINT

11:11 So Moses said to the LORD, "Why have You afflicted Your servant? And why have I not found favor in Your sight, that You have laid the burden of all these people on me?
12 "Did I conceive all these people? Did I beget them, that You should say to me, 'Carry them in your bosom, as a guardian carries a nursing child,' to the land which You swore to their fathers?
13 "Where am I to get meat to give to all these people? For they weep all over me, saying, 'Give us meat, that we may eat.'
14 "I am not able to bear all these people alone, because the burden *is* too heavy for me.
15 "If You treat me like this, please kill me here and now—if I have found favor in Your sight—and do not let me see my wretchedness!"

Num. 11:11–15

Moses' grievance, recorded in these verses, goes beyond the initial, precipitating cause of it, and it seems that the people's continual murmuring brought to a head in him an increasing disenchantment with them, making him expostulate vehemently with God regarding the fractious people. One renowned scholar thinks that Moses "discovered a sign of the burning wrath of Jehovah in the fact that, although the discontent of the people burst forth in loud cries, God did not help, but withdrew His help, and let the whole storm of the infuriated people burst upon him."[14] Noth draws attention to the kind of language Moses uses in these verses.[15] In placing this burden upon him God has dealt ill with him, Moses thinks (v. 11). Noth comments:

> Bold as this statement certainly is, it is surpassed in v. 12 by the assertion, cast in the form of a rhetorical question, that he, Moses, is, after all, not the people's mother and is, therefore, not obliged to fulfil maternal duties towards them. Implicit in this is the very unusual idea that Yahweh himself is Israel's mother. In view of the usual avoidance in the Old Testament of personal concepts of the relationship between God and people, such as are known in the religions of the surrounding peoples,

> even the statement that Israel is Yahweh's son is rare (Exod. 4:22; Hos. 11:1). It is, however, extremely rare to express the connection between Yahweh and Israel by the idea of motherhood, thereby, even indirectly, attributing to Yahweh the concept of femininity.

The reference to the word "conceive," essentially a feminine concept, recalls references such as Isaiah 49:15 and 66:13. In the Hebrew, the word for "compassion" is cognate with the word for "womb," a fact that protagonists of the "motherhood of God" debate are doubtless not slow to emphasize. Nor should we be slow to recognize that there is a rich vein of teaching, not only in the Old Testament, but also in the New, which stresses such qualities in God. No balanced or sensible exegesis, however, could possibly justify the extreme positions now taken in this debate. Extremism notwithstanding, however, the concept is a graphic and moving one, but it is perhaps particularly in the context of the congregational "family" of God's people that it becomes most meaningful. And when Paul's moving words to the Thessalonians on the same theme are taken into consideration (1 Thess. 2:7–12), we realize just how profound is Moses' understanding of the heart of the Lord toward His people. At all events Moses is not so much abdicating or throwing off his own responsibility for the people as he is pleading with God that the duty of providing for Israel's needs lies with Him as their Redeemer, rather than with himself.

The Divine Response

> 11:16 So the LORD said to Moses: "Gather to Me seventy men of the elders of Israel, whom you know to be the elders of the people and officers over them; bring them to the tabernacle of meeting, that they may stand there with you.
>
> 17 "Then I will come down and talk with you there. I will take of the Spirit that *is* upon you and will put *the same* upon them; and they shall bear the burden of the people with you, that you may not bear *it* yourself alone.
>
> 18 "Then you shall say to the people, 'Consecrate

yourselves for tomorrow, and you shall eat meat; for
you have wept in the hearing of the LORD, saying,
"Who will give us meat to eat? For *it was* well with us
in Egypt." Therefore the LORD will give you meat,
and you shall eat.
19 'You shall eat, not one day, nor two days, nor
five days, nor ten days, nor twenty days,
20 'but *for* a whole month, until it comes out of
your nostrils and becomes loathsome to you, because
you have despised the LORD who is among you, and
have wept before Him, saying, "Why did we ever
come up out of Egypt?"'"
21 And Moses said, "The people whom I *am*
among *are* six hundred thousand men on foot; yet
You have said, 'I will give them meat, that they may
eat *for* a whole month.'
22 "Shall flocks and herds be slaughtered for
them, to provide enough for them? Or shall all the
fish of the sea be gathered together for them, to
provide enough for them?"
23 And the LORD said to Moses, "Has the LORD's
arm been shortened? Now you shall see whether
what I say will happen to you or not."
24 So Moses went out and told the people the
words of the LORD,

Num. 11:16–24a

These verses give the divine response to the latter part of Moses' cry in verse 14 that he was unable to "bear all these people alone," and to the murmuring of the people about the manna. The difference in treatment meted out to Moses on the one hand and the people on the other is some indication of the qualitative difference in the two attitudes: that of Moses was a *plaint,* that of the people a *complaint.* The provision of help for Moses is gracious and generous, and seventy elders are set apart and anointed with the divine Spirit to enable them to share in the burden of governing the people.

Most commentators maintain that we are not to understand the anointing of the elders as implying that the fullness of the Spirit possessed by Moses was diminished in consequence, but Calvin disputes this, maintaining that "this division comprehends punishment in it,"[16] and that therefore a rebuke was administered to Moses in this regard. This, however, seems an arbitrary assumption to make, and one for which there is no real evidence in the text—indeed, the contrary, if we understand Moses' reaction in verse 29 correctly—and it is surely better to take the provision of the seventy as an evidence of divine grace at a time of difficulty and pressure in Moses' experience. One scholar remarks, "The Spirit of God is not something material, which is diminished by being divided, but resembles a flame of fire, which does not decrease in intensity, but increases rather by extension."[17] This certainly seems to be what happened on this occasion. God's answer to the need was a fresh outpouring of His Spirit into the midst of His people.

The divine response to the people's complaint, however, was very different. The language used in verses 19 and 20 makes it clear that the provision of food was to be very "double-edged": their craving for flesh would be satisfied, to be sure, but that very satisfaction would itself be an expression of divine wrath. Moses' mystification as to how this provision could possibly be made (vv. 21–22) is simply swept aside in the onward momentum of God's displeasure against the people. The command to them to sanctify themselves has a grim note in it: their chastisement was to be a religious act, and they were to have "the full treatment."

God's stern dealing with the murmuring people makes grim reading. As the psalmist puts it, "He gave them their request, but sent leanness into their soul" (Ps. 106:15). He was as good as His word. The flesh they had cried for and coveted came, as we shall see in verses 31ff., and it was the means of their destruction. While they were gorging themselves upon it, the plague came and devastated them. Was God, then, to blame, for letting them have what they were demanding? How careful we should be! What He forbids, He forbids in His mercy, for our good. He knows how bad it would be for us to have it. But when men insist, He sometimes says, "Very well, have your fill of it, if you are so set on it; have your own way." This was an attitude that developed into a fixed and unalterable reality later, when at Kadesh Barnea the people hung back from entering the land and God finally said, "You have made your choice, and I will accept it. Back you go into the wilderness." They disqualified themselves, because they rendered themselves increasingly incapable of fulfilling their destiny.

THE SPIRIT OF THE LORD

11:24b and he gathered the seventy men of the elders of
the people and placed them around the tabernacle.
25 Then the LORD came down in the cloud, and
spoke to him, and took of the Spirit that *was* upon
him, and placed *the same* upon the seventy elders;
and it happened, when the Spirit rested upon them,
that they prophesied, although they never did *so*
again.
26 But two men had remained in the camp: the
name of one *was* Eldad, and the name of the other
Medad. And the Spirit rested upon them. Now they
were among those listed, but who had not gone out to
the tabernacle; yet they prophesied in the camp.
27 And a young man ran and told Moses, and said,
"Eldad and Medad are prophesying in the camp."
28 So Joshua the son of Nun, Moses' assistant, *one*
of his choice men, answered and said, "Moses my
lord, forbid them!"
29 Then Moses said to him, "Are you zealous for
my sake? Oh, that all the LORD's people were
prophets *and* that the LORD would put His Spirit
upon them!"
30 And Moses returned to the camp, he and the
elders of Israel.

Num. 11:24b–30

The twofold word from God, in mercy and judgment, is now fulfilled. The elders are appointed and receive the anointing of the Spirit. Their prophesying (v. 25) is an evidence of the charisma they have received, in much the same way as "speaking in tongues" and "prophesying" were in the New Testament church. This seems, however, to have been a one-off manifestation, as the final words of the verse indicate. As a scholar remarks, however,

> We are not to infer from the fact, that the prophesying was not repeated, that the Spirit therefore departed from them after this one extraordinary manifestation. This miraculous manifestation of the Spirit was intended simply to give to the whole

nation the visible proof that God had endowed them with His Spirit, as helpers of Moses, and had given them the authority required for the exercise of their calling.[18]

An interesting incident occurred in relation to this divine anointing (vv. 26ff.). Two of the seventy elders had remained in the camp, instead of repairing to the tabernacle with the others (no reason is stated as to why they should not have been with the others, and speculation that they were unclean, or occupied with special labors, is fruitless). They also received the anointing and prophesied in the camp. This clearly caused excitement, and the matter was reported to Moses. Joshua, Moses' right-hand man, urged Moses to put a stop to this seemingly irregular and unauthorized exercise of the prophetic spirit. His motive in so doing was clearly worthy and creditable, for he felt that the honor—and the authority—of Moses was being challenged (cf. Mark 9:38, 39 for an obvious New Testament parallel). But Moses refused to do so, and dissociated himself from any spirit of jealousy shown on his account, uttering the memorable words, *"Oh, that all the Lord's people were prophets and that the Lord would put His Spirit upon them!"* (v. 29).[19]

The Quail

11:31 Now a wind went out from the LORD, and it brought quail from the sea and left *them* fluttering near the camp, about a day's journey on this side and about a day's journey on the other side, all around the camp, and about two cubits above the surface of the ground.

32 And the people stayed up all that day, all night, and all the next day, and gathered the quail (he who gathered least gathered ten homers); and they spread *them* out for themselves all around the camp.

33 But while the meat *was* still between their teeth, before it was chewed, the wrath of the LORD was aroused against the people, and the LORD struck the people with a very great plague.

34 So he called the name of that place Kibroth Hattaavah, because there they buried the people who had yielded to craving.

35 From Kibroth Hattaavah the people moved to Hazeroth, and camped at Hazeroth.

Num. 11:31–35

The remaining verses of the chapter describe the fulfillment of the grim promise given in verses 19 and 20 in the coming of the quails, and the plague which followed. The wind from the sea in verse 31 is referred to in Psalm 78 as both east wind and south wind (does this mean wind from a southeasterly direction?) which blew from the Arabian Gulf, bringing vast numbers of migratory birds from the south. The psalmist's description of meat raining on them "like the dust" and "like the sand of the seas" makes it clear that it was an unusual, indeed, miraculous manifestation in the natural realm. In what follows in verses 32 and 33, it becomes clear, as Calvin points out, that "God did not wait till satiety had produced disgust, but inflicted the punishment in the midst of their greediness."[20]

The Vindication of Moses

12:1 Then Miriam and Aaron spoke against Moses because of the Ethiopian woman whom he had married; for he had married an Ethiopian woman.

2 So they said, "Has the LORD indeed spoken only through Moses? Has He not spoken through us also?" And the LORD heard *it*.

3 (Now the man Moses *was* very humble, more than all men who *were* on the face of the earth.)

4 Suddenly the LORD said to Moses, Aaron, and Miriam, "Come out, you three, to the tabernacle of meeting!" So the three came out.

5 Then the LORD came down in the pillar of cloud and stood *in* the door of the tabernacle, and called Aaron and Miriam. And they both went forward.

6 Then He said, "Hear now My words:

If there is a prophet among you,
I, the LORD, make Myself known to him in a
vision;
I speak to him in a dream.
7 Not so with My servant Moses;
He *is* faithful in all My house.

8 I speak with him face to face,
Even plainly, and not in dark sayings;
And he sees the form of the LORD.
Why then were you not afraid
To speak against My servant Moses?"

9 So the anger of the LORD was aroused against
them, and He departed.
10 And when the cloud departed from above the
tabernacle, suddenly Miriam *became* leprous, as *white*
as snow. Then Aaron turned toward Miriam, and
there she was, a leper.

Num. 12:1–10

This passage records a further example of murmuring and disaffection in Israel, but with significant differences from that of the previous chapter. There, the trouble arose through the refusal of the worldlings among them to rise to a true spiritual calling; here, however, the opposition came from much nearer the center, from those nearest to Moses in natural and spiritual kinship, Miriam and Aaron, his sister and brother. It is clear that the heart of this issue lies in the challenge they made against Moses' position of supremacy as leader of the people, and his right to speak for God. Moses' marriage to the Ethiopian woman is therefore simply the pretext for the attack, an excuse to arouse opposition against him. The pretext in itself may have been a real enough issue so far as Miriam was concerned,[21] but it was nevertheless still a pretext, and we have to look beyond it for the real reason for this altercation, namely, resentment at Moses' undoubted authority.

Different interpretations of the identity of the Ethiopian (Heb. "Cushite") woman Moses is said to have married have been given, none of them either conclusive or satisfactory. The question is solved simply for Calvin, who maintains she is none other than Zipporah (following Augustine and others), since there is no mention of the death of Zipporah up to this point, and he regards it as "too absurd to charge the holy prophet with the reproach of polygamy."[22] It is true that the Hebrew "Cush" is used of two, possibly three, distinct districts or peoples—Ethiopia (the regular use of the word), a district east of Babylon, and also a north Arabian people, appearing in certain inscriptions as the Kusi. If this latter holds good, it could be reconciled with the word "Midianite" (cf. Exod. 2:15–21, Num. 10:29).

On the other hand, Zipporah may well have died, and the reference would then be to a genuine second marriage. Certainly the text seems to suggest that Miriam's complaint was against a recent marriage. The commentator Delitzsch bases his view that this wife cannot have been Zipporah on the fact that it is highly improbable Miriam had made Moses' marriage to Zipporah (which had taken place so many years before) the occasion of reproach at this particular point, and that it would have been much more likely for her to have done so if "a short time before, probably after the death of Zipporah, he had contracted a second marriage with a Cushite woman."[23] But, from a psychological point of view it is not necessary to suppose it must have been a recent marriage that had caused Miriam's petulant jealousy. It is by no means unknown in human relations for such a resentment to be harbored for years, and it would only need a certain combination of circumstances finally to bring what had been a secret attitude out into the open at last. The most one can say is that if we could accept the fact of Zipporah's death (for which there is no biblical evidence) it would be simplest to follow Delitzsch's viewpoint. If, however, the identity of "Ethiopian" (Cushite) with "Midianite" is valid, Calvin's is the more likely interpretation.

It has been pointed out that "Miriam and Aaron do not call in question Moses' prophetic position or his right to lead, but only the uniqueness of his prophetic position and his right to sole leadership,"[24] and that there is no suggestion in their question in verse 2 that he had done anything to forfeit a position originally held. This also serves to confirm that the issue of the Ethiopian marriage was simply a pretext, not a reason, for their challenge. Calvin's comment here provides a good analysis of the situation: "They pride themselves on their gift of prophecy, which ought rather to have schooled them to humility. But such is the natural depravity of men, not only to abuse the gifts of God unto contempt of their brethren, but so to magnify them by their ungodly and sacrilegious boasting, as to obscure the glory of their Author."[25]

The point of the reference in verse 3 to the humility of Moses is that it must surely be taken with the final sentence in verse 2, "*And the Lord heard it.*" The implication is that, although Moses through meekness and humility was prepared to submit to this unprovoked and hurtful attack without protest or defending himself, God was not prepared to let it pass (Calvin adds, "This passage teaches us that although the good and gentle refrain from reproaches and accusations, God nevertheless keeps watch for them and, whilst they are silent, the wickedness of the ungodly cries out to, and is heard by, God").

The Lord's intervention in the situation is swift and decisive. All three are summoned to the tabernacle. Miriam and Aaron are commanded to stand forward to receive the divine pronouncement on their challenge and complaint against Moses, a pronouncement Moses would hear, although he stands in the background. Two things are made very clear: the first, that there are various ways in which God speaks to man and makes Himself known to them; and the second, that there is a qualitative difference between the way in which He makes Himself known to people like Aaron and Miriam and the way in which He makes Himself known to Moses. What marked a man or a woman in those days as a prophet or prophetess was that they should be the recipients of dreams and visions, and this was an indication that the Lord "spoke" with them. It seems clear that both Aaron and Miriam fell into this category (cf. Exod. 4:16, 15:20), and that this was the basis of their claim in verse 2b.

By contrast, however, Moses' position was entirely different. The "*Not so*" in verse 7 is emphatic: he is "faithful in all My house" (RSV has "entrusted with all My house"), that is, as Noth points out, Moses' position is "compared with that of the chief slave who is at once the confidant of his master and the man to whom his master's whole 'house' is entrusted."[26] (This is the basis of the reference in Heb. 3:2–6, where Moses' position as servant is in terms contrasted with Christ's as Son.)

This is clearly a relationship of a different order, involving personal and intimate converse, described in the words "face to face" (cf. Exod. 33:11, Deut. 34:10). The further phrase in verse 8, "*he sees the form of the Lord*" serves to underline this unique intimacy the more graphically (cf. Exod. 33:18–23).

This distinction between Moses' position and that of the others is one that is of perennial relevance, and is indeed underlined in the New Testament itself (cf. Acts 21:8–14). The real criterion for judging whether a man speaks from God is not that he should have been the recipient of dreams and visions (although God has on occasion spoken through these) but that his word should be with power (cf. 1 Cor. 2:4) and that it should bear the unmistakable stamp of authority from on high upon it. This, as James Denney says, "is the hardest of all authorities to win, and the costliest to maintain, and therefore substitutes for it are innumerable."[27] And neither official standing, nor intellectual qualification as such, on the one hand, nor extravagant claims of immediacy of revelation through vision or dream on the other hand, will suffice to bestow it. The apostle Paul's teaching about the need to be "the fragrance of Christ" among men (2 Cor. 2:15) and "epistles of Christ" (2 Cor. 3:2, 3), and "by manifestation of the truth commending ourselves to every man's conscience in the sight of God" (2 Cor. 4:1ff.) is definitive in this regard: to carry about in the body the dying of the Lord Jesus, and to be always delivered to death for Jesus' sake (2 Cor. 4:10, 11) is the one unmistakable mark of authentic, authoritative ministry. The message of Christ crucified can be preached effectively only by crucified men.

It is the exposition of the relationship between Moses and the Lord that is made the basis of the divine condemnation. Aaron and Miriam should have been afraid to challenge this unparalleled intimacy, recognizing its superiority, and the qualitatively different authority that it had bestowed upon Moses. Because they failed to do so, Miriam, as the instigator of the rebellion, was immediately stricken with leprosy.[28]

MERCY SHOWN TO MIRIAM

12:11 So Aaron said to Moses, "Oh, my lord! Please do not lay *this* sin on us, in which we have done foolishly and in which we have sinned.

12 "Please do not let her be as one dead, whose flesh is half consumed when he comes out of his mother's womb!"

13 So Moses cried out to the LORD, saying, "Please heal her, O God, I pray!"

14 Then the LORD said to Moses, "If her father had but spit in her face, would she not be shamed seven days? Let her be shut out of the camp seven days, and afterward she may be received *again.*"

15 So Miriam was shut out of the camp seven

days, and the people did not journey till Miriam was
brought in *again.*
16 And afterward the people moved from Hazeroth
and camped in the Wilderness of Paran.

Num. 12:11–16

Aaron, on seeing the judgment of leprosy come upon his sister, beseeches Moses for mercy. There is surely in his prayer an implicit recognition of the different kind of authority that Moses had. Indeed, he is acknowledging that Moses possessed a power in intercession with God that he himself could not exercise, hence his appeal to his brother. The intercession is readily and willingly made by Moses, and secures the healing and restoration of Miriam, after a seven-day exclusion from the camp. According to Leviticus 14:2ff., a seven-day period of waiting was requisite before someone cleansed of leprosy could be restored to fellowship. Noth thinks this implies that the cleansing from the leprosy was immediate, and that the seven-day exclusion was in fact punishment; as such, the sentence of leprosy was reduced to a mere seven-day exclusion.[29] One esteemed scholar, however, regards the passage as meaning that "restoration and purification from her leprosy were promised to her after the endurance of seven days' punishment." He adds:

> Leprosy was the just punishment for her sin. In her haughty exaggeration of the worth of her own prophetic gift, she had placed herself on a par with Moses, the divinely appointed head of the whole nation, and exalted herself above the congregation of the Lord. For this she was afflicted with a disease which shut her out of the number of the members of the people of God, and thus actually excluded from the camp; so that she could only be received back again after she had been healed, and by a formal purification. The latter followed as a matter of course, from Lev xiii and xiv, and did not need to be specially referred to here.[30]

The forward march of the people was held up until Miriam was fully restored. This was but one of many hindrances on the way to the Promised Land.

The further instance of disaffection and murmuring recorded in this chapter is part of a general pattern which is shown to have a cumulative effect leading to the crisis-point at Kadesh Barnea (14:1 ff.). One by one, these incidents make their contribution to the general spirit of declination which finally brought Israel to disaster and relegation to the wilderness wandering until that whole generation died off. Critical failures do not come unheralded and unannounced, "out of the blue"—then or now—they usually have a considerable history and significant, not to say fateful, antecedents. Eventually, Kadesh Barnea became predictable, even inevitable, because Israel became incapable of avoiding such a refusal to enter the land.

But there are other, even more significant, lessons that the chapter teaches. The pretext of the disaffection, as has been noted, was Moses' marriage to the Ethiopian woman. Even if, however, Moses had committed a serious transgression of the law in terms of marrying outside the covenant, or even of committing bigamy (both of which suggestions are open to dispute), God nevertheless vindicated His servant. Even if Moses had on this occasion done wrong, it does not mean that the whole tenor of his life was wrong. One failure does not mar a whole life, when that life is basically aligned with the will and purpose of God—even when that failure is serious and terrible as was the case with King David's tragic lapse with Bathsheba. He could still be spoken of as the man after God's own heart, in spite of the fact that the consequences of his sin dogged his footsteps for the rest of his days.

But it is necessary, in order to gather the deepest lessons of the chapter, to look beyond the pretexts used by Miriam and Aaron to the deep, underlying reasons why they were so critical. It is surely clear in such circumstances that if the pretext of the Ethiopian woman had not been present, they would as likely have found another. It is instructive to consider the implications of their words in verse 2, "Has the Lord indeed spoken only through Moses? Has He not spoken through us also?" Why did they thus challenge Moses' leadership? It was because something else was true, deep down within them: they were reacting against the word that Moses spoke from the Lord, and against the "word" that his dedicated and consecrated life spoke to them. Moses was faithful in all God's house; that is to say, he was utterly true to the divine purpose, and had adhered unswervingly in obedience to it. But this is a costly way to live, and not everyone is prepared to pay such a price for an onward, forward movement of God. For Miriam and Aaron at this point, the price was apparently too great to pay. Ultimately, it is not even a question of ousting Moses from the leadership of the people, but one of ousting the word that Moses spoke from God in favor of another, easier one—less trenchant, less demanding, less devastating. There was a death that they were not prepared to die.

When Jesus taught His disciples the way of the cross, many said, "This is a hard saying; who can understand it?" and many walked with Him no more (John 6:60, 66). This, basically, is why God vindicated His servant, and visited Miriam so signally with His divine displeasure.

Here, then, are two kinds of opposition to the Lord's work: On the one hand, as we have seen in 11:1ff., resistance from the worldly rabble, and on the other, resistance from those who should have known better, those who knew the higher and chose the lower, the uncrucified trouble-makers within the camp, who refused the challenge of the cross where it hurt them. Which of the two grieved Moses and angered God the more, and which is more harmful to His work? The really dangerous problems facing the work of God arise not so much from the worldliness of a mixed multitude as from the refusal by God's own people of the word and the cross that alone can discipline, fashion, and transform their lives. And the real enemies of His work are not the unconverted and the graceless, but those who have a name that they live and are dead, who pay lip-service to evangelical truth but have said no to the heart-bruising, life-changing, character-forming word of the cross and have desired an easier way.

NOTES

1. For a long and detailed discussion of the geography of the region see Carl L. Keil and Franz Delitzsch, *Numbers,* Commentary on the Old Testament (Grand Rapids: Wm. B. Eerdmans, repr. 1971), pp. 57–59.

2. C. J. Ellicott, *Leviticus,* An Old Testament Commentary for English Readers (London: Cassell & Co., Ltd., 1897), p. 510.

3. This, substantially, is the viewpoint expressed by John Calvin, *Harmony of the Pentateuch,* 4:53ff.

Delitzsch comments: "When and why Hobab came into the camp of the

Israelites,—whether he came with his father Reuel (or Jethro) when Israel first arrived at Horeb, and so remained behind when Jethro left (Exod. xviii.27), or whether he did not come till afterwards,—was left uncertain, because it was a matter of no consequence in relation to what is narrated here."

4. L. Elliott Binns, *The Book of Numbers* (London: Methuen & Co., Ltd., 1927), p. 73.

5. G. B. Gray, *A Critical and Exegetical Commentary on Numbers,* International Critical Commentary (Edinburgh: T. & T. Clark, 1903), p. 95.

6. A. A. MacRae, *New Bible Commentary* (London: Inter-Varsity Press, 1953 Edition), p. 175.

7. Ibid.

8. Ibid.

9. Keil and Delitzsch, *Numbers,* p. 62.

10. Martin Noth, *Numbers, A Commentary,* Old Testament Library (London: SCM Press, 1968), p. 79.

11. Calvin, *Pentateuch,* 4:15: "Since the Hebrew root, *aven,* is sometimes trouble and labour, sometimes fatigue, sometimes iniquity, sometimes falsehood, some translate it, 'The people were, as it were, complaining or murmuring'. Others (though this seems to be more beside the mark) insert the adverb *unjustly;* as if Moses said, that their complaint was unjust, when they expostulated with God. Others render it, 'being sick', but this savours too much of affectation; others, 'lying, or dealing treacherously'. Some derive it from the root, *thonah,* and thus explain it, 'seeking occasion', which I reject as far fetched. To me the word fainting seems to suit best; for they failed, as if broken down with weariness. It is probable that no other crime is alleged against them than that, abandoning the desire to proceed, they fell into supineness and inactivity, which was to turn their back upon God, and repudiate the promised inheritance. This sense will suit very well, and thus the proper meaning of the word will be retained."

12. Keil and Delitzsch, *Numbers,* p. 64.

13. Ibid., p. 65.

14. Ibid., p. 67. Delitzsch quotes Kurtz as saying "the whole attitude of Moses shows that his displeasure was excited not merely by the unrestrained rebellion of the people against Jehovah, but also by the unrestrained wrath of Jehovah against the nation."

15. Noth, *Numbers,* p. 86.

16. Calvin, *Pentateuch,* 4:25.

17. Keil and Delitzsch, *Numbers,* p. 70.

18. Ibid., pp. 70–71.

19. Noth, *Numbers,* p. 90, thinks that "behind Eldad and Medad there stood 'prophets' or 'prophetic' groups who at one time or another had had

to battle for recognition in Israel." But the text as it stands makes it clear that the narrow spirit that would forbid them exercising such a ministry was not in Moses, but in others.

20. Calvin, *Pentateuch,* 4:39. Noth, *Numbers,* p. 91, says, "There is no explicit connection between the eating and the 'plague', but this is suggested in v.33; that is, it is indicated that the greedy and unrestrained eating of the 'covetous' people had brought about death." This, to say the least, is a doubtful interpretation; the plague could hardly have been caused so quickly by the mere eating of the quails—indeed, it is explicitly stated that the plague came *before* the meat was consumed. Calvin's acceptance of the obvious implication of the text is as so often the wisest and likeliest interpretation. Gray, *Numbers,* p. 119, adds "The rationalistic explanation, that the mortality among the people was due to the poisonous stuffs on which quails are said sometimes to feed, if intended as an interpretation of the meaning of the story, merely betrays a lack of literary sense on the part of those who offer it. This mortality is not the punishment with which Yahweh threatens the people in v. 18–24."

21. Binns, *Numbers,* p. 75, comments: "The reason for their complaint alleged in v.1 seems pointless unless the narrator intended to represent the whole affair as a product of female jealousy."

22. Calvin, *Pentateuch,* 4:43.

23. Keil and Delitzsch, *Numbers,* p. 76.

24. Gray, *Numbers,* p. 122.

25. Calvin, *Pentateuch,* 4:43–44.

26. Noth, *Numbers,* p. 96.

27. J. Denney, *2 Corinthians,* The Expositors' Bible (London: Hodder and Stoughton, 5th edition), p. 68.

28. Binns, *Numbers,* p. 77, points out that "According to the Talmud there were seven sins which incurred this punishment: denunciation, bloodshed, false oaths, immorality, haughtiness, robbery, and grudging."

29. Noth, *Numbers,* p. 97, adds, "This is an allusion to the fact that a punishment of this sort did in fact exist, namely in cases where a girl has become guilty in some shameful way or another so that her father has 'spit in her face' (cf. the somewhat different situation in Deut. 25:9, where there is no mention of exclusion) . . . . Presumably it is the clemency of the divine decision that is being brought out, a clemency which punishes Miriam only in the way in which a girl is punished who is guilty of an offense which is shameful, true, but is yet so trivial that the comparatively lenient punishment of a seven-day exclusion sufficed, whereas Miriam had turned against Yahweh's confidant, for which she should really have been punished by a lifetime of suffering from leprosy."

30. Keil and Delitzsch, *Numbers,* pp. 81–82.

CHAPTER NINE

The Spies at Kadesh Barnea

Numbers 13:1–14:45

The Choice of the Spies

13:1 And the LORD spoke to Moses, saying,
2 "Send men to spy out the land of Canaan, which I
am giving to the children of Israel; from each tribe of
their fathers you shall send a man, every one a leader
among them."
3 So Moses sent them from the Wilderness of Paran
according to the command of the LORD, all of them
men who *were* heads of the children of Israel.
4 Now these *were* their names: from the tribe of
Reuben, Shammua the son of Zaccur;
5 from the tribe of Simeon, Shaphat the son of
Hori;
6 from the tribe of Judah, Caleb the son of
Jephunneh;
7 from the tribe of Issachar, Igal the son of
Joseph;
8 from the tribe of Ephraim, Hoshea the son of
Nun;
9 from the tribe of Benjamin, Palti the son of
Raphu;
10 from the tribe of Zebulun, Gaddiel the son of
Sodi;
11 from the tribe of Joseph, *that is,* from the tribe
of Manasseh, Gaddi the son of Susi;
12 from the tribe of Dan, Ammiel the son of
Gemalli;
13 from the tribe of Asher, Sethur the son of
Michael;

14 from the tribe of Naphtali, Nahbi the son of Vophsi;
15 from the tribe of Gad, Geuel the son of Machi.
16 These *are* the names of the men whom Moses sent to spy out the land. And Moses called Hoshea the son of Nun, Joshua.
17 Then Moses sent them to spy out the land of Canaan, and said to them, "Go up this *way* into the South, and go up to the mountains,
18 "and see what the land is like: whether the people who dwell in it *are* strong or weak, few or many;
19 "whether the land they dwell in *is* good or bad; whether the cities they inhabit *are* like camps or strongholds;
20 "whether the land *is* rich or poor; and whether there are forests there or not. Be of good courage. And bring some of the fruit of the land." Now the time *was* the season of the first ripe grapes.

Num. 13:1–20

The narrative of the spies' expedition into Canaan is the prologue that leads to the story of the divine judgment upon Israel at Kadesh Barnea. Twelve men, one chosen from each of the twelve tribes, are sent in to spy out the land. They are sent, according to verse 1, at the command of the Lord, but according to Deuteronomy 1:22 it was the people who asked Moses to send the spies. This is taken by one scholar to be "a sign of their want of faith in Jehovah's leadership"; but another biblical scholar is nearer the mark when he maintains that this proposal of the congregation "pleased Moses, so that he laid the matter before the Lord, Who then commanded him to send out for this purpose the spies."[1] The spies were all men of rank in their tribes, "heads of the children of Israel" (v. 3) but different from the tribal princes mentioned in 1:3ff., 7:12ff.

The order of the listing of the tribes in 4–15 follows, in the main, that given in 1:5–15, with the minor alterations of Zebulun and Ephraim being reversed, also Gad and Naphtali. At the end of the list (v. 16b), there is added the statement that Moses called Hoshea, son of Nun, by the new name Joshua.[2]

The instructions given by Moses to the spies are recorded in verses 17–20. The commission was definite and specific. They were to penetrate the Negev (the south), and the hill country, and seek to make some assessment of the possible military strength of the people, and their aptitude for war, and estimate the economic resources of their land. This was an astute and businesslike proposal, with both the more immediate objective of conquest, and the longer term prospect of settlement in the land, in view.[3]

THE JOURNEY INTO CANAAN

> 13:21 So they went up and spied out the land from the Wilderness of Zin as far as Rehob, near the entrance of Hamath.
>
> 22 And they went up through the South and came to Hebron; Ahiman, Sheshai, and Talmai, the descendants of Anak, *were* there. (Now Hebron was built seven years before Zoan in Egypt.)
>
> 23 Then they came to the Valley of Eshcol, and there cut down a branch with one cluster of grapes; they carried it between two of them on a pole. *They* also *brought* some of the pomegranates and figs.
>
> 24 The place was called the Valley of Eshcol, because of the cluster which the men of Israel cut down there.
>
> 25 And they returned from spying out the land after forty days.
>
> *Num. 13:21–25*

The twelve spies went in, as they were bidden, and for forty days they searched out the land, obtaining in the course of that time a fairly clear and coherent picture of conditions there and of what would have to be faced by the people.[4] In verse 21 we are given a summary of the expedition, with what follows in verses 22–24 giving a particular detail of great importance to the congregation of Israel, as will be seen in what follows these verses, when the spies returned and made their report.[5] During the forty days—a length of time which really requires them to have ranged the length and breadth of the land—the spies made a full investigation of the terrain, from the Wilderness of Zin in the south, where Kadesh was situated, to Rehob in the north, near Hamath, a place generally identified with Beth-rehob at the head of the Jordan valley near to Dan and Mount Hermon. Visitors to Israel can well imagine such an itinerary and follow with engrossing interest the spies' progress northward through the Wilderness of Judaea, upward through Samaria, into Galilee and along the shores of the lake—what must their thoughts have been on seeing it for the first time!—and up the Jordan valley to the slopes of Mount Hermon. It is little wonder that in their report they should have spoken as they did in verse 27!

The Return of the Spies

13:26 Now they departed and came back to Moses
and Aaron and all the congregation of the children of
Israel in the Wilderness of Paran, at Kadesh; they
brought back word to them and to all the congregation, and showed them the fruit of the land.
27 Then they told him, and said: "We went to the
land where you sent us. It truly flows with milk and
honey, and this *is* its fruit.
28 "Nevertheless the people who dwell in the land
are strong; the cities *are* fortified *and* very large;
moreover we saw the descendants of Anak there.
29 "The Amalekites dwell in the land of the South;
the Hittites, the Jebusites, and the Amorites dwell
in the mountains; and the Canaanites dwell by the
sea and along the banks of the Jordan."
30 Then Caleb quieted the people before Moses,
and said, "Let us go up at once and take possession,
for we are well able to overcome it."
31 But the men who had gone up with him said,
"We are not able to go up against the people, for they
are stronger than we."
32 And they gave the children of Israel a bad report of the land which they had spied out, saying,
"The land through which we have gone as spies *is* a
land that devours its inhabitants, and all the people
whom we saw in it *are* men of *great* stature.
33 "There we saw the giants (the descendants
of Anak came from the giants); and we were like

grasshoppers in our own sight, and so we were in their sight."

Num. 13:26–33

On their return the spies reported back to Moses. Their testimony was unanimous (v. 27ff.): it was a good and fruitful land, flowing with milk and honey, and the grapes of Eshcol, a fertile valley north of Hebron, were produced as evidence of this. A note of great reserve, however, was sounded by the majority of the spies in verse 28: the land, they said, was inhabited by a very strong people, and their cities were large and well fortified (as the excavations at places like Jericho and Megiddo show today). In addition, the descendants of Anak were there, a giantlike people calculated to spread dismay and dread among the Israelites.[6]

The people seem to have gotten word of this gloomy report, and became agitated and discouraged by it—this is implied in verse 30, in the statement that *"Caleb quieted the people before Moses."* His attitude was positive and optimistic: all that the other spies had said was accepted, giants and all; nevertheless, Caleb declared, *"Let us go up at once and take possession, for we are well able to overcome it."*[7] The defeatist attitude of the other spies is underlined again in verses 32 and 33. It was as though, having once uttered their reserve, they were carried on by its momentum into an almost hysterical state of panic, which communicated itself inevitably to the congregation of the people, as is shown in the chapter that follows. (It will be best to complete the survey of both this and the next chapter before making general comment on the implications of this grave and critical crisis-point for Israel.)

Uproar and Revolt among the People

14:1 So all the congregation lifted up their voices and cried, and the people wept that night.

2 And all the children of Israel complained against Moses and Aaron, and the whole congregation said to them, "If only we had died in the land of Egypt! Or if only we had died in this wilderness!

3 "Why has the LORD brought us to this land to fall by the sword, that our wives and children should

become victims? Would it not be better for us to return to Egypt?"

4 So they said to one another, "Let us select a leader and return to Egypt."

5 Then Moses and Aaron fell on their faces before all the assembly of the congregation of the children of Israel.

6 But Joshua the son of Nun and Caleb the son of Jephunneh, *who were* among those who had spied out the land, tore their clothes;

7 and they spoke to all the congregation of the children of Israel, saying: "The land we passed through to spy out *is* an exceedingly good land.

8 "If the LORD delights in us, then He will bring us into this land and give it to us, 'a land which flows with milk and honey.'

9 "Only do not rebel against the LORD, nor fear the people of the land, for they *are* our bread; their protection has departed from them, and the LORD *is* with us. Do not fear them."

10 And all the congregation said to stone them with stones. Now the glory of the LORD appeared in the tabernacle of meeting before all the children of Israel.

Num. 14:1–10

The effect of the ten spies' report as it circulated among the people was to spread their defeatist attitude throughout the whole congregation of Israel. A movement of mass hysteria seems to have swept through them, but it was also more than this: it was, to change the metaphor, like putting a spark to dry tinder. Their history, recorded in the past few chapters, prepared for this, and the resultant conflagration was inevitable. The "murmuring" reached an ominous level (vv. 2–3), and broke out in open rebellion against Moses and Aaron (v. 4), as they opted for new leadership to take them back to Egypt. (Reference to this incident is made in Nehemiah 9:17, where it is explicitly stated that they "appointed a leader to return to their bondage." We may perhaps see a precedent for their action, not insignificantly, in the revolt by Aaron and Miriam against Moses' leadership in 12:1 ff.)

Moses' and Aaron's reaction to this is one of great distress and grief, and they fell on their faces before the assembled congregation (v. 5). As Calvin says, "In such a case of obduracy, nothing remained except to call upon God, yet in such sort that the prayer should be made in the sight of all, in order to influence their minds."[8] (Deut. 1:29–31, however, indicates that Moses first made an attempt to reassure the people and exhort them to go forward without fear.)

Joshua and Caleb, the other two spies, added their protest to Moses' and Aaron's, making an eloquent but vain appeal to the people, urging them to trust in the goodness and providence of God to fulfill His promise to them, and warning them of the danger of rebelling against Him (vv. 8–9). The congregation, however, were too far gone in their revolt to be influenced by this most eloquent of appeals, were all for stoning Caleb and Joshua, and would have done so but for the intervention of God (v. 10b), through the appearance of His glory in the tabernacle, to deal with the situation Himself. All in all, this is one of the saddest and most tragic experiences of Israel's long history, and one fraught with the most serious and far-reaching consequences, as we shall see in what follows.

The Intercession of Moses

14:11 Then the LORD said to Moses: "How long will these people reject Me? And how long will they not believe Me, with all the signs which I have performed among them?

12 "I will strike them with the pestilence and disinherit them, and I will make of you a nation greater and mightier than they."

13 And Moses said to the LORD: "Then the Egyptians will hear *it,* for by Your might You brought these people up from among them,

14 "and they will tell *it* to the inhabitants of this land. They have heard that You, LORD, *are* among these people; that You, LORD, are seen face to face and Your cloud stands above them, and You go before them in a pillar of cloud by day and in a pillar of fire by night.

15 "Now *if* You kill these people as one man, then the nations which have heard of Your fame will speak, saying,

16 'Because the LORD was not able to bring this
people to the land which He swore to give them,
therefore He killed them in the wilderness."
17 "And now, I pray, let the power of my LORD be
great, just as You have spoken, saying,
18 'The LORD is longsuffering and abundant in
mercy, forgiving iniquity and transgression; but He
by no means clears *the guilty,* visiting the iniquity of
the fathers on the children to the third and fourth
generation.'
19 "Pardon the iniquity of this people, I pray, according to the greatness of Your mercy, just as You
have forgiven this people, from Egypt even until now."
20 Then the LORD said: "I have pardoned, according to your word;
21 "but truly, as I live, all the earth shall be filled
with the glory of the LORD—
22 "because all these men who have seen My glory
and the signs which I did in Egypt and in the wilderness, and have put Me to the test now these ten
times, and have not heeded My voice,
23 "they certainly shall not see the land of which I
swore to their fathers, nor shall any of those who
rejected Me see it.
24 "But My servant Caleb, because he has a different spirit in him and has followed Me fully, I will
bring into the land where he went, and his descendants shall inherit it.
25 "Now the Amalekites and the Canaanites dwell
in the valley; tomorrow turn and move out into the
wilderness by the Way of the Red Sea."

Num. 14:11–25

There now follows a remarkable debate between Moses and the Lord. The patriarch interceded for the people, and with princely mediation won for them a reprieve. But, even with this, judgment could not be avoided (vv. 22–23). The land was closed to them, and the people were turned back into the wilderness, there to wander for forty years, one year for every day the spies were in the land, until that whole generation of adults should die off—Caleb, Joshua, and the children excepted. The distinction made here is that Israel *as a nation* was pardoned and still remained the people of God; but *that generation* of Israelites as individuals failed forever in the hope of their calling. For them, this was the end—not in the sense that they were no longer His people (for He still dealt with them in mercy in their wilderness wanderings), but in the sense that they missed their high destiny and entered a dreary "second-best."

This concept of a "second-best" is a solemn, even frightening thought, and it raises the question of whether our sin can after all defeat God's purpose for our lives. However difficult it may be to reconcile the reality of God's sovereign will with human responsibility for sin, it has to be conceded that this truth is too firmly embedded in the Scriptures of both the Old and New Testaments for it ever to be controverted. It is significant that the apostle Paul, in warning the Corinthian believers about the possibility of becoming "disqualified" (1 Cor. 9:27), amplifies his statement with a reference to the continuing murmuring and rebellion of Israel in the wilderness (1 Cor. 10:1–12). That being said, however, it has also to be affirmed that even when such "disqualification" takes place and a "second-best" situation arises, God still blesses His people *within the limits which they themselves place upon Him by their sin.* The "wilderness generation" of Israel experienced many outpourings of grace from the hand of their God, in the years that followed this tragic judgment upon them, as subsequent chapters will show.

Moses' intercession on this occasion, as he "stood in the breach" before God (Ps. 106:23), is similar to that in Exodus 32:10ff., with the addition here that he pleaded the honor of God's name among the heathen, which would be impugned in their sight if He destroyed them all. In addition to this consideration, Moses also pleaded the revelation that God had given of Himself as being "longsuffering and abundant in mercy, forgiving iniquity and transgression" (v. 18). This is powerful and effective pleading indeed. As Calvin puts it, "Moses was able to derive from thence a sure directive for prayer; for nothing can be more sure than his own word, on which if our prayers are based, there is no reason to fear that they will be ineffectual, or that the result should disappoint us, since He who has spoken will prove Himself to be true."[9]

Having pleaded the honor of God's name among the heathen, and the revelation that He had given of Himself as a long-suffering and merciful God, Moses finally bases his appeal on experience (v. 19):

> Pardon, (he says) as Thou hast so often done before. For since the goodness of God is unwearied and inexhaustible, the oftener we have experienced it, the more ought we to be encouraged to implore it; not that we may sink into the licentious indulgence of sin, but lest despair should overwhelm us, when we are lying under the condemnation of God, and our own conscience smites and torments us. In a word, let us regard this as a most effective mode of importunity, when we beseech God by the benefits which we have already experienced, that He will never cease to be gracious.[10]

This passage is one of several in Scripture which we should be encouraged to use as models for prayer and intercession (cf. Exod. 32:9–12, Ps. 51, Acts 4:24–30). It is the outward-looking aspects of the intercession that are so impressive—God's name, God's Word, God's covenant, God's faithfulness. The reminder to God of what He had said, and how He had pledged Himself in the grace of the covenant—this is the operative element in all true prayer. God loves to be reminded of His pledges in this way (cf. Isa. 43:26, "Put Me in remembrance"); and since His honor is involved, this is something that must prevail. He cannot be untrue to Himself; He will always keep His word, and when His children stand thus upon His promises, He delights to answer their prayers. It is because God is faithful to Himself that He proves Himself faithful to His people.

The divine response to Moses' intercession is immediate, and God pardons according to Moses' word (v. 20). This "change of mind" on God's part is remarkable (v. 12), but it poses problems.[11] It could be argued that the contradiction is only apparent, and that the sentence of disinheritance did not in itself exclude the possibility of forgiveness, and that this in fact is what took place: that generation did lose its inheritance, although it received the forgiveness of God (cf. Ps. 99:8). The truest thing, however, that can be said is that we have here one further evidence of the essential mystery inherent in the relationship of the divine sovereignty and human personality. As The Westminster Confession of Faith puts it: "God from all eternity, did by the most wise and holy counsel of His own will, freely and unchangeably ordain whatsoever comes to pass: yet so, as thereby neither is God the author of sin, nor is violence offered to the will of the creatures, nor is the liberty or contingency of second causes taken away, but rather established."[12]

The two sides of the antinomy must clearly be held in a polarity of truth rather than modifying the emphasis on the divine sovereignty on the one hand—or qualifying the reality of human responsibility on the other. Whatever the mystery involved, Moses' prayer clearly moved God on this occasion to change His dealings with His people.

The reference in verse 22 to their having *"put Me to the test now these ten times"* must surely be understood in general terms, ten being used as a number of completeness (although the Jewish Talmud takes it as a literal figure, and instances the following references in support of its contention: Exod. 14:11, 12, 15:23, 16:2, 17:1, 32; Num. 11:1, 4 ff., 14:1 ff.; Exod. 16:20, 27).

The Lord's testimony concerning Caleb in verse 24 is very moving: *"He has a different spirit in him and has followed Me fully"*—complete obedience and complete confidence are indicated. In such a context, this must surely have gladdened the heart of God!

The Sentence Passed on the People

14:26 And the LORD spoke to Moses and Aaron, saying,

27 "How long *shall I bear with* this evil congregation who complain against Me? I have heard the complaints which the children of Israel make against Me.

28 "Say to them, 'As I live,' says the LORD, 'just as you have spoken in My hearing, so I will do to you:

29 'The carcasses of you who have complained against Me shall fall in this wilderness, all of you who were numbered, according to your entire number, from twenty years old and above.

30 'Except for Caleb the son of Jephunneh and Joshua the son of Nun, you shall by no means enter the land which I swore I would make you dwell in.

31 'But your little ones, whom you said would be victims, I will bring in, and they shall know the land which you have despised.

32 'But *as for* you, your carcasses shall fall in this wilderness.

33 'And your sons shall be shepherds in the wilderness forty years, and bear the brunt of your infidelity, until your carcasses are consumed in the wilderness.

34 'According to the number of the days in which
you spied out the land, forty days, for each day you
shall bear your guilt one year, *namely* forty years,
and you shall know My rejection.
35 'I the LORD have spoken this. I will surely do so
to all this evil congregation who are gathered together against Me. In this wilderness they shall be
consumed, and there they shall die.'"
36 Now the men whom Moses sent to spy out the
land, who returned and made all the congregation
complain against him by bringing a bad report of the
land,
37 those very men who brought the evil report
about the land, died by the plague before the LORD.
38 But Joshua the son of Nun and Caleb the son of
Jephunneh remained alive, of the men who went to
spy out the land.

Num. 14:26–38

Moses and Aaron are now instructed to inform the people as to the details of the sentence passed upon them. The entire faithless generation of them, Caleb and Joshua excepted, were condemned to wander in the wilderness for forty years, one year for every day that the spies were in the land. There is a grim irony in the pronouncement that the Lord would take the people at their word: "If only we had died in this wilderness!" (v. 2), they had said, and so it was decided. The expression of their murmuring spirit became their sentence, and they had decided their own destiny by their faithlessness. The message of this section of the book is clear: They had brought their exclusion from the Promised Land upon themselves. "The punishment which befell the people was no merely arbitrary act: the unbelief and disobedience which they had repeatedly exhibited showed their unsuitability for the conquest of Canaan."[13] Even their children were not exempt from this visitation, for, although they were eventually to enter the land (v. 31) as a prey, this would be only after their prolonged period in the wilderness, a discipline which they must endure, to atone, as it were, for the apostasy and faithlessness of their fathers.

A grim footnote is added in verses 36–38 to the Lord's pronouncement of the sentence upon the people. The ten spies who had been instrumental in spreading the disaffection among the people and bringing them to the point of rebellion and revolt were stricken by plague and died before the Lord. This is the beginning of the Lord's "rejection" (the Hebrew word in v. 34 is variously translated: The KJV renders it "breach of promise," which is a more accurate translation of the original; the RSV has "displeasure"),[14] and as Calvin points out, "a kind of presage to all the others of the punishment which awaited them."[15] As the New Testament would put it, "God is not mocked; for whatever a man sows, that he will also reap" (Gal. 6:7).

The Defeat at Hormah

14:39 Then Moses told these words to all the children
of Israel, and the people mourned greatly.
40 And they rose early in the morning and went
up to the top of the mountain, saying, "Here we are,
and we will go up to the place which the LORD has
promised, for we have sinned!"
41 And Moses said, "Now why do you transgress
the command of the LORD? For this will not succeed.
42 "Do not go up, lest you be defeated by your enemies, for the LORD *is* not among you.
43 "For the Amalekites and the Canaanites *are*
there before you, and you shall fall by the sword;
because you have turned away from the LORD, the
LORD will not be with you."
44 But they presumed to go up to the mountaintop.
Nevertheless, neither the ark of the covenant of the
LORD nor Moses departed from the camp.
45 Then the Amalekites and the Canaanites who
dwelt in that mountain came down and attacked
them, and drove them back as far as Hormah.

Num. 14:39–45

What follows in the concluding verses of the chapter reminds us of the distinction that the apostle Paul draws between "godly sorrow" that "produces repentance to salvation, not to be regretted," and "the sorrow of the world" that "produces death" (2 Cor. 7:9f.). Instead of allowing the terrible sentence passed on them to work repentance in them, all that their "confession of sin" (v. 40) led to was a carnal resolve to enter the land. This was in spite of a warning from Moses that God's judgment in the matter was unalterable, and that they would certainly come to grief. That they were devoid of the presence of God in this ill-advised and ill-fated escapade is made plain in verse 44: *"Neither the ark of the covenant of the Lord nor Moses departed from the camp"* with them as they went up. The message of the verses is clear: their action simply confirmed the rebelliousness and obstinacy of their hearts against the will of God and underlined the inevitability of the divine judgment that came upon them. As one commentator has said, "It is human nature to neglect to serve God when He wills it, and then to attempt to serve Him when He forbids it."[16]

The truth is, God wanted more, far more, from His people than this abortive display could possibly indicate. All that they did was to demonstrate their natural perversity of heart, and their failure to understand the nature of repentance. Verse 44 says *"they presumed. . . ."* This is an eloquent and perhaps sufficient commentary on their state of heart, and it prompts us to remark that in such circumstances God is not really taken in by our protestations, though we ourselves may often be, and others also. The truth of the matter is that the willfulness, the disobedience, the hardhearted disregard of the divine will were all unchanged.

We must now pause to consider some of the lessons that this tragic crisis at Kadesh Barnea provides. It is clear that the solemn message it bears impressed itself deeply on the minds of New Testament writers. Two passages in particular, 1 Corinthians 10 and Hebrews 4, call for some comment.

The point of Paul's introduction of this subject in his epistle to the Corinthians (1 Cor. 10) is a general one. It is a warning to the Corinthian believers that if they persist in tempting God by their carnal worldliness and spiritual carelessness they would run the risk of being disqualified, as Israel was in this story. It is significant that Paul has just spoken (9:24–27) of the possibility of a believer, and a servant of the Lord, becoming through carelessness disqualified (Greek *adokimos*), castaway—not in the sense of being cut off from the mercies of God, or of losing salvation, but in the sense of losing one's reward, one's truest and highest destiny in the service and purposes of God. Paul could see in the life of the Corinthian church the same sinister pattern at work as had brought spiritual disaster upon the people of Israel: persistent and continuous dissension and disputing, and above all murmuring against the authority of the apostle. He is bidding them beware, saying, "See where all this is leading: your feet are on the slippery slope, and by and by you will not be able to stop. There is a predictable end to this attitude of yours. Remember the children of Israel at Kadesh Barnea."

To sin as the Corinthians were sinning was in Paul's eyes to refuse their calling to the spiritual purposes of God and to open the distinct possibility of disqualification. God could cast them off and choose another people as the instrument of His purposes. This is well illustrated in the dramatic words spoken by Mordecai to Esther (Esther 4:14). A moment of destiny had come for Esther, and she was wavering in her response to the challenge of God. Mordecai warned her, saying, "God has a purpose, He is intent on doing something, and He will do it, if not through you, through somebody else." His words are fraught with challenge: "For if you remain completely silent at this time, relief and deliverance will arise for the Jews from another place, but you and your father's house will perish. Yet who knows whether you have come to the kingdom for such a time as this?"

To those who are the called of God, and part of the divine purposes for their day and generation, this is an immense challenge. If through unwillingness, or fear, or timidity, or carelessness, they fail to recognize this to be their calling, and hang back for whatever reason, they will need to beware lest they fall as Israel fell, and God turn elsewhere to those who will dare to believe and venture out with Him.

In the other passage (Heb. 4:1–9) the apostle gives an impassioned appeal to his readers to enter into all that God has for them in Christ and guard against the danger and tragedy of not entering in because of an evil heart of unbelief. The statement he makes in 4:2—"For indeed the gospel was preached to us as well as to them; but the word which they heard did not profit them, not being mixed with faith in those who heard it"—refers not to the gospel of grace being preached to them of old time, but to the good news that Caleb and Joshua brought back from the Promised Land, when they said, "We are well able to overcome it." This is the message they heard and which did not benefit them.

The point of this parallel becomes clear when we remember to whom this epistle was written: believers who were wavering in faith and about to turn back because of their unwillingness to let go of the old tradition and Jewish beliefs and ways. In this they were just like the children of Israel on the borders of the Promised Land, and history was repeating itself in the spiritual sense, hence the apostolic exhortation, "Let us therefore be diligent to enter that rest, lest anyone fall after the same example of disobedience" (4:11).

This is a word of continuing relevance for the believer, especially when he is tempted to vacillate, selfishly holding back his allegiance from the full commitment to the work of God to which he is summoned. Its exhortation to him is to cast hesitation to the winds, and to go forward in the divinely appointed pattern, and "go on to perfection" (6:1), to go in and possess the land.

There are two directions along which all this can be followed: they can be described in terms of invitation and challenge.

As to the invitation it holds out, it has to be conceded that, on any estimate, the spies' expedition into the land, and their subsequent report, opened up an immense opportunity for Israel and provided an invitation to enter in to the blessing and enrichment that God had in mind for His people. In view of this, the fateful "nevertheless" in 13:28, stands in eloquent contrast, for it underlines the enormity of their failure in turning back, in spite of the undoubted and confessed attractiveness of the Promised Land. The refusals men make of the grace of God are always made in the face of such attraction. There are those who remain outside the covenant blessings of God in this way and never really enter His kingdom. They listen to the gospel, and they see the attractiveness of the new life—how could any man not see this?—they taste, so to speak, the grapes of Eschol, in the sense that they almost savor, by implication, the blessings of God's salvation, in the hearing of the Word; they stand, as it were, on the threshold of the kingdom—and yet they turn back and turn away refusing it.

One thinks of the sometimes irrational considerations that make men turn back. These Israelites swept aside the great prospect that stretched before them, that for which they had been called out of Egypt, prepared and trained, that for which their whole history had destined them and predisposed them. In one disastrous moment, in which they weighed the blessings of life against the doubtful attractions of the Egypt that their hearts hankered after—the "good old days," in which in fact they had suffered and languished in bondage. They hankered, and pined, and the blessing of God was outweighed. This is how men are lost; this is how men miss the gates of eternal life.

The story of Felix the governor, in Acts 24:24ff., is a case in point. Here is a man who was near to the kingdom, and who trembled at the approach of the eternal world. But his reply to Paul—and to God—was, "Go away for now." The pull of the unseen world was very real for him, but the "nevertheless" that betrayed him was his love of the world; and opportunity (Acts 24:25) did not knock again. Every preacher has seen this happening, has seen men and women, touched and drawn by the gospel, awakened and stirred, attracted by the message of salvation—but there has been a "nevertheless" that has put their souls in jeopardy.

This story makes its appeal to them, by the destiny that their upbringing has claimed for them, by the prayers that have surrounded them, and by the influences that have been brought to bear upon them, to listen to the invitation to enter in. "Let us go up at once," says Caleb (13:30) in this context, "for delay may be fatal." As Shakespeare puts it,

> There is a tide in the affairs of men,
> Which, taken at the flood, leads on to fortune;
> Omitted, all the voyage of their life
> Is bound in shallows and in miseries.
> On such a full sea are we now afloat,
> We must take the current when it serves,
> Or lose our ventures.
>
> *Julius Caesar,* Act 4

As to the challenge this story presents, there is no doubt that a formidable task awaited the people of Israel on entering the land, that would take all that there was of them to fulfill, as they confronted the sons of Anak and the walled cities that abounded there. In the same way, all the attractiveness of the gospel invitation does not conceal the resounding challenge and summons that it also presents to men. But a gospel that promises an easy time is not a gospel worthy of respect. It can be a temptation, in our preoccupation with commending our message to a generation that has become indifferent to it, to present the gospel in a false attractiveness that simply emasculates it and makes a caricature of it. This, however, is far from the biblical standpoint. There is a certain attitude of mind that has gained considerable currency in modern days. It is well expressed in the words, "The world owes me a living." It is deadly for the moral and spiritual welfare of church and nation alike. We have pampered and spoiled ourselves as a generation, until all that we can speak of is rights and privileges, never responsibilities and duties.

It is possible to capitulate to this spirit in such a way as to lose sight of the great horizons, and shrink the glory of the gospel to such an extent that it is made to play the role of a tranquilizer for sick and pining hypochondriacs, instead of a mighty, authentic word from on high about sin and forgiveness, new life, and everlasting hope. A shrewd, perceptive, and devastating critique of this attitude has been made by Rabbi Maurice Eisendrath, one time president of the Union of American Hebrew Congregations:

> Man is the beginning and end of present-day American religiosity—God is made to serve, or rather to subserve man, to subserve his every purpose and enterprise whether it be economic prosperity, free enterprise, security, or peace of mind. God thus becomes an omnipotent servant, a universal bellhop, to cater to man's every caprice: faith becomes a sure-fire device to get what we petulantly and peevishly crave. This reduction of God from master to slave has reached its height, or rather its depth of blasphemy, in the cult of the Man Upstairs—the friendly neighbour-god who dwells in the apartment just above. Call on him any time—especially if you are feeling blue. He does not get the least bit upset with your faults and failings and, as for your sins, not only does he not remember them . . . but the very word and concept of sin have been abolished and "adjustment" or "non-adjustment" have taken their places.[17]

What church and nation alike need—and what many secretly want and long for—is a challenge worth facing, a cause to live for and to die for. It is just such a cause that is represented in this story: "Go in and possess; fight with the sons of Anak; storm the walled cities and the strongholds." The church is not a wetnurse, appointed to soothe and pet the chronic immaturities of those who are not prepared to come to terms with themselves; it is rather the trumpet that summons men to battle. Winston Spencer Churchill's famous wartime summons to the British people to "blood and toil, tears and sweat," needs to have its spiritual counterpart. In Christian warfare the price does not come down: it asks everything of us. There is no cut-rate Christianity in the New Testament, no cheap grace. This is the standard, and the faithful few go forward in this spirit, even if, to continue the Churchillian metaphor, they have to "go it alone." There were only twelve disciples; but they turned the world upside down!

NOTES

1. Carl L. Keil and Franz Delitzsch, *Numbers,* Commentary on the Old Testament, vol. 3 (Grand Rapids: Wm. B. Eerdmans, repr. 1971), p. 84. Binn's suggestion surely misunderstands the situation; it need not have been any indication of want of faith in Jehovah's leadership that spies should be sent out, any more than it was want of faith on the apostle Paul's part to make use of his Roman citizenship in Acts 22:25, 25:11. The use of means is entirely legitimate, and consonant with the deepest faith and trust in God.

2. Ibid., pp. 85–86. Delitzsch comments: "This statement does not present any such discrepancy, when compared with Exodus 17:9, 13; 24:13; 32:17; 33:11; and Numbers 9:28, where Joshua bears this name as the servant of Moses at a still earlier period, as to point to any diversity of authorship. As there is nothing of a genealogical character in any of these passages, so as to warrant us in expecting to find the family name of Joshua in them, the name Joshua, by which Hoshea had become better known in history, could be used proleptically in them all. On the other hand, however, it is not distinctly stated in the verse before us, that this was the occasion on which Moses gave Hoshea the new name of Joshua . . . . the words may be understood without hesitation in the following sense: These are the names borne by the heads of the tribes to be sent out as spies, as they stand in the family registers according to their descent; Hoshea, however, was named Joshua by Moses; which would not by any means imply that the alteration in the name had not been made until then. It is very probable that Moses may have given him the new name either before or after the defeat of the Amalekites (Exod. 17:9 ff.), or

when he took him into his service, though it has not been mentioned before; whilst here the circumstances themselves required that it should be stated that Hoshea, as he was called in the list prepared and entered in the documentary record according to the genealogical tables of the tribes, had received from Moses the name of Joshua." See also Calvin, *Pentateuch,* 4:56. See note 3 below.

3. John Calvin, *Harmony of the Pentateuch,* 4:57. Calvin comments: "The counsel of Moses had this object, that the people might be made aware how rich and fertile the land was; for a barren country does not support a large population; and the healthfulness of a locality is inferred from the vigour of its inhabitants. He, therefore, chiefly insists on the goodness of the land and its abundant production of fruits. Still, perhaps, God would intentionally have the Israelites forewarned, that they would have to do with strong and powerful enemies; lest they might be alarmed and discouraged at suddenly beholding them. But the main point was, that the pleasantness and fertility of the land might allure them to take possession of it."

4. The critical hypothesis, which claims that there are two differing, and indeed contradictory, accounts of the spies' excursion fused together in this passage, maintains that there are two different starting points for the expedition mentioned: The wilderness of Paran on the one hand, and Kadesh, which is in the wilderness of Zin, on the other. But, as E. J. Young, *An Introduction to the Old Testament,* (Wheaton, Ill: Tyndale Press, 1949), p. 91 points out, "Nowhere is it explicitly stated that the spies started from Kadesh. The word Kadesh comes from v. 26 where it is identified as being in Paran. V. 26 should be translated 'and they went and came back—unto the wilderness of Paran, to Kadesh—.' Even if the critical partition were correct, it should be noted that the redactor wished to associate Kadesh and Paran. Since Kadesh was on the border of Paran and Zin, it might be said to be in either. Conclusion: The only starting point mentioned is Paran."

5. Critics maintain that one of the two accounts fused together in the narrative indicates that the spies went only as far as Hebron, and did not in fact traverse the whole land. But, even on this dubious hypothesis it can hardly be maintained that in verses 22–24 the spies are restricted to Hebron and Eschol. They followed Moses' command (v. 17) to go up not only to the Negeb but also into the hill country (i.e., the land proper) and even to investigate the cities, a term which can hardly be confined to the neighborhood of Hebron. Besides, if they had contented themselves with an exploration of the Negeb they must surely have returned long before the forty days were up. The length of time requires us to think in terms of the exploration of the whole land, and not even a redactor could have been unaware of this.

6. L. Eliott Binns, *The Book of Numbers* (London: Methuen & Co., Ltd., 1927), p. 85, in a note says: "Anak is not a personal name, its Heb. meaning is neck and the phrase sons of neck, by a common idiom, means long-necked or tall men. The sons named above represent probably not individuals but tribes of Amorite or North Arabian people settled round Hebron. Many traditions survived in Canaan of gigantic peoples most of whom were the original dwellers in the land; perhaps the sons of Anak in spite of their names were also pre-Canaanite: cf. Macalister's interesting remarks on these giant aborigines who, after being destroyed in Israel, survived in Gaza, Gath, and Ashdod (Jos xi.22) and perhaps amalgamated with the Philistines, giving them their gigantic champions."

7. Keil and Delitzsch, *Numbers,* pp. 90–91, adds: "The fact that Caleb only is mentioned, though, according to 14:6 Joshua also stood by his side, may be explained on the simple ground that at first Caleb was the only one to speak and maintain the possibility of conquering Canaan." Besides, as E. J. Young suggests, he was of the tribe of Judah, the leading tribe and it may be that Joshua allowed him as such to take the initiative, and kept himself in the background.

8. Calvin, *Pentateuch,* 4:66.

9. Ibid., p. 75.

10. Ibid., p. 76.

11. Ibid., p. 73. Calvin comments, "If the apparent contradiction offends any one, that God should declare the people to be cast off, when it was already decreed that He would pardon them, a reply may be sought from elsewhere in three words; for God does not here speak of His secret and incomprehensible counsel, but only of the actual circumstances, shewing what the people had deserved, and how horrible was the vengeance which impended, in respect of their wicked and detestable revolt, since it was not His design to keep Moses back from earnest prayer, but to put the sincerity of his piety and the fervency of his zeal to the proof. And, in fact, he does not contravene the prohibition, except upon the previous exhibition of some spark of faith. See Exodus xxxii."

12. The Westminster Confession of Faith, Ch. 3, 1.

13. Binns, *Numbers,* p. 96.

14. Delitzsch renders it "My turning away from you." Elliott Binns, with others, translates "My alienation" and adds, "the withdrawal of God's favour will be known by the disasters which will ensue." Calvin takes a different view, rendering the word as "vanity," deriving from a verb which signifies "to render ineffectual." He adds "Translators however extract from it various meanings. Some thus construe it: Ye shall know whether I am false or whether My word shall be vain. Others, rendering it 'prohibition,' depart more widely from the sense. But in my judgment, it is an

ironical concession, whereby God reproves their detestable pride, which had no other object than to accuse God of falsehood, and to charge Him calumniously with failing to fulfil His words . . . . I rather adopt this sense, that they should perceive by certain and experimental proof, whether God's promises were frivolous or vain."

15. Calvin, *Pentateuch,* 4:84.

16. Binns, *Numbers,* p. 98, quotes Pusey on Hosea 9:4.

17. Quoted in an article by Cecil Northcott, in *The Manchester Guardian Weekly,* 19 September 1957.

CHAPTER TEN

Various Laws and Regulations

Numbers 15:1–41

INSTRUCTIONS ON VARIOUS OFFERINGS

15:1 And the LORD spoke to Moses, saying,
2 "Speak to the children of Israel, and say to
them: 'When you have come into the land you are
to inhabit, which I am giving to you,
3 'and you make an offering by fire to the LORD, a
burnt offering or a sacrifice, to fulfill a vow or as
a freewill offering or in your appointed feasts, to
make a sweet aroma to the LORD, from the herd or
the flock,
4 'then he who presents his offering to the LORD
shall bring a grain offering of one-tenth *of an ephah*
of fine flour mixed with one-fourth of a hin of oil;
5 'and one-fourth of a hin of wine as a drink offering you shall prepare with the burnt offering or
the sacrifice, for each lamb.
6 'Or for a ram you shall prepare as a grain offering two-tenths *of an ephah* of fine flour mixed with
one-third of a hin of oil;
7 'and as a drink offering you shall offer one-
third of a hin of wine as a sweet aroma to the LORD.
8 'And when you prepare a young bull as a burnt
offering, or as a sacrifice to fulfill a vow, or as a
peace offering to the LORD,
9 'then shall be offered with the young bull a
grain offering of three-tenths *of an ephah* of fine
flour mixed with half a hin of oil;
10 'and you shall bring as the drink offering half a

hin of wine as an offering made by fire, a sweet
aroma to the LORD.
11 'Thus it shall be done for each young bull, for
each ram, or for each lamb or young goat.
12 'According to the number that you prepare, so
you shall do with everyone according to their number.
13 'All who are native-born shall do these things
in this manner, in presenting an offering made by
fire, a sweet aroma to the LORD.
14 'And if a stranger dwells with you, or whoever *is*
among you throughout your generations, and would
present an offering made by fire, a sweet aroma to the
LORD, just as you do, so shall he do.
15 'One ordinance *shall be* for you of the assembly
and for the stranger who dwells *with you,* an ordinance forever throughout your generations; as you
are, so shall the stranger be before the LORD.
16 'One law and one custom shall be for you and
for the stranger who dwells with you.'"

Num. 15:1–16

The transition from the narrative of the divine judgment at Kadesh Barnea and the relegation of that generation of Israel to forty years' wandering in the wilderness to the record of a miscellaneous series of cultic regulations that belonged to the Levitical pattern and system of sacrifices and offerings constituted by God for His people seems to have occasioned considerable bafflement for commentators, who see little in the way of any definite relation that they bear with their context. Why should such a record occur at this particular time? It will be noticed that the narrative is once again resumed at 16:1 ff., and the story of God's dealings with His people in the wilderness is continued. What is the significance of chapter 15 *here,* and in *this* place?

It is surely far from the mark to regard the chapter as "an interpolation which is singularly out of place in the narrative, and seems to have been substituted for a description of the disasters which followed on the abortive attempt of the Israelites to invade Canaan."[1] A possible, and much more likely explanation is to be found in verse 2, in the words "*When you have come into the land. . . .*" In chapter 14 it has just been said that none of that generation would enter into the land; therefore, the regulations here recorded must be for the new, younger generation (14:31), who were under twenty years of age at this point. And it is significant that the burden of the present chapter may be said to be with two matters: sins of ignorance on the one hand, and sins of presumption on the other. Here, it would seem, is the connection with the previous chapter. Sins of ignorance are pardoned, while sins of presumption are punished. Israel's sin at Kadesh was one of presumption—"with a high hand," as the Hebrew word is literally translated, and they were punished in this final way and excluded forever from entering the land. The chapter therefore stands as a meditative commentary on the serious and often fatal consequences of a life of sin and should be understood as such.[2]

The regulations set forth in the chapter are arranged carefully in three sections, each beginning with the words, *"The Lord spoke to Moses, saying, 'Speak to the children of Israel'"* (vv. 1, 17, 37). The present section sets forth the proper qualities of meal, oil, and wine to be offered with burnt offerings or peace offerings, and seem to have been given "for the purpose of reviving the hopes of the new generation that were growing up, and directing their minds to the Promised Land"[3] and to the sacrifices to be made there when they at last entered their inheritance. It was an evidence and assurance to them that, notwithstanding the judgment that had come upon this generation, the Lord was nevertheless committed to continuing relations with His people.

The Law of the Heave Offering

15:17 Again the LORD spoke to Moses, saying,

18 "Speak to the children of Israel, and say to them: 'When you come into the land to which I bring you,

19 'then it will be, when you eat of the bread of the land, that you shall offer up a heave offering to the LORD.

20 'You shall offer up a cake of the first of your ground meal *as* a heave offering; as a heave offering of the threshing floor, so shall you offer it up.

21 'Of the first of your ground meal you shall give to the LORD a heave offering throughout your generations.

Num. 15:17–21

Further regulations are added in these verses to those in verses 1–16, also looking forward to the people's settlement in Canaan. The subject of first fruits with which they deal comes up for fuller and more general treatment in 18:1 ff. Here, their mention follows naturally upon the stipulations given in the previous verses. Just as the reference to the main agricultural products of Canaan—meal, oil, and wine—symbolize every aspect of life, so here the principle of first fruits is brought into Israel's home life. When a housewife baked bread, the first fruits of it were to be set apart for the Lord "to cause a blessing to rest on your house" (Ezek. 44:30). Wenham in his Tyndale Commentary says, "After the fall of the second temple this custom was still maintained: pious Jews would throw a handful of the dough into the fire as a sort of mini-sacrifice, thereby making every hearth an altar and every kitchen a house of God."[4]

It is easy to see how such a ritual might well become an empty, legalistic bondage as seems certainly to have been the case with the Pharisees of our Lord's day (cf. Matt. 23:23); but our Lord does commend the proper practice of it, "These you ought to have done," thereby setting His seal upon the principle involved. It is the hallowing of the common life of man, whether at work or in the home, and its undergirding by an essentially religious dimension that is in view.

OFFERING FOR UNINTENTIONAL SIN

15:22 'If you sin unintentionally, and do not observe all these commandments which the LORD has spoken to Moses—

23 'all that the LORD has commanded you by the hand of Moses, from the day the LORD gave commandment and onward throughout your generations—

24 'then it will be, if it is unintentionally committed, without the knowledge of the congregation, that the whole congregation shall offer one young bull as a burnt offering, as a sweet aroma to the LORD, with its

> grain offering and its drink offering, according to the ordinance, and one kid of the goats as a sin offering.
>
> 25 'So the priest shall make atonement for the whole congregation of the children of Israel, and it shall be forgiven them, for it was unintentional; they shall bring their offering, an offering made by fire to the LORD, and their sin offering before the LORD, for their unintended sin.
>
> 26 'It shall be forgiven the whole congregation of the children of Israel and the stranger who dwells among them, because all the people *did it* unintentionally.
>
> 27 'And if a person sins unintentionally, then he shall bring a female goat in its first year as a sin offering.
>
> 28 'So the priest shall make atonement for the person who sins unintentionally, when he sins unintentionally before the LORD, to make atonement for him; and it shall be forgiven him.
>
> 29 'You shall have one law for him who sins unintentionally, *for* him who is native-born among the children of Israel and for the stranger who dwells among them.
>
> 30 'But the person who does *anything* presumptuously, *whether he is* native-born or a stranger, that one brings reproach on the LORD and he shall be cut off from among his people.
>
> 31 'Because he has despised the word of the LORD, and has broken His commandment, that person shall be completely cut off; his guilt *shall be* upon him.'"
>
> *Num. 15:22–31*

The subject of inadvertent or unintentional trespass and, by contrast, presumptuous or willful sin is now dealt with very fully. This, as has already been pointed out, is the real significance of the position of these regulations, following immediately upon Israel's sin at Kadesh Barnea. The subject is also dealt with in Leviticus 4 and 5, where however the offerings of the high priest and of the prince are separately provided for whereas here only the congregation (vv. 22–26) and the individual (v. 27f.) are distinguished. The emphasis here is clear and unequivocal: it is to be noted that sins committed deliberately and willfully ("with a high hand") were not capable of being atoned for, and punishment was the only recourse, and exclusion from the community, and even death itself. As has been pointed out, "The true Israelite would never think of sinning deliberately against Jehovah: so too the Christian is expected to avoid all sin (1 John 3:9)."[5]

It is obvious that this whole question raises some major issues, not least in attempting to define what relation this bears to the teaching of the New Testament. Does this distinction hold good for the New Testament era, and therefore for us? This is surely a matter of great concern, especially when we think of sins we have committed as believers that have not been, and could not honestly be said to be, sins of ignorance, but sins with a great deal of the willful and deliberate in them in rebellion against God's good and perfect will. In answer to this problem it is sometimes averred that whereas the Old Testament makes provision only for sins of ignorance, the New Testament provides for all sin, of ignorance and of presumption alike. But this is not perhaps the right or best way to put it. It is true that the new covenant is wider, broader, and greater than the old; but we do see surprising evidence in the New Testament itself of this distinction between sins of ignorance and sins of presumption (cf. Luke 23:34; Acts 3:17, 17:30; 1 Tim. 1:13). Indeed, the dire warnings in the epistle to the Hebrews (6:4ff., 10:26ff.) about the dangers of willful sinning (cf. Mark 3:29, 1 John 5:16) make it only too clear that the psalmist's prayer, "Keep back Your servant also from presumptuous sins" (Ps. 19:13) is of timeless validity and just as relevant for us as for him.

In fact, however, these references serve to raise *other* problems in our minds. Our Lord's words on the cross, "Father, forgive them, for they do not know what they do" (Luke 23:34), with the apostle Peter's comment in similar terms, "I know that you did it in ignorance, as did also your rulers" (Acts 3:17) highlight the issue for us. *Was* their crucifying of Christ a sin of ignorance? Did they not *mean* to crucify Him? What of the deliberate, calculated, malevolent plotting by the chief priests and scribes and elders of the people (Matt. 26:3ff.)? And what of the mad frenzy of persecution against the church by Saul of Tarsus? Was there not calculated and deliberate malignity there (1 Tim. 1:13)? Clearly, if we are to take our Lord's and the apostle's words seriously we have to accept that sins of ignorance embrace a wide range of sinful attitudes.

The truth of this difficult matter is this: there are always at least two elements in sin, ignorance and willfulness; and it is the presence of the element of ignorance (however partial) in *human* sin that makes it forgivable at all; whereas *demonic* sin, being pure willfulness and revolt against God, with no admixture of ignorance or weakness is neither forgivable nor can ever be. The artless question that a little girl once asked, "Why can't Satan be converted?" serves to underline this profound truth: it is because Satan's sin is pure spirit, and unalloyed willfulness and presumption, that his doom is fixed.

The terrible thing is that human sin can on occasion approximate more and more to the demonic, in such a way that it passes the point of no return, to become fixedly willful and presumptuous. This, we may say, is the sin against the Holy Ghost, for which there is no forgiveness, neither in this life nor in the next.

In human experience these two elements in sin are mixed in varying proportions, with now the one, and now the other, being more predominant. And none of us can ever really determine just how near to the point of no return we may be coming, in the sins that we allow in our lives (for has not sin a blinding power?). The only safe way, therefore, is to strive with all our might to see that we do not sin at all, and to determine (in the words of the saintly Murray McCheyne) to be as holy as it is possible for a forgiven sinner to be. In this connection, we should remember that Scripture speaks, explicitly as well as implicitly, of *culpable* ignorance (cf. 2 Peter 3:5, "For this they willfully forget. . . .").

An illustration may help to highlight this. A man has been brought up in church in a time of spiritual decline, when vital truths of salvation are all but eclipsed. He is in ignorance of the gospel, and of the way of salvation, "How shall they believe in Him of whom they have not heard? And how shall they hear without a preacher?" (Rom. 10:14). The man is in spiritual darkness and knows no better. This is a sin of ignorance. It is still sin, and ignorance does not excuse culpability, for—as Paul puts it in Rom. 1:18ff.—the light of nature and of conscience are there.

But then, the gospel is preached to him, in its fullness, and now he hears the good news in all its glory and power, proclaiming something that God has done for our salvation, not something that we must do. But now see the reaction: he bridles, he resists; his pride is touched, and he refuses to humble himself to receive salvation as a gift. And now the pendulum has begun to swing: it is no longer a matter of natural ignorance for him but a willing ignorance. Revolt against God and His way of salvation is now present; and the more he fights, under the conviction of the truth of God, the more willful his sin becomes, and indeed the more demonic, and the less purely ignorant. It is now a much more serious matter: he is allying himself with the devil against God.

This is seen supremely—and most frighteningly—in Judas Iscariot, of whom it is finally said that the devil entered into him "and he went out; and it was night." He made himself unforgivable, passing the point of no return, refusing even the Lord's final appeal to him at the Last Supper. This is what Israel did at Kadesh. And the point of these regulations given to the new generation here is that God was telling them, in effect, "Watch your step: Be very wary lest continuing in sin like your fathers will push you also past the point of no return." A solemn thought indeed!

VIOLATION OF THE SABBATH

> 15:32 Now while the children of Israel were in the wilderness, they found a man gathering sticks on the Sabbath day.
>
> 33 And those who found him gathering sticks brought him to Moses and Aaron, and to all the congregation.
>
> 34 They put him under guard, because it had not been explained what should be done to him.
>
> 35 Then the LORD said to Moses, "The man must surely be put to death; all the congregation shall stone him with stones outside the camp."
>
> 36 So, as the LORD commanded Moses, all the congregation brought him outside the camp and stoned him with stones, and he died.
>
> *Num. 15:32–36*

This incident is inserted here as a practical illustration of sinning "with a high hand." It had already been laid down clearly in Exodus

31:14, 15 and 35:2 that any breach of the law of the Sabbath should be punished by death; there could therefore be no extenuating plea of ignorance by this man about what he had done. In verse 34, "what should be done to him" refers only to the manner in which he was to be put to death, not to the sentence itself which, as the above references indicate, was unmistakable. The severity of the penalty imposed on Sabbath violation is "an indication of how the nation, as a whole, was impressed with the inviolable sanctity of the Lord's day."[6]

All the Old Testament evidence serves to indicate that this was something crucial in Israel's relationship with God—and for this reason, reverence for the Sabbath symbolized reverence for God Himself, and violation of its sanctity was therefore a sin against Him, an insult to His majesty.

It is in this regard that we can best understand the widespread contemporary neglect and desecration of the Lord's Day. It symbolizes our modern generation's neglect and contempt of the things of God. It is man's refusal of God, in the same way and for the same reasons as anti-semitism, the hatred of God's people, is man's rejection of God. As to the severity of the sentence—death by stoning—we should remember that it is not so very long since, in our own society, a man could be hanged for sheep-stealing. We do not do that nowadays, but we should realize that we must distinguish between the *form of punishment* (which varies from age to age and from society to society) and the *sanction of the law* (which does not change). It is *always* wrong to steal sheep even though the punishment for the offense may change. Similarly, it is always wrong to violate the Lord's Day, even though nowadays there is no penal consequence involved in the eyes of the law.

The Wearing of Tassels

> 15:37 Again the LORD spoke to Moses, saying,
> 38 "Speak to the children of Israel: Tell them to make tassels on the corners of their garments throughout their generations, and to put a blue thread in the tassels of the corners.

> 39 "And you shall have the tassel, that you may
> look upon it and remember all the commandments of
> the LORD and do them, and that you *may* not follow
> the harlotry to which your own heart and your own
> eyes are inclined,
> 40 "and that you may remember and do all My
> commandments, and be holy for your God.
> 41 "I *am* the LORD your God, who brought you out
> of the land of Egypt, to be your God: I *am* the LORD
> your God."
>
> *Num. 15:37–41*

The command to wear tassels on the corners of their garments appears to have been given in relation to the Sabbath incident recorded in the previous verses, as verse 39 makes explicit: they were to wear them as a reminder of the commandments of God and to prevent such presumptuous sin. The detailed nature of the instruction in verse 38, as to the inclusion of *"a blue thread,"* is striking. Wenham suggests it would remind the Israelite "that he belonged to a 'kingdom of priests and a holy nation' (Exod. 19:6)," and in adding that the tassels were to be reminders to Israel to be totally loyal to the Lord, points to the particular importance this regulation became for the Jews, even in our Lord's day (Matt. 23:5), forming part of the creedlike prayer, the Shema, recited every morning and evening.[7] The present-day practice of many Christians of wearing signs or badges of their faith, whether in dress or, for example, a cross as a pendant around the neck, must surely have its origin in this ancient regulation, as a reminder to the wearer of his commitment to deny himself, taking up his cross and walking in faithfulness and dedication to Christ.

NOTES

1. A. H. Sayce, *The Early History of the Hebrews* (London: Rivingtons, 1891), p. 207.
2. This is a view supported by Gordon J. Wenham, *Numbers,* Tyndale Old Testament Commentaries. (Leicester: Inter-Varsity Press, 1981), p. 127.

3. Carl L. Keil and Franz Delitzsch, *Numbers,* Commentary on the Old Testament, vol. 3 (Grand Rapids: Wm. B. Eerdmans, repr. 1971), p. 100.

4. Wenham, *Numbers,* p. 129.

5. L. Elliott Binns, *The Book of Numbers* (London: Methuen & Co., Ltd., 1927), p. 104.

6. Keil and Delitzsch, *Numbers,* p. 103.

7. Wenham, *Numbers,* p. 133.

CHAPTER ELEVEN

The Rebellion of Korah, Dathan, and Abiram

Numbers 16:1–17:13

THE ISSUES AT STAKE

16:1 Now Korah the son of Izhar, the son of Kohath,
the son of Levi, with Dathan and Abiram the sons of
Eliab, and On the son of Peleth, sons of Reuben, took
men;
2 and they rose up before Moses with some of the
children of Israel, two hundred and fifty leaders of
the congregation, representatives of the congregation, men of renown.
3 They gathered together against Moses and Aaron,
and said to them, "*You take* too much upon yourselves,
for all the congregation *is* holy, every one of them,
and the LORD *is* among them. Why then do you exalt
yourselves above the assembly of the LORD?"
4 So when Moses heard *it,* he fell on his face;
5 and he spoke to Korah and all his company, saying, "Tomorrow morning the LORD will show who *is*
His and *who is* holy, and will cause *him* to come near
to Him. That one whom He chooses He will cause to
come near to Him.
6 "Do this: Take censers, Korah and all your company;
7 "put fire in them and put incense in them before the LORD tomorrow, and it shall be *that* the man
whom the LORD chooses *is* the holy one. *You take* too
much upon yourselves, you sons of Levi!"

Num. 16:1–7

The historical narrative is now resumed, after the parenthesis on the various offerings and regulations in 15:1ff. What is recorded here in the account of a rebellion against Moses and Aaron by Korah, Dathan, and Abiram seems to continue the topic of presumptuous sin dealt with in the last section, for here was a revolt which brought summary judgment from God upon it. We need not suppose that it took place immediately following the events of Kadesh. Commentators suggest that it may well have taken place at a time not near either the beginning or the end of the forty years of wilderness wandering. It is placed here in the meantime, however, by the Holy Spirit for our learning and admonition, as a further illustration of presumptuous sin. The words in verse 7, *"You take too much upon yourselves, you sons of Levi!"* are rendered significantly by the RSV, "You have gone too far. . . ." This is what presumptuous sin means—going too far, and reaching the point of no return.

A careful reading of the chapter shows that it records what might be called a composite rebellion—that is, it is made up of more than one strand and issue. On the one hand, it is clear that one party was led by Korah and was composed principally of Levites, and that their quarrel was with the fact that the family of Aaron had been specially set apart for the duties and privileges of the priesthood (cf. vv. 8–10 especially).

On the other hand, Dathan's and Abiram's complaint (cf. Ps. 106:16, 17) was against the authority they considered Moses and Aaron to have arrogated to themselves (vv. 3, 13). It is interesting to see that while a *united* complaint was made against Moses, he in reply divided it up into its component parts. As one commentator puts it, "A rebellion against ecclesiastical authority and another against political authority are associated together, and the strength of each is greatly enhanced by cooperation with the other."[1]

This twofold factor has led critical scholars to suppose that what we have here is an amalgam of two different stories, from different sources, combined to form one. But it is not only unnecessary to make such an assumption, it also misses the point that is being made, and it comes to grief as a theory on the rock of practical human considerations. In fact, the account as it stands is true to life, true also to human nature and its darker aspects, and this is one of the important lessons it has to teach.

Here are two groups of people, widely different, it would seem, in their background, and having little in common with one another, but uniting and making common cause against Moses and against God. There is something basically contemptible and lacking in integrity and in character, in such an attitude—people with nothing in common, and perhaps having otherwise little time for one another, save a common antagonism to the truth of God. Here are strange bedfellows indeed! Nor is this something confined to those far-off days, for we see the same pattern repeating itself in the New Testament, in the strange and unnatural alliance of the Pharisees and the Sadducees against our Lord. Traditionally, these two groups had little in common. In origin they were very different from one another. The Pharisees began as a deeply devoted "breakaway" group protesting against the deadness of the spiritual life of their day. It was only in their later development that they lost the vision and became hardened, but even then they were the backbone of orthodoxy, to whom the very sticks and stones of the synagogue were dear. The Sadducees, however, were the rationalists of their day: they sat lightly with regard to real spiritual values, disbelieving the cardinal doctrines of their faith, and were held in contempt for their indifference by the Pharisees. Yet both united in a grand alliance in their hatred of Jesus.

Nor must we forget Pilate and Herod who, formerly enemies, were made friends (Luke 23:12) over their condemnation of Jesus. Is it not very sinister that the grim reality of opposition against our Lord and His gospel should cement a friendship between two so very different people, who could not naturally stand one another? Such associations are certainly not unknown in the life of the church today, when religious-minded people without a religious experience, with a taste *for* religion but no taste *of* it are quite prepared to unite forces with the indifferent for whom the church is simply "a social club," in a common opposition to the living gospel when it is preached.

MOSES REBUKES THE LEVITES

16:8 Then Moses said to Korah, "Hear now, you sons of Levi:

9 "*Is it* a small thing to you that the God of Israel has separated you from the congregation of Israel, to

> bring you near to Himself to do the work of the tabernacle of the LORD, and to stand before the congregation to serve them;
> 10 "and that He has brought you near *to Himself*, you and all your brethren, the sons of Levi, with you? And are you seeking the priesthood also?
> 11 "Therefore you and all your company *are* gathered together against the LORD. And what *is* Aaron that you complain against him?"
>
> *Num. 16:8-11*

We may learn from these verses that Korah, Dathan, and Abiram did not state the real ground of their complaint against Moses and Aaron in what they said in verse 3, for Moses pinpoints the heart of the issue in his challenge to them in verse 10: "Are you seeking the priesthood also?" It is as if the patriarch had said, "This (v. 3) is what you are saying, but this (v. 10) is what I see lies at the root of it. This is why you are complaining." How very significant that the man of God could see behind the pretext and recognize the real nature of the opposition.

Clearly, this coveting of place by the rebels represented a serious crisis among the people of God, which merited the serious dealing with it that followed. It is a familiar enough experience in the life of the church even though it does not always reach crisis proportions. The apostle Paul himself seems well aware of its danger, in the way in which he expounds the idea of differentiation of function within the body of Christ, in such passages as Romans 12:4 ff. The whole point, he means, is that we are all different from one another, and meant to be so, in function and service. It is not a question of superiority or inferiority. We have all different duties, and we must be intent on doing to the best of our ability what God has given us to do. The gifts that men have *are* gifts, and not to be taken pride in, or used for personal advancement, but for the good of the body, the church. And since this is so, it is both useless and dangerous for one member to covet another's place or gift, for in so doing he is both trespassing beyond bounds and at the same time neglecting his own. To see things in this light is to come to a true assessment of one's importance—we all have a part to play, and only a part, and if God has appointed us not only a small, but also an unobtrusive, part, then we must content ourselves with it, and realize that only in glad acceptance of it will true happiness and peace—and wholeness—ever be found. After all, we cannot be more useful to God than He chooses to make us. We might well remember in this connection the wise words spoken by Jeremiah to his servant of old: "Do you seek great things for yourself? Do not seek them" (Jer. 45:5).

Moses Defied

> 16:12 And Moses sent to call Dathan and Abiram the sons of Eliab, but they said, "We will not come up!
> 13 "*Is it* a small thing that you have brought us up out of a land flowing with milk and honey, to kill us in the wilderness, that you should keep acting like a prince over us?
> 14 "Moreover you have not brought us into a land flowing with milk and honey, nor given us inheritance of fields and vineyards. Will you put out the eyes of these men? We will not come up!"
> 15 Then Moses was very angry, and said to the LORD, "Do not respect their offering. I have not taken one donkey from them, nor have I hurt one of them."
> *Num. 16:12–15*

The terms in which the rebels' defiance of Moses were expressed are very significant. It is true that their words in verse 13 can be described as a harking-back to "the good old days" of Egypt, similar to that expressed by the people in 11:4ff. (see commentary *in loc*); but now there is something more. For sin, when persisted in, always assumes more serious and sinister proportions. Sins of ignorance and human frailty sometimes develop into presumptuous sins; and from "harking back to the good old days" these men came to the point of calling evil good and good evil. Now they were calling their bondage in Egypt *"a land flowing with milk and honey."* This was the measure of the distortion of their thinking. And God says, "Woe to those who call evil good, and good evil; Who put darkness for light, and light for darkness; Who put bitter for sweet, and sweet for bitter!" (Isa. 5:20). This is to come very near the point of no return, and it is surely this that explains the severity of the judgment that came upon them. As Jesus put it, "This is the condemnation, that the light has come into the world, and men loved darkness rather than light, because their deeds were evil" (John 3:19).

And, of course, their accusation against Moses in verse 14 that he had failed to bring them into the Promised Land falls rather flat when we remember why this was so: they had refused to go in. They could hardly blame Moses, when in fact God had simply taken them at their word when they had shown so clearly their unwillingness to enter. But then, opposition to God is never a very rational or consistent matter, is it?

The Showdown

16:16 And Moses said to Korah, "Tomorrow, you and
all your company be present before the LORD—you
and they, as well as Aaron.
17 "Let each take his censer and put incense in it,
and each of you bring his censer before the LORD,
two hundred and fifty censers; both you and Aaron,
each *with* his censer."
18 So every man took his censer, put fire in it, laid
incense on it, and stood at the door of the tabernacle
of meeting with Moses and Aaron.
19 And Korah gathered all the congregation against
them at the door of the tabernacle of meeting. Then
the glory of the LORD appeared to all the congregation.
20 And the LORD spoke to Moses and Aaron, saying,
21 "Separate yourselves from among this congregation, that I may consume them in a moment."
22 Then they fell on their faces, and said, "O God,
the God of the spirits of all flesh, shall one man sin,
and You be angry with all the congregation?"
23 So the LORD spoke to Moses, saying,
24 "Speak to the congregation, saying, 'Get away
from the tents of Korah, Dathan, and Abiram.'"

Num. 16:16–24

Moses challenges Korah and his company to put their calling to the test by the offering of incense. Korah seems to have been confident of being vindicated in this confrontation and is duly discomfitted.

Judgment is announced upon the whole congregation, but Moses' and Aaron's intercession saves the people, urging them in verse 24 to separate themselves from the rebels, whose punishment is described in the verses that follow.

Severe though the punishment proved to be, it is difficult to see what other alternative there could have been. The challenge they threw at Moses and Aaron was too total to admit of half measures, for it struck at the very root of their divine appointment as leaders of the people. The charge in verse 3, "You take too much upon yourselves. . . . Why then do you exalt yourselves above the assembly of the Lord?" is always one to which those who are intent on wholly following the Lord lay themselves open. This is unavoidable, for the very good reason that men are always pricked in their conscience by the testimony of total obedience in another's life. It is the resentment caused by the awareness of a standard they cannot reach without being prepared to be changed and made different by the grace of God. And this they are not prepared to allow. In these terms, any believer, let alone a God-appointed leader, is likely to be accused of "going too far," and of being narrow, extreme, dogmatic, and fanatical. For those who oppose it, "religion"—and particularly that form of it which presents itself as a thoroughgoing consecration to God—is something that must be kept strictly in its place; it must never on any account be allowed to interfere with life. How difficult for such an attitude to realize that the Christian gospel has only one way—"going the whole way": it is all or nothing. There can be no halfway house.

The Punishment of the Rebels

> 16:25 Then Moses rose and went to Dathan and Abiram, and the elders of Israel followed him.
>
> 26 And he spoke to the congregation, saying, "Depart now from the tents of these wicked men! Touch nothing of theirs, lest you be consumed in all their sins."
>
> 27 So they got away from around the tents of Korah, Dathan, and Abiram; and Dathan and Abiram came out and stood at the door of their tents, with their wives, their sons, and their little children.

28 And Moses said: "By this you shall know that
the LORD has sent me to do all these works, for *I have*
not *done them* of my own will.
29 "If these men die naturally like all men, or if
they are visited by the common fate of all men, *then*
the LORD has not sent me.
30 "But if the LORD creates a new thing, and the
earth opens its mouth and swallows them up with all
that belongs to them, and they go down alive into the
pit, then you will understand that these men have
rejected the LORD."
31 Now it came to pass, as he finished speaking all
these words, that the ground split apart under them,
32 and the earth opened its mouth and swallowed
them up, with their households and all the men with
Korah, with all *their* goods.
33 So they and all those with them went down
alive into the pit; the earth closed over them, and
they perished from among the assembly.
34 Then all Israel who *were* around them fled at
their cry, for they said, "Lest the earth swallow us up
also!"
35 And a fire came out from the LORD and consumed the two hundred and fifty men who were offering incense.

Num. 16:25–35

The punishment that fell on the rebels was awesome and terrible. The drama of the challenge with which Moses confronted them must have been well nigh unbearable, and it shows just how sure Moses was of God, to commit himself in the way he did. The words in verse 28, *"By this you shall know . . ."* are sublime in the confidence they express that the Lord would create "a new thing," making the earth open to swallow up the rebels, as a conclusive proof that Moses was the Lord's chosen leader, and that they, the rebels, were imposters.

No sooner had Moses spoken thus, when his words were literally and in exact detail fulfilled. Point by point the predicted judgment of God's "new thing" overtook them (vv. 31–33).

One readily thinks of a similar confrontation between Elijah and the prophets of Baal on Mount Carmel (1 Kings 18). The circumstances, and the issues, were much the same on that occasion. If the predicted judgment did not take place, this would prove that the Lord had not sent either Moses or Elijah, and each would have been discredited in the eyes of their enemies. But both were equally sure of God, and their lonely faith was instantly vindicated.

We might be tempted to shrink from such a story thinking "what a harsh and terrible thing to have happened." This is a favorite pastime for those who seek to belittle the Old Testament and say that the Old Testament God is not the Christian God, but rather a bloodthirsty Jewish Deity, and that Jesus came to correct such false notions about Him. But one has only to look at the account given in Acts 5 of the summary judgment upon Ananias and Sapphira by the holy God of the early church to realize how wide of the mark such a facile and superficial interpretation is. The parallel is a true one: danger was threatening God's sovereign, ongoing purposes in and for His church, and He could not allow it to go unchecked. If He had, a poison would have spread that could well have destroyed the life of the young church. This is why the hapless couple were struck down for their sin. And so it was here: for this spirit of rebellion to have continued among the people would have meant that the whole onward march of Israel would have been jeopardized, indeed overturned. Such a challenge to the divine authority *had to be* dealt with summarily.

The message, then, is this: "Hands off My work," says God. As the Epistle to the Hebrews puts it (10:31) "It is a fearful thing to fall into the hands of the living God." This is the real issue: God does business with men. He is something more than a status-symbol, more than a comfortable and comforting idea "up there." He is the living God: He is good, but He is a God who stands no nonsense, and He is not prepared to let anything or anybody stand in the way of His sovereign purposes. C. S. Lewis conveys this thought very powerfully in his children's book *The Lion, the Witch, and the Wardrobe.* In a discussion about Aslan, the great lion, Susan, one of the children, asks,

> "Is he—quite safe? I shall feel rather nervous about meeting a lion."
>
> "That you will, dearie, and no mistake," said Mrs. Beaver, "if there's anyone who can appear before Aslan without their knees knocking, they're either braver than most or else just silly."
>
> "Then he isn't safe?" said Lucy.

"Safe?" said Mr. Beaver. "Don't you hear what Mrs. Beaver tells you? Who said anything about safe? 'Course he isn't safe. But he's good. He's the King, I tell you."[2]

The Censer Memorial

16:36 Then the LORD spoke to Moses, saying:
37 "Tell Eleazar, the son of Aaron the priest, to pick
up the censers out of the blaze, for they are holy, and
scatter the fire some distance away.
38 "The censers of these men who sinned against
their own souls, let them be made into hammered
plates as a covering for the altar. Because they presented them before the LORD, therefore they are holy;
and they shall be a sign to the children of Israel."
39 So Eleazar the priest took the bronze censers,
which those who were burned up had presented,
and they were hammered out as a covering on the
altar,
40 *to be* a memorial to the children of Israel that no
outsider, who *is* not a descendant of Aaron, should
come near to offer incense before the LORD, that he
might not become like Korah and his companions,
just as the LORD had said to him through Moses.

Num. 16:36–40

The censers of the rebels, since they had been offered before the Lord, were regarded as having become holy, even though they had been offered irregularly, and the men involved were not authorized to do so, because they did not belong to the Aaronites. Eleazar, Aaron's son, was commanded to gather the censers and make of them a covering for the altar, and to scatter the burning coals, that no further use, particularly common use, might be made of them. Two points may be made here: The first is that "this passage exhibits in a striking way the priestly conception of holiness as being contagious."[3] An interesting contrast to this idea, however, is found in Haggai 2:10ff., where the prophet is emphasizing the contagious properties of sin rather than holiness, as a warning against the over-facile application of the levitical law (Lev. 6:20) in any way that would engender complacency. The other point is that the use of the rebels' censers in this way became a sign, or memorial (v. 40), to all who approached the sanctuary, to warn them of the danger of intruding into the priestly office, and grasping at priestly prerogatives.[4]

The Plague

16:41 On the next day all the congregation of the children of Israel complained against Moses and Aaron,
saying, "You have killed the people of the LORD."
42 Now it happened, when the congregation had
gathered against Moses and Aaron, that they turned
toward the tabernacle of meeting; and suddenly the
cloud covered it, and the glory of the LORD appeared.
43 Then Moses and Aaron came before the tabernacle of meeting.
44 And the LORD spoke to Moses, saying,
45 "Get away from among this congregation, that I
may consume them in a moment." And they fell on
their faces.
46 So Moses said to Aaron, "Take a censer and put
fire in it from the altar, put incense *on it*, and take it
quickly to the congregation and make atonement for
them; for wrath has gone out from the LORD. The
plague has begun."
47 Then Aaron took *it* as Moses commanded, and
ran into the midst of the assembly; and already the
plague had begun among the people. So he put in
the incense and made atonement for the people.
48 And he stood between the dead and the living;
so the plague was stopped.
49 Now those who died in the plague were fourteen thousand seven hundred, besides those who
died in the Korah incident.
50 So Aaron returned to Moses at the door of the
tabernacle of meeting, for the plague had stopped.

Num. 16:41–50

One would have thought that the grim events recorded in the previous verses would have brought the people to a more sober and reflective frame of mind, but not so. Moses and Aaron are not at the end of their troubles yet, for now they are blamed and murmured against for the deaths of Korah and the others. The basis of the accusation made against them is, as Elliott Binns observes: "that Moses and Aaron in order to vindicate their own position had caused the death of those who opposed them. Thus quickly was any sense they might have had that the judgment of God was upon them dissipated, and their querulous spirit renewed."[5] This is all too true to human psychology: it is frequently the case that when crisis or disaster first strikes there is a readiness to accept at least some responsibility for what has happened; but then, attitudes may harden and responsibility may be shrugged off and even completely denied.

We have known this to happen in the context of a marriage breakdown crisis: at first there was a readiness on the part of the wife to accept at least some responsibility for attitudes and behavior which finally precipitated the breakdown; but as time went on when no sign of reconciliation seemed likely, she back-tracked, and ended by laying the whole blame upon her estranged husband.

The people's murmuring led to a swift reaction from the Lord: His glory appeared, and He announced His intention of destroying the entire congregation (v. 45): a deadly plague broke out among them (of what kind it was, nothing is said) and the people began to die. Moses and Aaron reacted characteristically, and fell on their faces in intercession. Aaron at Moses' behest offered incense in his censer (v. 46), to make atonement for the people, and the plague was stayed, although not before many had died. The phrase in verse 48, *"he stood between the dead and the living"* is a particularly moving and dramatic one, and underlines the vicarious, even mediatorial, function that he fulfilled as high priest. There could hardly have been a more telling or effectual vindication of his office in the sight of Israel, or a more practical demonstration of the power and authority with which he had been invested by God.

AARON'S ROD THAT BUDDED

17:1 And the LORD spoke to Moses, saying:
2 "Speak to the children of Israel, and get from
them a rod from each father's house, all their leaders

according to their fathers' houses—twelve rods. Write each man's name on his rod.

3 "And you shall write Aaron's name on the rod of Levi. For there shall be one rod for the head of *each* father's house.

4 "Then you shall place them in the tabernacle of meeting before the Testimony, where I meet with you.

5 "And it shall be *that* the rod of the man whom I choose will blossom; thus I will rid Myself of the complaints of the children of Israel, which they make against you."

6 So Moses spoke to the children of Israel, and each of their leaders gave him a rod apiece, for each leader according to their fathers' houses, twelve rods; and the rod of Aaron *was* among their rods.

7 And Moses placed the rods before the LORD in the tabernacle of witness.

8 Now it came to pass on the next day that Moses went into the tabernacle of witness, and behold, the rod of Aaron, of the house of Levi, had sprouted and put forth buds, had produced blossoms and yielded ripe almonds.

9 Then Moses brought out all the rods from before the LORD to all the children of Israel; and they looked, and each man took his rod.

10 And the LORD said to Moses, "Bring Aaron's rod back before the Testimony, to be kept as a sign against the rebels, that you may put their complaints away from Me, lest they die."

11 Thus did Moses; just as the LORD had commanded him, so he did.

12 So the children of Israel spoke to Moses, saying, "Surely we die, we perish, we all perish!

13 "Whoever even comes near the tabernacle of the LORD must die. Shall we all utterly die?"

Num. 17:1–13

The incident recorded in these verses continues and concludes the story of the rebellion of Korah, Dathan, and Abiram, which began in 16:1 ff. It is the second part, so to speak, of the divine vindication of Moses and Aaron, and completes the picture of God's dealings with His people in the matter.

The emphasis in chapter 16 was a negative one, involving the rejection of the offerings of the sons of Korah, and speaking of judgment which, as Calvin points out is ever God's "strange" work. But here the emphasis is positive: it is a vindication, in an unmistakable manner, of God's choice of Aaron and his posterity for the priesthood. One commentator, referring to the judgment of the rebel leaders says, "Great issues are rarely decided by force alone. Reasonable proof is also requisite, if a decision is to be lasting."[6] This is a legitimate way of looking at the issue. At all events, the double indication of the divine will—the judgment of Dathan, Abiram, and Korah on the one hand, and the unmistakable seal on Aaron's priesthood on the other—was meant to convince the people finally, and finish their murmuring against God and His servants. The fact that it seems to have failed to do so—for in later chapters we see more of this unhallowed spirit—is some indication of the irrational and even demonic nature of the opposition that men show against God and His will and purposes. Some people are not prepared to be convinced of the truth, however unmistakable and convincing, persuasive and unanswerable God's indications may be.

But the proof does not fall to the ground on that account. For it shows to any reasonable consideration that God is saying, "This is the way: this is right; this is the man of My choice, and the leader that I appoint." It is a testimony to everything rational in the universe, to the moral foundation of the world, if not to irrational stubbornness, that right is right and God is God.

The "sign" itself was simple enough: the leader of each tribe was to bring a rod to be placed in the Tabernacle, with each man's name upon his rod. Aaron's name was to be on the rod of Levi. God undertook to show, by unmistakable sign, whose rod was His sovereign choice. And in the morning, when the rods were examined, Aaron's rod was found to be bearing buds, blossoms, and fruit of almond, while those of the other tribes were barren and bare.

As to what is signified by the "sign," several things may be said. It may be taken, first of all, as a simple sign, in the sense that "something happened" to Aaron's rod that did not happen to the others, and that God thus indicated His choice of Aaron rather than any of the others. This is a good understanding of the story as such. Aaron was singled out and shown as different from the others, and this was the indication of God's will for the people.

But there is also something more. There is a symbolic significance in the nature of the sign itself, and that in two ways: first, in that it was a *rod* that was chosen by God; and second, in that the rod was made to show life at the behest of God. The "rod" was a symbol of power and of authority, in the Old Testament economy, and certainly in the early history of God's people. One readily recalls the rod of Moses (Exod. 4:1 ff.), which became the symbol of divine authority in his hand, and how he smote the waters of the Red Sea and parted them with it, and how he drew water from the rock by means of it (Exod. 14:21, 17:5 ff.). This, then, was God's way of saying that His authority, so far as the priesthood was concerned, was vested in Aaron, and that Aaron's authority was a living reality.

In the second place, in that the rod was made to show life by the hand of God, and that it budded, blossomed, and bore fruit, was God's way of saying that the priesthood under Aaron would be a living thing, a source of life, blessing, and benediction to the people whom it served. What is more, God was saying that this family that had in fact budded and blossomed in blessing among the people—as had been so dramatically demonstrated in the mediation that had stopped the plague in 16:46 ff.—was the one He had chosen. This is the one infallible and indisputable test: where life and fruitfulness and blessing are, let none presume to challenge or oppose.

This is an impressive lesson. Aaron was by no means perfect; he had his faults, and some very real weaknesses, as indeed had Moses. But their lives had the seal of God upon them, and they were fruitful in His sovereign purposes. It was this consideration that overrode all others. This is what the people needed—and were meant—to see in the "sign" from God. It was meant to silence once and for all the murmurings and the incipient revolt in their hearts.

The test is still the same today. God makes the rod of His chosen and ordained servants to bud and blossom and bear fruit. This is the overriding consideration in any work of the Spirit. What matter if it does not follow the expected patterns? What matter if it leads in strange directions? The question is: Is the seal of God manifestly upon it? If so, be content and follow.

In this connection, Matthew Henry, the Puritan commentator, has a very penetrating and shrewd comment to make on the story: "Here were not only almonds for the present, but buds and blossoms promising more hereafter. Thus has Christ provided in His church that a seed should serve Him from generation to generation."[7]

The *fruit* represented Aaron's priesthood then; the *blossoms* his sons who even then were "in training," so to speak, for future responsibilities; the *buds* represented the generation to come, the children who would yet take their place in the succession. Here is a word of enormous hopefulness and encouragement, for a work on which God lays His hand. Fruit now, blossoms promising much as they become fruit later; and buds breaking out, in the young lives committed to the church's care.

In this light it becomes clear how serious a thing it was for anyone to have challenged and disputed a work on which God had so manifestly laid His hand. The message that comes through in all this is surely clear and plain: "Hands off My work," says God; "Do not touch My anointed ones, and do My prophets no harm" (Ps. 105:15).

One wonders whether the sign of the "branch of an almond tree" given to Jeremiah at the beginning of his ministry (Jer. 1:11) was intended to convey to the prophet just this message given here, as if God were saying to him, "Remember Aaron's rod that budded, and take heart in the difficult task that I have appointed for you. Fear not: be not discouraged: for in due time you will reap if you faint not. I will make your ministry to bud and blossom and bring forth fruit. Beyond death there is resurrection; and although there may be a dark night to pass through, with much weeping, *joy cometh in the morning!* "

Older commentators have delighted in this story as seeing in it a type of Christ, our great High Priest, and this is surely a legitimate application of it, especially in view of the New Testament's insistence that the Old Testament Scriptures' central theme is their witness to Christ (cf. Introduction). Christ's eternal priesthood is also challenged today, by men who do not care to bow to His authority. And God has vindicated that priesthood by raising Him from the dead. The Resurrection is the budding and blossoming of the almond rod all over again. The New Testament writers make much of this in their preaching. Peter, in his great sermon on the day of Pentecost, preached the Resurrection, and it was this that made the rebels tremble and cry out, "Men and brethren, what shall we do?" (Acts 2:37). Paul, preaching to the Athenians, holds up the authority of Christ and calls for repentance, asserting that God had vindicated that authority in that He raised Him from the dead (Acts 17:30, 31). In the Epistle to the Romans (1:4) the apostle likewise asserts that Jesus was "declared to be the Son of God with power . . . by the resurrection from the dead."

One final point may be made: there is a real sense in which the story of Aaron's rod that budded may be regarded as a figure of things to come. God's purpose in leading the people back to the wilderness was to purge their hearts of sin. In verse 5 it is said that the miracle of the budding rod was meant to make the people's murmurings cease.[8] And it did, for the time being. But this was only a token—all it did was to point forward to the one great miracle which does give the final answer to the problem of sin and man's rebellion against God—the death and resurrection of Christ. He, Christ, is the almond rod that is laid, barren and alone, in death, and buds and blossoms in newness of life. It is this victory, this vindication by God of the sacrifice which He made on the Cross, that alone constitutes the final answer to the murmurings and rebellions of men's hearts, for in His death and resurrection there is wrought a full and final reconciliation between God and man.

NOTES

1. A. A. MacRae, *New Bible Commentary* (London: Inter-Varsity Press, 1953), p. 182.

2. C. S. Lewis, *The Lion, the Witch, and the Wardrobe* (London: Geoffrey Bles), chapter 8.

3. L. Elliott Binns, *The Book of Numbers* (London: Methuen & Co., Ltd., 1927), p. 115.

4 Gordon J. Wenham, *Numbers*, Tyndale Old Testament Commentaries, (Leicester: Inter-Varsity Press, 1981), p. 139, adds: "The importance of visual aids to prevent men sinning is an important theme in Numbers. The tassels on garments (15:38–41) and Aaron's rod (17:10) also serve the same purpose (cf. Exod. 13:9; 31:13, 17; Deut. 6:8; 11:18; Josh. 4:7).

5. Binns, *Numbers*, p. 117, observes in verse 46 that "atonement without bloodshed is unusual although not unknown elsewhere: cf. Exod. 30:15." Delitzsch, however, (op. cit.), p. 112, has a valuable comment, "The means resorted to by Moses to stay the plague showed afresh how the faithful

servant of God bore the rescue of his people upon his heart. All the motives which he had hitherto pleaded, in his repeated intercession that this evil congregation might be spared, were now exhausted. . . . There was but one way left of averting the threatened destruction of the whole nation, namely, to adopt the means which the Lord Himself had given to His congregation, in the high-priestly office, to wipe away their sins, and recover the divine grace which they had forfeited through sin—viz. the offerings of incense which embodied the high-priestly prayer, and the strength and operation of which were not dependent upon the sincerity and earnestness of subjective faith, but had a firm and immovable foundation in the objective force of the Divine appointment. This was the means adopted by the faithful servant of the Lord, and the judgment of wrath was averted in its course; the plague was averted."

6. MacRae, *New Bible,* p. 183.

7. Matthew Henry, *Genesis-Deuteronomy,* Commentary on the Whole Bible (Old Tappan, N.J.: Fleming H. Revell Co.), 1:648.

8. Carl L. Keil and Franz Delitzsch, *Numbers,* Commentary of the Old Testament (Grand Rapids: Wm. B. Eerdmans, repr. 1971), 3:114, in underlining the supernatural, miraculous nature of what happened to Aaron's rod, and discounting any natural interpretations, adds: "As a severed branch, the rod could not put forth shoots and blossom in the natural way. But God could impart new vital powers even to the dry rod. And so Aaron had naturally no pre-eminence above the heads of the other tribes. But the priesthood was founded not upon natural qualifications and gifts, but upon the power of the Spirit, which God communicates according to the choice of His wisdom, and which He had imparted to Aaron through his consecration with holy anointing oil. It was this which the Lord intended to show to the people, by causing Aaron's rod to put forth branches, blossom, and fruit, through a miracle of His omnipotence; whereas the rods of the other heads of the tribes remained as barren as before."

CHAPTER TWELVE

The Service of the Priests and Levites

Numbers 18:1–32

The Duties of Levi

18:1 Then the LORD said to Aaron: "You and your sons and your father's house with you shall bear the iniquity *related to* the sanctuary, and you and your sons with you shall bear the iniquity *associated with* your priesthood.

2 "Also bring with you your brethren of the tribe of Levi, the tribe of your father, that they may be joined with you and serve you while you and your sons *are* with you before the tabernacle of witness.

3 "They shall attend to your needs and all the needs of the tabernacle; but they shall not come near the articles of the sanctuary and the altar, lest they die—they and you also.

4 "They shall be joined with you and attend to the needs of the tabernacle of meeting, for all the work of the tabernacle; but an outsider shall not come near you.

5 "And you shall attend to the duties of the sanctuary and the duties of the altar, that there *may* be no more wrath on the children of Israel.

6 "Behold, I Myself have taken your brethren the Levites from among the children of Israel; *they are* a gift to you, given by the LORD, to do the work of the tabernacle of meeting.

7 "Therefore you and your sons with you shall attend to your priesthood for everything at the altar and behind the veil; and you shall serve. I give your

priesthood *to you* as a gift for service, but the outsider who comes near shall be put to death."
Num. 18:1–7

The last two verses of the previous chapter (17:12, 13) provide the connection with what now follows in these verses. The events described in chapters 16 and 17 have shown the deadly danger of unauthorized persons encroaching on the realm of the "holy" and the disastrous judgments which followed such presumption; and now as a corrective, to prevent any further violation a statement is made about the solemn duties and responsibilities, fateful indeed in their implications as well as blessed, of divinely appointed priests and Levites.[1]

The association of ideas between these verses and what precedes them should be noted. The rebels had just challenged Aaron in the priesthood. They had clearly, for their own reasons and motives, coveted his place and his position and privileges. And here, God paints a clearer picture of the priesthood for them, to show them it is not something to covet. He unfolds the responsibilities of priesthood, as a warning, so to speak, against carnal coveting of the office.

The truth is, it is possible to covet place in the work and service of God, and to do so as a means of self-expression, or for the gratification of personal ambition, or as the indication of a lust for power, or even merely for the prestige it seems to bestow. It is oddly impressive to realize that what so often attracts from the outside is the kudos, the glory and the dignity that position seems to offer; the "other side" seldom seems to be seen, with solemn responsibilities matching every privilege.

The Scriptures warn very clearly against the natural tendency to hanker after the attractions of position or authority in spiritual life. "Do you seek great things for yourself?" asked Jeremiah of his servant Baruch, "Do not seek them" (Jer. 45:5). In Hebrews 5:4 we read, "No man takes this honor to himself, but he who is called by God, just as Aaron was." And in 1 Corinthians 12 (cf. also 1 Cor. 7:20ff.), Paul stresses the complementary nature of the various callings within the church, the body of Christ, and warns against trespassing upon another's calling, urging us to be content with what God has called us to do, and to do it with all our might. That will be solemn enough responsibility to be accountable for in His sight, without coveting another's place.

Thus, God gently and firmly reminds His people that there are solemn responsibilities attached to the priestly and levitical offices. Aaron and the Levites, it is pointed out, were to bear the iniquity of the sanctuary, and the iniquity of the priesthood. This means that if the sanctuary were profaned by the intrusion of strangers, or by persons in their uncleanness, the blame should lie on the priests and on the Levites, whose responsibility was to have prevented it. Or, if any of the offices of the sanctuary were neglected, or any service not done in accordance with the divine will they were held accountable for it. Or, if any part of the priestly office itself were neglected, they would bear the blame.

Here is a word for the servant of God, with a vengeance! The defilement of the sanctuary, the intrusion of alien things, the neglect of the true work of the ministry—these are the things for which a minister is held accountable to God! To be answerable to God in such a way is a solemn burden indeed. This is why a man cannot afford to fear the face of men, and why he must be prepared ultimately to be at odds with whole sections of his people. He fears the face of God more than that of any man, for it is to Him that he must in the end give account. If as ministers and servants of Christ's church we are held responsible for the purity of the church's life and activity, this is burden enough for any man and will make him more concerned to please God than please any other, whatever the cost.

Nor is it to ordained ministers only that this word speaks; it is of wider application. There is such a thing in the Christian church as the priesthood of all believers—this, contrary to what some suppose, is not to be interpreted as the *ministry* of all believers, and does not constitute a calling to all believers to preach (only some are called to do so, Eph. 4:11ff.) but has reference to the right and responsibility every believer has to approach God. The application, then, is to the ministry of prayer. All believers have responsibility here, and the neglect of our priestly duties in congregational life must also be regarded as being accountable to God.

The Revenues of the Priests

> 18:8 And the LORD spoke to Aaron: "Here, I Myself
> have also given you charge of My heave offerings, all

the holy gifts of the children of Israel; I have given
them as a portion to you and your sons, as an ordinance forever.
9 "This shall be yours of the most holy things *re-*
served from the fire: every offering of theirs, every
grain offering and every sin offering and every trespass offering which they render to Me, *shall be* most
holy for you and your sons.
10 "In a most holy *place* you shall eat it; every male
shall eat it. It shall be holy to you.
11 "This also *is* yours: the heave offering of their
gift, with all the wave offerings of the children of
Israel; I have given them to you, and your sons and
daughters with you, as an ordinance forever. Everyone who is clean in your house may eat it.
12 "All the best of the oil, all the best of the new
wine and the grain, their firstfruits which they offer
to the LORD, I have given them to you.
13 "Whatever first ripe fruit is in their land, which
they bring to the LORD, shall be yours. Everyone who
is clean in your house may eat it.
14 "Every devoted thing in Israel shall be yours.
15 "Everything that first opens the womb of all
flesh, which they bring to the LORD, whether man or
beast, shall be yours; nevertheless the firstborn
of man you shall surely redeem, and the firstborn of
unclean animals you shall redeem.
16 "And those redeemed of the devoted things you
shall redeem when one month old, according to your
valuation, for five shekels of silver, according to the
shekel of the sanctuary, which *is* twenty gerahs.
17 "But the firstborn of a cow, the firstborn of a
sheep, or the firstborn of a goat you shall not redeem; they *are* holy. You shall sprinkle their blood on
the altar, and burn their fat *as* an offering made by
fire for a sweet aroma to the LORD.
18 "And their flesh shall be yours, just as the wave
breast and the right thigh are yours.
19 "All the heave offerings of the holy things,
which the children of Israel offer to the LORD, I have
given to you and your sons and daughters with you
as an ordinance forever; it *is* a covenant of salt

forever before the LORD with you and your descendants with you."

20 Then the LORD said to Aaron: "You shall have no inheritance in their land, nor shall you have any portion among them; I *am* your portion and your inheritance among the children of Israel."

Num. 18:8–20

There now follows in these verses a list of what the priests (and, in vv. 21–24, the Levites) receive in recognition of their service, and in return for taking upon themselves the responsibility of bearing the iniquity of the sanctuary and the priesthood (v. 1). They were to receive parts of the sacrifices, the firstfruits of the harvest, and the firstborn of animals. This repeats, substantially, what has already been legislated for in Leviticus 6–7 and 27. A distinction is made between "most holy things" (vv. 9–10), which were the priests' sole perquisite and could be partaken of only by the priest and his sons, and "holy things" (vv. 17–18), which could be eaten by any members of the priest's family.[2] The various details of these priestly provisions repeat earlier regulations laid down in Leviticus (cf. Lev. 2:1ff., 3:1ff., 4:1–6:7, 6:14–7:7, 7:31–34, 11:1ff., 27:26ff.; cf. also Exod. 22:29, 23:16, 19).

Wenham points out that the binding and permanent nature of these obligations is underlined by calling them *a covenant of salt,*[3] that is to say, this covenant is indestructible, like salt.[4] Significantly, however, the passage concludes with a further explanation of the reason for these offerings being allocated to the priests, as being on account of their having no landed possessions or inheritance in Canaan. As this applied in equal measure to the Levites also (v. 24), it will be appropriate to leave comment on this particular point until we have dealt with the Levites' apportionment in verses 21–24.

THE REVENUES OF THE LEVITES

18:21 "Behold, I have given the children of Levi all the tithes in Israel as an inheritance in return for the work which they perform, the work of the tabernacle of meeting.

22 "Hereafter the children of Israel shall not come

near the tabernacle of meeting lest they bear sin and die.
23 "But the Levites shall perform the work of the tabernacle of meeting, and they shall bear their iniquity; *it shall be* a statute forever, throughout your generations, that among the children of Israel they shall have no inheritance.
24 "For the tithes of the children of Israel, which they offer up *as* a heave offering to the LORD, I have given to the Levites as an inheritance; therefore I have said to them, 'Among the children of Israel they shall have no inheritance.'"

Num. 18:21–24

The assignment of "all the tithes in Israel" (v. 21) to the Levites appears to be something new, as Wenham points out,[5] and is not found, in contrast to the priestly provisions, in the Levitical legislation (but cf. later references in Deut. 14:29; Neh. 10:37–39). Tithing was an ancient institution, antedating the Mosaic law by centuries, as we see from Genesis 14:20, 28:22. The regulation here laid down clearly has reference to Israel's future settlement in Canaan, when in a settled agricultural economy the tithing of the produce of the land would become possible. Here again, as with the priests in the previous verses, the twofold point is made that the tithe was a payment both as a return for service and a recognition of the dangers involved in their responsibilities, on the one hand, and on the other as a compensation from the Lord for their lack of territorial inheritance.

We now take up this latter issue, common to both Levites and priests, namely the nature of their inheritance. It is here in particular that the deepest implications in relation to reward for service are to be found. When responsibility in the service of God is fulfilled and honored worthily and with a full and pure heart, the privileges and recompense that come from His hand are incontrovertible and blessed beyond all telling. God is no man's debtor: He abundantly provides for those who serve Him faithfully and in love. "Those who honor Me, I will honor," says the Lord. The point that is being made in the central verses of this chapter is that not only do the priests and Levites have high responsibilities in their office, but their calling involves sacrifices. They are not as other men. The reason they are to have no inheritance as the other tribes is that the Lord is their inheritance. They are separated unto Him, and what are rightful and natural privileges for others are denied to them by virtue of their office and calling.

The enactments recorded here were made so that they should be disentangled from the affairs of this life (cf. 2 Tim. 2:4). As Matthew Henry puts it, "They had no grounds to occupy, no land to till, no vineyards to dress, no cattle to tend, no visible estate to take care of."[6] But from the natural point of view, this is sacrificial living. And no man who is not prepared thus to count all things loss ("for the excellence of the knowledge of Christ Jesus my Lord," Phil. 3:8, to use New Testament categories) is likely to be either faithful to his calling or fruitful in it. But those who do, find the reward of God rich and satisfying. The priests and Levites had no inheritance; but God's provision for them, even in material things, was bountiful and generous, and they were more than amply cared for by a faithful God (it is helpful to look at the apostle Paul's treatment of this, in the context of the new covenant, in 1 Cor. 9:13, 14).

An important point here is to realize that the provision God made for the Levites, and makes also for those who serve Him, is simply the material symbol of the spiritual enrichment He also gives them, when they are dedicated to His service (cf. 12 particularly, which may be taken both literally and metaphorically). A faithful priest or minister of God is a much blessed man, and He keeps him as the apple of His eye, blessing him with His best blessings (as we may gather from the apostle Paul's well-known words in 2 Cor. 6:9ff. ". . . as poor, yet making many rich; as having nothing, and yet possessing all things." The whole context of the apostle's words here is worthy of study as embodying both the burdens and hazards, as well as the rewards of service for God). God is truly no man's debtor, and what applies to priests and Levites here surely also applies to the priesthood of all believers, as we may gather from our Lord's words in Mark 10:29ff.: "Assuredly, I say to you, there is no one who has left house or brothers or sisters . . . for My sake and the gospel's, who shall not receive a hundredfold now in this time. . . ." "Seek first the kingdom of God and His righteousness," He says in another place, "and all these things shall be added to you."

THE PRIESTS' TITHE

18:25 Then the LORD spoke to Moses, saying,
26 "Speak thus to the Levites, and say to them: 'When you take from the children of Israel the tithes which I have given you from them as your inheritance, then you shall offer up a heave offering of it to the LORD, a tenth of the tithe.
27 'And your heave offering shall be reckoned to you as though *it were* the grain of the threshing floor and as the fullness of the winepress.
28 'Thus you shall also offer a heave offering to the LORD from all your tithes which you receive from the children of Israel, and you shall give the LORD's heave offering from it to Aaron the priest.
29 'Of all your gifts you shall offer up every heave offering due to the LORD, from all the best of them, the consecrated part of them.'
30 "Therefore you shall say to them: 'When you have lifted up the best of it, then *the rest* shall be accounted to the Levites as the produce of the threshing floor and as the produce of the winepress.
31 'You may eat it in any place, you and your households, for it *is* your reward for your work in the tabernacle of meeting.
32 'And you shall bear no sin because of it, when you have lifted up the best of it. But you shall not profane the holy gifts of the children of Israel, lest you die.'"

Num. 18:25–32

The tithe paid to the Levites was itself to be subject to a tithe which they in turn were to pay to the priests. Noth's comment is helpful here:

> In this respect the Levites appear in a strange intermediate position between priests and "laymen". On the one hand they are, as cultic personnel, recipients of dues, of the tithes; on the other hand they are, in turn, obliged to pay dues to the priests who are the real representatives of the sanctuary. . . .This

> "tithe of the tithe" . . . is to be treated like the ten per cent levy on the natural products of the Israelites and must then be used by the priests in accordance with the rule laid down in 12, 13. . . .[7]

Once this was done, they were free to eat the rest of the provision without restriction, as the reward for their service at the tabernacle, without any penalty or blame being attached to them by so doing (vv. 31, 32).

Something may at this point be said about the basic presupposition underlying this whole arrangement of the divine provision—tithing. It is plain to see that everything in the Israelite economy really depended upon the principle of tithing being adopted and strictly adhered to. Only thus would the system work.

The significance of the tithe is that it is similar in principle to the institution of the Sabbath day of rest. Israel was to keep the Sabbath day holy and devote it entirely to God as a symbol that all days belonged to Him.[8] In the same way the tithe is the symbol that all we have is the Lord's; to practice tithing is therefore a standing witness of our recognition that this is so.

A good case could be made for maintaining that one reason for the spiritual impoverishment of the church in our time lies in the fact that it does not practice this kind of discipline and stewardship in any substantial way. When one thinks of the vast sums of money that would become immediately available for the work of God in the world if even a proportion of His people were to tithe their income, then one begins to see the measure of the real spiritual impoverishment we suffer from today in the "Christian" West. "Will a man rob God?" cried Malachi long ago (Mal. 3:8). The question still stands today.

It is worth remembering that this regulation must certainly have been included in the teaching on the law that Israelite parents would give to their children. This is a practice that the church should also teach its young people. These verses are a challenge and an invitation to them to adopt God's appointed way right from the outset of responsible Christian living, as soon as they begin to earn money at all. When they do, they will soon get into the way of it, and it will become second nature to them; soon they will not even regard it as their own, but God's, belonging as of right to Him, and regard it as stealing if they withhold it. The church has yet to experience the general enrichment that a wholehearted adoption of the principle of tithing can bring to it.

NOTES

1. L. Elliott Binns, *The Book of Numbers* (London: Methuen & Co., Ltd., 1927), p. 120. More a re-statement than a statement, as Binns comments in his introductory note to the chapter: "This ch. opens with a reference to the holiness and danger of the sanctuary, an obvious connexion with xvii. 12f., and then goes on to define the duties of the Levites, introducing them almost as if they had not previously been mentioned. There are close parallels between vv. 1–7 and i. 50ff., iii. 5–10, 38; and between the rest of the ch. and Lev. ii. 3, 10, vi. 16ff."

2. Ibid., p. 121: "A distinction between holy and *most holy things* is definitely drawn in Lev. xxi. 22, perhaps because the latter offerings 'obtained a higher consecration.' According to Lev. vi. 27 anyone touching *most holy* flesh became infected by it, but such was not the case apparently with holy flesh (Hag. ii.10). It is probable as Gray suggests that the two terms were not always used very strictly (cf. v. 10a and 10b)."

3. Gordon J. Wenham, *Numbers*, Tyndale Old Testament Commentaries (Leicester: Inter-Varsity Press, 1981), p. 144.

4. Binns, *Numbers*, p. 123.

5. Wenham, *Numbers*, p. 144.

6. Matthew Henry, *Genesis-Deuteronomy*, Commentary on the Whole Bible (Old Tappan, N.J.: Fleming H. Revell Co., n.d.), 1:651.

7. Martin Noth, *Numbers: A Commentary*, Old Testament Library (London: SCM Press, 1968), p. 137.

8. The Sabbath, of course, antedated the existence of Israel by many centuries, and belongs to the order of Creation itself.

CHAPTER THIRTEEN

The Laws of Purification

Numbers 19:1–22

The Ashes of the Red Heifer

19:1 Now the LORD spoke to Moses and Aaron, saying,

2 "This *is* the ordinance of the law which the LORD has commanded, saying: 'Speak to the children of Israel, that they bring you a red heifer without blemish, in which there *is* no defect *and* on which a yoke has never come.

3 'You shall give it to Eleazar the priest, that he may take it outside the camp, and it shall be slaughtered before him;

4 'and Eleazar the priest shall take some of its blood with his finger, and sprinkle some of its blood seven times directly in front of the tabernacle of meeting.

5 'Then the heifer shall be burned in his sight: its hide, its flesh, its blood, and its offal shall be burned.

6 'And the priest shall take cedar wood and hyssop and scarlet, and cast *them* into the midst of the fire burning the heifer.

7 'Then the priest shall wash his clothes, he shall bathe in water, and afterward he shall come into the camp; the priest shall be unclean until evening.

8 'And the one who burns it shall wash his clothes in water, bathe in water, and shall be unclean until evening.

9 'Then a man *who is* clean shall gather up the ashes of the heifer, and store *them* outside the camp in a clean place; and they shall be kept for the

congregation of the children of Israel for the water of purification; it *is* for purifying from sin.

10 'And the one who gathers the ashes of the heifer shall wash his clothes, and be unclean until evening. It shall be a statute forever to the children of Israel and to the stranger who dwells among them.'

Num. 19:1–10

Most commentators see no connection between this chapter and what precedes or follows it, and regard it as an "independent unit which has been inserted immediately before the Pentateuchal narrative is resumed once more in 20:1." G. J. Wenham, however, relates it to the previous chapter in a likely and persuasive way, in that while chapter 18 dealt with the responsibilities and privileges of the priests and Levites in relation to the protection of the tabernacle against trespass, here it is the divine provision for the other social division in Israel, the ordinary people, that is outlined.[1]

The ritual, nevertheless, is an unusual one, and without parallel elsewhere in the Old Testament. The slaying of the heifer is not part of a sacrificial action, although done in the presence of the priest, nor is it within but outside the sanctuary; nor is the animal itself given to God, but totally burned and used to provide the ashes in the water; nor does the priest participate in the burning, although it is done in his presence. Wenham thinks that since offering a sacrifice was a difficult and expensive procedure, which would greatly add to the distress of family and friends when someone died, the ritual provides "an alternative remedy which marked the seriousness of the pollution caused by death, yet dealt with it without the cost and inconvenience of sacrifice."[2]

The ritual itself was as follows: A red heifer (the color probably chosen as being that of blood), a young cow without blemish, on which no yoke had come, was to be taken outside the camp, and slain in the presence of the priest, who was to sprinkle its blood with his finger seven times before the tabernacle of the congregation. The carcass of the animal was to be burned entirely, and into the midst of the fire which consumed it the priest was to throw cedar wood, hyssop, and scarlet. When the carcass was completely consumed, the ashes were to be collected and preserved for future use. On a person contracting ceremonial defilement through touching a dead body, a portion of these ashes was to be mixed with running water, and a clean person, dipping a bunch of hyssop in the mixture was to sprinkle it on him who was unclean.[3]

General Rules As to Purification

> 19:11 'He who touches the dead body of anyone shall be unclean seven days.
> 12 'He shall purify himself with the water on the third day and on the seventh day; *then* he will be clean. But if he does not purify himself on the third day and on the seventh day, he will not be clean.
> 13 'Whoever touches the body of anyone who has died, and does not purify himself, defiles the tabernacle of the LORD. That person shall be cut off from Israel. He shall be unclean, because the water of purification was not sprinkled on him; his uncleanness *is* still on him.'
>
> *Num. 19:11–13*

Thus instituted, the ordinance provided a ready-made, instant sin offering. Clearly, it was to be taken seriously, and the ritual required the application of the remedy twice, on the third and on the seventh day of the seven-day period of uncleanness. Failure to do so meant that the tabernacle would be defiled, and just as this led in chapter 18 to death for the rebels, so here the offending Israelites would be cut off from Israel (vv. 13, 20), a punishment usually signifying in the Pentateuch a sudden death at the hands of God.

Special Rules of Purification

> 19:14 'This *is* the law when a man dies in a tent: All who come into the tent and all who *are* in the tent shall be unclean seven days;
> 15 'and every open vessel, which has no cover fastened on it, *is* unclean.
> 16 'Whoever in the open field touches one who is slain by a sword or who has died, or a bone of a man, or a grave, shall be unclean seven days.

> 17 'And for an unclean *person* they shall take some of the ashes of the heifer burnt for purification from sin, and running water shall be put on them in a vessel.
>
> 18 'A clean person shall take hyssop and dip *it* in the water, sprinkle *it* on the tent, on all the vessels, on the persons who were there, or on the one who touched a bone, the slain, the dead, or a grave.
>
> 19 'The clean *person* shall sprinkle the unclean on the third day and on the seventh day; and on the seventh day he shall purify himself, wash his clothes, and bathe in water; and at evening he shall be clean.
>
> 20 'But the man who is unclean and does not purify himself, that person shall be cut off from among the assembly, because he has defiled the sanctuary of the LORD. The water of purification has not been sprinkled on him; he *is* unclean.
>
> 21 'It shall be a perpetual statute for them. He who sprinkles the water of purification shall wash his clothes; and he who touches the water of purification shall be unclean until evening.
>
> 22 'Whatever the unclean *person* touches shall be unclean; and the person who touches *it* shall be unclean until evening.'"
>
> *Num. 19:14–22*

Details are next given as to what is to be done in particular instances of death. The main point to note is that all who lived in the same tent as the person who died, and all those who came into the tent, were regarded as defiled whether or not they had come in actual contact with the dead body. It is a testimony to the widespread effect of defilement brought by death that even vessels in the home were regarded as having partaken of the infection (v. 15), and graves themselves (v. 16), hence the need for whitewashing them, so that the ritually pious could avoid touching them inadvertently (cf. Matt. 23:27, Luke 11:44). In verse 20 the threat of punishment for the neglect of purification is repeated (cf. 13), and this is a measure of the seriousness of the issue for Israel.

The use that the writer of the Epistle to the Hebrews makes of this ordinance (9:13, 14) indicates that it has significance and importance for the Christian in the type which it gives of the New Testament and of Christ. The apostle says: "For if the blood of bulls and goats and the ashes of a heifer, sprinkling the unclean, sanctifies for the purifying of the flesh, how much more shall the blood of Christ, who through the eternal Spirit offered Himself without spot to God, purge your conscience from dead works to serve the living God?" Some verses later (10:4) he adds: "For it is not possible that the blood of bulls and goats could take away sins," and goes on to speak of the sacrifice of Christ which alone can deal with the problem of sin. In this regard, we must say that the sacrifices in Old Testament times had no intrinsic worth, but were shadows cast on the course of history by the Lamb slain from the foundation of the world. This does not mean, however, that these Old Testament sacrifices had no efficacy. If we believe in the doctrine of the Trinity, we must necessarily recognize that Christ the Savior was at work in the Old Testament time as in the New, blessing and sanctifying His people. Very properly, The Westminster Confession of Faith (7.5) says:

> This covenant (of grace) was differently administered in the time of the law, and in the time of the gospel; under the law it was administered by promises, prophecies, sacrifices, circumcision, the paschal lamb, and other types and ordinances delivered to the people of the Jews, all foresignifying Christ to come, which were for that time sufficient and efficacious, through the operation of the spirit, to instruct and build up the elect in faith in the promised Messiah, by whom they had full remission of sins, and eternal salvation.

But they were efficacious in an indirect way, in what they signified, rather than in themselves, and by virtue of what they signified, namely the death of Christ; whereas the New Testament ordinances are directly efficacious. It is therefore only partially true to say that in the Old Testament era sins were "covered," whereas in the New, they are "removed," for forgiveness was something that could be genuinely experienced in olden time just as in the present. Indeed, in the last analysis we must recognize that the cross of Christ was planted in the center of history, and that it casts its gracious shadow both backward to the beginning of history and forward to its consummation. In whichever dispensation men may have lived, there is ever only one way of forgiveness and reconciliation, through faith in the blood of the cross. This is why Christ could say, "Abraham rejoiced to see My day, and he saw it and was glad" (John 8:56).

In both the Old Testament and in the New distinctions are made between different aspects of cleansing. On the one hand, there is the once-and-for-all cleansing of the guilt of sin. This is typified for us in the provision of the bronze altar in the tabernacle, signifying the putting away of sin once-and-for-all by Christ through the sacrifice of Himself. When once we come to the fountain open for sin and for uncleanness, we receive a full, free, and final cleansing from the guilt of our sin. This corresponds to justification, which covers the whole of life, past, present, and future. The believer is a justified man, and remains so, unalterably. When he sins, as he will, the question of his *standing* is never again raised; judicial guilt is once-and-for-all dealt with and put away. His subsequent sins as a believer are dealt with as a family matter, within the family of God, and there is provision for this. But his standing is not affected, nor can it ever be. As to the judicial guilt of sin, we are forgiven persons, and remain so.

But as to the other aspects of sinning, much still is to be said. For example, there is the fact that it is not possible, in our daily walk through the world, but that we shall contract defilement from contact with the dust and grime of the world. This seems to be suggested in John 13, in the story of Christ washing the disciples' feet. The imagery is that of a man returning from the public baths to his house, when his feet would contract defilement, but not his body, and would thus need cleansing. So the believer, once-for-all washed, needs no further cleansing; but needs to bring his daily sins to the Father for cleansing and forgiveness, so that he may remain in unbroken fellowship with Him. This is typified in the contrast between the bronze altar (in the tabernacle) and the laver.

On the other hand, as perhaps a special case of the oft-needed and oft-repeated cleansing, there is the case of the believer whose conscience has again become defiled by contact with something unclean. It is here that the idea of the "ashes of the heifer" comes in. In this regard, we see how everything in the ordinance points to Christ. The heifer is taken outside the camp, as Christ was (Heb. 13:13); the cleansing was based on, and depended on, the slaying of the animal, that is, on atonement. Every kind of cleansing goes back to the Cross, and there is no cleansing apart from that blessed place.

But the ashes were mingled with water. The ashes obviously speak of the once-for-all sacrifice that has continuing efficacy, but what of the water? Water symbolizes in Scripture both the Word and Spirit of God, and we may therefore say that the symbolism means something like this: The believer who contracts defilement is convicted of his sin by the Holy Spirit (cf. John 16:8) speaking in and through the Word, and he is thus brought afresh to the Cross for cleansing and renewal. Furthermore, it is in the Word and by the Spirit that the efficacy of the Cross comes home afresh to us.

Significantly, the blood of Christ, the Word, and the Spirit of God, are all associated with cleansing in the New Testament (cf. John 15:3; 1 John 1:7, 5:6–8). We should not—and need not—differentiate these in the different aspects of cleansing, for all are active in each, whether in the initial, once-for-all cleansing by which we enter into the kingdom of God, or the constant daily cleansing we all need to keep us in fellowship with the Father and with the Son, and in the specific instances in which we become defiled by contact with some uncleanness.

We should not be concerned to press this threefold distinction in cleansing too far, but it does correspond to basic realities in our experience: the once-and-for-all cleansing by which we become children of God; the continual cleansing by which we are maintained in fellowship with Him (in this regard we may recall Paul's words in 1 Cor. 4:4, "I know nothing against myself, yet I am not justified by this," for this indicates that even when we may not be conscious of things that are wrong, we still stand in need of constant daily cleansing); and thirdly, the specific cleansing in any particular matter. There is a distinction, after all, between a believer who is conscious that he is not perfect and therefore needs continual, daily cleansing by the blood of Christ (cf. 1 John 1:7) and one who has gotten out of touch with the Lord because of some specific transgression. David was "out of touch" for a whole year, before and until he sought the "purging with hyssop" mentioned in Psalm 51 (a clear reference to this ordinance in Num. 19).

The specific matter mentioned here is defilement by contact with a dead body—ceremonial defilement, to be sure, but what does it represent, or typify, in spiritual life? Any dead thing—the dead hand of the world on a believer's life, the deadness of some unhallowed thing that leaves its mark upon the life, blighting and marring it, and robbing it of its fine edge of consecration. Can such defilement ever remain secret, as to its effects? Is it not sadly true that others can often discern that something is amiss, and could say to us, "Brother, sister, what is it that has taken the fire from your testimony, the light from your eye, the joy from your heart?" When this obtains, and the Word and Spirit of God bring home a solemn conviction about it to the believer's heart, there is need for a fresh experience of Calvary, of repentance, of a new death to be died, and a new consecration to be made. The provision is there; God waits to be gracious, and by His mercy things may become new again.

NOTES

1. Gordon J. Wenham, *Numbers*, Tyndale Old Testament Commentaries (Leicester: Inter-Varsity Press, 1981), p. 145. Wenham adds: "Even if laymen avoided blatant trespass like Korah's, they could still pollute the tabernacle through being unclean close to the tent. For this reason those who were unclean had earlier been expelled from the camp (5:2–4, 12:14, Lev. 13:45–46). The most serious and obvious type of human uncleanness was that caused by death. . . . The death of someone in the camp could pollute all those in it, and this would *defile the tabernacle of the LORD* (vv. 13, 20) unless preventive measures were taken."

2. Ibid., p. 146.

3. L. Elliott Binns, *The Book of Numbers* (London: Methuen & Co., Ltd., 1927), p. 128, comments, "The Rabbis regarded uncleanness arising from contact with the dead as the greatest of all defilements (Kelim I)." Even Jehovah Himself was unclean after burying Moses and had to be purified by fire: see on 31:23.

CHAPTER FOURTEEN

From Kadesh to Moab

Numbers 20:1–21:35

THE INCIDENT AT MERIBAH

20:1 Then the children of Israel, the whole congregation, came into the Wilderness of Zin in the first month, and the people stayed in Kadesh; and Miriam died there and was buried there.

2 Now there was no water for the congregation; so they gathered together against Moses and Aaron.

3 And the people contended with Moses and spoke, saying: "If only we had died when our brethren died before the LORD!

4 "Why have you brought up the assembly of the LORD into this wilderness, that we and our animals should die here?

5 "And why have you made us come up out of Egypt, to bring us to this evil place? It *is* not a place of grain or figs or vines or pomegranates; nor *is* there any water to drink."

6 So Moses and Aaron went from the presence of the assembly to the door of the tabernacle of meeting, and they fell on their faces. And the glory of the LORD appeared to them.

7 Then the LORD spoke to Moses, saying,

8 "Take the rod; you and your brother Aaron gather the congregation together. Speak to the rock before their eyes, and it will yield its water; thus you shall bring water for them out of the rock, and give drink to the congregation and their animals."

9 So Moses took the rod from before the LORD as He commanded him.

10 And Moses and Aaron gathered the assembly
together before the rock; and he said to them, "Hear
now, you rebels! Must we bring water for you out of
this rock?"
11 Then Moses lifted his hand and struck the rock
twice with his rod; and water came out abundantly,
and the congregation and their animals drank.
12 Then the LORD spoke to Moses and Aaron,
"Because you did not believe Me, to hallow Me in the
eyes of the children of Israel, therefore you shall not
bring this assembly into the land which I have given
them."
13 This *was* the water of Meribah, because the children of Israel contended with the LORD, and He was
hallowed among them.

Num. 20:1–13

The various ritual regulations having been delineated and completed, Israel's journey from Kadesh to Moab is about to begin. The events recorded in this chapter—the death of Miriam, the murmuring of the people against Moses and Aaron, the miraculous provision of water from the rock, Edom's refusal to allow Israel passage through their territory, and the death of Aaron—carry the narrative to the close of Israel's wanderings in the wilderness. They form an introduction to the account of the march toward the Promised Land, the beginning of which is noted in verse 22, and is continued in the following chapters.

The section begins with the record of the death of Miriam, Moses' sister. It is therefore against the background of a personal sorrow that we should look at the murmuring of the people (vv. 2ff.). It was surely an evidence of heartlessness and insensitivity on the part of the people that they should have allowed their bitter complaining to surface once again when Moses' sorrow was so fresh. It was an inopportune time, and singularly inappropriate, for them to have done so. The truth is, however, that when people are "out of sorts" with God, they become clumsy and insensitive, and intrude unceremoniously at all manner of unsuitable times, causing needless hurt and distress that could, and should, have been avoided. It lends particular seriousness to this evidence of murmuring and disaffection and serves to show how far wrong in spirit they were. The picture is one that has grown familiar in these studies of the journeying and wanderings of Israel: each time anything seemed to go wrong for them, this is how they reacted, in a grumbling, querulous, and faithless spirit that blamed Moses and Aaron, who were the constant scapegoats for an ugly and vindictive attitude against God. We find ourselves asking, "Do these people *never* learn? Have they not learned *any* wisdom from their past experience of God's dealings with them?" And well might we ask this, for God's dealings with them up to this point were all such as to inspire them with a faith and trust in His goodness and love (see Deut. 8:2–6 for a description of the divine grace toward them. It was in face of *this* that they sinned yet again).

The divine reaction to their querulous and faithless spirit is—not wrath, but grace (vv. 7 ff.). Moses is commanded to take his rod, and "*speak to the rock*" in the presence of all the people, and it would give forth water to satisfy their thirst. This provision for their need is yet another signal evidence of the meaning of the grace of God—undeserved, unmerited kindness and goodness, free and unearned. "Grace for the rebellious" would be an apt title for the passage, and F. W. Faber's well-known words come readily to mind:

> And the heart of the Eternal
> Is most wonderfully kind.

Water for the thirsty, bread for the hungry, home for the homeless, rest for the weary, pardon for the sinful—this is grace, and in the story of these verses we have an illustration of something that is fulfilled and magnified in the gospel of Christ. It is this that makes the gospel good news—good news for those who have failed and been a disappointment to themselves and to God, for those who despair of themselves in His sight. Everything in the New Testament confirms this. One thinks of Peter, and his black denial of Jesus—no unexpected happening, but something that was entirely predictable, for all along his heart had refused the discipline of discipleship. One can readily imagine the dark despair and desolation that must have gripped his soul after his denial. Yet, one of the first statements of the resurrection narrative is, "Go and tell His disciples—*and Peter*. . . ." This was a special reassurance from the risen Lord that there was grace for failures, grace for poor, broken, dejected Peter, to reach deeper than the depths of self-despair to lift him up, and back, into fellowship with the Lord.

But there is another emphasis also in these verses which must not be missed. There is no room for complacency in the knowledge of such a love and grace as God displayed toward His people. He means us to take His grace seriously, on pain of punishment. We may not presume upon it; when we do, we shall suffer for it. This is the lesson which Moses' experience in verses 12–13 has to teach us. A judgment was passed upon him because of his sin of *striking* the rock rashly and presumptuously, when God had told him to *speak* to it,[1] and the privilege of leading the people into the Promised Land was withdrawn from this great leader and given to another (cf. Ps. 106:32, 33; Deut. 32:48ff., 3:24ff.). Whatever the nature of the transgression—and we may suppose it was serious indeed—it brought dire consequences upon him. Moses was disobedient in the matter, through irritation, anger, and resentment, not to say bitterness, with the people; and disobedience is no less serious in the man of God than in the people of God. And he paid dearly for it.

The lesson is clear: grace is never a ground for complacency or presumption. By our carelessness, by our sinful neglect, we can sin away forever some of the privileges of our calling—not salvation itself, but our opportunities for service, our possibility for usefulness, our contribution to the ongoing purposes of God. Can a man take fire into his bosom and not be burned? The answer, ringing from a hundred pages in Scripture, is never! The fact that this happened to Moses teaches us that there is no height to which we may rise in spiritual life where this will not be a possibility or danger. The message that comes through, loud and clear, in these verses is, "Do not be haughty (high-minded), but fear" (Rom. 11:20).

Edom's Refusal

20:14 Now Moses sent messengers from Kadesh to the king of Edom. "Thus says your brother Israel: 'You know all the hardship that has befallen us,

15 'how our fathers went down to Egypt, and we dwelt in Egypt a long time, and the Egyptians afflicted us and our fathers.

16 'When we cried out to the LORD, He heard our
voice and sent the Angel and brought us up out of
Egypt; now here we are in Kadesh, a city on the edge
of your border.
17 'Please let us pass through your country. We
will not pass through fields or vineyards, nor will
we drink water from wells; we will go along the
King's Highway; we will not turn aside to the right
hand or to the left until we have passed through your
territory.'"
18 Then Edom said to him, "You shall not pass
through my *land*, lest I come out against you with the
sword."
19 So the children of Israel said to him, "We will
go by the Highway, and if I or my livestock drink any
of your water, then I will pay for it; let me only pass
through on foot, nothing *more*."
20 Then he said, "You shall not pass through." So
Edom came out against them with many men and
with a strong hand.
21 Thus Edom refused to give Israel passage through
his territory; so Israel turned away from him.

Num. 20:14–21

This section gives the account of an approach Moses made to the king of Edom for permission to pass through his country on Israel's onward march to the land of Canaan. An interesting and instructive episode is here unfolded. Israel is refused a passage through Edom's territory, and not all the assurances Moses can give the king of Edom suffice to make right of way for them. One biblical scholar's comments on the incident seem to suggest that Edom's refusal was due largely to prudential considerations, and that it was natural for Edom to refuse to allow them through.[2] But this does much less than justice to the importance and significance that later Old Testament writers undoubtedly place upon the incident. The enmity—for such it was between Edom and Israel—had ancient roots, as is evident from the earlier chapters of Genesis onwards. Edom's intransigence on this occasion is simply one of a number of subsequent incidents in the ongoing history of God's people which underline not only the hereditary enmity between these two nations (with a common ancestry in the patriarch Isaac), but also the implacable hatred that

Edom showed toward Israel. This brought upon them the pronouncements of doom by Isaiah (21:11, 12), Jeremiah (49:7ff.), Ezekiel (25:12ff.), Amos (1:11), and Obadiah (1ff.).

The message emerging from all this, particularly in relation to the divine retribution that ultimately came upon Edom for their cruelty to Israel, is this: He who touches God's people touches the apple of His eye. *God* could chastise His people, judge them or discipline them, but woe betide anyone *else* who did them harm and ill. For all their querulousness and rebelliousness, they were precious to Him, and for anyone to harm them was to ask for trouble. This also is the grace of God: He would buffet and bruise them, sending judgment after judgment upon them, but He cared for them. He would never let them go, and He would allow no other to touch them with impunity. This is a phenomenon that has remained true throughout history to the present time. In our own day any nation that has done despite to God's covenant people has fallen into trouble.

The following quotation serves to underline the miraculous preservation of God's people, against all the attempts of their enemies to destroy them:

> Four hundred years in Egypt; forty in the wilderness; a long dark and terrible period of warfare, backsliding and idolatry; a brief gleam of sunshine in the reigns of David and Solomon, a rapid downward career of apostacy, discord and sin, to the time of the Babylonian captivity; seventy years' exile, a long interval of darkness and oppression; the great rejection of the Lord of glory, the frightful sufferings and downfall of Jerusalem, and nineteen centuries of shame, oppression, dispersion, and above all, unbelief, blindness, hatred to God's dear Son, the only Saviour. . . .
>
> Why do they exist after all the persecutions that they have endured? Pharaoh tried to drown them, but they could not be drowned; Nebuchadnezzar tried to burn them, but they could not be burned; Haman tried to hang them, but it was of no avail. All the nations of the earth have persecuted them, but here they are, and more numerous at the present day than ever before. Why? Because God calls them an everlasting nation.[3]

And we could well add to these words the horrors of the Holocaust and Nazi Germany's "final solution," to which the answer of

God has been the establishment of modern Israel as a nation, after so many centuries of dispersion.

It is an interesting commentary on the nature of the life of pilgrimage that Edom should not have allowed Israel to travel through their land. The world is never slow to spurn and despise the people of God. This bears witness to the "separate" character of true Christian life. As Christians we are in the world, but not of it. It is true that Israel in many ways all but obscured her pilgrim character, and in view of this it would be well for us if as Christians we were to take seriously as our aim and intention the sentiments of Moses expressed in verse 17, *"We will go along the King's Highway; we will not turn aside to the right hand or to the left. . . ."*

THE DEATH OF AARON

20:22 Now the children of Israel, the whole congregation, journeyed from Kadesh and came to Mount Hor.

23 And the LORD spoke to Moses and Aaron in Mount Hor by the border of the land of Edom, saying:

24 "Aaron shall be gathered to his people, for he shall not enter the land which I have given to the children of Israel, because you rebelled against My word at the water of Meribah.

25 "Take Aaron and Eleazar his son, and bring them up to Mount Hor;

26 "and strip Aaron of his garments and put them on Eleazar his son; for Aaron shall be gathered *to his people* and die there."

27 So Moses did just as the LORD commanded, and they went up to Mount Hor in the sight of all the congregation.

28 Moses stripped Aaron of his garments and put them on Eleazar his son; and Aaron died there on the top of the mountain. Then Moses and Eleazar came down from the mountain.

29 Now when all the congregation saw that Aaron was dead, all the house of Israel mourned for Aaron thirty days.

Num. 20:22–29

The record of the death of Aaron, Israel's first high priest, is a strangely moving one, in the association it must have had for Moses.[4] We should not miss the significant fact that the chapter which ends with the report of his death began with an account of Miriam's death. Her death took place, we are told (v. 1), in the first month and Aaron's in the first day of the fifth month (33:38) of the fortieth year. It seems likely, therefore, that this year held a double bereavement for God's appointed leader, and the passage invites us, so to speak, to consider what this must have meant to Moses in terms of bleak desolation and loneliness. It says something about Moses' stature that he should have continued without interruption in his divinely ordained work, even in such a context of sorrow and grief.

The reason for Aaron's death at this juncture is emphasized again in verse 24 (cf. 12, 13), but there is almost a gentleness—and certainly a solemn dignity—in the Lord's word about his being "gathered to his people." This phrase is peculiar to the Pentateuch (cf. Gen. 25:8, 17, 35:29, 49:33; Num. 27:13, 31:2; Deut. 32:50), although a similar phrase, "gathered to their fathers," is used elsewhere.[5] But it is surely a misunderstanding to interpret it merely as a reference to the family sepulchre. Wenham must be right in insisting that "it describes a central Old Testament conviction about life after death, that in Sheol, the place of the dead, people will be reunited with other members of their family," quoting as he does in support of his interpretation of David's words in 2 Samuel 12:23: "I shall go to him, but he shall not return to me"—a reference to the death of Bathsheba's child.

There is also a beautiful sense of continuity in Aaron's son Eleazar being invested with the priestly garments and authority on Mount Hor, prior to Aaron's death. This is a solemn ritual indeed, and one which must have brought a sense of quiet assurance and comfort to Aaron's heart rather than any consciousness that he was being deprived of his priestly commission. It has been said, "God buries His workers, and carries on His work." There was to be no interruption of the divine provision for His people. They were not to be without a high priest.

This serves to remind us of the wonderful words in Hebrews 7:23–24 about the imperfection of the Levitical priesthood: "And there were many priests, because they were prevented by death from continuing. But He, because He continues forever, has an unchangeable priesthood."

The Victory at Hormah

> 21:1 The king of Arad, the Canaanite, who dwelt in the South, heard that Israel was coming on the road to Atharim. Then he fought against Israel and took *some* of them prisoners.
> 2 So Israel made a vow to the LORD, and said, "If You will indeed deliver this people into my hand, then I will utterly destroy their cities."
> 3 And the LORD listened to the voice of Israel and delivered up the Canaanites, and they utterly destroyed them and their cities. So the name of that place was called Hormah.
>
> *Num. 21:1–3*

The opening verses of this chapter record an encounter that Israel had with the king of Arad. It has a twofold significance, both because it was Israel's first victory over the Canaanites, and because it was won at Hormah, for it was there that their abortive attempt to enter the land after the tragedy of Kadesh Barnea ended in disastrous defeat (14:45). The context seems to be the onward movement of the people following the episode with Edom (20:14–21). Undeterred by Edom's refusal to let them pass through their territory, they resolved to find another way. Perhaps the most significant thing about what is told us here is the new spirit shown by the people. In the initial encounter, they experienced a setback, in which some were taken prisoner. Undismayed, however, they betook themselves to the Lord in prayer with determination and firm resolve, and God wonderfully heard their prayer and gave them victory.

It is true that in the verses immediately following this incident we again see the people discouraged and grumbling, but at least there is the beginning of a new attitude that paid dividends in no uncertain way. We may learn from this that so often the Lord is simply waiting for some sign of firmness and fortitude in His people, in order to bless them by His grace and enabling. Low-spiritedness is seldom ever justified in face of such a willing God. If only we would realize that even a spark of spirit in us will be met with all the resources of the Godhead to help and prosper us!

In this sense it is certainly true that God helps those who help themselves. Perhaps it is that we sometimes need time to become disenchanted with our own spinelessness in the spiritual life and realize how fragile and "precious" we have all unconsciously become, in order to be gripped by a new determination to be "up and doing." This is the context in which God delights to answer our prayers; this prompts the question—is it possible for prayer to become so doleful that it is incapable of being answered?

The Bronze Serpent

> 21:4 Then they journeyed from Mount Hor by the Way of the Red Sea, to go around the land of Edom; and the soul of the people became very discouraged on the way.
>
> 5 And the people spoke against God and against Moses: "Why have you brought us up out of Egypt to die in the wilderness? For *there is* no food and no water, and our soul loathes this worthless bread."
>
> 6 So the LORD sent fiery serpents among the people, and they bit the people; and many of the people of Israel died.
>
> 7 Therefore the people came to Moses, and said, "We have sinned, for we have spoken against the LORD and against you; pray to the LORD that He take away the serpents from us." So Moses prayed for the people.
>
> 8 The the LORD said to Moses, "Make a fiery *serpent,* and set it on a pole; and it shall be that everyone who is bitten, when he looks at it, shall live."
>
> 9 So Moses made a bronze serpent, and put it on a pole; and so it was, if a serpent had bitten anyone, when he looked at the bronze serpent, he lived.
>
> *Num. 21:4–9*

These verses describe the last recorded occasion on which Israel expressed their grumbling discontentment about their desert food and their yearning for the fleshpots of Egypt, describing the divine provision of manna as *"this worthless bread"* (v. 5). On this occasion it did not lead to a further divine provision of food and water, but instead precipitated an act of divine judgment. Fiery serpents were sent among the people, and many suffered fatally from their bites. A confession of sin on the part of those who had spoken against the Lord and against Moses enabled Moses to make intercession for them. This was heard and answered, and Moses was instructed to *"make a fiery serpent, and set it on a pole."* Moses made it of bronze, holding it up as instructed so that the people could see it. Those who looked upon this bronze replica were healed of the serpent bites and lived.

Such is the story; it has raised many questions among scholars, and something must be said about these now. Critical commentators make much of the superstitious beliefs of ancient time about the alleged magical properties of images of serpents and other animals in the preservation against disease and demonic influence, referring for example to the practice of the Philistines of making images of mice when their land was infested with such vermin (1 Sam. 6:5). They remind us of the story in 2 Kings 18:4 of how the children of Israel burned incense to Moses' bronze serpent in the time of Hezekiah, in consequence of which it was destroyed. It is doubtless true that the serpent may have been a symbol of life and fertility among the Canaanite peoples, and that in Egypt serpent symbols were worn to ward off serpent bites (in much the same way as copper bracelets are sometimes worn today to alleviate rheumatic pain!); but these observations do not explain why this particular symbolism was enjoined by the Lord and enacted by the people.

Gordon J. Wenham's comments are particularly helpful in this regard as he seeks for the clue to the symbolism in the general principles underlying the sacrifices and purificatory rites in the Old Testament. Briefly, his view is as follows: just as animals were killed so that sinful men who deserved to die might live, and as in such sacrifices an inversion operated, by which normally polluting substances or actions had the opposite effect in a ritual context and served to purify, so also in the case of the bronze serpent, those dying through the serpent bites were restored to life by the dead image of the bronze serpent. And, just as in the ordinary sacrifices, the participant had to identify with the sacrifice by laying his hand on the animal's head, so in this instance with the bronze serpent, "looking at it" was the equivalent of the manual contact.[6]

Wenham maintains that if this is a valid interpretation, it makes it clear how our Lord could use the story as an apt picture of His own saving ministry, in which men dying in sin are saved by the dead body of a man suspended on the cross.

The particular and special value of this story lies in the fact that our Lord Himself chose it to illustrate perhaps the greatest utterance in the whole of Scripture about the gospel, in John 3:14–16, where the correspondence is made in unmistakable terms: "And as Moses lifted up the serpent in the wilderness, even so must the Son of Man be lifted up, that whoever believes in Him should not perish but have eternal life. For God so loved the world that He gave His only begotten Son, that whoever believes in Him should not perish but have everlasting life."

Here, then, is the best possible of illustrations to bring out the meaning of salvation. We must remember that the Old Testament is "God's picture book," compiled to teach us the truths of grace. And we must realize that in His providence and mercy some of these old records throw wonderful illumination upon the New Testament doctrine of salvation, helping us who are so slow to understand the Scriptures to grasp them more fully and truly. One recalls our Lord's post-resurrection words to the disciples, "O foolish ones, and slow of heart to believe in all that the prophets have spoken. . . . And beginning at Moses and all the prophets, He expounded to them in all the Scriptures the things concerning Himself." Was *this* story included? One can hardly think it would have been omitted, when He had already used it, to such effect, with Nicodemus.

The story illustrates two aspects of the nature of sin. On the one hand, in the fact that the Israelites were bitten by fiery serpents, Jesus means to tell us that sin is like the mortal bite of a poisonous serpent. One readily thinks of Genesis 3 and the story of the Fall in this connection. Sin bites like a serpent and stings like an adder, inflicting terrible wounds on man's soul. To be a sinner means therefore to stand in urgent need of healing. With snake bite, time is of the essence, if life is to be saved. This is the aspect of sin that calls forth the compassion and pity of God, and the tender care of the great Physician Himself.

On the other hand, in the fact that the serpents were sent to Israel as a punishment for their murmurings and rebelliousness, Jesus means to tell us that sin is revolt against God and His good and perfect will. This was surely one element in Nicodemus's situation: his was a willing blindness. He did not want to see the truth about the necessity for rebirth, because seeing it would have been at that point much too costly a thing for him. He resisted the truth because his heart was in rebellion against God, as much as the Israelites were.

In the same way, the provision God made for Israel illustrates the great gospel provision for sin. As has already been indicated in the exposition, the significance of the uplifted bronze serpent is that bronze speaks of sin judged (cf. the bronze altar in the tabernacle, where the burnt offering for sin was made), and as Matthew Henry puts it, "That which cured was shaped in the likeness of that which wounded." As Israel was given this symbol of substitutionary atonement—their sin, represented by the bronze serpent, was cursed and cancelled, and it was this they were bidden to look upon—so also Christ, for our sakes, and for our healing, was made in the likeness of sinful flesh, and made sin for us, and was lifted up from the earth, when He bore in His own body the judgment of a holy God upon sin. And, since judgment cannot come where judgment has already been, we are bidden to look upon the uplifted Christ for our salvation. As the old hymn puts it, "There is life for a look at the Crucified One."

The Journey

21:10 Now the children of Israel moved on and camped in Oboth.

11 And they journeyed from Oboth and camped at Ije Abarim, in the wilderness which *is* east of Moab, toward the sunrise.

12 From there they moved and camped in the Valley of Zered.

13 From there they moved and camped on the other side of the Arnon, which *is* in the wilderness that extends from the border of the Amorites; for the Arnon *is* the border of Moab, between Moab and the Amorites.

14 Therefore it is said in the Book of the Wars of the LORD:

"Waheb in Suphah,
The brooks of the Arnon,
15 And the slope of the brooks
That reaches to the dwelling of Ar,
And lies on the border of Moab."
16 From there *they went* to Beer, which *is* the well
where the LORD said to Moses, "Gather the people
together, and I will give them water."
17 Then Israel sang this song:
"Spring up, O well!
All of you sing to it—
18 The well the leaders sank,
Dug by the nation's nobles,
By the lawgiver, with their staves."
And from the wilderness *they went* to Mattanah,
19 from Mattanah to Nahaliel, from Nahaliel to
Bamoth,
20 and from Bamoth, *in* the valley that *is* in the
country of Moab, to the top of Pisgah which looks
down on the wasteland.

Num. 21:10–20

These verses describe Israel's journey stage by stage around the land of Edom, past Ije Abarim and the eastern part of the territory of Moab and across the river Arnon and northward to the headland of Pisgah, overlooking Jeshimon. This brief travel narrative seems to anticipate the outcome of the battles with Sihon and Og described in the next verses (vv. 21 ff.), and this is confirmed by the fuller account given of these battles in Deuteronomy 2–3. This serves in part at least to explain the two fragments (vv. 14–15 and vv. 17–18) which are consonant with the spirit of rejoicing and indeed celebration that must have animated Israel in their onward advance.

"The Book of the Wars of the Lord" (v. 14) is mentioned only here in Scripture; it is probably a collection of popular songs of the time, from which the "well" song in verses 17–18 is also likely to have been taken. The names "Wahab" and "Suphah" are unknown as place names, and attempts have been made through emendation of the Hebrew text to make it read "the Lord came in a whirlwind."[7] But this is pure conjecture and cannot be substantiated, even if it does read more intelligibly. But intelligibility at the cost of accurate

translation is scarcely an advantage or improvement, and it is better to accept references to those places now unknown.

The account of Israel's continuing journeyings is punctuated by the record of a beautiful incident in verses 16ff., which relates the Lord's further provision for His people's needs, and well illustrates Isaiah's famous words, "Before they call, I will answer" (Isa. 65:24), for on this occasion they did not even voice their need of water to the Lord. It was He who took the initiative and told Moses to gather them together so that He might provide them with water. More importantly, perhaps, the divine initiative forestalled any possible complaint from them so that, instead of murmuring, songs of praise rang out from them. In the comment on 21:1–3 reference was made to a new spirit among the people, and this is exemplified to a marked degree here.

The overriding impression throughout these verses is that of movement, from one place to another. This is surely a parable of deeper spiritualities, for the impression is given that Israel was now "getting somewhere." It is always this that makes hearts sing for joy.

The song of the wells (vv. 17–18) is a lovely fragment. One commentator says that it "refers not to the discovery of a specific well, but is rather a popular song addressed to a well by the women who gathered round it," and remarks that such songs are still sung by the Bedouin even today. Sturdy, in the Cambridge Bible Commentary, quotes one such, as follows:

> Flow, water, spread abundantly!
> Wood, camel, do not scorn it!
> With sticks we have dug it![8]

Pisgah (v. 20) was the mount from which Moses was later to view the land (Deut. 3:27), and where he was to die (Deut. 34:1ff.). One can readily imagine the sense of anticipation that must have gripped both him and the people as they finally came within sight of their longed-for destination. This also is surely reflected in the spirit of rejoicing that these song fragments convey.

Matthew Henry adds a characteristic comment on the phrase in verse 17, *"Spring up, O well"*: "As the brazen serpent was a figure of Christ, who is lifted up for our cure, so is this well a figure of the

Spirit, who is poured forth for our comfort, and from whom flow to us *rivers of living waters* (John 7:38). Does this well spring up in our souls? We should sing to it; take the comfort to ourselves, and give the glory to God."[9]

Holy Spirit, Joy Divine,
Gladden Thou this heart of mine;
In the desert ways I sing,
"Spring, O Well, for ever spring!"

The Defeat of Sihon and Og

21:21 Then Israel sent messengers to Sihon king of
the Amorites, saying,
22 "Let me pass through your land. We will not
turn aside into fields or vineyards; we will not drink
water from wells. We will go by the King's Highway
until we have passed through your territory."
23 But Sihon would not allow Israel to pass through
his territory. So Sihon gathered all his people together
and went out against Israel in the wilderness, and he
came to Jahaz and fought against Israel.
24 Then Israel defeated him with the edge of
the sword, and took possession of his land from the
Arnon to the Jabbok, as far as the people of Ammon;
for the border of the people of Ammon *was* fortified.
25 So Israel took all these cities, and Israel dwelt in
all the cities of the Amorites, in Heshbon and in all
its villages.
26 For Heshbon *was* the city of Sihon king of the
Amorites, who had fought against the former king of
Moab, and had taken all his land from his hand as far
as the Arnon.
27 Therefore those who speak in proverbs say:
"Come to Heshbon, let it be built;
Let the city of Sihon be repaired.
28 "For fire went out from Heshbon,
A flame from the city of Sihon;
It consumed Ar of Moab,
The lords of the heights of the Arnon.

29 Woe to you, Moab!
You have perished, O people of Chemosh!
He has given his sons as fugitives,
And his daughters into captivity,
To Sihon king of the Amorites.
30 "But we have shot at them;
Heshbon has perished as far as Dibon.
Then we laid waste as far as Nophah,
Which *reaches* to Medeba."
31 Thus Israel dwelt in the land of the Amorites.
32 Then Moses sent to spy out Jazer; and they took
its villages and drove out the Amorites who *were*
there.
33 And they turned and went up by the way to
Bashan. So Og king of Bashan went out against them,
he and all his people, to battle at Edrei.
34 Then the LORD said to Moses, "Do not fear
him, for I have delivered him into your hand, with
all his people and his land; and you shall do to him
as you did to Sihon king of the Amorites, who dwelt
at Heshbon."
35 So they defeated him, his sons, and all his people, until there was no survivor left him; and they
took possession of his land.

Num. 21:21–35

The incidents recorded in these verses are similar in content and significance to Israel's earlier experience in 20:14–22 with Edom. Once again, as on the previous occasion, Moses declared his intention of going *"by the King's Highway"* (v. 22); but to no avail, and the Amorites confronted Israel just as Edom had earlier done, but with this difference, that whereas on the former occasion Israel skirted their opponents, here confrontation took place, and battle was joined. There was no alternative to this, indeed, since there was no other route for Israel to take to the Jordan river. Further advance by Israel brought a similar conflict with Og, king of Bashan, who was likewise defeated and his territory possessed.

These two victories are referred to and looked back upon in later books of the Old Testament as deeply significant in the settlement of Canaan by Israel, as may be seen from Deuteronomy 1:4, 2:24ff., 3:1–11, 4:47, 29:7; Joshua 9:10, 12:4; and Judges 11:19ff. As Numbers

32:1 ff. indicates, these were the territories that were first to be settled, and "their settlement was an assurance that the Promised Land of Canaan would also be conquered and settled by Israel."[10]

The song or poem which forms the centerpiece of this passage (vv. 27–30) presents problems for interpretation. Gray maintains that "the one thing that is clear is that the poem celebrates a victory over Moab. Everything else is more or less uncertain."[11] Wenham says his own suggestion, that it was apparently composed by Amorite bards to celebrate Sihon's defeat of Moab, follows the traditional Jewish view and has recently returned to scholarly favor. He adds:

> It is probably inserted here to justify Israel's right to hold the land. It appears that at one time Moab had occupied the land lying between the Arnon and the Jabbok, but Sihon had defeated Moab, as this song recalls, Now, Israel had conquered Sihon. Thus Israel showed itself superior to Moab as well as to the Amorites, and therefore Moab had no right to claim it back from Israel.[12]

This incident, like that recorded in 20:14–22, symbolizes the conflict between the people of God and the world. It is, ultimately, an irreconcilable conflict, and one that is fought to the death. What is said in verse 34 is ever the heritage of God's people in the ongoing battle. It is God's battle, and the victory is His. All that is needed is for His people to be at one with Him in His purposes in the world. Given this, no power on earth can finally resist or oppose them. But the work of God always advances by the way of conflict whether in Old Testament times or in New, or today, and it is unrealistic for us to think otherwise, or to imagine that we will ever get by in our Christian experience without encountering opposition of one kind or another. As the apostle Paul puts it, "We must through many tribulations enter the kingdom of God."

NOTES

1. Critical commentators do not seem to know what to make of the judgment passed on Moses here. L. Elliott Binns, *The Book of Numbers*

(London: Methuen & Co., Ltd., 1927), p. 131. Binns's comment is: "The reason for the exclusion of Moses and Aaron from the land of promise is exceedingly obscure and from the present story no real clue can be discovered: there is no lack of faith, no disobedience, or rebellion against Jehovah. It looks as if the sources, if they contained originally some sin of the two leaders, had been toned down, and the real reason lost."

G. B. Gray, *A Critical and Exegetical Commentary on Numbers,* International Critical Commentary (Edinburgh: T. & T. Clark, 1903), p. 262. Gray says, "Whether the use Moses makes of (the rod) was also in accordance with Yahweh's command cannot be determined, for the Divine instructions as to the use of the rod are now missing from the story."

Gordon J. Wenham, *Numbers,* Tyndale Old Testament Commentaries (Leicester: Inter-Varsity Press, 1981), p. 150. Wenham, however, while finding the incident puzzling is in substantial agreement with the interpretation we have given: "Though this (the striking of the rock) brought forth water, it was not produced in the divinely intended way, and counted as rebelling against God's command and unbelief."

2. Binns, *Numbers,* p. 133, "Edom was a land of narrow defiles and passes, and to introduce a large body of foreigners into it, revealing to them the secret ways, would have been highly dangerous. The wide promises of Moses would have been difficult to carry out with a large and badly disciplined host like the Israelites."

3. Adolph Saphir, *Christ and Israel,* p. 165.

4. Wenham, *Numbers,* p. 153, thinks differently about this. His comment, "Clinically, without a hint of emotion until verse 29, the death of Israel's first high priest is recorded. This low-key description emphasizes the inevitability of the Judgment of Aaron (24; cf. 12) for his disobedience at Meribah," seems uncharacteristically lacking in perception.

5. Binns, *Numbers,* p. 135.

6. Wenham, *Numbers,* pp. 157–158.

7. Ibid., p. 159, quoting Christensen's translation.

8. J. Sturdy, *Numbers,* The Cambridge Bible Commentary (Cambridge: Cambridge University Press, 1976), p. 151.

9. Matthew Henry, *Genesis–Deuteronomy,* Commentary on the Whole Bible (Old Tappan, N.J.: Fleming H. Revell Co.), p. 667.

10. Wenham, *Numbers,* p. 163.

11. Gray, *Numbers,* p. 300.

12. Wenham, *Numbers,* p. 161 (note).

CHAPTER FIFTEEN

The "Balaam" Incident

Numbers 22:1–24:25

INVITATION AND REFUSAL

22:1 Then the children of Israel moved, and camped
in the plains of Moab on the side of the Jordan *across*
from Jericho.
2 Now Balak the son of Zippor saw all that Israel
had done to the Amorites.
3 And Moab was exceedingly afraid of the people
because they *were* many, and Moab was sick with
dread because of the children of Israel.
4 So Moab said to the elders of Midian, "Now this
company will lick up everything around us, as an ox
licks up the grass of the field." And Balak the son of
Zippor *was* king of the Moabites at that time.
5 Then he sent messengers to Balaam the son of
Beor at Pethor, which *is* near the River in the land
of the sons of his people, to call him, saying: "Look, a
people has come from Egypt. See, they cover the face
of the earth, and are settling next to me!
6 "Therefore please come at once, curse this people for me, for they *are* too mighty for me. Perhaps
I shall be able to defeat them and drive them out
of the land, for I know that he whom you bless *is*
blessed, and he whom you curse is cursed."
7 So the elders of Moab and the elders of Midian
departed with the diviner's fee in their hand, and
they came to Balaam and spoke to him the words of
Balak.
8 And he said to them, "Lodge here tonight, and I

will bring back word to you, as the LORD speaks to
me." So the princes of Moab stayed with Balaam.
9 Then God came to Balaam and said, "Who *are*
these men with you?"
10 So Balaam said to God, "Balak the son of Zippor,
king of Moab, has sent to me, *saying,*
11 'Look, a people has come out of Egypt, and they
cover the face of the earth. Come now, curse them for
me; perhaps I shall be able to overpower them and
drive them out.'"
12 And God said to Balaam, "You shall not go with
them; you shall not curse the people, for they *are*
blessed."
13 So Balaam rose in the morning and said to the
princes of Balak, "Go back to your land, for the
LORD has refused to give me permission to go with
you."
14 And the princes of Moab rose and went to
Balak, and said, "Balaam refuses to come with us."

Num. 22:1–14

This chapter marks the beginning of the final part of the Book of Numbers, and from this point to the end of the book a miscellaneous collection of narratives, laws, and regulations are presented as having taken place or having been formulated during Israel's encampment in the plains of Moab. The first of these narratives, and undoubtedly the most striking, concerns Balaam, a Gentile seer who was hired by Balak, king of Moab, to curse Israel and frustrate their onward march. Balak was led by the Spirit of God in a most remarkable way to utter words concerning Israel and her future in the divine purposes which on any interpretation must rank as among the most striking ever uttered.

The story is remarkable and impressive in the range of its teaching, but it is not without its problems in interpretation. What is recorded in it emerges directly from the account given in the previous chapter of the triumphs of Israel over Sihon and Og. It is in the context of the forward march of the people of God that Balak's attempt to bring a curse on them must be seen. This gives one very valuable key to a proper interpretation, for it indicates that here was an attempt to hinder, frustrate, and destroy the work and the people of God. There is no doubt that this is the significance which the New Testament gives to the story (cf. 2 Peter 2:15, Jude 11, Rev. 2:14). Hitherto, the attacks on Israel had been direct, and these had been repulsed; but now this was a more subtle attack, and all the more dangerous because it was indirect. The story is therefore important for the light it throws upon the unseen warfare against the principalities and powers arrayed against the work and purpose of God—and on the way in which the evil one uses his wiles to hinder and frustrate that work. It will be best, however, to leave further comment until we look at the details of the narrative.

The custom of cursing an enemy before battle was widespread in the ancient world, and Balaam seems to have gained a reputation as an effective operative who could be relied upon, on the payment of an appropriate fee (v. 7), to give satisfaction. We are quickly made to see, however, that this is no ordinary transaction, for, as verse 8 indicates, Balaam is conscious of being under some constraint, and he bids the elders of Moab to tarry for a night until he receives some word from the Lord. The use of the divine names in these verses is perplexing. Balaam using the revealed name "Jehovah" in verse 8, but the narrator using "Elohim" in verses 9 and 10. It would seem from verse 12 that Balaam was ignorant of the special relationship in which Israel stood with Jehovah and needed to be told that they were a people "blessed" by Him and were not to be cursed. The implication is clear, nevertheless, that the Lord had made Himself known in some definite way to Balaam, and that he was conscious of a divine overruling in the whole matter.

The divine instruction given to Balaam was unequivocal: He was forbidden to go with the princes of Moab, and he told them so without hesitation (v. 13). If the matter had been left there, there would have been no problem, but as we will see in the verses which follow, Balak refused to accept this rejection. Some commentators suggest that there was more to Balaam's refusal at this point than meets the eye, and that he may well have adopted this apparently uncompromising attitude with a view to the possibility of further and more generous offers being made to him by Balak.[1] It is fair to say, however, that there is no support in the text at this point for attributing avarice and greed to Balaam: this is a judgment that can be made only from reading the story as a whole and taking into consideration the New Testament comments made upon it.

THE WARNING VOICE OF GOD

> 22:15 Then Balak again sent princes, more numerous and more honorable than they.
> 16 And they came to Balaam and said to him, "Thus says Balak the son of Zippor: 'Please let nothing hinder you from coming to me;
> 17 'for I will certainly honor you greatly, and I will do whatever you say to me. Therefore please come, curse this people for me.' "
> 18 Then Balaam answered and said to the servants of Balak, "Though Balak were to give me his house full of silver and gold, I could not go beyond the word of the LORD my God, to do less or more.
> 19 "Now therefore, please, you also stay here tonight, that I may know what more the LORD will say to me."
> 20 And God came to Balaam at night and said to him, "If the men come to call you, rise *and* go with them; but only the word which I speak to you—that you shall do."
> 21 So Balaam rose in the morning, saddled his donkey, and went with the princes of Moab.
>
> *Num. 22:15–21*

It is at this point in the narrative that the complications begin to arise. Balak, as has been indicated, was not prepared to accept Balaam's original pronouncement, and sent another, more highly powered, delegation to the prophet promising further inducements. Balaam's response to this (v. 18) was entirely in harmony with his earlier attitude in verse 13, and what he said must surely be regarded as being in harmony with the best prophetic tradition of later times in Israel. It is all the more perplexing, therefore, that he should have asked Balak's delegates to stay with him overnight in order to see whether the Lord would have more to say to him (v. 19). What more could have been said than had been said in verse 12, in such unequivocal terms? The suspicion inevitably arises that Balaam had at least some hopes that the situation might change. It is here that questions about his moral character begin to arise for us.

It is surely in this light that we must seek to interpret the remarkable change in the divine instructions to the prophet (v. 20), when he was given permission to go with Balak's emissaries. Wenham's comments here are interesting: "Balaam may go, but he may say and do only what God permits. The listener or reader is meant to be surprised and to ask himself why this apparent change of mind on God's part? Will Balaam really be allowed to curse Israel after all? The next scene answers such questions beyond ambiguity."[2] One source regards Balak "as persisting after God's first refusal and so bringing ruin upon himself."[3] If there is substance in these observations, as there certainly seems to be, they can only mean that God was reading the prophet's heart and, seeing the mixed motives there, and the desire for gain, said to him in effect, "Very well, have your own way, and go with them"—in the spirit of Psalm 106:15, "He gave them their request, but sent leanness into their soul." This seems to be confirmed in the statement in verse 22 about God's anger being aroused because he went.

The Donkey and the Angel

22:22 Then God's anger was aroused because he went, and the Angel of the LORD took His stand in the way as an adversary against him. And he was riding on his donkey, and his two servants *were* with him.

23 Now the donkey saw the Angel of the LORD standing in the way with His drawn sword in His hand, and the donkey turned aside out of the way and went into the field. So Balaam struck the donkey to turn her back onto the road.

24 Then the Angel of the LORD stood in a narrow path between the vineyards, *with* a wall on this side and a wall on that side.

25 And when the donkey saw the Angel of the LORD, she pushed herself against the wall and crushed Balaam's foot against the wall; so he struck her again.

26 Then the Angel of the LORD went further, and stood in a narrow place where there *was* no way to turn either to the right hand or to the left.

27 And when the donkey saw the Angel of the LORD, she lay down under Balaam; so Balaam's anger was aroused, and he struck the donkey with his staff.

28 Then the LORD opened the mouth of the donkey, and she said to Balaam, "What have I done to
you, that you have struck me these three times?"
29 And Balaam said to the donkey, "Because you
have abused me. I wish there were a sword in my
hand, for now I would kill you!"
30 So the donkey said to Balaam, "*Am* I not your
donkey on which you have ridden, ever since *I became* yours, to this day? Was I ever disposed to do
this to you?" And he said, "No."
31 Then the LORD opened Balaam's eyes, and he
saw the Angel of the LORD standing in the way with
His drawn sword in His hand; and he bowed his
head and fell flat on his face.
32 And the Angel of the LORD said to him, "Why
have you struck your donkey these three times? Behold, I have come out to stand against you, because
your way is perverse before me.
33 "The donkey saw Me and turned aside from Me
these three times. If she had not turned aside from
Me, surely I would also have killed you by now, and
let her live."
34 And Balaam said to the Angel of the LORD, "I
have sinned, for I did not know You stood in the way
against me. Now therefore, if it displeases You, I will
turn back."
35 Then the Angel of the LORD said to Balaam, "Go
with the men, but only the word that I speak to you,
that you shall speak." So Balaam went with the
princes of Balak.

Num. 22:22–35

The critical, albeit complicated, part of the story is unfolded in these verses. If the above interpretation is valid, and Balaam had a secret hankering after gain, the confrontation described here was surely inevitable. It is an eloquent commentary on the deceitfulness of the human heart that men should allow their estimation of what is God's will to be colored and decided by their own secret hankerings and determinations.

There were two elements in the confrontation: on the one hand, it was the expression of the divine anger (this is the force of "adversary" in v. 22) against Balaam for what he was intent on doing; on the other hand, it was designed to restrain him from advancing further on a road that was inevitably to lead him headlong into disaster. The impressive—and frightening—thing, however, is that although Balaam's donkey could "see" the angel (the animal's reaction to the sense of the supernatural is entirely convincing, in this regard), Balaam himself remained entirely unaware of the angel's presence until he was abruptly brought to his senses by the speaking of the animal (another supernatural and miraculous manifestation). One feels for the donkey in this story, clearly terrified as it was by the presence of the angel, on the one hand, and harassed and ill-treated by Balaam on the other. It was, as we say, caught between two fires. As such it may be said to represent the suffering brought upon the entirely innocent by those who are out of joint and at odds with God. The blight that unconsecrated lives inevitably spread all around them is one of the uglier and more shameful aspects of sin.

Wenham makes a similar point about the donkey when he says that "its acts and words anticipate the problems Balaam is about to face. The ass was caught three times between the angel's sword and Balaam's stick. Soon Balaam will find himself trapped three times between Balak's demands and God's prohibitions."[4]

The phenomenon of talking animals is an intriguing one, commentators making reference to frequent occurrences of this in classical literature. There was a common Jewish belief that before the Fall, the beasts and man had a common speech.[5] One readily thinks in this connection of St. Francis of Assisi's extraordinary rapport with birds. Also, C. S. Lewis's *Narnia* books make the point about talking animals in a plausible way that reminds us we do not have sufficient knowledge about pre-fallen creation to dismiss the concept out of hand.

We do not know whether the word "donkey" had the same kind of connotation as it sometimes has for us today, but it does seem that there is a certain fitness for our thinking that it took a donkey to demonstrate to Balaam the real nature of what he was doing. One thinks in this connection of the psalmist's words, "O God, You know my foolishness" (Ps. 69:5). It would almost seem as if the Lord was grimly determined to show Balaam just how foolish and ill-guided he was.

We should not underestimate the nature and extent of his blindness, however—it is a solemn and frightening reminder of what sin when deliberately indulged can do to our powers of perception, and how it can "put out our eyes" and render us insensitive to spiritual realities. The later dialogue between Balaam and the angel (vv. 32ff.) shows that grace was still nevertheless at work in this strange and unusual incident; for the angel points out (v. 33) that but for the donkey's reaction Balaam would have been destroyed. His eyes, it seems, had been opened just in time. How humiliating it must have been for the seer, who prided himself on having eyes for divine revelation, to realize that he had not been able to see what his dumb donkey had seen. Truly, as Paul says in 1 Corinthians 1:27, "God has chosen the foolish things of the world to put to shame the wise."[6]

Balaam and Balak

22:36 Now when Balak heard that Balaam was coming, he went out to meet him at the city of Moab, which *is* on the border at the Arnon, the boundary of the territory.
37 Then Balak said to Balaam, "Did I not earnestly send to you, calling for you? Why did you not come to me? Am I not able to honor you?"
38 And Balaam said to Balak, "Look, I have come to you! Now, have I any power at all to say anything? The word that God puts in my mouth, that I must speak."
39 So Balaam went with Balak, and they came to Kirjath Huzoth.
40 Then Balak offered oxen and sheep, and he sent *some* to Balaam and to the princes who *were* with him.
41 So it was, the next day, that Balak took Balaam and brought him up to the high places of Baal, that from there he might observe the extent of the people.

Num. 22:36–41

The last verses of the chapter recount the eventual meeting between Balaam and Balak, who was understandably somewhat cool and reproachful of the seer for his delay in coming, and for his, to Balak, unaccountable reluctance to "perform" in response to the generous overtures made to him (v. 37). Balaam's answer to the king simply repeated what he had already said to the king's messengers in verse 18. By indicating to him that he was "under orders" to speak only what the Lord allowed him to speak he showed he had learned his lesson from the donkey (v. 38); but it may have been better, and safer, for him to have said something to Balak about his dramatic encounter with the angel of the Lord, for that would surely have impressed upon Balak the futility of his desire to bring a curse on the people whom God was determined to bless. That Balaam did not do so may well be an indication that, even then, he was still not utterly reconciled to the divine will and still, it may be, hankering after some gain from the transaction. At all events, the hint of asperity in his voice in verse 38 is disquieting and may not be unconnected with the fact that later in the story his "counsel" (see 31:16, and compare 25:1 ff., and Rev. 2:14) led Israel into grave and terrible sin. What he could not do by cursing the people of God he succeeded in doing by deceit. This is a solemn and frightening thought, and due consideration should be given to it in our understanding of the story.

THE FIRST ORACLE

23:1Then Balaam said to Balak, "Build seven altars for me here, and prepare for me here seven bulls and seven rams."

2 And Balak did just as Balaam had spoken, and Balak and Balaam offered a bull and a ram on *each* altar.

3 Then Balaam said to Balak, "Stand by your burnt offering, and I will go; perhaps the LORD will come to meet me, and whatever He shows me I will tell you." So he went to a desolate height.

4 And God met Balaam, and he said to Him, "I have prepared the seven altars, and I have offered on *each* altar a bull and a ram."

5 Then the LORD put a word in Balaam's mouth, and said, "Return to Balak, and thus you shall speak."

6 So he returned to him, and there he was, standing by his burnt offering, he and all the princes of
Moab.

7 And he took up his oracle and said:
"Balak the king of Moab has brought me from
Aram,
From the mountains of the east.
'Come, curse Jacob for me,
And come, denounce Israel!'
8 "How shall I curse whom God has not cursed?
And how shall I denounce *whom* the LORD has
not denounced?
9 For from the top of the rocks I see him,
And from the hills I behold him;
There! A people dwelling alone,
Not reckoning itself among the nations.
10 "Who can count the dust of Jacob,
Or number one-fourth of Israel?
Let me die the death of the righteous,
And let my end be like his!"

11 Then Balak said to Balaam, "What have you done
to me? I took you to curse my enemies, and look, you
have blessed *them* bountifully!"

12 So he answered and said, "Must I not take heed
to speak what the LORD has put in my mouth?"

Num. 23:1–12

In this and in the next chapter we have on record the four oracles or prophecies uttered by Balaam under the constraint of the Spirit of God. They are remarkable for their insight and are indicative of the sovereign control that the living God had over this recalcitrant and double-dealing seer.

It is interesting and striking to realize that throughout the whole of the Balaam incident Israel was unaware of anything happening behind the scenes. Here was a battle taking place in the unseen, in which the powers of darkness vied with the covenant grace of God to overthrow God's people and do them ill, and an instance of how God protected them from hidden dangers and foes. The Watcher of Israel, who neither slumbers nor sleeps, was fulfilling His promised role on their behalf.

The preparations recorded in verses 1–3 show that Balaam was "going through the motions of" seeking the face of the Lord. This may have been to convince Balak of the genuineness of his approach, and therefore to absolve him, so to speak, of any responsibility of what the Lord would say. A case could well be made for suggesting that the wily seer was "hedging his bets" so as to safeguard his own position against any possible repercussions that might follow an adverse answer from the Lord. At all events, we should certainly recognize that Balaam had put himself in considerable danger, in being obliged to prophesy blessing instead of cursing upon Israel, as he was about to do, with the king and all his nobles and their attendant forces around him. He must have realized he was in jeopardy of his life. This prompts the reflection that it would have been so much easier for Balaam to have said no at the beginning, and refused to go to the king in the first place. Ah yes! But when we willfully take a wrong turning, God is intent upon teaching us in painful fashion that our own way is fraught with complication, embarrassment, and even danger to life. It is as if God had said to him, "I told you not to go with these men, at the beginning; but you *would* go, and you must now take the consequences of your foolish and ill-considered determination. You will have to say no to them several times in much more difficult circumstances than you would have needed to do at the beginning." Well might Jesus say, "*My* yoke is easy, and *My* burden is light." We often make spiritual life far more complicated for ourselves than it need have been, and than it was meant to have been.

Once Balaam had started on his own way, however, he was not permitted to turn back. Doubtless, after his encounter with the angel of the Lord, he would have far preferred to have turned back into the wilderness of Pethor, and washed his hands of Balak and his nobles. But, once begun on the forbidden course, he was obliged to keep to it. This is the only way we will sometimes learn properly that God means His will to be taken seriously, and that it is good and acceptable and perfect, and that no other way is either safe or salutary for us. We find ourselves in a prison of our own making, and there is not often a remission of sentence.

The Lord seemed to be impatient of Balaam's ritual in verses 1–3, however, and ignored Balaam's reference to the sacrifices he had prepared (v. 4), thrusting His word into the seer's mouth and commanding him to go and speak it to the king (v. 5).

Balaam's prophecy "is in the form of a poem of seven couplets after the manner of Hebrew parallelism, the second line merely repeating, in different language, the thought of the first."[7] The prophet begins with a brief statement of how he comes to be prophesying about Israel, and points out that he had been summoned by Balak from Aram (Mesopotamia) for the purpose of pronouncing a curse on the people of God. But how, he says, could he curse a people for whom God had very different ideas and intentions? Thus early in his utterances Balak was given the indication that things were not to be as he had planned and intended.

Under the constraint of the Spirit, Balaam uttered a plain word about Israel in verse 9: *"A people dwelling alone, not reckoning itself among the nations."* Balaam clearly discerned the separated character of this people whom God had called to be His own. It is a word that has been marvelously fulfilled and literally true of Israel down thirty long centuries of turbulent history, in which empires have waxed and waned, and nation after nation has tried to destroy them, but in vain. It is impressive and wonderful that so long ago such a clear delineation of the future should be given to man. This is what God does when evil men presume to threaten and sidetrack His purposes and His people. It is almost as if God, being challenged concerning His chosen people, went out of His way to make it clear, not only to Balak, but to all posterity, that here was a people for whom He had the most wonderful and far-reaching purposes.

What we have in Balaam's prophecies is an uncovering of the divine plan of the ages, that which underlies the whole redemptive history of the Bible, the plan of redemption fulfilled in Christ, but prepared for and foreshadowed down the centuries until the fullness of the time when He should come, to give Himself as a ransom for the sins of many.

In verse 10, the words *"Who can count the dust of Jacob?"* are a clear allusion to Genesis 13:16, a remarkable evidence that this seer from Mesopotamia must have had access to some history of God's people; and what follows at the end of the verse, *"Let my end be like his,"* is an expression of Balaam's desire to be included in the promise given to Abraham in Gen. 12:3: "In you all the families of the earth shall be blessed."

Balak's irritation and anger in verse 11 is entirely understandable, but Balaam reiterates his earlier insistence that he must speak only what the Lord put into his mouth.

THE SECOND ORACLE

23:13 Then Balak said to him, "Please come with me
to another place from which you may see them; you
shall see only the outer part of them, and shall not
see them all; curse them for me from there."
14 So he brought him to the field of Zophim, to the
top of Pisgah, and built seven altars, and offered a
bull and a ram on *each* altar.
15 And he said to Balak, "Stand here by your burnt
offering while I meet *the* LORD over there."
16 Then the LORD met Balaam, and put a word in
his mouth, and said, "Go back to Balak, and thus you
shall speak."
17 So he came to him, and there he was, standing
by his burnt offering, and the princes of Moab were
with him. And Balak said to him, "What has the
LORD spoken?"
18 Then he took up his oracle and said:
"Rise up, Balak, and hear!
Listen to me, son of Zippor!
19 "God *is* not a man, that He should lie,
Nor a son of man, that He should repent.
Has He said, and will He not do?
Or has He spoken, and will He not make it
good?
20 Behold, I have received a *command* to bless;
He has blessed, and I cannot reverse it.
21 "He has not observed iniquity in Jacob,
Nor has He seen wickedness in Israel.
The LORD his God *is* with him,
And the shout of a King *is* among them.
22 God brings them out of Egypt;
He has strength like a wild ox.
23 "For *there is* no sorcery against Jacob,
Nor any divination against Israel.

It now must be said of Jacob
And of Israel, 'Oh, what God has done!'
24 Look, a people rises like a lioness,
And lifts itself up like a lion;
It shall not lie down until it devours the prey,
And drinks the blood of the slain."
25 Then Balak said to Balaam, "Neither curse them
at all, nor bless them at all!"
26 So Balaam answered and said to Balak, "Did I
not tell you, saying, 'All that the LORD speaks, that
I must do'?"

Num. 23:13–26

The second prophecy or oracle was prepared for and given to Balaam in the same way as the first (vv. 14, 16). There are two things in particular to notice in it, but before dealing with them it is as well to consider the mysterious fact that such authentic words from God should have been spoken by, and through, a man of such questionable character. For we can hardly suppose, in view of what ultimately followed at the end of the story, that Balaam was walking in fellowship with God. All the evidence seems to point in the opposite direction, and to the fact that his double-dealing, wily nature was sovereignly overruled by God. It is clear that Balaam's words were what we would term an ecstatic prophetic utterance, and this, as has been pointed out, does not in itself signify particular spirituality, nor does it follow that those thus prophesying are necessarily good and faithful servants of God, as this story, and a similarly graphic one in 1 Samuel 19:18–24 (which see) make plain. Nor must we forget our Lord's solemn reminder in Matthew 7:21–23 that prophesying in His name does not even guarantee acceptance with Him at the last.

The first point for us to notice is Balaam's conviction as to the unchanging nature of God's covenant promises to Israel stated as clearly and plainly as it was centuries later by the apostle Paul in Romans 11:29: "The gifts and the calling of God are irrevocable." Balaam's way of putting it (v. 19) is impressive: *"God is not a man, that He should lie,/Nor a son of man, that He should repent./Has he said, and will He not do? Or has He spoken, and will He not make it good?"* This is surely a word that we need to take to ourselves day by day and, in looking at how faithfully it has been fulfilled to Israel, be assured that what He has said to us, He will also do. It was, in fact, a resounding rebuke to Balak for supposing that he could manipulate the living God, either by bribe or by magic or any other means.

The second point to note is what is said of Israel in verse 21. This does not mean that the people of God were sinless, or that God overlooked their sins—we have seen in this ongoing history only too clearly that this is not true—but rather that no sin of theirs could weary His exhaustless mercy, or cause Him to abrogate His covenant or His purposes with them. Many times He sorely punished them for their sins, but He never left them or forsook them, for His covenant's sake. He was indeed with them, and the shout of a King was among them (this last has reference to their triumphant progress into the Promised Land, with the ark in their midst). The Lord was indeed their King, as well as their God but, as Wenham adds, "He was no distant emperor: He lived and reigned among them. The tabernacle was set up to be a portable palace, with the ark as God's throne."[8]

That this is the true interpretation of verse 21 is borne out in verses 22ff. which explicitly refer to the beginning of their pilgrimage from Egypt to the Promised Land. It was this demonstration of divine power on behalf of Israel that made any attempt, by sorcery or divination, to harm the people of God a futile and fruitless exercise. The purposes of God for His people were to give them complete victory over all their enemies (v. 24). Some awareness of this seems to have gotten through to Balak, who now began to think it would be better for Balaam to say nothing either for or against Israel (v. 25), than to speak in such positive terms about them. But Balaam was under divine constraint: speak he must, as God commanded him (v. 26), as the next section clearly shows.

The Third Oracle

> 23:27 Then Balak said to Balaam, "Please come, I will take you to another place; perhaps it will please God that you may curse them for me from there."
>
> 28 So Balak took Balaam to the top of Peor, that overlooks the wasteland.
>
> 29 Then Balaam said to Balak, "Build for me here seven altars, and prepare for me here seven bulls and seven rams."

30 And Balak did as Balaam had said, and offered
a bull and a ram on *every* altar.
24:1 Now when Balaam saw that it pleased the
LORD to bless Israel, he did not go as at other times,
to seek to use sorcery, but he set his face toward the
wilderness.
2 And Balaam raised his eyes, and saw Israel encamped according to their tribes; and the Spirit of
God came upon him.
3 Then he took up his oracle and said:
"The utterance of Balaam the son of Beor,
The utterance of the man whose eyes are
opened,
4 The utterance of him who hears the words of
God,
Who sees the vision of the Almighty,
Who falls down, with eyes wide open:
5 "How lovely are your tents, O Jacob!
Your dwellings, O Israel!
6 Like valleys that stretch out,
Like gardens by the riverside,
Like aloes planted by the LORD,
Like cedars beside the waters.
7 He shall pour water from his buckets,
And his seed *shall be* in many waters.
"His king shall be higher than Agag,
And his kingdom shall be exalted.
8 "God brings him out of Egypt;
He has strength like a wild ox;
He shall consume the nations, his enemies;
He shall break their bones
And pierce *them* with his arrows.
9 'He bows down, he lies down as a lion;
And as a lion, who will rouse him?'
"Blessed *is* he who blesses you,
And cursed *is* he who curses you."
10 Then Balak's anger was aroused against Bal-
aam, and he struck his hands together; and Balak
said to Balaam, "I called you to curse my enemies,
and look, you have bountifully blessed *them* these
three times!
11 "Now therefore, flee to your place. I said I

would greatly honor you, but in fact, the LORD has
kept you back from honor."
12 So Balaam said to Balak, "Did I not also speak
to your messengers whom you sent to me, saying,
13 'If Balak were to give me his house full of silver
and gold, I could not go beyond the word of the
LORD, to do good or bad of my own will. What
the LORD says, that I must speak'?

Num. 23:27–24:13

Balak, however, for all his misgiving, was nothing if not persistent, and he tried yet again to get Balaam to curse Israel by suggesting another place from which to do so. Apparently, he had not as yet realized that there was no place from which the people of God could be cursed. But Balaam was certainly getting the message, and on this occasion changed his tack (v. 1) by going into the wilderness, where he viewed the encamped Israelites spread out before him. The sight seems to have moved him deeply, and the Spirit of God came upon him, causing him to prophesy once again. On the two earlier occasions, it was a case of the word of the Lord being given him, whereas here the seer was brought into an ecstatic state, in which he began to prophesy. Perhaps we are meant to regard this variation in procedure as a cumulative effect of some significance, as if to underline that God was really intent on blessing, and not cursing, His people. In any event, the blessing Balaam pronounced on Israel in this third oracle was very definite, and of a twofold nature: on the one hand, he spoke of the glorious prosperity of Israel and the exaltation of their kingdom (vv. 5–7); on the other, he spoke of the terrible power, so fatal to all their foes, of this people who had been sent to be a curse or a blessing to all the nations (vv. 8–9).

The first part of the vision (vv. 5–7) presents an impressive picture of an ideal Israel, so to speak—Israel as seen in the mind and purpose of God. It is a picture of beauty and prosperity, of a land that God was bountifully to bless, and it reminds us of another moving description, given in Deuteronomy 11:11–12, of "a land for which the Lord your God cares." The words in verse 7 are particularly graphic: the nation is personified as a man carrying two buckets of water—"that leading source of all blessing and prosperity in the burning east."[9] This is a beautiful picture, of the true Israel "pouring out the living waters of salvation, the pure streams of the spirit, and making the wilderness of the world to rejoice and be glad."[10] This is fulfilled ultimately only in Christ, in and through whom rivers of living water flow out to mankind.

In the second part of the blessing (vv. 8–9), it is the power of Israel that is described. As put by one scholar, "The fulness of power that dwelt in the people of Israel was apparent in the force and prowess with which their God brought them out of Egypt" (cf. 23:22).[11] Not only the wild ox, however, but also the lion figures in the metaphor describing the strength of Israel. It is almost as if Balaam were rebuking the temerity of Balak for presuming to want to curse such a people. "You are treading on perilous ground, Balak," he seems to say, "and you must beware. If you rouse the lion, it will be to your cost."

One or two further points may be made before we leave this passage. It is clear that Balaam underwent a visionary experience here, although his viewing of the Israel encampment in verse 2 is clearly to be taken literally. It was the site of their encampment, however, that seems to have brought about the vision, in which he *"saw"* this ideal Israel and *"heard"* God's words about them. Balaam is spoken of in verse 3 as a man *"whose eyes are opened."* However, the word translated *"opened"* occurs only here, and its meaning, according to Noth, is uncertain,[12] and Elliott Binns translates it as "closed." Either way, however, the sense is not materially changed, since the closing of the bodily eye and the opening of the inward eye may be said to be complementary aspects of the same experience.

The somewhat oblique and cryptic reference to a future king for Israel in verse 7b is developed more fully in the next oracle (24:17). Here, the reference seems simply to be to a future defeat of Israel's oldest enemy, Amalek, but in view of the later reference in the next oracle a Messianic "hint" can hardly be discounted.[13]

The Farewell Message

24:14 "And now, indeed, I am going to my people.
Come, I will advise you what this people will do to
your people in the latter days."
15 So he took up his oracle and said:
"The utterance of Balaam the son of Beor,

And the utterance of the man whose eyes are opened;
16 The utterance of him who hears the words of God,
And has the knowledge of the Most High,
Who sees the vision of the Almighty,
Who falls down, with eyes wide open:
17 "I see Him, but not now;
I behold Him, but not near;
A Star shall come out of Jacob;
A Scepter shall rise out of Israel,
And batter the brow of Moab,
And destroy all the sons of tumult.
18 "And Edom shall be a possession;
Seir also, his enemies, shall be a possession,
While Israel does valiantly.
19 Out of Jacob One shall have dominion,
And destroy the remains of the city."
20 Then he looked on Amalek, and he took up his
oracle and said:
"Amalek *was* first among the nations,
But *shall be* last until he perishes."
21 Then he looked on the Kenites, and he took up
his oracle and said:
"Firm is your dwelling place,
And your nest is set in the rock;
22 Nevertheless Kain shall be burned.
How long until Asshur carries you away captive?"
23 Then he took up his oracle and said:
"Alas! Who shall live when God does this?
24 But ships *shall come* from the coasts of Cyprus,
And they shall afflict Asshur and afflict Eber,
And so shall *Amalek,* until he perishes."
25 So Balaam rose and departed and returned to
his place; Balak also went his way.

Num. 24:14–25

Balak, blind to the warning implicit in the seer's words in verses 3–9, became still angrier with him, as verses 10ff. indicate, and summarily indicated his dismissal of the unobliging prophet. But before the dismissal could take place Balaam fell into another trance and uttered a further, final prophecy which in content surpassed all the others for its profound depths and insights. It is an extraordinary word. Not only did Balaam become the mouthpiece of God to declare the divine purpose for the chosen people, but also the vehicle of revelation of His ultimate design in choosing them as His people, namely the preparation and coming forth of a Redeemer. One has only to read these verses, especially 17 and 19, to sense the high dignity and mystery of their message. The Star from Jacob and the Scepter from Israel point forward to Christ Himself, who is the fulfillment of these wonderful words. To say this is not of course to minimize or call in question earlier and partial fulfillments of the prophecy. Noth is right when he says, "It is highly probable that what is conceived of here is the future glory of King David and that it is the historical emergence of David that forms the background of this discourse,"[14] some three hundred years after this time. But as Wenham observes, "traditional Jewish and Christian interpreters have seen another and fuller realization of these prophecies in the Messiah."[15] Thus early in history, therefore, the gospel was proclaimed in prophecy—not to Israel, but to the Gentile nations. One can only marvel that such clear vision should have come so anciently, and through such a man!

The prophecy itself is a fourfold one divided by the repetition of the words, "he took up his oracle," in verses 15, 20, 21, and 23. The first part refers to Edom and Moab (vv. 17, 19), the two nations that were related to Israel; the second to Amalek, the ancient archenemy of Israel (v. 20); the third to the Kenites, who were allied to Israel (vv. 21–22); and the fourth to the great powers of the world that were to be overthrown (vv. 23–24). It is true that these prophecies received at least partial fulfillment in the time of the early monarchy, especially in the reign of David. However, as the later historical books (1 and 2 Samuel) make clear, these subjugations were temporary. Hence the repeated oracles in the pre-exilic prophets foretelling further doom for them. It is surely implicit in Balaam's words that the divine kingdom which he foresaw would be realized in David only in its first and imperfect beginnings, and that its completion would not be attained until the coming of "great David's greater Son," the Messiah Himself "who breaks in pieces all the enemies of Israel, and founds an everlasting kingdom, to which all the kingdoms and powers of this world are to be brought into subjection."[16]

One or two further comments of a general nature may be made by way of postscript to this remarkable story. Reference was made earlier (see p. 243) to the way in which the Balaam incident throws light upon the unseen warfare against the principalities and powers that are arrayed against the work and purpose of God, and on the way in which the evil one uses his wiles to hinder and frustrate that work. We may add that one of the most important things for us to see is that Satan found his tool in a "servant of God" who was out of joint spiritually, and who wanted the best of both worlds. This was the doorway through which Satan was able to attack the people of Israel. This contains its own warning for us: we may never know just how much harm and injury we may do the work of God—and the people of God—if we are out of joint spiritually, and therefore become the unwitting tool of the devil. He is never slow to grasp an opportunity, or to jump at any chance we give him. Renegades, of whatever sort, usually succeed in doing much more harm than ordinary enemies of the faith.

One of the impressive lessons of the story is the way in which God overruled this attempt to bring evil on Israel and turned the curse into blessing. This serves to emphasize just how sovereignly God was determined to protect and preserve His people, in spite of all their waywardness and rebellion. It reveals the strength of the bond that existed between Him and His people. His mercy was ever toward them, and it went ill with any who tried to harm those whom He was determined to bless. Perhaps the chief lesson here, however (and that which the New Testament writers take up in their application), is the character study it gives of Balaam himself. It is a remarkable picture of the battle that went on in his own heart—a battle for integrity of character, a battle which he eventually lost, if we interpret the last stage of the story aright. Thus, within the battle to harm and hurt Israel, there was also this hidden battle for the soul of a man.

Balaam was not a Hebrew; yet he was a worshiper of the living God. He was one of those outside the covenant who "found" the Lord and served Him, like Jethro, priest of Midian, and others. He was clearly known to Balak of Moab as a man with a reputation for spiritual power. We have here an interesting commentary on the misunderstanding of spiritual power that can grow in a man's mind. Balaam seems to think that the power could be exercised thus unscrupulously and wantonly, without reference to the moral nature of the God who was supposed to be the source of it! How little some men discern about the nature of God!

One perplexing aspect of the story is that, tool of the devil though he was, Balaam was nevertheless genuinely wrought upon by the Spirit of God. He was used by Him, however reluctant a messenger he may have been. This also reflects the reality of the divine sovereignty: God can and does take up men who are not in, or who have gotten out of, His best, directive will. He is prepared to bless us and use us within the limits which we ourselves impose upon Him by our sinfulness and willfulness. We may think of this in relation to men who have failed and perhaps permanently jeopardized God's purposes for them. Jeremiah's remarkable parable about the potter's vessel illustrates this well (Jer. 18:1 ff.): when the vessel was marred in the hand of the potter, he made it again into another vessel—not the one he had first designed and planned, but another, and still usable, although in a different way. This is a solemn and sobering thought and is often reflected both in personal life and on a larger scale. We should not forget that God is still using His chosen people Israel in the world today in spite of themselves, even in their rejection of the Messiah, as a signpost in the world.

By the same token, however, this fact stands as a solemn warning, in the reminder it gives us that "having a word from the Lord" does not of itself necessarily mean that a man must be a great saint.

However paradoxical, not to say contradictory, this may be, it is nevertheless true that men who have spoken a true word from the Lord may also be seriously defective and deficient in character. I recall a ministerial colleague commenting on this mystery and speaking of a man known to him as an effective soul-winner whose life was marked by manifest moral blemishes. The truth is, prophecy is one of the gifts of the Spirit, and gifts are not graces. As Samuel Rutherford once said, "Gifts neither break nor humble; grace does both." Nor should we forget our Lord's solemn warning in Matthew 7:22–23 that prophesying and casting out demons in His name is no guarantee of acceptance with God on the Great Day. It is only too possible to have gifts and be deficient in the grace that makes men Christlike. It is not only more important, it is infinitely more important to magnify the Savior in a humble, lowly walk with God than to possess the greatest gifts. Well might the apostle Paul say, "Let him who thinks he stands take heed lest he fall" (1 Cor. 10:12).

NOTES

1. L. Elliott Binns, *The Book of Numbers* (London: Methuen & Co., Ltd., 1927), p. 154. "The negotiations seem definitely to be closed, though oriental methods of bargaining may have led Balaam—taking the lowest view of his character—to anticipate fresh efforts to re-open them; Balak evidently took this view of the matter." Wenham (op. cit.), pp. 167–168, suggests a similar possibility, particularly in view of the dubious light in which New Testament writers speak of Balaam.

2. Gordon J. Wenham, *Numbers,* Tyndale Old Testament Commentaries (Leicester: Inter-Varsity Press, 1981), p. 170.

3. Binns, *Numbers,* p. 155. Binns quotes Dean Stanley.

4. Wenham, *Numbers,* p. 171.

5. Binns, *Numbers,* p. 157.

6. Martin Noth, *Numbers,* Old Testament Library (London: SCM Press, 1968), p. 178. Noth's introductory comment on the episode is interesting: "With its clarity, with its artistic presentation of suspense and of dramatic heightening, the episode of the ass is a masterpiece of ancient Israelite narrative art. At the heart of it lies the idea that an unprejudiced animal can see things to which a man in his willfulness is blind; there is certainly also in this respect the presupposition that Yahweh's messenger was in himself 'visible' in the usual way, just as elsewhere in the Old Testament the messenger of Yahweh, when he appears, is thought of as visible in human form and, in the present context, with a drawn sword held threateningly in his hand."

7. Binns, *Numbers,* p. 160.

8. Wenham, *Numbers,* p. 175.

9. Carl L. Keil and Franz Delitzsch, *Numbers,* Commentary on the Old Testament (Grand Rapids: Wm. B. Eerdmans, repr. 1971), 3:188.

10. C. J. Ellicott, *Leviticus,* An Old Testament Commentary for English Readers (London: Cassell & Co., Ltd., 1897), p. 547. Ellicott is quoting Bishop Wordsworth's observations.

11. Keil and Delitzsch, *Numbers,* p. 190.

12. Noth, *Numbers,* p. 190.

13. Keil and Delitzsch, *Numbers,* p. 190. "The king of Israel, whose greatness was celebrated by Balaam, was therefore neither the Messiah exclusively, nor the earthly kingdom without the Messiah, but the kingdom of Israel that was established by David, and was exalted in the Messiah into an everlasting kingdom, the enemies of which would all be made its footstool (Ps. ii. and cx.)."

14. Noth, *Numbers,* p. 192.

15. Wenham, *Numbers,* p. 178. He goes on: "This is characteristic of

many messianic passages in the Old Testament. On one level they are but expressions of hope for a good and righteous king. But on another plane, they must be looking for something more, for no real king ever came up to the ideals expressed (e.g., Ps. 72; Is. 11, etc.). In interpreting these last words of Balaam both perspectives must be respected. Primarily they refer to royal triumphs in the period of the early monarchy, but these victories prefigure the greater conquests of Christ at his first and second advents."

16. Keil and Delitzsch, *Numbers,* p. 200.

CHAPTER SIXTEEN

Various Laws and Incidents

Numbers 25:1–31:54

The Sin of Baal-peor

25:1 Now Israel remained in Acacia Grove, and the people began to commit harlotry with the women of Moab.

2 They invited the people to the sacrifices of their gods, and the people ate and bowed down to their gods.

3 So Israel was joined to Baal of Peor, and the anger of the LORD was aroused against Israel.

4 Then the LORD said to Moses, "Take all the leaders of the people and hang the offenders before the LORD, out in the sun, that the fierce anger of the LORD may turn away from Israel."

5 So Moses said to the judges of Israel, "Every one of you kill his men who were joined to Baal of Peor."

Num. 25:1–5

In stark contrast to the wonderful prophecies uttered by Balaam concerning Israel, these verses describe yet another moral and spiritual declension on the part of God's people. Wenham usefully points out that there are clear parallels in the arrangement of Numbers between the events at Sinai and those in the plains of Moab. In both, the revelation of God was followed by a flouting of basic covenant principles: the giving of the Law was followed by the making of the golden calf, and Balaam's prophecies were followed by the idolatry and immorality of Baal-peor.[1] The verses indeed make sad reading. They occur at this point, at the end of the Balaam incident because of a connection with it indicated by Moses in 31:16 where it is said that the women of Moab "caused the children of Israel, *through the counsel of Balaam,* to trespass against the Lord in the incident at Peor." It would seem from this that Balaam, before quitting the country, had suggested to Balak that if the Israelites could be seduced into the idolatry and impurity of the worship practiced at Baal of Peor by the Moabites, they might even yet come under the curse of the Lord. This evil course was followed: Israel was duly tempted, was corrupted, and in the war that followed, Balaam was slain by the sword (31:8).

There is a timely warning for us in this. There is a superficial attitude to the idea of Balaam being in God's "second best" that might make us complacently settle for this ourselves, so long as He will still bless us (within the limits we ourselves impose on Him by our sin). Some men are not overconcerned about being in God's "second best," and indeed would be content with much less. But it is much easier to fall and to make mistakes when in this shadow-land of spiritual experience. That is how it was with Balaam. He had not crucified his double motives and had not learned to hate his sin; and in the end, events went out of his control. The evil thing rose up again within him, and he fell tragically, coming to an inglorious end on the battlefield and bringing woe upon Israel. And so he leaves the stage of history, having at the last done devil's work, a total dupe of Satan, when he might have been an example and inspiration to succeeding ages (cf. 1 Cor. 10:12).

THE ZEAL AND REWARD OF PHINEHAS

25:6 And indeed, one of the children of Israel came and presented to his brethren a Midianite woman in the sight of Moses and in the sight of all the congregation of the children of Israel, who *were* weeping at the door of the tabernacle of meeting.

7 Now when Phinehas the son of Eleazar, the son of Aaron the priest, saw *it,* he rose from among the congregation and took a javelin in his hand;

8 and he went after the man of Israel into the tent and thrust both of them through, the man of Israel,

and the woman through her body. So the plague was
stopped among the children of Israel.
9 And those who died in the plague were twenty-
four thousand.
10 Then the LORD spoke to Moses, saying:
11 "Phinehas the son of Eleazar, the son of Aaron
the priest, has turned back My wrath from the children of Israel, because he was zealous with My zeal
among them, so that I did not consume the children
of Israel in My zeal.
12 "Therefore say, 'Behold, I give to him My covenant of peace;
13 'and it shall be to him and his descendants after
him a covenant of an everlasting priesthood, because
he was zealous for his God, and made atonement for
the children of Israel.'"
14 Now the name of the Israelite who was killed,
who was killed with the Midianite woman, *was* Zimri
the son of Salu, a leader of a father's house among
the Simeonites.
15 And the name of the Midianite woman who was
killed *was* Cozbi the daughter of Zur; he *was* head of
the people of a father's house in Midian.

Num. 25:6–15

The extent of the corruption that afflicted Israel is well demonstrated in these verses. From verse 8 we may gather that a plague had been sent on them as a judgment on their evil ways, and this had produced at least some semblance of contrition (v. 6b). But not enough, as the ugly incident recorded in verse 6a makes clear. It is the brazenness of Zimri's action that was so sinister and was an indication of just how far the poison had spread within the nation. It is generally in the later and more advanced stages of the corruption of society that sin becomes blatant and open. For long enough, it is concealed and covered in the murky and hidden dens of vice; but when it parades itself arrogantly and shamelessly in its contempt for accepted convention and for the standards of God, it is revealed for what it really is—rejection of God and rebellion against Him. That Zimri was the son of a noble house (v. 14) serves to compound the sin, for he was one who by his status must surely have been in a position to exercise an influence over many in Israel.

Those in prominent positions in society need to recognize that privilege involves responsibility. They are not in any sense free to live as they like, but rather are accountable to the God who gave them their privileges. They would do well to remember this.

The action and reaction of Phinehas was radical and extreme, and as one scholar remarks, his zeal became proverbial.[2] Doubtless he would have had his critics who would seriously have questioned whether the sin merited such harsh treatment, but we should take note of the fact that God vindicated him in no uncertain fashion (vv. 11–13). He, at least, was in no doubt as to the seriousness and heinousness of what Zimri had done; and this prompts the reflection that when men differ in their views from God's estimate of the situation and take issue with Him, it is they who are making the error of judgment, not God. It is refreshing to have this divine testimony concerning what we might call a "hard line" attitude to sin. God is, apparently, not in the least afraid of being thought censorious—or of His servants and champions being thought censorious, either. Rather, it is a question of calling some ugly things by their proper names and dealing with them accordingly. In this permissive and morally decadent age, we could certainly do with some of this spirit.

It is true, of course, that acts of a brutal and barbarous nature, such as Phinehas's and numbers of others in the Old Testament (e.g., the assassinations of Eglon and Sisera in Judg. 3:21f., 4:21) raise grave moral issues, as Wenham rightly points out, true also that they may be a reflection of the barbarism of the times.[3] But what we must beware of is the danger of falling into the simplistic expedient of branding them as sub-Christian, as if they belonged to an era when "they did not know any better." One has only to think of some of the desperate exploits of World War II, and the many cruelties and atrocities that took place on both sides, and which raise many moral problems for the Christian today. Even to mention this is to indicate that we are touching on vast and complex moral questions involving the whole question of whether war with its attendant evils is ever justified. Is assassinating a heathen monarch in such a brutal way worse, or better, or different from using napalm or bombing civilian targets? These are very real questions, and we must not yield to the temptation of giving merely "emotional reaction" answers to them. Primitive, Old Testament barbarities are mere dilettantism by comparison with the horrors of twentieth-century inhumanity to man.

The all-important consideration here is the divine approval given to Phinehas's act, as indicating that he was zealous with God's own zeal in the matter, as a result of which atonement was made for the children of Israel, so that they were not consumed (vv. 11, 13).

The Punishment of the Midianites

25:16 Then the LORD spoke to Moses, saying:
17 "Harass the Midianites, and attack them;
18 "for they harassed you with their schemes by which they seduced you in the matter of Peor and in the matter of Cozbi, the daughter of a leader of Midian, their sister, who was killed in the day of the plague because of Peor."

Num. 25:16–18

The final verses of the chapter tell of God's command to Moses to fight against the Midianites and smite them because of the strategem they had practiced on the Israelites by tempting them to idolatry. One authority says that this was "in order that the practical zeal of Phinehas against sin, by which expiation had been made for the guilt, might be adopted by all the nation."[4] Wenham is right to remind us that "for Paul, the main point of the story is that Christians should beware of the dangers of immorality. Like the other stories of judgment from the wilderness, 'these things are warnings for us' (1 Cor. 10:6–8)."[5]

The Command to Moses and Eleazar

26:1 And it came to pass, after the plague, that the LORD spoke to Moses and Eleazar the son of Aaron the priest, saying:
2 "Take a census of all the congregation of the children of Israel from twenty years old and above, by their fathers' houses, all who are able to go to war in Israel."
3 So Moses and Eleazar the priest spoke with them in the plains of Moab by the Jordan, *across from* Jericho, saying:

> 4 "*Take a census of the people* from twenty years old and above, just as the LORD commanded Moses and the children of Israel who came out of the land of Egypt."
>
> *Num. 26:1–4*

After the fascinating and dramatic chapters unfolding the story of Balaam, we come to the record of another census. Moses and Eleazar are commanded to take the numbers of the people, from twenty years old and above, to ascertain the military strength of Israel for warfare against Midian (cf. 25:16ff.) and for the conquest of Canaan. The previous census took place forty years earlier, in the Wilderness of Sinai (cf. chs. 1–4); this one is taken in the plains of Moab, "*after the plague*" (v. 1). Wenham suggests a particular reason for this census as being "to determine the relative size of the tribes so that they should each receive a proportionate share of territory in the promised land (26:52–56)."[6] In the first census a man taken out of every tribe, the head of his father's house, was appointed to assist Moses and Aaron. Here, however, no mention is made of this, although it may be implied in verse 4, and some such similar arrangement is likely to have operated (the words "*take a census of the people*" in verse 4 are missing from the Hebrew, and are to be understood on the basis of what was said in verse 2, which is recapitulated in greater detail, in verse 4).

THE SECOND CENSUS

> 26:5 Reuben *was* the firstborn of Israel. The children of Reuben *were*: *of* Hanoch, the family of the Hanochites; *of* Pallu, the family of the Palluites;
>
> 6 *of* Hezron, the family of the Hezronites; *of* Carmi, the family of the Carmites.
>
> 7 These *are* the families of the Reubenites: those who were numbered of them were forty-three thousand seven hundred and thirty.
>
> 8 And the son of Pallu *was* Eliab.
>
> 9 The sons of Eliab *were* Nemuel, Dathan, and Abiram. These *are* the Dathan and Abiram, representatives of the congregation, who contended against

Moses and Aaron in the company of Korah, when they contended against the LORD;

10 and the earth opened its mouth and swallowed them up together with Korah when that company died, when the fire devoured two hundred and fifty men; and they became a sign.

11 Nevertheless the children of Korah did not die.

12 The sons of Simeon according to their families *were: of* Nemuel, the family of the Nemuelites; *of* Jamin, the family of the Jaminites; *of* Jachin, the family of the Jachinites;

13 *of* Zerah, the family of the Zarhites; *of* Shaul, the family of the Shaulites.

14 These *are* the families of the Simeonites: twenty-two thousand two hundred.

15 The sons of Gad according to their families *were: of* Zephon, the family of the Zephonites; *of* Haggi, the family of the Haggites; *of* Shuni, the family of the Shunites;

16 *of* Ozni, the family of the Oznites; *of* Eri, the family of the Erites;

17 *of* Arod, the family of the Arodites; *of* Areli, the family of the Arelites.

18 These *are* the families of the sons of Gad according to those who were numbered of them: forty thousand five hundred.

19 The sons of Judah *were* Er and Onan; and Er and Onan died in the land of Canaan.

20 And the sons of Judah according to their families were: *of* Shelah, the family of the Shelanites; *of* Perez, the family of the Parzites; *of* Zerah, the family of the Zarhites.

21 And the sons of Perez were: *of* Hezron, the family of the Hezronites; *of* Hamul, the family of the Hamulites.

22 These *are* the families of Judah according to those who were numbered of them: seventy-six thousand five hundred.

23 The sons of Issachar according to their families *were: of* Tola, the family of the Tolaites; of Puah, the family of the Punites;

24 of Jashub, the family of the Jashubites; of Shimron, the family of the Shimronites.

25 These *are* the families of Issachar according to those who were numbered of them: sixty-four thousand three hundred.

26 The sons of Zebulun according to their families *were:* of Sered, the family of the Sardites; of Elon, the family of the Elonites; of Jahleel, the family of the Jahleelites.

27 These *are* the families of the Zebulunites according to those who were numbered of them: sixty thousand five hundred.

28 The sons of Joseph according to their families, by Manasseh and Ephraim, *were:*

29 The sons of Manasseh: of Machir, the family of the Machirites; and Machir begot Gilead; of Gilead, the family of the Gileadites.

30 These *are* the sons of Gilead: *of* Jeezer, the family of the Jeezerites; of Helek, the family of the Helekites;

31 *of* Asriel, the family of the Asrielites; *of* Shechem, the family of the Shechemites;

32 *of* Shemida, the family of the Shemidaites; *of* Hepher, the family of the Hepherites.

33 Now Zelophehad the son of Hepher had no sons, but daughters; and the names of the daughters of Zelophehad *were* Mahlah, Noah, Hoglah, Milcah, and Tirzah.

34 These *are* the families of Manasseh; and those who were numbered of them *were* fifty-two thousand seven hundred.

35 These *are* the sons of Ephraim according to their families: of Shuthelah, the family of the Shuthalhites; of Becher, the family of the Bachrites; of Tahan, the family of the Tahanites.

36 And these *are* the sons of Shuthelah: of Eran, the family of the Eranites.

37 These *are* the families of the sons of Ephraim according to those who were numbered of them: thirty-two thousand five hundred. These *are* the sons of Joseph according to their families.

38 The sons of Benjamin according to their families

were: of Bela, the family of the Belaites; of Ashbel, the
family of the Ashbelites; of Ahiram, the family of
the Ahiramites;
39 of Shupham, the family of the Shuphamites; of
Hupham, the family of the Huphamites.
40 And the sons of Bela were Ard and Naaman: *of
Ard,* the family of the Ardites; *of* Naaman, the family
of the Naamites.
41 These *are* the sons of Benjamin according to their
families; and those who were numbered of them *were*
forty-five thousand six hundred.
42 These *are* the sons of Dan according to their
families: of Shuham, the family of the Shuhamites.
These *are* the families of Dan according to their
families.
43 All the families of the Shuhamites, according to
those who were numbered of them, *were* sixty-four
thousand four hundred.
44 The sons of Asher according to their families
were: of Jimna, the family of the Jimnites; of Jesui,
the family of the Jesuites; of Beriah, the family of
the Beriites.
45 Of the sons of Beriah: of Heber, the family of
the Heberites; of Malchiel, the family of the
Malchielites.
46 And the name of the daughter of Asher *was*
Serah.
47 These *are* the families of the sons of Asher according to those who were numbered of them: fifty-three thousand four hundred.
48 The sons of Naphtali according to their families
were: of Jahzeel, the family of the Jahzeelites; of
Guni, the family of the Gunites;
49 of Jezer, the family of the Jezerites; of Shillem,
the family of the Shillemites.
50 These *are* the families of Naphtali according to
their families; and those who were numbered of them
were forty-five thousand four hundred.
51 These *are* those who were numbered of the children of Israel: six hundred and one thousand seven
hundred and thirty.

Num. 26:5–51

At first glance it might seem that there is little to be learned and still less to be gathered and extracted of any relevant spiritual value from this "statistical return," which records the disposition of the various tribes of Israel, with but few additional comments of historical interest, such as on the story of Korah, Dathan, and Abiram (vv. 9–11), Er and Onan (v. 19), and Zelophehad (v. 33). But when we remember that the Scriptures yield their best treasures to reverent and painstaking inquiry, we begin to realize that the Holy Spirit has His own purposes in recording this detailed tribal analysis.

As Wenham points out, there are two differences between the second census and the first: one is that in the first, only the total number of men in each tribe is given, whereas here the totals include the families that make up each tribe; the other lies in the census figures themselves, where there are considerable variations.[7] Most of the tribes increased in size during the wilderness wanderings, but five show a decrease: Reuben, from 46,500 to 43,730; Gad from 45,650 to 40,500; Ephraim from 40,500 to 32,500; Naphtali from 53,400 to 45,400; and Simeon from 59,300 to 22,200. Nothing is said as to the reason for these decreases, and we are left to come to our own conclusions about them. One wonders whether the decrease in the tribe of Reuben may have to do with the incident recorded about Dathan and Abiram in 16:1 ff. (compare what is said in vv. 9–10 with the earlier account). And has the catastrophic decrease in the tribe of Simeon something to do with the fact that Zimri (25:14), a Simeonite, was involved in the Baal of Peor disaster? And is Gad's decrease due to the fact that they were associated with Reuben and Simeon in the order of the tribes?

It is a remarkable fact that the overall decrease is relatively small, from 603,550 to 601,730, even minimal, and this is surely a monument to the faithfulness of God to His promises concerning Israel. For, in spite of their many disobediences and rebellions, and the judgments that these brought upon them, God remained unchangingly true to them. He buffeted and bruised them, dealing severely with them because of their sins, but He did not let them go. At the beginning of our study of this book, we stressed that in the historical context of the divine drama of redemption some of the most important lessons to be learned were those of the sovereignty of God and His faithfulness. This is what is stressed and underlined afresh in these census figures, particularly the faithfulness to His Word and to His promise: His covenanted promises to the patriarchs might be delayed by human sin, but they could not be ultimately frustrated. The meaning and significance of Balaam's words in 23:19 are therefore brought out very clearly, and the apostle Paul underlines this basic truth just as emphatically in Romans 11:29.

It has been suggested, in connection with the words in verse 1, *"after the plague,"* that the judgment at Baal of Peor probably destroyed the remnant of the generation that had come out of Egypt. If this is so, one can see in a very graphic way the sovereignty of God at work fulfilling His will through the very actions and attitudes of His people that flouted and transgressed it. Evil was made the unwilling and unwitting tool of the divine purposes.

It has also been suggested that the decrease in numbers of the various above-mentioned tribes reads like a statistical return in an Assembly or Presbytery report, recording a decline in church membership. Perhaps there is a lesson for us here. Ellicott quotes Bishop Wordsworth as commenting, "When the Israelites were suffering persecution in Egypt they 'multiplied exceedingly' (Exod. 1:7, 20): but after their deliverance from Egypt they rebelled against God, and 'He consumed their days in vanity, and their years in trouble' (Ps. lxxviii. 33). . . . Here there is comfort and warning to the church and every soul in it—comfort in time of affliction, and warning in days of prosperity."[8]

It is an incontrovertible fact that oppression and persecution do bring life and vitality to the church. So far as my own church is concerned, Scottish history shows that the church was far more vital when she suffered persecution than in times of prosperity. And one has only to think of contemporary situations today, in churches behind the Iron Curtain, in Eastern Europe, and in Russia, where vital Christian testimony is not only being maintained but making substantial advances in spite of increasing repression and persecution; while in China, after so many years of determined efforts made by Chinese communism to stamp out the Christian faith, church growth has been quite phenomenal. Jesus said, "I will build My church, and the gates of Hades shall not prevail against it (Matt. 16:18)."

THE FAITHFULNESS OF GOD

26:52 Then the LORD spoke to Moses, saying:
53 "To these the land shall be divided as an inheritance, according to the number of names.
54 "To a large *tribe* you shall give a larger inheri-
tance, and to a small *tribe* you shall give a smaller inheritance. Each shall be given its inheritance according to those who were numbered of them.
55 "But the land shall be divided by lot; they shall
inherit according to the names of the tribes of their fathers.
56 "According to the lot their inheritance shall be
divided between the larger and the smaller."
57 And these *are* those who were numbered of the
Levites according to their families: of Gershon, the family of the Gershonites; of Kohath, the family of the Kohathites; of Merari, the family of the Merarites.
58 These *are* the families of the Levites: the family
of the Libnites, the family of the Hebronites, the family of the Mahlites, the family of the Mushites, and the family of the Korathites. And Kohath begot Amram.
59 The name of Amram's wife *was* Jochebed the
daughter of Levi, who was born to Levi in Egypt; and to Amram she bore Aaron and Moses and their sister Miriam.
60 To Aaron were born Nadab and Abihu, Eleazar
and Ithamar.
61 And Nadab and Abihu died when they offered
profane fire before the LORD.
62 Now those who were numbered of them were
twenty-three thousand, every male from a month old and above; for they were not numbered among the other children of Israel, because there was no inheritance given to them among the children of Israel.
63 These *are* those who were numbered by Moses
and Eleazar the priest, who numbered the children of Israel in the plains of Moab by the Jordan, *across from* Jericho.
64 But among these there was not a man of those
who were numbered by Moses and Aaron the priest

when they numbered the children of Israel in the Wilderness of Sinai.

65 For the LORD had said of them, "They shall surely die in the wilderness." So there was not left a man of them, except Caleb the son of Jephunneh and Joshua the son of Nun.

Num. 26:52–65

Moses is now given instructions concerning the apportionment of the land, which was to be divided among the tribes in proportion to their size: larger tribes received a larger inheritance while smaller tribes received a smaller inheritance. Presumably in cases of dispute or disagreement, the division was to be by lot, a favorite means of deciding difficult or complicated questions in ancient times[9] (the implementation of these commands is given us in Josh. 15:1 ff.).

The census of the Levites is taken separately, as at the first census. Their distinctive function and duties are repeatedly underlined. As verse 62 indicates, no tribal territory was allocated to them (we read in 35:1–8 that forty-eight villages scattered throughout the territories belonging to the other tribes were assigned to them).

In the final verses of the chapter (vv. 63–65) one significant conclusion is drawn from the record of the census—namely, that none of the former generation of Israel were left, save the two permitted exceptions, Caleb and Joshua. The wheel has now come around full circle, and a new generation of God's people is ready to enter the Promised Land.

Some concluding observations may be made before we leave this chapter. Its main, central lesson has to do with the faithfulness of God. He is faithful to His Word and to His promise. He said that none of the earlier generation of Israel would enter into the Promised Land because of their sin and unbelief, and none of them did (vv. 64–65). For thirty-eight years, God kept the nation wandering in the wilderness until the sinning generation died off. *Then,* He proceeded to lead them on and in. This is a solemn consideration, and it serves to complete the picture. The truth is, the biblical idea of divine faithfulness is two-sided, two-edged, and is so in the very nature of the case. It is impossible to have the one without the other.

Reference has already been made to Balaam's words in 23:19, "Hath He said, and shall He not do it?" There are many occasions on which we could take these words as a source of the most wonderful assurance and comfort. But this story reminds us that there is also a grimness about them that is very terrible. And it is not that *God* changes. He changes not. The change is in us. It is our attitude to Him, not His to us, that determines whether His faithfulness is a comfort or a terror to us. And, nothing can alter this inescapable fact of human existence and experience, because God cannot change His nature.

Israel's own history provides a graphic illustration of this truth. The pillar of cloud and fire was one of the great realities of their ongoing experience. To them it was a source of comfort and strength and assurance; but that same pillar was, at the same time, a source of terror to their enemies. This does not mean God was a different God to Israel than to their enemies. He was one and the same God to both: it was *they* who were different. His love and grace were anathema to them. It was this that was their condemnation.

It is a question, then, of one's attitude to God and His ways that determines whether we find Him a God of love and a source of comfort, hope, and joy, or One who is unbearable. This is the point Peter takes up in his first epistle (1 Peter 2:6ff.), when he speaks of those who find that the God who is a sanctuary to many is a stumbling stone and a rock of offense to others. Emil Brunner observes, in a passage dealing with the reality of human guilt, "The constancy, the self-consistency of God, which is primarily one of the comforting and glorious things about Him, is a terrible thing in this connection. . . . Just as previously it was comforting to know that we could reckon on God, so now it strikes terror to the heart of man to know that we *must* reckon with Him."[10] This is a lesson that Israel had to learn the hard way, in their heart-sore experience in the wilderness.

The reference to Caleb and Joshua in verse 65 is an additional indication to us of the faithfulness of God, for He was faithful to those who had been faithful to Him. Of these two faithful warriors of God the following comment has been made with impressive perception:

> What were they doing all these forty years of wandering? They were waiting for God's day to come. Like their fellows they had stood on the borders of Canaan and had been aware of the enemies and the costly conflict that had awaited the

> advancing Israelites. But they had also seen with the eyes of faith the vision of God's land and God's work going into the ever more glorious future. Their hearts responded and consented to the command to go forward, but it could not be, because of the refusal of the vast majority of the people. Being part of Israel they had to share Israel's rebuke, but all these years their hearts had neither been lured away by the deceitfulness of sin nor filled with unworthy fears regarding God's capacity and willingness to bring them to victory in the land (13:30). It must have been sore indeed for them to watch the fading away of a whole generation of people to whom such hopeful possibility had been presented, but their hearts remained loyal to God and they still looked in faith for the day of entry to come as God had promised. If ever there was an elect remnant bridging the gap from the past to the future through a derelict present, it was Joshua and Caleb.[11]

As 1 Samuel 2:30 puts it, "Those who honor Me I will honor, and those who despise Me shall be lightly esteemed."

THE INHERITANCE OF DAUGHTERS

> 27:1 Then came the daughters of Zelophehad the son of Hepher, the son of Gilead, the son of Machir, the son of Manasseh, from the families of Manasseh the son of Joseph; and these *were* the names of his daughters: Mahlah, Noah, Hoglah, Milcah, and Tirzah.
>
> 2 And they stood before Moses, before Eleazar the priest, and before the leaders and all the congregation, *by* the doorway of the tabernacle of meeting, saying:
>
> 3 "Our father died in the wilderness; but he was not in the company of those who gathered together against the LORD, in company with Korah, but he died in his own sin; and he had no sons.
>
> 4 "Why should the name of our father be removed from among his family because he had no son? Give us a possession among our father's brothers."
>
> 5 So Moses brought their case before the LORD.
>
> 6 And the LORD spoke to Moses, saying:

7 "The daughters of Zelophehad speak *what is*
right; you shall surely give them a possession of inheritance among their father's brothers, and cause
the inheritance of their father to pass to them.
8 "And you shall speak to the children of Israel,
saying: 'If a man dies and has no son, then you shall
cause his inheritance to pass to his daughter.
9 'If he has no daughter, then you shall give his
inheritance to his brothers.
10 'If he has no brothers, then you shall give his
inheritance to his father's brothers.
11 'And if his father has no brothers, then you
shall give his inheritance to the relative closest to
him in his family, and he shall possess it.'" And it
shall be to the children of Israel a statute of judgment, just as the LORD commanded Moses.

Num. 27:1–11

The subject matter of these verses is the right of daughters to inherit in the case where a man has no sons. It is an interesting and important passage in that it shows what happened when an issue arose for which there was no precedent established within the known and declared legislation at that time. The rules of inheritance up to that time in Hebrew law did not include any provision for daughters, a father's property being divided between his sons after his death, with the eldest son receiving twice as much as his brothers (cf. Deut. 21:15–17; 25:5–10). Land was kept within the family by the custom of Levirate marriage, as the references in Deuteronomy show. But the Levirate law would not apply in this instance, since on his death Zelophehad's inheritance would be transferred to his nearest male relative. His daughters' concern was that their father's name would be forgotten (v. 4).

It is clear that this whole issue must have set an important precedent, for the case of Zelophehad's daughters must have been far from unique. Here, then, was a situation in which an unprotected, defenseless family of daughters, who seemed to have no provision made for them within existing legislation, appealed to the justice and faithfulness of God for recognition and redress, and their appeal was heard and honored. The Lord made a definitive pronouncement on the matter, and this became incorporated within the legislative system of Israel. Further reference is made to the incident in Joshua 17:3ff., where this ruling was appealed to and ratified in the context of the actual apportionment of land after the conquest of Canaan.

It is remarkable to find this piece of humanitarian legislation at such an early date, when the rights of minorities, let alone minorities of women, were so little recognized or noticed, and it emphasizes once again how advanced the Mosaic code really was. But it does something far greater: it underlines the reality of the fatherly care of God for all those who have been hardly used by life, those whom misfortune has buffeted, who are the poor of the land, who tend to be forgotten in the mad whirl of life, who have few to care for them, and fewer still to plead their cause.

Here, then, is a word of encouragement for all who have found themselves in such a position of helplessness and need, lonely, unprotected, underprivileged, unprovided for, and deprived of the protection and sustaining that menfolk can give: *There is a God in heaven who cares,* who sees and understands, and will move in answer to our cries, and will provide for our needs. No one is too insignificant for Him. His tender mercies are over all His works. This is embodied supremely in the gospel narratives themselves, where we see the Son of God, Friend of sinners, making good this word to the insignificant, the poor, the oppressed—the widow of Nain, blind Bartimaeus, the women of Samaria, the lepers. He was their Champion as well as their Savior. This is a word that requires to be taken without reserve, for it is an assurance about what God is like. When we bring our pleas to Him and spell them out before Him, we may be sure that nothing of concern to us will fail to be a concern to Him. We should particularly note what is said in verse 7, "*The daughters of Zelophehad speak what is right. . . .*" They had only to speak, to explain their case, for it to be given immediate and full redress.

Wonderfully reassuring as this is, there are other, even more important, lessons the incident has to teach. We should bear in mind that Israel was still very much in the wilderness; the Promised Land was as yet a dream for them. It was not theirs at that point to apportion to the tribes. Yet, here is a group of people, Zelophehad's daughters, laying claim to an allotted part as if it had been all conquered and made over to the chosen people. Here is faith indeed! Faith in the word of promise. They did not doubt that what God had promised He would assuredly perform. And they were determined to be in on it. It is wonderful to think that in the midst of so much faithlessness, backsliding, and worldliness in Israel there should be this kind of unquestioning faith in the promises of God. This is a good example of the idea of the faithful remnant, and it reminds us that even in the darkest moments God has His seven thousand who have not bowed the knee to Baal.

Nor is it difficult to see a spiritual parallel in the incident. The Promised Land in the Old Testament is a type and illustration of salvation and eternal life, and if this is so, then the five daughters of Zelophehad were staking their claim to eternal life and laying hold upon it. This is a graphic and telling illustration of how to enter the kingdom of God. They considered the promises of God, they interpreted them in relation to their own case, and then they applied them personally to their own needs and desires. To take God at His word and deed is to make the promises one's own by claiming them, laying hold on them by simple faith. Matthew Henry, in his own penetrating way, suggests that in this respect these five daughters of Zelophehad were indeed five wise virgins, and one wonders whether in fact our Lord may conceivably have had them in mind when He told the parable in Matthew 25.[12]

Moses and His Successor

27:12 Now the LORD said to Moses: "Go up into this Mount Abarim, and see the land which I have given to the children of Israel.

13 "And when you have seen it, you also shall be gathered to your people, as Aaron your brother was gathered.

14 "For in the Wilderness of Zin, during the strife of the congregation, you rebelled against My command to hallow Me at the waters before their eyes." (These *are* the waters of Meribah, at Kadesh in the Wilderness of Zin.)

15 Then Moses spoke to the LORD, saying:

16 "Let the LORD, the God of the spirits of all flesh, set a man over the congregation,

17 "who may go out before them and go in before

them, who may lead them out and bring them in,
that the congregation of the LORD may not be like
sheep which have no shepherd."
18 And the LORD said to Moses: "Take Joshua the
son of Nun with you, a man in whom *is* the Spirit,
and lay your hand on him;
19 "set him before Eleazar the priest and before all
the congregation, and inaugurate him in their sight.
20 "And you shall give *some* of your authority to
him, that all the congregation of the children of
Israel may be obedient.
21 "He shall stand before Eleazar the priest, who
shall inquire before the LORD for him by the judgment of the Urim; at his word they shall go out, and
at his word they shall come in, *both* he and all the
children of Israel with him, all the congregation."
22 So Moses did as the LORD commanded him. He
took Joshua and set him before Eleazar the priest and
before all the congregation.
23 And he laid his hands on him and inaugurated
him, just as the LORD commanded by the hand of
Moses.

Num. 27:12–23

The word about Moses in verses 12–14 stands in marked contrast—a contrast that can hardly be accidental—to the account of Zelophehad's daughters in the previous verses. They were promised an inheritance in the land, but Moses is excluded. The reference in verse 14 is to the incident recorded in 20:1–13, when he rebelled against God and "spoke rashly with his lips" (Ps. 106:33). For further elaboration of this see Deuteronomy 3:23–28 and 32:48–52, particularly the first of these references, where the anger of the Lord against the patriarch is specifically mentioned. It is clear that this was a deeply serious infringement on Moses' part, and it had fateful consequences for him.

His "sentence" needs to be properly understood and assessed, however. There was no question, in his being forbidden entry of the Promised Land, of his being excluded from the blessings of eternal life (any more than the original generation of Israel were because of their sin at Kadesh Barnea, 14:22ff.), but Moses' ill-considered irritation and anger at the waters of Meribah was a costly mistake for him in that it excluded him from the privilege of leading Israel into the Promised Land.

We may learn from this that the sins of the saints, though they will never lead to forfeiture of eternal life, can affect their ultimate reward (cf. 1 Cor. 3:12–15, 9:25–27; 1 John 2:28), and can affect also their continuing usefulness and serviceableness to God. This solemn story stands in Scripture as a timely warning to all who believe on Him that we may never presume upon His grace. Carelessness and neglectfulness in spiritual things, although forgiven, may nevertheless cost the children of God dearly. It is sobering to realize that in the scriptural record we have several instances of servants of God, honored and owned of Him in the most signal of ways, falling sadly and tragically in the later days of their lives—Noah, Moses, David, Solomon. If this has a lesson for us, it is that there are dangers concealed in the spiritual life for those who have advanced beyond the elementary stages and have been going on faithfully and steadily for many years. Well might the prophet pray, "O Lord, revive Your work *in the midst of the years*"—the middle years, when we are at the height of our powers. *There* is the danger point!

It might be thought that this judgment on Moses was rather harsh—and disproportionate to the offense. But we may be sure that God did not deal arbitrarily with His honored servant.[13] Who shall know whether Moses' sin may have done something to him that made him incapable of furthering the divine purpose with His people? This is the point at issue—incapacitation for future work. If, in fact, the ongoing work of the Lord requires continual enlargement of capacity for its fulfillment, no one can afford to jeopardize or impair the possibility of that enlargement through sin.

A simple illustration, of the kind the apostle Paul was in the habit of using, may make this point: In the field of athletics, if a world-class runner damages a muscle, and it heals leaving a weakness, he may still be a very fine athlete, but he may no longer be able to give the superb, classical performance as before. Something will have come in to disqualify him permanently from that exalted place where only two or three names are mentioned. So it was with Moses: sin in the believer is forgiven, but it may do permanent damage to his usefulness and disqualify him forever from the kind of purpose God has for him. This is frightening—and God means it to be so—to warn us to beware, and at all costs guard and battle against sin.

Moses' almost matter-of-fact acceptance of the fact that someone else would lead Israel into the Promised Land should not conceal from us the costliness to him of such a verdict (as the reference in Deut. 3:23 ff. surely makes clear), but it says much for the stature of the man that he should have addressed himself so humbly and with all submission to the appointment of a successor (v. 15 ff.). His pastoral care for the people is very moving: his chief concern is that Israel be not left as sheep without a shepherd, and Joshua is chosen as the next undershepherd of Israel. It seems clear from verses 18–21 that his leadership was not to be quite the same as that of Moses: he was to bear a similar authority (v. 20), but whereas the Lord spoke to Moses face to face (12:6–8), Joshua was to have the word of the Lord mediated to him through Eleazer the priest in the use of the Urim and Thummim (v. 21).[14] For all that, however, there can be no doubt about the sense of continuity in this succession, as the laying on of Moses' hands is meant to indicate (v. 18).

Just as in the case of Moses' sin we spoke of disqualification, so now in Joshua's case we may speak of qualification. To be sure, grace is ever the principle on which the work of God operates, and we cannot ever speak of "qualifying" for grace. At the same time, however, just as sin reduces our capacity for the kind of enlargement that God's work needs, so in the same way obedience and responsiveness to the grace of God and to His good and perfect will creates the possibility of enlargement of capacity. This sets us in the way of further positive service. Jesus said, "Whoever has, to him more will be given" (Luke 8:18), and these words are particularly true in this connection. God had had His hand on young Joshua from the beginning, and had destined him for a work of strategic significance. Early on in the record of Numbers, the young warrior passed a test that did something to him (cf. the account of the spies' expedition and Joshua's spirited testimony at Kadesh Barnea in 14:6 ff.). It enlarged his capacity and led him on in the things of God. And in the fullness of the time, God called him forward. As Isaiah 49:2 puts it, "In the shadow of His hand He has hidden me and made me a polished shaft; in His quiver He has hidden me"—until the appointed time.

Here, then, is the Old Testament "apostolic succession"; and we should note particularly the spiritual qualifications involved (v. 18). There was nothing arbitrary, still less hereditary in the choice.

Joshua had shown himself worthy, and now the mantle of Moses was to rest on him (v. 20). It may be going too far for us to assert that Moses was set aside by God in the sense that Paul uses the word "disqualified" in 1 Corinthians 9:27, and we cannot say how long he might have gone on as leader of Israel if he had not spoken rashly with his lips; but what we do see here is that God's work goes on, none hindering. Soon Moses was to climb up Mount Pisgah, his work over, and lie down to rest, being gathered to his fathers. As the saying has it, "God buries His workmen, but carries on His work." And we see in the appointment and anointing of Joshua the steady, onward movement of the divine purposes. God's work goes on. He invites our cooperation and participation; when we are obedient, the work is carried forward, and we are blessed and enriched in sharing it. When we disobey, it still goes on—but we are hurt and damaged by our folly. God help us to learn and to obey at all costs, in humble submission and surrender to His holy and perfect will.

Daily Offerings

28:1 Now the LORD spoke to Moses, saying,
2 "Command the children of Israel, and say to them, 'My offering, My food for My offerings made by fire as a sweet aroma to Me, you shall be careful to offer to Me at their appointed time.'
3 "And you shall say to them, 'This *is* the offering made by fire which you shall offer to the LORD: two male lambs in their first year without blemish, day by day, as a regular burnt offering.
4 'The one lamb you shall offer in the morning, the other lamb you shall offer in the evening,
5 'and one-tenth of an ephah of fine flour as a grain offering mixed with one-fourth of a hin of pressed oil.
6 '*It is* a regular burnt offering which was ordained at Mount Sinai for a sweet aroma, an offering made by fire to the LORD.
7 'And its drink offering *shall be* one-fourth of a hin for each lamb; in a holy *place* you shall pour out the drink to the LORD as an offering.
8 'The other lamb you shall offer in the evening;

as the morning grain offering and its drink offering,
you shall offer *it* as an offering made by fire, a sweet
aroma to the LORD.

Num. 28:1–8

The subject matter of this chapter and the one which follows relates to public worship and the various regulations concerning it. Sacred feasts and the offering of sacrifices lie at the heart of the religion of Israel and indeed of the whole concept of biblical worship, and numerous chapters throughout the Pentateuch are devoted to the various regulations involved. In an extended and valuable introductory note to this chapter Gordon J. Wenham makes mention of earlier references in Exodus, Leviticus, and in Numbers itself (15:1 ff.), but points out that the central concern here is different since these chapters prescribe the type and number of sacrifices to be offered on every day of the year, and that it is the priestly duties that are paramount. He also discusses why these laws about sacrifice should come at this point in the book and suggests that they stand as a strong re-affirmation of the promise to Joshua and the rest of the people that God really meant what He said when He promised to bring them into the land of Canaan: "These laws about sacrifices then contribute to the note of triumph that grows ever louder as the border of Canaan is reached."[15]

But this also must be said: it should be borne in mind just where in the story of God's dealings with His people we now stand. The old generation of Israel, which had sinned away its opportunity to enter into the land by its failure and unbelief at Kadesh Barnea, had now all died off. God was dealing with the new generation that was about to go in to possess it, under the leadership of Joshua. It is significant that, just as He had given the original generation detailed instructions as to the observing of feasts and ordinances at Sinai, so now He does likewise with the new generation. In other words, God underlined once more the foundations for Israel's life. "If you are to be My people," He seems to say, "then this is how it must be with you. This is the priority, and this must be the basis and foundation of all your experience."

Here, then, is a lesson at the outset: one generation had failed, and in taking up another, God was saying in effect that the only hope of averting failure was the establishing of a true pattern of worship.

The significance of this is that at the heart of these instructions for worship lies the matter of a right relationship with God. It is here that everything hopeful begins, as it is the lack of such a relationship that spells foreboding and disaster for the people of God.

In this connection one recalls an interesting comment made by James S. Stewart in his fine book *Heralds of God* on the centrality of worship. He quotes the late Archbishop of Canterbury William Temple as once having propounded a thesis which he admitted many people would feel to be outrageous and fantastic: "This world can be saved from political chaos and collapse by one thing only, and that is worship." And Dr. Temple proceeded to define worship as follows: "To worship is to quicken the conscience by the holiness of God, to feed the mind with the truth of God, to purge the imagination by the beauty of God, to open the heart to the love of God, to devote the will to the purpose of God."[16]

One can easily see, looking back, how this lay at the heart of the failure and loss that the first generation of Israel experienced. Their long history of murmuring, their hankering after the old ways, their secret desires for the fleshpots of Egypt—all this indicated a wrong relationship with God. They were not right with Him; Kadesh Barnea was simply the summing up of their continual spiritual sickness, the inevitable culmination and fruit of past disobedience and rebellion. They had failed to discern the heart and essence of all God had said to them in the earlier enactments—namely, that He wanted a people for Himself, to walk in fellowship with Him. This is the purpose of creation. God has not willed to be alone in His universe: He seeks the fellowship of the creatures He has made. Indeed, He has made us in such a way that *only* in fellowship with Him do we find ourselves and attain our true destiny as human beings.

And, having failed with one generation, God began again. What could underline more graphically the reality of the patience and long-suffering of God than this? And what lessons there are to be learned from this, the chief of which is the same for us as it was for Israel. Everything true and hopeful and fruitful in Christian life begins with a spirit of worship, indicative of a right relationship with God!

We should notice particularly the implication in these verses of the emphasis on the offerings being made both morning and evening. It is that Israel's day was to be bounded and compassed on all sides by worship. Life was to begin and end with God. This is not merely a matter of starting and ending the day with prayer, for it is of course possible to do this and still live a practically godless life. Rather, what it means is that the whole of life is to be set in the context of God, lived for God and lived unto God. This is life as it was meant to be, and as it was designed to be—inter-penetrated by the dimension of the eternal, touched and suffused by the supernatural—the life, indeed, of heaven upon earth.

Certainly, this is the only life that ultimately tells for God: only thus can we truly serve Him and bring forth fruit unto Him, for His glory. At the same time, however, we must beware of the danger of regarding this merely as a means to an end. Fellowship with God, regarded as a means to an end, the end being fruitfulness of service, can become a great snare, and will ultimately lead to the same kind of failure to which the first generation of Israel succumbed. Fellowship with God is an end in itself, and service for Him is the incidental, though inevitable, fruit of it.

This is emphasized in the New Testament, in the record of our Lord's calling of His disciples, in Mark 3:14: "He appointed twelve, *that they might be with Him* and that He might send them out to preach." In this respect, the familiar catch-phrase "saved to serve" may be called in question. This is not the biblical emphasis: rather, it is "saved for Himself." We are redeemed *unto God,* primarily, and only afterward unto service.

Such, then, is the *rationale* behind the sacrificial offerings ordained for Israel in these verses. It remains to make only two further observations before leaving them. The first concerns the phrase in verse 2, "*as a sweet aroma to Me.*" Underlying the whole sacrificial system is the idea of atonement. The sacrifices were essentially propitiatory in nature: they bear witness to the fact that some solemn and decisive transaction must be accomplished for any relationship with God to become possible. Brunner finely expresses it thus: "The atoning sacrifice represents the truth that something must happen, if there is to be peace between God and man, if the communion which has been broken by sin is to be restored. Indeed, there is a further truth behind the shedding of blood in the atoning sacrifice: blood must actually flow, for man has forfeited his life by his rebellion against his Creator and Lord."[17] The sacrifice turns away the divine anger provoked by human sin, making peace and fellowship possible.

The second point is to remind ourselves that the New Testament views all the sacrifices of the old covenant as pointing forward to Christ and finding their fulfillment in Him. They had no intrinsic worth, as such, but were but shadows cast upon the course of history by the Lamb slain from the foundation of the world.[18]

Offerings for Sabbath and New Moon

> 28:9 'And on the Sabbath day two lambs in their first year, without blemish, and two-tenths *of an ephah* of fine flour as a grain offering, mixed with oil, with its drink offering—
>
> 10 '*this is* the burnt offering for every Sabbath, besides the regular burnt offering with its drink offering.
>
> 11 'At the beginnings of your months you shall present a burnt offering to the LORD: two young bulls, one ram, and seven lambs in their first year, without blemish;
>
> 12 'three-tenths *of an ephah* of fine flour as a grain offering, mixed with oil, for each bull; two-tenths *of an ephah* of fine flour as a grain offering, mixed with oil, for the one ram;
>
> 13 'and one-tenth *of an ephah* of fine flour, mixed with oil, as a grain offering for each lamb, as a burnt offering of sweet aroma, an offering made by fire to the LORD.
>
> 14 'Their drink offering shall be half a hin of wine for a bull, one-third of a hin for a ram, and one-fourth of a hin for a lamb; this *is* the burnt offering for each month throughout the months of the year.
>
> 15 'Also one kid of the goats as a sin offering to the LORD shall be offered, besides the regular burnt offering and its drink offering.
>
> *Num. 28:9–15*

The Sabbath was to be distinguished from other days, both by laymen, who rested from their normal work (cf. Exod. 20:8–11, Deut. 5:12–15) and by the priests, who offered special sacrifices in addition to those made by them on other days. One scholar observes that "this ordinance is new, and indeed is the only law relating to a sabbath offering in the Pentateuch, though its observance is repeatedly insisted upon (Exod. 20:8ff.)."[19] The clear importance attached here to the Sabbath is mirrored in many parts of the Old Testament, especially by the prophets, who repeatedly warned the people of God in later times of the danger of desecrating the Sabbath and neglecting its ordinances.

The sacrifices to be made at the beginning of each month, at the time of the new moon, were equally important, and indeed new moon and Sabbath seem to have been linked together in the thinking of Israel (cf. Isa. 1:13, Ezek. 46:4ff.). Noth points out that this is the first time that bulls and rams appear as sacrificial animals along with the lambs, hence the exact details given about the precise quantities for the grain and drink offerings that are to accompany them.[20] The elaborate description given puts the new moon celebrations on much the same level as the Feast of Unleavened Bread and the Feast of First Fruits, or the Feast of Weeks. Like these, this was also an occasion of celebration and joy, and this is an important consideration: religious commitment for Israel was not incompatible with pleasure and joy in temporal things conceived as gifts of God. It is abundantly clear that by these feasts Israel not only acknowledged God as their provider but also celebrated His favor and covenant mercy toward them as His chosen people. This is particularly true with regard to the Passover and the Feast of Weeks, which are next dealt with in the verses that follow.

OFFERINGS AT PASSOVER

28:16 'On the fourteenth day of the first month *is* the Passover of the LORD.

17 'And on the fifteenth day of this month *is* the feast; unleavened bread shall be eaten for seven days.

18 'On the first day *you shall have* a holy convocation. You shall do no customary work.

19 'And you shall present an offering made by fire as a burnt offering to the LORD: two young bulls, one ram, and seven lambs in their first year. Be sure they are without blemish.

20 'Their grain offering shall be of fine flour mixed with oil: three-tenths *of an ephah* you shall offer for a bull, and two-tenths for a ram;
21 'you shall offer one-tenth *of an ephah* for each of the seven lambs;
22 'also one goat *as* a sin offering, to make atonement for you.
23 'You shall offer these besides the burnt offering of the morning, which *is* for a regular burnt offering.
24 'In this manner you shall offer the food of the offering made by fire daily for seven days, as a sweet aroma to the LORD; it shall be offered besides the regular burnt offering and its drink offering.
25 'And on the seventh day you shall have a holy convocation. You shall do no customary work.

Num. 28:16–25

This passage is based on Leviticus 23:5–8, which is repeated substantially here. The actual Passover ceremony was distinct from the Feast of Unleavened Bread, although the latter followed immediately upon the former. No mention is made here of the Passover sacrifices, since they were made by individual families, and do not properly belong in a section dealing with ordinances pertaining to the community as a whole. Wenham usefully points out that the New Testament makes full use of the Passover imagery to explain the significance of our Lord's death: "He called it his exodus that he was to accomplish at Jerusalem (Luke 9:31). John points out that, like the passover lamb, none of his bones was broken (John 19:36), while Paul says Christians must be as ruthless in expelling sin from their lives as the Jews are in throwing out leaven prior to passover (1 Cor. 5:7–8)."[21]

Offerings at the Feast of Weeks

28:26 'Also on the day of the firstfruits, when you bring a new grain offering to the LORD at your *Feast of* Weeks, you shall have a holy convocation. You shall do no customary work.
27 'You shall present a burnt offering as a sweet aroma to the LORD: two young bulls, one ram, and seven lambs in their first year,

28 'with their grain offering of fine flour mixed
with oil: three-tenths *of an ephah* for each bull, two-
tenths for the one ram,
29 'and one-tenth for each of the seven lambs;
30 '*also* one kid of the goats, to make atonement
for you.
31 'Be sure they are without blemish. You shall
present *them* with their drink offerings, besides the
regular burnt offering with its grain offering.

Num. 28:26–31

This is the second of the great national feasts, called also the Feast of Harvest (Exod. 23:16), and here spoken of as "*the day of the first-fruits.*" It celebrated the conclusion of the barley harvest. In the account of it given in Leviticus 23:15 ff. we see that it was celebrated fifty days after the Feast of Unleavened Bread. Hence the name "Pentecost" in New Testament times. It was marked by a holy convocation and by the offering of the same number of sacrifices as at the Feasts of New Moon and Unleavened Bread.

The Feast of Trumpets and the Day of Atonement

29:1 'And in the seventh month, on the first *day* of
the month, you shall have a holy convocation. You
shall do no customary work. For you it is a day of
blowing the trumpets.
2 'You shall offer a burnt offering as a sweet
aroma to the LORD: one young bull, one ram, *and*
seven lambs in their first year, without blemish.
3 'Their grain offering *shall be* fine flour mixed
with oil: three-tenths *of an ephah* for the bull, two-
tenths for the ram,
4 'and one-tenth for each of the seven lambs;
5 'also one kid of the goats *as* a sin offering, to
make atonement for you;
6 'besides the burnt offering with its grain offering for the New Moon, the regular burnt offering
with its grain offering, and their drink offerings, according to their ordinance, as a sweet aroma, an offering made by fire to the LORD.

7 'On the tenth *day* of this seventh month you shall have a holy convocation. You shall afflict your souls; you shall not do any work.

8 'You shall present a burnt offering to the LORD *as* a sweet aroma: one young bull, one ram, *and* seven lambs in their first year. Be sure they are without blemish.

9 'Their grain offering *shall be of* fine flour mixed with oil: three-tenths *of an ephah* for the bull, two-tenths for the one ram,

10 'and one-tenth for each of the seven lambs;

11 'also one kid of the goats *as* a sin offering, besides the sin offering for atonement, the regular burnt offering with its grain offering, and their drink offerings.

Num. 29:1–11

The amount of space devoted to the feasts of the seventh month (vv. 1, 7, 12), with the great detail about the offerings, particularly in the Feast of Tabernacles (vv. 12ff.), makes it clear that this was a most important, indeed climactic, month. It had a special character for the people of God. The fact that this month included both the Day of Atonement and the Feast of Tabernacles may be the reason why it was ushered in with a special ritual of trumpet-sounding. In Leviticus 23:23ff. this is called a "memorial." The reason for this is not clear: some think that, as the seventh month was the beginning of the civil year, it was a particularly suitable time for recollection (in much the same way as we today tend to "look back" at New Year time). Others think it kept the creation in mind, echoing the "sons of God shouting with joy" (Job 38:7) at the foundation of the world; others think the trumpet sound, "which is so often connected with the voice of God, was a special memorial of God having, in former days, spoken with man—a sound more joyful far than all the shoutings of the sons of God."[22] However, Bonar inclines to the view that "memorial" has more the sense of "a reminding" of something present or just at hand. The meaning would therefore be that it represented God's solemn call to attention in view of the very special causes for joy in this month, such as the Day of Atonement and the Feast of Tabernacles. In type, therefore, it represents the proclamation and declaring (i.e., preaching, as by a herald) of the sufferings (the Day of Atonement) and the glory (the Feast of Tabernacles) of the Savior.

The Feast of the Day of Atonement, described briefly in verses 7–11, was perhaps the most solemn of all the ordinances, and called by one commentator "the crown of the whole sacrificial system."[23] It needs to be studied along with the much fuller accounts given elsewhere in Scripture (cf. Lev. 16 and Heb. 9:6–14, the New Testament anti-type; also Lev. 23:26–32). It was to be a time of afflicting of the soul; that is, of sorrow for sin, when Israel was to recall the shame and the guilt of sin, as a necessary preparation leading to the joy of the Feast of Tabernacles. Another writer elaborates:

> *Sorrow for sin* seems to be like the rough sand that a man uses to rub off rust from iron; sorrow searches and rubs sore on the soul, but at the same time effectually removes what cleaved to the soul before. The vessel is thus rinsed of the flavour of former wines, and left quite clean for the new wine of the kingdom. *Sorrow* does not take away the sin, but it takes away the taste for it, and the pleasant taste of it; it does not empty out the vessel, but it frees the emptied vessel (the pardoned soul) from the former relish it had for earth. It is thus that the Lord's children pass through fire and water to the wealthy place.[24]

The Feast of Tabernacles

29:12 'On the fifteenth day of the seventh month you shall have a holy convocation. You shall do no customary work, and you shall keep a feast to the LORD seven days.

13 'You shall present a burnt offering, an offering made by fire as a sweet aroma to the LORD: thirteen young bulls, two rams, *and* fourteen lambs in their first year. They shall be without blemish.

14 'Their grain offering *shall be of* fine flour mixed with oil: three-tenths *of an ephah* for each of the thirteen bulls, two-tenths for each of the two rams,

15 'and one-tenth for each of the fourteen lambs;

16 'also one kid of the goats *as* a sin offering, besides the regular burnt offering, its grain offering, and its drink offering.

17 'On the second day *present* twelve young bulls,
two rams, fourteen lambs in their first year without
blemish,
18 'and their grain offering and their drink offerings for the bulls, for the rams, and for the lambs, by
their number, according to the ordinance;
19 'also one kid of the goats *as* a sin offering, besides the regular burnt offering with its grain offering, and their drink offerings.
20 'On the third day *present* eleven bulls, two rams,
fourteen lambs in their first year without blemish,
21 'and their grain offering and their drink offerings for the bulls, for the rams, and for the lambs, by
their number, according to the ordinance;
22 'also one goat *as* a sin offering, besides the regular burnt offering, its grain offering, and its drink
offering.
23 'On the fourth day *present* ten bulls, two rams,
and fourteen lambs in their first year, without blemish,
24 'and their grain offering and their drink offerings for the bulls, for the rams, and for the lambs, by
their number, according to the ordinance;
25 'also one kid of the goats *as* a sin offering, besides the regular burnt offering, its grain offering,
and its drink offering.
26 'On the fifth day *present* nine bulls, two rams,
and fourteen lambs in their first year without blemish,
27 'and their grain offering and their drink offerings for the bulls, for the rams, and for the lambs, by
their number, according to the ordinance;
28 'also one goat *as* a sin offering, besides the regular burnt offering, its grain offering, and its drink
offering.
29 'On the sixth day *present* eight bulls, two rams,
and fourteen lambs in their first year without blemish,
30 'and their grain offering and their drink offerings for the bulls, for the rams, and for the lambs, by
their number, according to the ordinance;
31 'also one goat *as* a sin offering, besides the regular burnt offering, its grain offering, and its drink
offering.
32 'On the seventh day *present* seven bulls, two

rams, *and* fourteen lambs in their first year without
blemish,
33 'and their grain offering and their drink offerings for the bulls, for the rams, and for the lambs, by
their number, according to the ordinance;
34 'also one goat *as* a sin offering, besides the regular burnt offering, its grain offering, and its drink
offering.
35 'On the eighth day you shall have a sacred assembly. You shall do no customary work.
36 'You shall present a burnt offering, an offering
made by fire as a sweet aroma to the LORD: one bull,
one ram, seven lambs in their first year without
blemish,
37 'and their grain offering and their drink offerings for the bull, for the ram, and for the lambs, by
their number, according to the ordinance;
38 'also one goat *as* a sin offering, besides the regular burnt offering, its grain offering, and its drink
offering.
39 'These you shall present to the LORD at your
appointed feasts (besides your vowed offerings and
your freewill offerings) as your burnt offerings
and your grain offerings, as your drink offerings and your peace offerings.'"
40 So Moses told the children of Israel everything,
just as the LORD commanded Moses.

Num. 29:12–40

The Feast of Tabernacles, further details for the celebration of which are given in Leviticus 23:34–36 and 39–43, was the greatest festival of joy of all the feasts. It had a twofold significance. On the one hand, following the completion of the ingathering of the fruits of harvest, it marked the sense of gratitude and joy toward the Lord, the giver of such bountiful provision, who had blessed the people's work and industry (Deut. 16:13–15). On the other, as the name "tabernacles" or "booths" indicates, it had a historical reference to the exodus from Egypt and reminded the people of God of their wandering and dwelling in booths in the wilderness (Lev. 23:42). The historical seems to have been the foundation of the agricultural, as if to suggest that it was the mighty intervention of God on behalf of His people that was the all-important evidence of the divine favor upon them. The blessing of fruitfulness and harvest flowed from this. As Paul says in Romans 8:32, "He who did not spare His own Son, but delivered Him up for us all, how shall He not with Him also freely give us all things?" If God delivered His people from bondage, how should it be thought that He would fail to bless their harvests also? Thus, Israel remembered in the feasts not only God's goodness in the fruits of the earth but also His goodness in the fruits of redemption.

A rather mysterious point emerges in the diminishing number of bulls to be sacrificed on each of the seven days, from thirteen in verse 13 to seven in verse 32. Various suggestions have been advanced to account for this, although Noth maintains that it can no longer be explained with any certainty. Another commentator thinks the arrangement was probably made for the purpose of securing the holy number seven for the final day, and indicating at the same time, through the gradual diminution in the number of sacrificial oxen, the gradual decrease in the festal character of the seven festal days.[25] This, to say the least, can be nothing more than conjecture. Perhaps we should look for the reason in the "type" of things to come that the ritual affords, pointing to the passing of all "shadow" sacrifices when the perfect Sacrifice appears in the person of Christ.

The eighth day (v. 35) was reckoned the great day of the feast, and is so described in John 7:37, and it is difficult not to allow our thoughts to turn to the moving scene in the temple at Jerusalem described by the apostle John. The hidden significance implicit in our Lord's appearance at the feast is very considerable, as the following considerations will show.

A careful examination of the chronology in Luke 1:5 ff. reveals an interesting fact. Zacharias, the father of John the Baptist, was "of the division of Abijah," and it was while he was executing his priestly office "in the order of his division" (Luke 1:8) that the angel of the Lord appeared to him, and announced the forthcoming birth of his son. The order of divisions for the priests is given in 1 Chronicles 24:7–19. It will be seen that Abijah's lot was eighth in the twenty-four divisions. Taking the first division as being at the beginning of the first month (Nisan or Abib, Deut. 16:1), Abijah's duty, being eighth in order, would fall in the second part of the fourth Jewish month. It was then that John the Baptist was conceived in the womb of Elizabeth who, we are told in Luke 1:24, hid herself for five months. Then, in the sixth month (i.e., six months after Elizabeth's experience), the angel Gabriel appeared to Mary, the mother of our Lord, foretelling the birth of Jesus. This, the sixth month after Elizabeth's experience, makes it the tenth month of the Jewish year, which would make the time of Jesus' birth during the second half of the seventh month in the Jewish calendar (i.e., at the time of the Feast of Tabernacles which, as Leviticus 23:34 tells us, was celebrated from the fifteenth to the twenty-first of the seventh month).

Can this really be a coincidence? Must there not be some deep spiritual significance in these dates? The Son of God, the Savior of the world, is likely to have been born at the time of the Feast of Tabernacles, and probably at the climax of the feast. In this connection it is not out of place to mention that the literal translation of John 1:14 is, "The Word was made flesh and *tabernacled* among us."

Whichever, therefore, of the two emphases in the Feast we take, the agricultural or the historical, a great light shines here for us. For on the one hand, in the thanksgiving for harvest in which the people gave thanks for the fruits of the earth, we have the marvelous thought that the birth of the Son of God is the fruition of God's loving purposes in the fulfillment of His promises of redemption. The seed of the woman, He had promised, would bruise the head of the serpent, and the promised harvest from that precious Seed was now evident, in the presence of the Son of God in the temple that day. On the other hand, there is the historical reference to the exodus from Egypt and the deliverance of God's people from bondage. It is one of the accepted interpretations of this Old Testament story by New Testament writers, that it points forward to a greater deliverance, that of the redemption wrought by Christ in His precious blood. And here, in the midst of the Feast of Tabernacles which commemorated that deliverance, the real deliverer was born.

It surely adds a new dimension to our understanding of John's reference to the great day of the Feast to realize that it may have been the birthday of our Lord. It does not require much imagination to think of the solemn self-consciousness with which He would stand up in the temple, knowing that the Feast spoke of Him, and that He was the truth and fulfillment of all it promised and prophesied. "For this I was born," He cried in effect, "for this I have come. It is for Me that you should be giving thanks. Do not be content with praising God for something long past in your history, but realize that that ancient deliverance points forward to another and greater, which I have come to inaugurate and accomplish."

Further comment on the ritual points out that in post-exilic times, and almost certainly in our Lord's day, one part of the ceremony involved water being taken from the pool of Siloam by the priests and poured out in the temple, the priests singing during the procession the words of Isaiah 12:3, "Therefore with joy will you draw water from the wells of salvation." It is likely that it was during this ritual that our Lord stood up and cried, "If anyone thirsts, let him come to Me and drink. . . ." Also, at a particular point in the festival the temple precincts were flooded, so that all the little back courts of Jerusalem were illuminated. And Jesus said, "I am the Light of the world. He who follows Me shall not walk in darkness, but have the light of life" (John 8:12). The tragedy was that so often, and particularly in our Lord's day, Israel rested in the type and shadow, and sought their full joy from the mere feast and its glad ceremonies, instead of pressing through to what lay behind it, Christ Himself. He is the Water of life and the Light of the world.

As a final footnote to this long section dealing with the various offerings (28:1–29:40) and in relation to its central thrust, namely the *worship* of God's people, this may be said: There are two phrases and ideas in common usage in our thinking, and especially in our hymnology—the Fatherhood of God, and the Lover of our souls. Both ideas underline and emphasize the reality of fellowship and relationship. The important thing in a family—and Israel was the family of God—is not *work* or *service*, but *relationship*. A father *takes pleasure* in his family. In a true family the important thing is not the getting or the giving by the one or the other, but the relationship of love, care, and concern between its members. And in particular, a bond of love, such as that implied in the phrase, "the Lover of our souls," is a relationship that is paramount and supreme. Alongside it, service simply pales into insignificance. When this is paramount and central, everything else is right, for everything is then rightly related to God.

This is the real point made in the oft-repeated phrase, "a sweet aroma to Me." The chief aim of our worship should be giving pleasure to Him. This may be seen supremely in the pleasure given by the Son to the Father in the worship He gave Him, as the story of the

Transfiguration well illustrates, when the love of the Son for the Father and the passion in His heart for His holy will broke through the bonds and barriers of human nature in a grand oblation to the Father of lights, as He was transfigured before His wondering disciples. This is the real test. Do we think of giving to God the pleasure in us that He desires? Do we enter His house week by week with this thought primarily in view?

This is surely a much-needed emphasis today, and a necessary corrective to another, which has been distorted almost beyond all biblical recognition. We refer to our Lord's words in Matthew 25:40: "Inasmuch as you did it to one of the least of these My brethren, you did it to Me." Of course Jesus spoke these words to underline an important truth, but we are very sure He did not mean them to be set in opposition to what has just been said about the centrality of fellowship with God. And we must at all costs beware of making this a substitute for that personal relationship with Him. For this would mean, in effect, that good works—works of compassion and mercy—could take the place of fellowship with God and "become" Christianity for us.

This danger is present in a twofold way. On the one hand, it is possible for service to *displace* fellowship. It is perilously easy for believers to become so involved in Christian service that fellowship with God is neglected. We must beware of the spiritual barrenness of a busy life. "My son," says God, "give Me your heart (Prov. 23:26)—not the work of your hands, not your time, talents, or money, but your heart." On the other hand, service can become a *substitute* for fellowship altogether. So many seek to serve a God they do not really know. The story of Mary and Martha (Luke 10:38–42) is meant to show us what ought to come first. It was Mary, not Martha, who was commended by Jesus. And we must disavow "clever" interpretations of that story which seek to vindicate Martha's "practical Christianity" as against Mary's "sitting at Jesus' feet." Our Lord rebuked Martha's "practical Christianity" because, however sincerely it was meant to please Him, it did not. She missed what He really wanted to impart to her because she was too busy to sit still and give Him pleasure by hearing His word. The service that really counts is one which issues from fellowship with Him. Where fellowship with Him declines and is displaced, service becomes less and less useful or fruitful, becoming subject to the law of diminishing returns.

The Law Concerning Vows

30:1 Then Moses spoke to the heads of the tribes concerning the children of Israel, saying, "This *is* the thing which the LORD has commanded:

2 "If a man makes a vow to the LORD, or swears an oath to bind himself by some agreement, he shall not break his word; he shall do according to all that proceeds out of his mouth.

3 "Or if a woman makes a vow to the LORD, and binds *herself* by some agreement while in her father's house in her youth,

4 "and her father hears her vow and the agreement by which she has bound herself, and her father holds his peace, then all her vows shall stand, and every agreement with which she has bound herself shall stand.

5 "But if her father overrules her on the day that he hears, then none of her vows nor her agreements by which she has bound herself shall stand; and the LORD will release her, because her father overruled her.

6 "If indeed she takes a husband, while bound by her vows or by a rash utterance from her lips by which she bound herself,

7 "and her husband hears *it,* and makes no response to her on the day that he hears, then her vows shall stand, and her agreements by which she bound herself shall stand.

8 "But if her husband overrules her on the day that he hears *it,* he shall make void her vow which she took and what she uttered with her lips, by which she bound herself, and the LORD will release her.

9 "Also any vow of a widow or a divorced woman, by which she has bound herself, shall stand against her.

10 "If she vowed in her husband's house, or bound herself by an agreement with an oath,

11 "and her husband heard *it,* and made no response to her *and* did not overrule her, then all her vows shall stand, and every agreement by which she bound herself shall stand.

12 "But if her husband truly made them void on
the day he heard *them,* then whatever proceeded
from her lips concerning her vows or concerning the
agreement binding her, it shall not stand; her husband has made them void, and the LORD will release
her.
13 "Every vow and every binding oath to afflict
her soul, her husband may confirm it, or her husband
may make it void.
14 "Now if her husband makes no response whatever to her from day to day, then he confirms all her
vows or all the agreements that bind her; he confirms
them, because he made no response to her on the day
that he heard *them.*
15 "But if he does make them void after he has
heard *them,* then he shall bear her guilt."
16 These *are* the statutes which the LORD commanded Moses, between a man and his wife, and
between a father and his daughter in her youth in
her father's house.

Num. 30:1–16

The subject matter of this chapter relates to the sanctity of vows. It is an unvarying principle in the Old Testament that vows once having been made ought to be kept. That being said, however, there is the recognition that there are vows which for one reason or another are unfulfillable, and regulations are given as to what the person making such a vow must do instead. The rules by which vows were to be legally regulated, so far as their objects and their discharge were concerned, are to be found in other Scriptures, such as Leviticus 27, which should be read in conjunction with this chapter (cf. also Deut. 23:21–22, which emphasizes the importance of keeping vows that are made, while making plain that they are purely voluntary, and that there is no compulsion involved).

Here, another kind of problem relating to vows is discussed: the vows made by women. The greater part of the chapter (vv. 3–16) is devoted to this subject. Significantly, this theme is taken up following upon the account of the feasts in the previous two chapters, and it may be assumed from this that the vows were related substantially to the presentation of sacrifices and made in the context of worship.[26] In this connection, one recalls the words of the psalmist,

"What shall I render to the Lord for all His benefits toward me? . . . I will pay my vows to the Lord now in the presence of all his people" (Ps. 116:12–14).

A woman's vows, in contrast to a man's, are subject to certain qualifications, and four distinct cases are envisaged in these verses: an unmarried girl, under the jurisdiction of her father (in her youth, i.e., "not yet of age," vv. 3ff.); a woman unmarried at the time of her vow but having entered marriage before the vow is fulfilled (vv. 6ff.); the widow or the divorced woman (v. 9); and finally the married woman (vv. 10–12).

We should note this at the outset: it is presupposed that women have the right to undertake on their own initiative obligations of this nature. Their validity, however, depends on the assent of the man in question. The point in these instructions is surely clear: it is the assertion of the headship of the man in the life of the family. The man, as father or husband, is regarded as having jurisdiction over the other members of the household, and even over the vows they make. If the man concerned heard about the vow, but said nothing, it was regarded as binding; but if he objected or discouraged the vow it was not to be carried out.

There is more than a suggestion here of the father or husband acting as a restraint against the making of unwise or rash vows and disallowing them for that reason. On the other hand, if he did disallow them, the responsibility would lie on him. That is to say, he could prevent a rash or bad vow; but if he discouraged or hindered a good and legitimate one he became accountable to God for his actions, the implication being that he should not do so.

When a woman married (vv. 6–8), she passed from her father's jurisdiction to her husband's. The same regulations now applied as in the previous case. If her husband learned of the vow and said nothing, it would be binding; but if he objected to the vow, it would be nullified.

In the third case, that of a woman widowed or divorced, the situation was different. Even if she returned to her father's house, or went to stay with a son, neither the son nor the father could annul her vow. She was regarded as standing independently of them.

In the final case, that of married women making vows after marriage (vv. 10–16), husbands could veto these vows so long as the veto was applied as soon as they heard about them. A man's silence on the subject would indicate consent and would establish his wife's vow and make it binding. It is clear from these regulations, as Gordon J. Wenham observes: "Neither wives nor children may substitute self-imposed religious obligations for God-given duties."[27]

There is a substantial measure of comfort and encouragement in all this for sensitive and vulnerable spirits who may have been led into unwise and rash courses of action, willing and sincere of heart as they may have been in making their vows. It is an evidence of the pastoral care of God for His children, exercised in this case through those appointed over us in the Lord, in delivering us from the foolishness of our own actions. In an age which is impatient of authority, this is something which shows the positive values of that much-maligned word. We should be grateful and thankful to God that He cares to rescue us from the consequences of our youthful (and sometimes not so youthful) follies.

The whole question of making vows as such arises in relation to the Christian life, and whether there is any place for vows in the new economy. The New Testament church did, in fact, keep up the practice of vows and fasts (Matt. 6:16; Mark 2:20; Acts 13:2, 18:18, 21:23), and Christians have made vows of a variety of kinds and in a variety of contexts. It will be useful to look into this whole matter from the Christian perspective.

It is a striking and impressive fact, however, that Bible concordances show that while the word "vow" is found almost everywhere in the Old Testament, it is seldom used in the New. It may not be possible to draw firm conclusions from this, but it might in fact be *prima facie* evidence that what was needed in the Old Testament economy (because of the limitations of the old covenant, which could make nothing perfect) was not in the same way needed in the New, which is the era of the Spirit. In this respect, it compares with the phenomenon of "lots," which were extremely common in the Old Testament, as a means of discerning the Lord's will, but virtually unknown in the New, when the leading of the indwelling Spirit superseded them. Be that as it may, it will he helpful at this point to look at three vows recorded in Scripture, which serve to illuminate the whole question: Jacob's vow at Bethel (Gen. 28); Jephthah's vow (Judg. 11); and Paul's vow (Acts 18:18 and 21:18–26).

The well-known story of Jacob at Bethel has been interpreted in two different ways, and both illustrate different facets of the question before us. On the one hand, it is interpreted as if Jacob were bargaining with God. "If . . . if . . . if . . . then the Lord will be my God." If this represents conditional consecration on Jacob's part, then Jacob is rightly to be criticized, for it is certainly not the highest ground to take. God always requires of us unconditional surrender. We *owe* Him our devotion and loyalty, as His creatures, apart from anything He chooses to bestow on us. In the New Testament sense, this is the challenge and summons of the gospel. It is not an optional extra, but the logical response we make to the mercies of God in Christ (Rom. 12:1–2)—"the least we can do." And rightly understood, this is just what the gospel does lay upon us, and there is in this sense no need for further vows on the matter, as if some specially consecrated people should give God this kind of response while others did not. Vows, as special, advanced expressions of one's consecration, can be highly misleading and erroneous. It is this false aspect that lies behind much of the Catholic monastic vow idea.

On the other hand, Jacob's vow may be taken as his reaction and response to God's revelation of Himself to the patriarch. "*Since* God has done this. . . . and will be my God, therefore I will (in gratitude to Him) raise this stone, and give a tenth of all I possess to Him." This illustrates the vow of lifelong consecration and obedience to God which is the hallmark of a true and living faith. In this respect, we can see the importance of "paying our vows to the most High," for consecration must be real and utter: far better *not* to vow at all than to do so and go back on the vow.

The story of Jephthah's vow in Judges 11 is in many ways a very moving and disturbing one. A good deal of discussion has taken place in the commentaries as to whether what is referred to in the story is a literal blood-sacrifice of Jephthah's daughter (the view held by the early fathers) or that Jephthah simply confined his daughter to a perpetual virginity (the view held by one of the commentators, who maintains that since human sacrifice was forbidden in the Old Testament, it is inconceivable that Jephthah could have even contemplated a vow which violated the law of God).[28] With any interpretation, however, the question is whether Jephthah was right in keeping to his vow. And the answer we must certainly give, in the light of the teaching of this chapter, is that he should have broken it, because it was a wrong and unwise one to have made. Wrong vows should be renounced and ignored, for it is never right to do wrong.

Calvin's words on this subject are worth noting:

> As timid and inexperienced consciences, even after they are dissatisfied with a vow, and convinced of its impropriety, nevertheless feel doubts respecting the obligation, and are grievously distressed, on the one hand, from a dread of violating their promise to God, and on the other, from a fear of incurring greater guilt by observing it, it is necessary here to offer them some assistance to enable them to extricate themselves from this difficulty. Now, to remove every scruple at once, I remark, that all vows, not legitimate or rightly made, as they are of no value with God, so they ought to have no force with us. For if in human contracts no promises are obligatory upon us, but those to which the party with whom we contract wishes to bind us; it is absurd to consider ourselves constrained to the performance of those things which God never requires of us: especially as our works cannot be good unless they please God, and are accompanied with the testimony of our conscience that He accepts them. . . .
>
> Therefore, if it be not lawful for a Christian man to attempt anything without this assurance, and if any one through ignorance has made a rash vow, and afterwards discovered his error, why should he not desist from the performance of it? Since vows inconsiderately made, not only are not binding, but ought of necessity to be cancelled. . . . Hence we may conclude, that vows which have originated in error and superstition, are of no value with God, and ought to be relinquished by us.[29]

The apostle Paul's vow in Acts 18:18 was, it would seem, a Nazirite vow made, as has been said, to reassure himself that underlying the routine of daily life he was devoted to God. Such a vow usually lasted for thirty days, after which, by a series of sacrifices, the participant was discharged from it and returned to ordinary life (for detailed exposition of this vow see commentary on Num. 6:1–21). The principle underlying it certainly seems still to have relevance for Christian life today. One thinks, for example, of Paul's teaching about the use of the good things of life—"I will not be brought under the power of any" (1 Cor. 6:12), and "using the world, as not misusing it" (1 Cor. 7:31). But the question in all this is: how can we be sure that such an attitude of detachment obtains, at any given time? How other than by applying a temporary discipline to life, to reassure ourselves that underlying the daily routine of life we are after all really devoted to God, and not beguiled and snared by the good things of life? There is both a need for detachment in Christian life and a need to prove it to be a reality in our experience. Are we able to say with the psalmist, "Like a weaned child is my soul within me" (Ps. 131:2)? And how to be sure of this? Only by putting it to the test by means of a temporary discipline, to prove to ourselves that this is really where we are.

The Defeat of Midian

31:1 And the LORD spoke to Moses, saying:

2 "Take vengeance on the Midianites for the children of Israel. Afterward you shall be gathered to your people."

3 So Moses spoke to the people, saying, "Arm some of yourselves for war, and let them go against the Midianites to take vengeance for the LORD on Midian.

4 "A thousand from each tribe of all the tribes of Israel you shall send to the war."

5 So there were recruited from the divisions of Israel one thousand from *each* tribe, twelve thousand armed for war.

6 Then Moses sent them to the war, one thousand from *each* tribe; he sent them to the war with Phinehas the son of Eleazar the priest, with the holy articles and the signal trumpets in his hand.

7 And they warred against the Midianites, just as the LORD commanded Moses, and they killed all the males.

8 They killed the kings of Midian with *the rest of* those who were killed—Evi, Rekem, Zur, Hur, and Reba, the five kings of Midian. Balaam the son of Beor they also killed with the sword.

9 And the children of Israel took the women of Midian captive, with their little ones, and took as spoil all their cattle, all their flocks, and all their goods.

10 They also burned with fire all the cities where
they dwelt, and all their forts.
11 And they took all the spoil and all the booty—
of man and beast.
12 Then they brought the captives, the booty, and
the spoil to Moses, to Eleazar the priest, and to the
congregation of the children of Israel, to the camp in
the plains of Moab by the Jordan, *across from* Jericho.
Num. 31:1–12

The confident pronouncements by some commentators that this account of a war with Midian is a *midrash,* a story invented to illustrate a point of religious significance, and not intended to be taken as historical (so Snaith, Sturdy, Noth, and others) seems to me an arbitrary assumption based on entirely inadequate evidence. Apart from any other consideration, the list of Midianite kings named in verse 8, whose names appear elsewhere in the Old Testament, seems to confer a historicity which there seems little reason to question.

The war against the Midianites is clearly meant to be understood as a holy war, that is to say, a war ordained by God to be a punishment and judgment upon them because of their sins. This is the only thing that will help us to see meaning and significance in what is undoubtedly a chapter which presents considerable moral difficulties to our minds.

Moses is commanded by God to avenge Israel on Midian (v. 2). That it was a war initiated at the command of the Lord is stressed at the outset, and in fact reinforced in verse 3, where the operation is described as being *"vengeance for the Lord."* We need to recall in this connection the incident mentioned in 25:17, in the story of Balaam (significantly, Balaam was killed in this battle, v. 8). A small army was selected to go out against Midian and devastated it, slew its five kings, and took an enormous amount of booty (concerning the apportionment of which a good part of the rest of the chapter is occupied). This near-destruction of an entire people makes grim reading, and it is hard for the modern mind to accept that such a thing could have been commanded by God. Yet this is what is asserted by the writer of Numbers, and we must look at it as he undoubtedly did, however great the problems that this raises for us. The problems, indeed, become even greater in the following verses, and it will be convenient to look at them before making further comment.

THE RETURN OF THE WARRIORS

31:13 And Moses, Eleazar the priest, and all the leaders of the congregation, went to meet them outside the camp.

14 But Moses was angry with the officers of the army, *with* the captains over thousands and captains over hundreds, who had come from the battle.

15 And Moses said to them: "Have you kept all the women alive?

16 "Look, these *women* caused the children of Israel, through the counsel of Balaam, to trespass against the LORD in the incident of Peor, and there was a plague among the congregation of the LORD.

17 "Now therefore, kill every male among the little ones, and kill every woman who has known a man intimately.

18 "But keep alive for yourselves all the young girls who have not known a man intimately.

Num. 31:13–18

On the return of the warriors from the battlefield with their booty, Moses expostulated angrily (vv. 14–15) at the sight of the women they had taken captive and, like Samuel on the return of Saul from the slaughter of Amalek (1 Sam. 15:10 ff.), insisted on further destruction still, and commanded that all save those who were innocent girls be slain, along with the male children. The reason given for this by Moses was that the whole trouble at Peor (25:1 ff.) was caused by the women of Midian. The further slaughter took place at Moses' behest. The extreme severity of this action compounds the moral issues that the story raises and poses questions of concern which it would be neither honest nor honorable to pass by without some attempt to understand them.

First of all, a general word may be said about the grim and sometimes gruesome accounts we find in the earlier books of the Old Testament of the slaughters perpetrated by the Israelites on the nations of Canaan. What we must understand clearly—and this includes the incident about Midian—is that, as already indicated, these were holy wars commanded by God. The only way to make sense of these bloody carnages, and to see any moral ground for

Israel's displacement of the nations of Canaan from the land, is to realize that God was using His people as the rod of His anger against peoples whose cup of iniquity was full to overflowing. They were being judged for their sins and their depravities. This is, of course, stated explicitly more than once in the Old Testament itself (cf. Gen. 15:16 and Lev. 18:24–30). The time of their destruction was ripe. This is why they were thus dealt with, and it was no arbitrary act of injustice that drove them out of their land. They had forfeited the right to live as nations in Canaan by the extremes of their debauchery and depravity, just as Sodom and Gomorrah had done (Gen. 19), and just as the Cainite civilization as a whole had done, bringing upon itself the judgment of the Flood (Gen. 6). Furthermore, it should be remembered that God dealt with His own people in similar fashion when they proved themselves unworthy to life in the land of promise, and He brought them into the captivity of Babylon in 586 B.C. To understand God's burning passion for righteousness in His creatures is to understand the basic reason for these judgments upon men and nations that refused to be righteous, and who rendered themselves incapable of being so by their continued sin.

That is the first consideration. The second, concerning Midian itself, is that Midian, an implacable enemy of Israel down through her history, at that time constituted a threat to Israel's very existence as a spiritual people. Balaam had shown the way to corrupt God's people, and the ugly incidents recorded in 25:1 ff. are sufficient to show just how great a demoralizing power this became in the life of Israel. We must always bear in mind the overall divine strategy in choosing the Israelites and bringing them into the land of Canaan. Redemption was the culminating concern, and the bringing forth of the promised Seed. The corrupting influence of Midian was therefore threatening the very existence of the line of promise. It had to be rooted out.

What are we to say, however, about the harsh barbarities committed, particularly the slaughter of the women and the children? The usual answer given to this question is to say that "of course a good deal of the Old Testament is sub-Christian, and we could never hold with many of the things—such as this—that are written in the history books of the Old Testament and the Psalms. These were primitive times, and they did not know any better." But this is not only too simple a conclusion to come to; it is also silly, as a moment or two's reflection will show, and it raises far more serious problems than it solves. For what such an approach does is to dismiss certain portions of Scripture as not inspired by God. But this is to make one's own moral judgment the sole criterion of what is inspired in the Scriptures and what is not. And this is to claim inspiration for oneself; another man may apply his judgment in other directions, and soon there will be little left but a Bible of shreds and patches.

But the idea that these "barbarities" took place in primitive times when "they did not know any better" is at variance with the facts. For it was not the people who initiated this "slaughter of the innocents." If it had been, we might see the force of such a charge, for the people were a dubious company, with much that was unlovely about them. But it was Moses who remonstrated the people for *not* slaying the women and the children. And Moses walked with God; he was the spiritual giant among them, with whom God spoke face to face. Clearly, if it had simply been the expression of primitive and savage brutality on the part of a backward people the story would have read the other way around, with Moses protesting violently against their barbarity. This surely indicates that there is something far more in this than at first meets the eye.

As for saying they did not know any better, this is simply not true. One has only to think of the legislation given elsewhere in the Pentateuch to realize the compassion of God toward women and children, and His special care for them, and for the strangers outside the covenant (cf. Lev. 19:10, 17, 18; Exod. 22:21–23, 23:4–5). Moses was not acting in a barbaric manner, and it is not possible to square his conduct here with other Scriptures on this thesis. What he was doing—and what he was conscious of doing—was acting as a theocratic leader of the people of God, acting as a legal judge in relation to the Midianites, an executor of divine justice. This is the truth of the position, and some things need to be said about such an idea.

There were no courts of law as such in Moses' day. But justice was administered through Moses, the God-appointed leader of the people. It was never a case of taking the law into his own hands, for he habitually acted as the Lord's representative and spokesman. Grim justice, we might say; but what has already been said about the heathen nations helps to explain why it was so necessary.

Furthermore, we need to bear in mind that Israel was in a particular situation. They were an emergent people, in the sense that they were about to come into their own as the people of God, with a destiny, a calling, in the world. And always in emergent nations, one finds a certain stringency in their discipline that is not found in more static or degenerating situations. Thus, in Exodus 22 we see the death penalty exacted for crimes other than murder. This has been mirrored in modern situations also, as for example in Russia and China, where the death penalty has been known to be exacted for things like industrial sabotage. It is, it seems, essential for the very existence of a new emergent community that discipline be harsh and stringent. One thinks in this connection of the extremely severe judgment that fell on Ananias and Sapphira in Acts 5, when the purity of the church required the death of these two whose continued existence could have threatened its very life. And so it was here also. Issues were clearly being seen as black and white. The sentence had to be executed on Midian.

But little children? Could God have ordained this? Some things need to be said in this connection. We must insist that it was not mere wanton brutality, for the slaughter was not indiscriminate. Not all the children were slain, only the males. They were the future "Midian," a potential danger and peril for Israel if allowed to grow up. What we must realize is that there are such things as national character and national traits and propensities. We speak of such and such a people being a military people, and as such liable to be warlike and belligerent. So it was with the Midianites.

That is the first thing, and the second is this: we have to remember something much closer to our own time, the extirpation and destruction of whole cities during World War II by huge bombing raids on Germany. We estimated, rightly or wrongly, that the only way for the Nazi menace to be destroyed was to have done this, when doing it involved innocent civilians, children included.

C. S. Lewis has a striking passage in his *Reflections in the Psalms* in a chapter on "Second Meanings in the Psalms," in which he discusses the stark and seemingly brutal and barbarous words of Psalm 137:9, "Happy shall he be who takes and dashes your little ones against the rock." He writes, "I know things in the inner world which are like babies; the infantile beginnings of small indulgences, small resentments, which may one day become dipsomania or settled hatred, but which woo us and wheedle us with special pleadings and seem so tiny, so helpless that in resisting them we feel we are being cruel to animals. . . ."[30] And his advice is: Kill them. Show them no mercy. For they will grow, and rend you, and perhaps destroy you.

This is one of the values of the passage for spiritual life. Israel's experiences are a "picture" of the Christian pilgrimage; and from this we must learn to "resist beginnings," however sweet, alluring, and charming they may be. For they will finally grow into ugly and dangerous enemies.

The Purification of the Army

> 31:19 "And as for you, remain outside the camp seven days; whoever has killed any person, and whoever has touched any slain, purify yourselves and your captives on the third day and on the seventh day.
>
> 20 "Purify every garment, everything made of leather, everything woven of goats' *hair,* and everything made of wood."
>
> 21 Then Eleazar the priest said to the men of war who had gone to the battle, "This *is* the ordinance of the law which the LORD commanded Moses:
>
> 22 "Only the gold, the silver, the bronze, the iron, the tin, and the lead,
>
> 23 "everything that can endure fire, you shall put through the fire, and it shall be clean; and it shall be purified with the water of purification. But all that cannot endure fire you shall put through water.
>
> 24 "And you shall wash your clothes on the seventh day and be clean, and afterward you may come into the camp."
>
> *Num. 31:19–24*

Moses next instructed all who had been defiled from contact with the dead to remain outside the camp for a period of seven days until the ordained purification rites had been fulfilled (cf. 5:1–4; 19:11–12, 16–19). What is new here, however, is that the booty taken in battle was itself to be purified. This elaborate procedure seems to indicate that, even though the war in which they had been engaged was a holy war ordained by God, uncleanness had been incurred and required cleansing. G. J. Wenham's comment on this is, we think, a true one: "Over every war, however glorious its outcome from the victor's point of view, hangs the shadow of death. These purification rules reminded Israel that the death of one's fellow men was a catastrophic disruption of God's creation, even though in some cases it was the Creator himself who demanded the execution of the sinner."[31]

THE DIVISION OF THE SPOIL

31:25 Now the LORD spoke to Moses, saying:
26 "Count up the plunder that was taken—of man
and beast—you and Eleazar the priest and the chief
fathers of the congregation;
27 "and divide the plunder into two parts, between
those who took part in the war, who went out to battle, and all the congregation.
28 "And levy a tribute for the LORD on the men of
war who went out to battle: one of every five hundred of the persons, the cattle, the donkeys, and the
sheep;
29 "take *it* from their half, and give *it* to Eleazar
the priest as a heave offering to the LORD.
30 "And from the children of Israel's half you shall
take one of every fifty, drawn from the persons, the
cattle, the donkeys, and the sheep, from all the livestock, and give them to the Levites who keep charge
of the tabernacle of the LORD."
31 So Moses and Eleazar the priest did as the LORD
commanded Moses.
32 The booty remaining from the plunder, which the
men of war had taken, was six hundred and seventy-
five thousand sheep,
33 seventy-two thousand cattle,
34 sixty-one thousand donkeys,
35 and thirty-two thousand persons in all, of women
who had not known a man intimately.
36 And the half, the portion for those who had
gone out to war, was in number three hundred and
thirty-seven thousand five hundred sheep;

37 and the LORD's tribute of the sheep was six
hundred and seventy-five.
38 The cattle *were* thirty-six thousand, of which
the LORD's tribute *was* seventy-two.
39 The donkeys *were* thirty thousand five hundred, of which the LORD's tribute *was* sixty-one.
40 The persons *were* sixteen thousand, of which
the LORD's tribute *was* thirty-two persons.
41 So Moses gave the tribute *which was* the LORD's
heave offering to Eleazar the priest, as the LORD commanded Moses.
42 And from the children of Israel's half, which
Moses separated from the men who fought—
43 now the half belonging to the congregation was
three hundred and thirty-seven thousand five hundred sheep,
44 thirty-six thousand cattle,
45 thirty thousand five hundred donkeys,
46 and sixteen thousand persons—
47 and from the children of Israel's half Moses took
one of every fifty, drawn from man and beast, and
gave them to the Levites, who kept charge of the tabernacle of the LORD, as the LORD commanded Moses.
48 Then the officers who *were* over thousands of
the army, the captains of thousands and captains
of hundreds, came near to Moses;
49 and they said to Moses, "Your servants have
taken a count of the men of war who *are* under our
command, and not a man of us is missing.
50 "Therefore we have brought an offering for the
LORD, what every man found of ornaments of gold:
armlets and bracelets and signet rings and earrings
and necklaces, to make atonement for ourselves before the LORD."
51 So Moses and Eleazar the priest received the
gold from them, all the fashioned ornaments.
52 And all the gold of the offering that they offered
to the LORD, from the captains of thousands and captains of hundreds, was sixteen thousand seven hundred and fifty shekels.
53 (The men of war had taken spoil, every man for
himself.)

> 54 And Moses and Eleazar the priest received the gold from the captains of thousands and of hundreds, and brought it into the tabernacle of meeting as a memorial for the children of Israel before the LORD.
>
> *Num. 31:25–54*

The regulations for the division of the booty won in the war with the Midianites are now given. Half of it was to go to the twelve thousand men of war who had taken part in the campaign and half to the congregation of the Lord, those who had remained in the camp. This division was reasonable and just, reflecting not only the solidarity of the people of God in their campaigns and warfare but also the recognition of the rest of the people's involvement and participation in the logistics of the campaign. The twelve thousand warriors, nevertheless, received proportionally more than those who had not been engaged in the battle; moreover, the proportion they gave to Eleazar as an offering to the Lord—and which the latter received on behalf of the whole company of priests—was one five-hundredth part (one-fifth of one percent) compared with the one-fiftieth that was given to the Levites from the congregation's half of the booty. Priests and Levites, then, received a share of the booty in the ratio of one to ten.

It became a general rule that those who remained at home should receive a share of the booty in a successful campaign (cf. Josh. 22:8; 1 Sam. 30:24–25), thus demonstrating, as has already been said, the essential unity of the congregation of the Lord. Indeed, as is pointed out in 1 Samuel 30:24, those who stayed "by the supplies" would doubtless have had duties and responsibilities behind the scenes, which necessarily involved them in the action as a whole. They were therefore entitled to their share.

This is a consideration of wide significance and encouragement. God sees to it that the unseen, hidden workers in His service are not overlooked or devalued. Every faithful servant receives his reward (cf. Heb. 6:10). It is interesting, however, to see the concept of differentials being established here. There is a real recognition of different responsibilities, and greater and lesser burdens borne. But there were no strikes when the arrangements were made known to the people! Acceptance was the order of the day.

On a roll call being taken of the army (vv. 48ff.), it was found that not a single Israelite soldier had been lost in the campaign. Such a miraculous preservation called forth from them an expression of thanksgiving in the form of a sacrificial gift to the Lord from their own portion of the booty. In view of the fact that so many of the lessons presented to us by the experience of the Israelites are sad and grim ones, it is good to note here that in some respects at least they were "getting the message" as to what being a true people of God really meant. Here they did the right thing and expressed their gratitude to God, acknowledging in a spirit of generous giving His goodness to them.

The Lord, as the apostle Paul reminds us in 2 Corinthians 9:7, loves a cheerful giver, and it must have been a source of joy to Him that His people should have shown such a spirit of thankfulness. That this is the true basis of liberality is seen in the apostle's teaching on the subject in the Corinthian epistle. We should note that there was nothing niggardly in their giving (v. 50): they gave generously and even lavishly of their hard-won spoils. It is almost a truism to say that a thankful heart is a generous heart; perhaps if the church were more conscious of the mercies of God in Christ, there would be more generous and sacrificial giving on the part of His people. The financial problems of any congregation are always, in the last analysis, spiritual.

NOTES

1. Gordon J. Wenham, *Numbers,* Tyndale Old Testament Commentaries (Leicester: Inter-Varsity Press, 1981), p. 184.

2. L. Elliott Binns, *The Book of Numbers* (London: Methuen & Co., Ltd., 1927), p. 177f., "The zeal of Phinehas here exhibited became proverbial (cf. Ps. cvi. 30; 1 Macc. ii. 24ff., 54; 1 Cor. x. 8) and he was taken as a model by the Zealots (4 Macc. xviii. 12). According to a late tradition he was granted immortality (see Fabricius Cod. Pseudep. I pp. 893f.); at the end of Jos. xxiv., however, LXX states that he was buried in Gibeah."

3. Wenham, *Numbers,* p. 188.

4. Carl L. Keil and Franz Delitzsch, *Numbers,* Commentary on the Old Testament, vol. 3 (Grand Rapids: Wm. B. Eerdmans, repr. 1971), p. 207. Delitzsch quotes Baumgarten.

5. Wenham, *Numbers*, p. 189.
6. Ibid.
7. Ibid.
8. C. J. Ellicott, *Leviticus*, An Old Testament Commentary for English Readers (London: Cassell & Co., Ltd., 1897), p. 554.
9. Binns, *Numbers*, p. 185.
10. Emil Brunner, *The Mediator* (London: Lutterworth Press, 1934), p. 463.
11. George Philip, *Sandyford Henderson Congregational Record and Bible Readings*, October 1978, p. 29.
12. Matthew Henry, *Genesis-Deuteronomy*, Commentary on the Whole Bible (Old Tappan, N. J.: Fleming H. Revell Co.), 1:694.
13. Binns, *Numbers*, p. 189, says: "It would be easy to criticise the representation of the character of God contained in this narrative: according to which a lifetime of faithful service is apparently wiped out by a single lapse. But the divine majesty had to be vindicated, and a public failure atoned for, by a striking and impressive punishment: moreover there was another Land of Promise from which Moses was not excluded by his offence."
14. Ibid., p. 191: "The position of Joshua is practically that of a military commander under the direction of the high-priest; the high-priest himself gives direction through the use of the divine oracle."
15. Wenham, *Numbers*, pp. 195–99.
16. James S. Stewart, *Heralds of God* (London: Hodder and Stoughton, 1946), p. 73.
17. Emil Brunner, *The Christian Doctrine of Creation and Redemption*, Dogmatics II (London: Lutterworth, 1952), p. 284.
18. But cf. Westminster Confession of Faith, ch. 7.5: "Under the law (the covenant) was administered by promises, prophecies, sacrifices, circumcision, the paschal lamb, and other types and ordinances delivered to the people of the Jews, all foresignifying Christ to come, which were for that time sufficient and efficacious, through the operation of the spirit, to instruct and build up the elect in faith in the promised Messiah, by whom they had full remission of sins, and eternal salvation."
19. Binns, *Numbers*, p. 194.
20. Martin Noth, *Numbers: A Commentary*, Old Testament Library (London: SCM Press, 1968), p. 222.
21. Wenham, *Numbers*, p. 201.
22. Andrew A. Bonar, *Commentary on Leviticus 23:24* (London: Nisbet & Co., 1861), p. 413.
23. Binns, *Numbers*, p. 197.
24. Bonar, *Leviticus*, p. 417.

25. Keil and Delitzsch, *Numbers,* p. 222.
26. Ibid., p. 223.
27. Wenham, *Numbers,* p. 208.
28. Keil and Delitzsch, *Numbers.*
29. John Calvin, *Harmony of the Pentateuch,* Bk. 4. 13:20.
30. C. S. Lewis, *Reflections on the Psalms* (London: Geoffrey Bles, 1958), p. 136.
31. Wenham, *Numbers,* p. 212.

CHAPTER SEVENTEEN

Miscellaneous Topographical Narratives

Numbers 32:1–36:13

The remaining chapters of the Book of Numbers deal with the settlement of the two and a half tribes, Reuben, Gad, and half of Manasseh on the east side of Jordan (32:1–42), the route taken by Israel on their way from Egypt to the borders of Canaan, with the various encampments on the way (33:1–56), the settlement of the rest of the tribes on the west side of Jordan, in Canaan proper (34:1–29), the Levitical cities, including the cities of refuge (35:1–34), and finally, a further statement about the daughters of Zelophehad (36:1–13), to supplement the legislation of 27:1–11.

Request for the Territory of East Jordan

32:1 Now the children of Reuben and the children of Gad had a very great multitude of livestock; and when they saw the land of Jazer and the land of Gilead, that indeed the region *was* a place for livestock,

2 the children of Gad and the children of Reuben came and spoke to Moses, to Eleazar the priest, and to the leaders of the congregation, saying,

3 "Ataroth, Dibon, Jazer, Nimrah, Heshbon, Elealeh, Shebam, Nebo, and Beon,

4 "the country which the LORD defeated before the congregation of Israel, *is* a land for livestock, and your servants have livestock."

5 Therefore they said, "If we have found favor in your sight, let this land be given to your servants as a possession. Do not take us over the Jordan."

6 And Moses said to the children of Gad and to the children of Reuben: "Shall your brethren go to war while you sit here?

7 "Now why will you discourage the heart of the children of Israel from going over into the land which the LORD has given them?

8 "Thus your fathers did when I sent them away from Kadesh Barnea to see the land.

9 "For when they went up to the Valley of Eshcol and saw the land, they discouraged the heart of the children of Israel, so that they did not go into the land which the LORD had given them.

10 "So the LORD's anger was aroused on that day, and He swore an oath, saying,

11 'Surely none of the men who came up from Egypt, from twenty years old and above, shall see the land of which I swore to Abraham, Isaac, and Jacob, because they have not wholly followed Me,

12 'except Caleb the son of Jephunneh, the Kenizzite, and Joshua the son of Nun, for they have wholly followed the LORD.'

13 "So the LORD's anger was aroused against Israel, and He made them wander in the wilderness forty years, until all the generation that had done evil in the sight of the LORD was gone.

14 "And look! You have risen in your fathers' place, a brood of sinful men, to increase still more the fierce anger of the LORD against Israel.

15 "For if you turn away from following Him, He will once again leave them in the wilderness, and you will destroy all these people."

Num. 32:1–15

The fact that the tribes of Reuben, Gad, and half of Manasseh settled on the east side of Jordan is repeatedly referred to in the Pentateuch (cf. Deut. 3:12ff., 4:43, 29:8; Josh. 12:6, 13:29, 31, 14:3, 18:7), and it is clear from this that what took place here was of considerable, even fateful, significance in later times. The situation is described as follows: Reuben and Gad came to Moses requesting permission to make the land of Gilead on the east side of Jordan (which had already been acquired through conquest from Sihon and

Og, Num. 21:21–35) their permanent settlement and dwelling place, instead of going across Jordan and into Canaan itself with the rest of the tribes. The basis of their request, according to these verses, was the fact that they had large herds of cattle, and they saw that Gilead was ideal cattle country.

Moses (vv. 6ff.) reacted angrily to this suggestion, immediately comparing and identifying it with the spirit of Kadesh Barnea (Num. 13–14), when the children of Israel were unwilling to go in to possess the land and hung back from fulfilling their calling and destiny as the chosen people of God.[1] This heated exchange between Moses and the tribes is quite understandable when we recall the earlier situation at Kadesh and all the pain and anguish it caused Moses, not to say the judgment it brought upon a whole generation of Israel. It can hardly be doubted that it filled the man of God with a sense of foreboding at the prospect of what he feared was to be another situation of backsliding and rebellion on the part of these tribes, for it must have seemed to him, and with some justification, that for them to consider settling anywhere outside the land promised to Abraham was tantamount to showing indifference and contempt toward the divine purposes for them, and to opt out of the part God had for them to play in the conquest of Canaan.

There is much to say by way of comment on this situation, but it will be convenient to look at the rest of the chapter before doing so.

The Promises Made by Reuben and Gad

32:16 Then they came near to him and said: "We will build sheepfolds here for our livestock, and cities for our little ones,

17 "but we ourselves will be armed, ready *to go* before the children of Israel until we have brought them to their place; and our little ones will dwell in the fortified cities because of the inhabitants of the land.

18 "We will not return to our homes until every one of the children of Israel has received his inheritance.

19 "For we will not inherit with them on the other side of the Jordan and beyond, because our inheritance has fallen to us on this eastern side of the Jordan."

20 Then Moses said to them: "If you do this thing,
if you arm yourselves before the LORD for the war,
21 "and all your armed men cross over the Jordan
before the LORD until He has driven out His enemies
from before Him,
22 "and the land is subdued before the LORD, then
afterward you may return and be blameless before
the LORD and before Israel; and this land shall be
your possession before the LORD.
23 "But if you do not do so, then take note, you
have sinned against the LORD; and be sure your sin
will find you out.
24 "Build cities for your little ones and folds for
your sheep, and do what has proceeded out of your
mouth."
25 And the children of Gad and the children of
Reuben spoke to Moses, saying: "Your servants will
do as my lord commands.
26 "Our little ones, our wives, our flocks, and all
our livestock will be there in the cities of Gilead;
27 "but your servants will cross over, every man
armed for war, before the LORD to battle, just as my
lord says."
28 So Moses gave command concerning them to
Eleazar the priest, to Joshua the son of Nun, and
to the chief fathers of the tribes of the children of
Israel.
29 And Moses said to them: "If the children of Gad
and the children of Reuben cross over the Jordan
with you, every man armed for battle before the
LORD, and the land is subdued before you, then you
shall give them the land of Gilead as a possession.
30 "But if they do not cross over armed with you,
they shall have possessions among you in the land of
Canaan."
31 Then the children of Gad and the children of
Reuben answered, saying: "As the LORD has said to
your servants, so we will do.
32 "We will cross over armed before the LORD into
the land of Canaan, but the possession of our inheritance *shall remain* with us on this side of the Jordan."
33 So Moses gave to the children of Gad, to the

> children of Reuben, and to half the tribe of Manasseh the son of Joseph, the kingdom of Sihon king of the Amorites and the kingdom of Og king of Bashan, the land with its cities within the borders, the cities of the surrounding country.
>
> *Num. 32:16–33*

Reuben and Gad responded to Moses' angry outburst by protesting that they had no intention of neglecting their responsibilities in the wars of the Lord in the conquest of Canaan, and that they would go over to fight, but leave their wives and children in fenced cities in Gilead, then return to their families when the campaign was over. In other words, they now indicated that it was concern for their families that had activated them in their desire and request to Moses to be given this territory. Such seems to be the implication of their words in verses 16–19. This assurance—which really constituted a "revised version" of their earlier request in verses 3–5—was accepted by Moses, and their wish was granted, subject to the strict condition of honoring their promise to take their due part in the campaign (vv. 20–24). Reuben and Gad hastened to reassure Moses that they would fulfill his requirements to the letter; whereupon he formally made over to them the territories of the Amorites and the kingdom of Og, king of Bashan (v. 33).

The Conquest of Gilead by Manasseh

> 32:34 And the children of Gad built Dibon and Ataroth and Aroer,
> 35 Atroth and Shophan and Jazer and Jogbehah,
> 36 Beth Nimrah and Beth Haran, fortified cities, and folds for sheep.
> 37 And the children of Reuben built Heshbon and Elealeh and Kirjathaim,
> 38 Nebo and Baal Meon (*their* names being changed) and Shibmah; and they gave *other* names to the cities which they built.
> 39 And the children of Machir the son of Manasseh went to Gilead and took it, and dispossessed the Amorites who *were* in it.

> 40 So Moses gave Gilead to Machir the son of Manasseh, and he dwelt in it.
> 41 Also Jair the son of Manasseh went and took its small towns, and called them Havoth Jair.
> 42 Then Nobah went and took Kenath and its villages, and he called it Nobah, after his own name.
>
> *Num. 32:34–42*

The list of cities given in these verses as allocated to and inhabited by Gad (vv. 34–36), Reuben (vv. 37–38), and Manasseh (vv. 39–42) with the agreement of Moses includes those mentioned in verse 3. But the details given here differ from the fuller account of the final distribution of the land in Joshua 13:15ff., where Reuben was settled in the territory east of the Dead Sea, and Gad east of Jordan between the Dead Sea and the Sea of Galilee, and Manasseh in the northern part of Gilead. It may be that the arrangements mentioned here were merely temporary, as to detail, and subject to later and more permanent adjustment after the conquest was completed, with particular cities changing hands in the process. The incidents mentioned in verses 39, 41, and 42 are accounts of individual conquests, similar to those mentioned in Judges 1. Jair (v. 41) is the same "Jair the Gileadite" of Judges 10:3, whose judgeship preceded that of Jephthah.

Such is the outline of the chapter. As to interpretation, there can be little doubt that Reuben, Gad, and Manasseh committed a grave error here, and that their action was in fact correctly estimated by Moses in his initial reaction to it (vv. 6ff.). We consider first of all some very revealing notes in the text itself. For one thing, we must compare verses 1 and 4 with verses 16 and 17. There is a discrepancy here: the latter verses indicated that the reason for their request was concern for their families and little ones. But the record in verse 1 speaks very differently: *"They saw . . . that . . . the region was a place for livestock,"* and they said this, moreover, to Moses, and made this the ground of their request (vv. 4–5). What can this mean but that they saw something materially profitable, and that they lost interest in going over Jordan in their desire for it?

One is reminded of the story in Genesis 13:10, when Lot lifted up his eyes toward the plain of Jordan and, seeing that it was well-watered everywhere, chose it for himself despite the fact that he was thereby choosing an environment that was spiritually and morally dangerous. The very wording of verse 1 is reminiscent of that earlier, fateful choice made by Lot, to his ultimate discomfiture and loss. This choice was likewise fateful for Reuben, Gad, and Manasseh; for repeatedly, in later years, that was the portion of Israel that bore the *first* brunt of enemy attack, *because* they were so vulnerable, and because they did not have the protection of the river they refused to cross (see Judges 10:8, 17, 18; 1 Kings 22:3; 2 Kings 10:32–33, 15:29; 1 Chron. 5:26).

One readily recalls the patriarch Jacob's final words about his sons recorded in Genesis 49, in relation to Reuben of whom he said, "Unstable as water, you shall not excel." How truly this estimate is substantiated in the record before us! The words in verses 11–12 are pivotal here. It was a failure *wholly* to follow the Lord that lay at the root of this attitude of theirs, just as Caleb's and Joshua's determination in the other direction was definitive of all their future. Our Lord's words in Mark 8:36, "What will it profit a man if he gains the whole world, and loses his own soul?" find graphic illustration in the tribes' attitude, and should remind us that there is a price to be paid—sometimes a very great one—for allowing oneself to be controlled by worldly considerations.

If this is a valid interpretation of the situation, as we believe it to be, Moses' second response to them (vv. 20ff.) must therefore be regarded as permissive of what was certainly a compromise. We may wonder at this, but we have seen enough already in the Book of Numbers to know this people and their determination to go their own way. Moses had reminded them of Kadesh Barnea and the refusal of their fathers to rise to their spiritual destiny. It is as if God was saying to them once again, "Very well, if you are set on this, after all I have brought you through, I will accept the situation as you have delineated it. Gilead shall be yours—to your cost!" In the words of Psalm 106:15, "He gave them their request, but sent leanness into their soul." How often have these words applied to Israel's behavior (cf. Judg. 5:15–17 for a significant comment and illustration of Reuben's attitude here).

There is something inexpressibly sad about the picture given in this chapter of a company of God's people lacking in real enthusiasm for the goal to which they have been called, and opting for something less than God willed for them, but we can hardly doubt that this is something that often takes place in Christian experience, in the church, and in the life of a congregation of God's people. We sometimes speak of Christians living "in the shallows" when they should be launching out "into the deep," but this is something even more critical. For a Christian to opt for an easier, less arduous, less demanding way is to be in a backslidden state. It is to have no enthusiasm for the things of God to which He calls us. And it means putting other things in their place, things that become substitutes for the good and acceptable and perfect will of God. Indeed, it is often precisely these "other things" which lead to the failure. It was the fertile plains of Gilead that beguiled the hearts of Reuben, Gad, and Manasseh from the Promised Land. This story asks us some pointed and disturbing questions: Have we opted for an easier, alternative way in spiritual things? And is it because of some beguiling attraction that has come to mean more to us than the kingdom of God? Something that would certainly have to go, and would go, if we really pressed on as God is calling and challenging us to do?

The same factors that hinder some people in spiritual life are those that keep others out of the kingdom of God altogether. One thinks readily of the rich young ruler: he stood at the very gates, so to speak, of the Promised Land, viewing it and being inexpressibly drawn to it; but love of the world held him back from entering in, and he went away sorrowful. We do not know whether an absolute distinction can be made between those who are irreconcilably opposed to the message of the gospel and those whose hearts have been divided within themselves, one part of them longing for the blessings of its peace, the other resisting and holding back because of the claims of the world. But both, sadly, may end in the same way, without Christ and without hope.

But when we think of how suddenly God can cut men off from the little, paltry things that blind their eyes to the eternal world, we should realize that *none* of these things, whatever they are, are worth the price we often pay for them, in terms of spiritual values. Sometimes it is a *way of life* that keeps men from the true riches, and a whole way of life may need to be radically changed—this is what would have been involved for the rich young ruler, and plainly it was something he was not prepared to face. But a way of life can very soon pass away: how tragic then, to be clinging stubbornly to it until it slips through our nerveless fingers, and how much better to cast it aside resolutely, in order to lay hold on eternal life!

Perhaps the most frightening thing of all, however, is that such an attitude, described so trenchantly by the apostle James in his epistle (1:8) in the words, "He is a double-minded man, unstable in all his ways" (could he have been thinking of Jacob's description of Reuben?) leads to a double life in which we deceive ourselves and begin to live a lie. Reuben said one thing, but he meant another. His concern for his little ones, however genuine in itself it may have been, was only an excuse to hide his carnal desire for the plains of Gilead. This is what happens in a Christian context. We tell ourselves and others one thing, but the real reasons for not going over to Jordan are different. The tragedy is that the real reasons become hidden for us, because they are too uncomfortable to face, and no longer remain conscious in our mind.

This is how the unhappy, unsatisfactory, and spiritually barren state of compromise comes to pass, in which it is quite possible to pay lip service to the call of God, yet live at odds with it; to be under arms, it may be, and fighting the battles of the Lord, as Reuben was intending to do, but not with a full, unreserved commitment, and on a different footing from the real warriors of God. Such people seldom suspect that others may see how it is with them, or that such a compromising position, however subtly disguised, is impossible of concealment. They do not realize that there is something in the very nature of the warfare itself that serves to expose anything less than full and wholehearted surrender. We should not forget Moses' words in verse 23: "Be sure your sin will find you out"—not, be it noted "your sin will be found out," but something more serious—it will find *you* out, search *you* out, hunt *you* out, and be your destroyer. The plains of Gilead cost Reuben dearly in the end. Compromise always costs!

THE JOURNEYS OF ISRAEL

> 33:1 These *are* the journeys of the children of Israel,
> who went out of the land of Egypt by their armies
> under the hand of Moses and Aaron.
> 2 Now Moses wrote down the starting points of

> their journeys at the command of the LORD. And these *are* their journeys according to their starting points:
>
> 3 They departed from Rameses in the first month, on the fifteenth day of the first month; on the day after the Passover the children of Israel went out with boldness in the sight of all the Egyptians.
>
> 4 For the Egyptians were burying all *their* firstborn, whom the LORD had killed among them. Also on their gods the LORD had executed judgments.
>
> *Num. 33:1–4*

The chapter which begins with these verses is largely taken up with a retrospective account of the journeyings of Israel from the time they left Egypt until they stood on the plains of Moab, about to cross into the Promised Land. In this introductory section we are told of the date and the circumstances of Israel's departure from Egypt on their journeys, and that Moses made this summary of them at the express command of the Lord. The word "journeys" in verse 1 is rendered "stages" in some margins and is said by one commentator more nearly to represent the Hebrew which literally means "pluckings up," a reference to "the taking up of the tent-pegs before beginning the march."[2] Some forty of these "stages" or camping sites are listed, at which Israel encamped, between their departure from Rameses in Egypt (v. 3) and their arrival at the plains of Moab (v. 49). Eleven stages are mentioned from Rameses to the Wilderness of Sinai (vv. 3–15); twenty stages from there to Ezion Geber (vv. 16–35); one stage from Ezion Geber to the Wilderness of Zin (v. 36); and nine from there to the plains of Moab (vv. 37–49). It is clear that this record was to stand as an important reminder to Israel of all that had taken place.

A number of problems arise in a consideration of this catalog of stopping places, and reference will be made to them in the course of the exposition, but something must be said now about the significance of its inclusion at this point in the narrative. Wenham suggests that "since Moses' great achievements took place at the stations mentioned, this list serves as a sort of obituary for him" and that it also "reminds the reader of the great obstacles that the nation has overcome in escaping from Egypt and crossing the Sinai desert."[3] There is probably a real significance in the fact that the journey is summed up in these forty stages, for it took, all told, forty years to accomplish. We do not mean by this that they completed one stage per year—the first eleven stages were completed in a period of two months (Exod. 19:1)—but rather that there seems to be some symbolism involved in the coincidence of the numbers. And, of course, this is the point: it should not have taken anything like this time to accomplish it. The journey from Egypt to Horeb (Sinai) on a rough estimate could not have been more than, say, 220–240 miles, and from there to Kadesh 150–170 miles (in Deut. 1:2, 3 we are told that from Horeb to Kadesh was eleven days' journey). The whole thing could have been done in little more than a month!

The lesson of the chapter seems aptly summed up in the contrast between the eleven days' journey (Deut. 1:2, 3) and the forty years it took them to get to this present point in the plains of Moab. What seems implied is that the great part of their journeyings was not really necessary, but was made necessary by their failure and sin. They were on the move, but they did not get anywhere for so very long.

It is possible, too, to journey thus through the spiritual life, being constantly on the move without getting anywhere, going around in circles—and all because of disobedience and sin. If the Old Testament is God's "picture book" of the spiritual life, the question this poses for us is whether we see ourselves portrayed in this chapter. Is this the story of our lives—at a standstill spiritually, although showing a great deal of movement and activity? Have we gotten *anywhere* in the past while?

FROM RAMESES TO SINAI

33:5 Then the children of Israel moved from Rameses and camped at Succoth.

6 They departed from Succoth and camped at Etham, which *is* on the edge of the wilderness.

7 They moved from Etham and turned back to Pi Hahiroth, which *is* east of Baal Zephon; and they camped near Migdol.

8 They departed from before Hahiroth and passed through the midst of the sea into the wilderness, went three days' journey in the Wilderness of Etham, and camped at Marah.

9 They moved from Marah and came to Elim. At Elim *were* twelve springs of water and seventy palm trees; so they camped there.
10 They moved from Elim and camped by the Red Sea.
11 They moved from the Red Sea and camped in the Wilderness of Sin.
12 They journeyed from the Wilderness of Sin and camped at Dophkah.
13 They departed from Dophkah and camped at Alush.
14 They moved from Alush and camped at Rephidim, where there was no water for the people to drink.
15 They departed from Rephidim and camped in the Wilderness of Sinai.

Num. 33:5–15

In his commentary, Gray remarks of these verses that "for aught that appears to the contrary, (they) presuppose a simple direct line of march from Egypt to Sinai," but in fact opinions differ as to the route followed after Israel crossed the Red Sea. The main question centers on the exact location of Mount Sinai. The traditional site identifies Gebel Musa with Mount Sinai at the southern end of the Arabian Peninsula. The fact, however, that Sinai is spoken of in Exodus 3:1ff., 5:3, 8:27 and elsewhere as being only three days' journey from Egypt, and in Deuteronomy 1:2 as eleven days from Kadesh, has prompted scholars to consider alternative sites, such as Jebel Sin Bisher, some thirty miles southwest of present-day Suez. Arguments for and against either interpretation with greater or lesser plausibility are given in modern commentaries, but are not our immediate concern here.[4]

These verses stand parallel to the account of the journey given in Exodus 12:37–19:2. One commentator points out that "with the exception of Dophkah and Alush all the places named are well known."[5] It is interesting that in this record of the first part of the journey not only are the camping sites mentioned, but also important events that occurred at some of them (e.g., the experiences at Elim, v. 9, and Rephidim, v. 14), in contrast to the later verses, which are a simple record of place-names.

From Sinai to Ezion Geber

33:16 They moved from the Wilderness of Sinai and camped at Kibroth Hattaavah.

17 They departed from Kibroth Hattaavah and camped at Hazeroth.

18 They departed from Hazeroth and camped at Rithmah.

19 They departed from Rithmah and camped at Rimmon Perez.

20 They departed from Rimmon Perez and camped at Libnah.

21 They moved from Libnah and camped at Rissah.

22 They journeyed from Rissah and camped at Kehelathah.

23 They went from Kehelathah and camped at Mount Shepher.

24 They moved from Mount Shepher and camped at Haradah.

25 They moved from Haradah and camped at Makheloth.

26 They moved from Makheloth and camped at Tahath.

27 They departed from Tahath and camped at Terah.

28 They moved from Terah and camped at Mithkah.

29 They went from Mithkah and camped at Hashmonah.

30 They departed from Hashmonah and camped at Moseroth.

31 They departed from Moseroth and camped at Bene Jaakan.

32 They moved from Bene Jaakan and camped at Hor Hagidgad.

33 They went from Hor Hagidgad and camped at Jotbathah.

34 They moved from Jotbathah and camped at Abronah.

35 They departed from Abronah and camped at Ezion Geber.

Num. 33:16–35

The great majority of the names in this section of Israel's journey, which deals with the wanderings in the wilderness, are entirely unknown, and with the exception of Kibroth Hattaavah and Hazeroth, which are mentioned in 11:34, 35, are not found elsewhere, although Wenham suggests that verses 31–33 appear to find an echo in Deuteronomy 10:6, 7.[6] Gray, recognizing the problems in the distances between Sinai and Ezion Geber and between the latter and Kadesh, whichever site may be determined for Sinai, draws the interesting conclusion: "The stations in this section can therefore scarcely be given as points on a route; they are rather points scattered over a district of which 'Esion-Geber and Kadesh' may be taken as being respectively the southern and northern points. Thus section 2 probably gives the places visited during the period of wandering; they correspond in the itinerary to the wilderness of Paran."[7]

FROM EZION GEBER TO MOAB

33:36 They moved from Ezion Geber and camped in the Wilderness of Zin, which *is* Kadesh.

37 They moved from Kadesh and camped at Mount Hor, on the boundary of the land of Edom.

38 Then Aaron the priest went up to Mount Hor at the command of the LORD, and died there in the fortieth year after the children of Israel had come out of the land of Egypt, on the first *day* of the fifth month.

39 Aaron *was* one hundred and twenty-three years old when he died on Mount Hor.

40 Now the king of Arad, the Canaanite, who dwelt in the South in the land of Canaan, heard of the coming of the children of Israel.

41 So they departed from Mount Hor and camped at Zalmonah.

42 They departed from Zalmonah and camped at Punon.

43 They departed from Punon and camped at Oboth.

44 They departed from Oboth and camped at Ije Abarim, at the border of Moab.

45 They departed from Ijim and camped at Dibon
Gad.
46 They moved from Dibon Gad and camped at
Almon Diblathaim.
47 They moved from Almon Diblathaim and
camped in the mountains of Abarim, before Nebo.
48 They departed from the mountains of Abarim
and camped in the plains of Moab by the Jordan,
across from Jericho.
49 They camped by the Jordan, from Beth Jesimoth
as far as the Abel Acacia Grove in the plains of
Moab.

Num. 33:36–49

In this list of stages from Ezion Geber to the plains of Moab there is a change again from the pattern in verses 16–35 in that it includes a historical reference, to the death of Aaron (vv. 38–39), which summarizes the fuller account given in Numbers 20:22–29. The reference in verse 40 to the king of Arad is similarly taken from Numbers 21:1ff. The date given in verse 38, the fortieth year of Israel's pilgrimage, makes it clear that the entire period of the wilderness wanderings is assumed to have been covered in this chapter of retrospect, even although there has been no mention of the historic crisis at Kadesh Barnea (Num. 13–14), when a whole generation of Israel was forbidden entrance into the Promised Land and condemned to wilderness wandering until their death. This fact alone must surely make it clear that the point of this record was not primarily to give a step-by-step geographical and historical account of Israel's journeys. The writer could hardly have been so obtuse, if this had been his purpose, as to omit such an important element in the story. His purpose must have lain elsewhere. This lends credence to the view expressed by Wenham that the writer was concerned to assure his readers that if God had helped Israel thus far, He would surely enable them also, now that they were on the borders of the land of Canaan, to reach their goal and to conquer the Promised Land.[8] The chapter therefore has a didactic rather than a geographical purpose.

This serves to explain why, for example, none of the murmurings of the people find mention throughout. It is not merely because it might be considered out of place to mention such incidents in a catalog of this nature, for in fact other incidents, such as the provision

God made for His needy people at Elim in the fountains of water and the palm trees, are particularly noted. This may be meant to indicate that more important than all the sorry history of sin and failure is the divine provision of grace. When the story is ultimately told, it will be the latter, not the former, that will adorn the permanent record of the pilgrimage. F. B. Meyer, in a comment on this, says, "When we get to heaven and study the way-book, we shall find all the deeds of love and self-denial carefully recorded, though we have forgotten them; and all the sins blotted out, though we remember them."[9]

In similar fashion, the reference to the death of Aaron in verses 38–39 has its lesson to teach. No mention is made of the reason why Aaron was gathered home to God at this point, as in 20:24; rather, it is related to the completion of the forty-year period of Israel's wanderings, suggesting an integral connection with the divine purposes. His work was done, his course run, and God took him to be with Himself. Always it is the ongoing purposes of God that are central, and this is what should take up our minds and hearts also—not vain, regretful tears for the past, though never without a due sense of being unprofitable servants, but rather a looking forward to the future with confidence, resolution, and courage. After all, as someone has said, "Tomorrow is the first day of the rest of our lives" (cf. 1 Peter 4:2–3).

Instructions for the Conquest of Canaan

33:50 Now the LORD spoke to Moses in the plains of Moab by the Jordan, *across from* Jericho, saying,

51 "Speak to the children of Israel, and say to them: 'When you have crossed the Jordan into the land of Canaan,

52 'then you shall drive out all the inhabitants of the land from before you, destroy all their engraved stones, destroy all their molded images, and demolish all their high places;

53 'you shall dispossess *the inhabitants of* the land and dwell in it, for I have given you the land to possess.

54 'And you shall divide the land by lot as an

inheritance among your families; to the larger you
shall give a larger inheritance, and to the smaller
you shall give a smaller inheritance; there everyone's
inheritance shall be whatever falls to him by lot. You
shall inherit according to the tribes of your fathers.
55 'But if you do not drive out the inhabitants of
the land from before you, then it shall be that those
whom you let remain *shall be* irritants in your eyes
and thorns in your sides, and they shall harass you in
the land where you dwell.
56 'Moreover it shall be *that* I will do to you as I
thought to do to them.'"

Num. 33:50–56

The lessons to be learned by Israel from this historical retrospect have become clearer as we have proceeded through the chapter. The reason why they had to remain for so long in the wilderness was their basic resistance to God's will, which is always certain to bring spiritual advancement to a standstill. This was highlighted for Israel by the fact of the mighty acts of God on their behalf by which they were brought out of Egypt into freedom. In this connection, one readily thinks of Exodus 4:31 and 12:27—if only they had maintained *this* spirit as the proper response of glad and humble acceptance of God's word of promise! But their subsequent history showed a tragic falling away from that spirit, with the inevitable consequences that followed. The apostle Paul once wrote to the Galatians, "You ran well. What hindered you from obeying the truth?" This is one of the tragedies of spiritual life, that so many *begin* well, but trail off after a few years into a barren and chilling mediocrity of experience. Israel did so. This is the warning note that rings through the chapter.

It is against this background of failure that we can best understand what now follows in these verses and in the next chapter. For the discipline of the long years in the wilderness had now come to an end, and God was about to bring His people into the land. And He had two words in particular for them, which require to be viewed in the light of their past failure, one in these verses, the other in 34:1–15. On the one hand, they were to drive out all the inhabitants of the land; on the other, they were to take possession of all God had given them in His promise and extend the borders of their inheritance to the utmost of the promise. That is to say, there was both a negative and a positive command. It is as if God, in bringing this twofold command into juxtaposition with the retrospect of Israel's past failures, was saying to them, "Remember your past failures, and see that you do not fail in this that I now set before you. You suffered needlessly during these long years; see that you do not, by another disobedience, bring more needless suffering and deprivation upon your hearts." One thinks of the words of Psalm 85:8, "He will speak peace to His people and to His saints; but let them not turn back to folly." This is exactly the spirit of these verses. It is impressive how, often in one brief sentence, the psalmist sums up the essence of a situation and goes to the heart of it, giving an inspired and authoritative interpretation of Old Testament history.

The Canaanites were to be uprooted and utterly destroyed because they were depraved, and because they were therefore a possible, nay certain, source of contamination for Israel. Hence the radical and inexorable nature of the command given here. Subsequent history proves that Israel often found the Canaanite nations rather too interesting and fascinating, to her own loss, for sometimes they were spared, and they became *"irritants"* in her eyes and *"thorns"* in her side, as God had warned them (v. 55); and it was this that led finally to the Israelites being exiled from their own land (v. 56).

Wenham points out that "Christian commentators have often drawn parallels between Israel's war against pagan religion and the Christian's call to subdue the vices of the old Adam in himself (cf. Rom. 6; Col. 3)."[10] This is surely a valid exercise, and one that is always relevant. We are to cast out all the warring factions in our lives, for if we do not, they will yet rise up against us and do us despite. We must deal with them without delay, and not wait until they get the advantage over us. If there are enemies of our souls with whom we have made friends, with whom we have made the equivalent of a "non-aggression pact," we had better beware, for they will yet prove perilous, if not fatal, for our spiritual life and service. We should recall our Lord's action in the temple with the scourge of small cords, and seek to follow His example and cleanse the temple of the Holy Spirit which is our body, and make it a worthy place for His gracious indwelling.

THE APPOINTED BOUNDARIES OF CANAAN

34:1 Then the LORD spoke to Moses, saying,
2 "Command the children of Israel, and say to
them: 'When you come into the land of Canaan, this
is the land that shall fall to you as an inheritance—
the land of Canaan to its boundaries.
3 'Your southern border shall be from the Wilderness of Zin along the border of Edom; then your
southern border shall extend eastward to the end of
the Salt Sea;
4 'your border shall turn from the southern side
of the Ascent of Akrabbim, continue to Zin, and be
on the south of Kadesh Barnea; then it shall go on to
Hazar Addar, and continue to Azmon;
5 'the border shall turn from Azmon to the Brook
of Egypt, and it shall end at the Sea.
6 'As for the western border, you shall have the
Great Sea for a border; this shall be your western
border.
7 'And this shall be your northern border: From
the Great Sea you shall mark out your *border* line to
Mount Hor;
8 'from Mount Hor you shall mark out *your border*
to the entrance of Hamath; then the direction of the
border shall be toward Zedad;
9 'the border shall proceed to Ziphron, and it
shall end at Hazar Enan. This shall be your northern
border.
10 'You shall mark out your eastern border from
Hazar Enan to Shepham;
11 'the border shall go down from Shepham to
Riblah on the east side of Ain; the border shall go
down and reach to the eastern side of the Sea of
Chinnereth;
12 'the border shall go down along the Jordan, and
it shall end at the Salt Sea. This shall be your land
with its surrounding boundaries.'"
13 Then Moses commanded the children of Israel,
saying: "This *is* the land which you shall inherit by
lot, which the LORD has commanded to give to the
nine tribes and to the half-tribe.

> 14 "For the tribe of the children of Reuben according to the house of their fathers, and the tribe of the children of Gad according to the house of their fathers, have received *their inheritance;* and the half-tribe of Manasseh has received its inheritance.
> 15 "The two tribes and the half-tribe have received their inheritance on this side of the Jordan, *across from* Jericho eastward, toward the sunrise."
>
> *Num. 34:1–15*

The thoroughness and rigor with which Israel was to possess the land of Canaan having been enjoined upon them by the Lord (33:50–56), the extent of the operation was next defined. The delineation of the borders-to-be of Israel is given in these verses. Not all of the place-names are now identifiable with any certainty, and some are quite unknown; but on any estimate and interpretation, the "Canaan" that was the inheritance given to Israel was larger and more extensive than they were ever able to possess, even in David's and Solomon's time. One theologian speaks of the passage as an ideal representation, and compares it with the similarly ideal picture given in Ezekiel 47.[11] There are other references elsewhere in the Old Testament about the extent of the divine promise concerning the land to be given Israel, as for example Genesis 15:18, "from the river of Egypt to the great river, the River Euphrates"; "from Dan to Beersheba" in Judges 20:1, and frequently elsewhere in the historical books; "from the entrance of Hamath to the Brook of Egypt" in 1 Kings 8:65; and these should be compared with what is indicated here (cf. also Josh. 15–19).

As to the various boundaries, the southern border described in verses 3–5 is the same as that given in Joshua 15:2–4 as the boundary of the tribe of Judah's territory (as also in Ezek. 47:19), and reaches down into the Negev some miles south of Beersheba, and across south of Kadesh to the Brook of Egypt, the present-day Wadi el Arish, at the southern end of the Gaza strip. The western boundary (v. 6) is the Mediterranean coastline which, as Binns and others point out, was at no time the boundary of Israel, and Israel never occupied any of the seacoast until the time of the Maccabees in the second century B.C., when Simon the Maccabee captured Joppa (1 Macc. 14:5).[12] In the south, the Philistines stood between Judah and the sea throughout the period of the monarchy.[13]

The northern border (vv. 7–9), so far as identifiable place-names are concerned, seems to have encompassed much of present-day Lebanon, and some think that it reached well north of the border of the tribe of Dan. Binns observes, "Though Dan, south of the mountains (of Lebanon), is, as Gray says, 'the proverbial northern town,' the tide of Israelite conquest in the reigns of David (1 Kings 8:65) and of Jeroboam II (2 Kings 14:25) seems to have flowed far beyond it."[14] Another writer gives a useful pointer at the end of an extended discussion of verses 7–9 as follows: "We may look for Hazar-enan (fountain-court), which is mentioned as the end of the northern boundary, and the starting-point of the eastern, near the fountain of Lebweh. This fountain forms the water-shed in the Bekaa, between the Orontes, which flows to the north, and the Leontes, which flows to the south. . . ."[15] The eastern frontier presents problems almost impossible of solution. The only reasonably definite statement one can make is that, as Gray points out, the mention of intermediate points between Hazar-enan and the Lake of Galilee (Chinnereth) shows that the former was some distance away from (north or north-east of) the latter. From the Sea of Galilee, it followed the Jordan valley down to the Dead Sea.[16]

The land thus delineated was therefore very extensive, and God's command to Israel was to take possession of all He had given them in His promise. The tragedy is that by their failure to cast out and destroy their enemies (according to 33:51 ff.) Israel failed to make her own all that God had in store for them. It is a simple fact that the children of Israel never entered into their full inheritance because of their inability or refusal to be thorough enough in dealing with their enemies, and because they were content with small things (as Reuben, Gad, and Manasseh were). They could have been a much greater nation, with their borders extending far beyond the furthest they ever reached, if only they had risen fully to the challenge of the divine promise.

The spiritual parallel in this is very plain, in both general and specific ways. In its specific application what must be said is this: When we allow the "enemies of our souls" to remain unmolested in our hearts and lives, make pacts with them, indulge them, they not only become irritants in our eyes and thorns in our sides but—much worse—they prevent us from possessing the true riches that God wills us to have, and from being what we could be, and were destined to be, for God. This is as true for unbelievers as for believers. Many a man has been beguiled from his true destiny by some worldly consideration that has become too dear for him to consider parting from without the greatest pain. He clings to it, thinking the loss of it would make life meaningless and dull, whereas by clinging to it he is preventing himself from entering the real riches of life. He is content with tawdry tinsel, when God is holding out pure gold to him. And—as Jesus Himself said—"What will it profit a man if he gains the whole world, and loses his own soul?" (Mark 8:36).

The more general application of this passage is this: there is far, far more for us in the gift of Christ than ever we have yet appropriated or made our own. We are too easily satisfied. The biblical testimony (Rev. 1:6) is that God has made us kings and priests to Him, but we often fall far short of living like sons and daughters of a King. We do not have a royal demeanor, nor do we make the resources of His royal treasure-house our own. We have not stretched God by our demands upon Him. We are not restricted in Him: He is restricted in us (cf. 2 Cor. 6:12). The challenge of these verses is well expressed in Henry Francis Lyte's fine hymn, "Jesus, I My Cross Have Taken,"

Take, my soul, thy full salvation,
  Rise o'er sin and fear and care;
Joy to find in every station
  Something still to do or bear;
Think what Spirit dwells within thee,
  What a Father's smile is thine,
What a Saviour died to win thee:
  Child of heaven, shouldst thou repine?

Such is the open door that God sets before us in the gospel, saying "Son, you are always with me and *all that I have is yours*" (Luke 15:31). God forbid that we should ever be satisfied with small things when God wants us to extend the borders of our "promised land" to the utmost of His promise.

The Appointment of Supervisors

34:16 And the LORD spoke to Moses saying,
17 "These *are* the names of the men who shall

divide the land among you as an inheritance: Eleazar
the priest and Joshua the son of Nun.
18 "And you shall take one leader of every tribe to
divide the land for the inheritance.
19 "These *are* the names of the men: from the tribe
of Judah, Caleb the son of Jephunneh;
20 "from the tribe of the children of Simeon,
Shemuel the son of Ammihud;
21 "from the tribe of Benjamin, Elidad the son of
Chislon;
22 "a leader from the tribe of the children of Dan,
Bukki the son of Jogli;
23 "from the sons of Joseph: a leader from the
tribe of the children of Manasseh, Hanniel the son of
Ephod,
24 "and a leader from the tribe of the children of
Ephraim, Kemuel the son of Shiphtan;
25 "a leader from the tribe of the children of
Zebulun, Elizaphan the son of Parnach;
26 "a leader from the tribe of the children of
Issachar, Paltiel the son of Azzan;
27 "a leader from the tribe of the children of
Asher, Ahihud the son of Shelomi;
28 "and a leader from the tribe of the children of
Naphtali, Pedahel the son of Ammihud."
29 These *are* the ones the LORD commanded to divide the inheritance among the children of Israel in
the land of Canaan.

Num. 34:16–29

In these verses we are given the names of those appointed to oversee the allotment of the territories in Canaan. The fact that they are spoken of in verse 17 as having been appointed by God Himself is an indication of the importance of the task given them. They were, in fact, entrusted with the implementation of the divine will for His people. They were chosen on the same principle as those who superintended the census in 1:1–15, but Eleazar and Joshua (v. 17) were to take the place of Moses and Aaron (1:3). Since only ten tribes were to share in the land west of Jordan, Gad and Reuben and half of Manasseh having already been settled in trans-Jordan, only ten leaders are mentioned here.

The ten tribes are mentioned in geographical order according to their situation in Canaan, from south northward, but Judah is given precedence over Simeon, in violation of this geographical order (either because of its importance or because of the importance of its appointed leader, Caleb, who along with Joshua and Eleazar were the only survivors of that earlier generation). One writer comments, "The names provide interesting insight into Israel's name system, (such as) Shemuel, name of God; Elidad, God has loved; Hanniel, favour of God; Elizaphan, my God protects; Paltiel, God is my deliverance; Pedahel, God has redeemed."[17] This may indicate to us that they were men whose character and integrity matched their names in such a way that the work of responsibility and importance was entrusted to them. It could well be, although there is no actual scriptural evidence for this, that they had proved themselves previously, as Caleb had done, to be worthy of trust. Thus their faithfulness was now being recognized. Men who have God not merely in their names but in their lives as a controlling principle are men who can be trusted to serve Him worthily.

Cities for the Levites

35:1 And the LORD spoke to Moses in the plains of
Moab by the Jordan *across from* Jericho, saying:
2 "Command the children of Israel that they give
the Levites cities to dwell in from the inheritance of
their possession, and you shall *also* give the Levites
common-land around the cities.
3 "They shall have the cities to dwell in; and their
common-land shall be for their cattle, for their herds,
and for all their animals.
4 "The common-land of the cities which you will
give the Levites *shall extend* from the wall of the city
outward a thousand cubits all around.
5 "And you shall measure outside the city on the
east side two thousand cubits, on the south side two
thousand cubits, on the west side two thousand cubits, and on the north side two thousand cubits. The
city *shall be* in the middle. This shall belong to them
as common-land for the cities.

6 "Now among the cities which you will give to the Levites *you shall appoint* six cities of refuge, to which a manslayer may flee. And to these you shall add forty-two cities.

7 "So all the cities you will give to the Levites *shall be* forty-eight; these *you shall give* with their common-land.

8 "And the cities which you will give *shall be* from the possession of the children of Israel; from the larger *tribe* you shall give many, from the smaller you shall give few. Each shall give some of its cities to the Levites, in proportion to the inheritance that each receives."

Num. 35:1–8

Wenham usefully points out that directions about the Levites regularly follow directions about the other tribes (cf. 1:47–54 after 1:1–46; 3:1–49 after 2:1 ff.; 26:57–62 after 26:1–56), and he adds: "So here, after the remarks in chapter 34 about the allocation of land to the other tribes, the tribe of Levi is dealt with."[18] The main part of the chapter concerns the appointment of cities of refuge, but these verses deal with the cities for the Levites to dwell in, and it was from these that the cities of refuge were set apart. We have already seen that the Levites were to have no inheritance (cf. Num. 3–4 and, particularly, 18:21–24) since the Lord was to be their inheritance. They were called to be separate, to be different from the other tribes. The extent of that "difference" is seen further here. They were to be dispersed throughout the land in forty-eight cities set apart for them by the twelve tribes (cf. Joshua 21, where a detailed account of the fulfillment of this command is given: thirteen cities from Judah, Simeon, and Benjamin allocated to the priests; ten cities from Ephraim, Dan, and west-Manasseh allocated to the Kohathites; thirteen cities from Issachar, Asher, Naphtali, and east-Manasseh allocated to the Gershonites; and twelve cities of Reuben, Gad, and Zebulun allocated to the Merarites).

In other words, the Levites were to have no corporate existence *as a tribe,* but were rather fragmented in this way in a God-appointed isolation. Furthermore, the purpose of this dispersion, as we may learn from Deuteronomy 33:10, was with a view to the instruction of the people of God in the law of the Lord.

This consideration serves to put the Levites' calling in a true spiritual perspective. Even with the pasture lands around the cities allocated to them, the total area of actual land given them could have amounted only to one-tenth of the 1 percent of the whole of Canaan, as Wenham points out,[19] so that relative to the other tribes it could be substantially said that they had "no inheritance among the children of Israel" (18:23). Their spiritual function was therefore regarded as paramount.

This has a twofold significance: on the one hand, it underlines the fact that the separated life, so far as those called to the ministry of the Word is concerned, either then or now, is likely to be a life of loneliness and isolation and that it is in the context of such a loneliness that the Lord's work is to be done. There is a sense in which God cannot afford a strong concentration of His servants in one place, when a whole land, and a whole people, have to be served in the gospel. And if there are, relatively speaking, few who are people after His own heart, it can hardly be surprising if they are not stationed alongside each other. But often they are far apart, with only occasional meetings for fellowship and sharing. We should spare a thought, then, for those laboring in lonely places, and pray for them. And—in the matter of vacation times—it might perhaps fulfill a ministry of real encouragement to visit with them and to sit under their ministry, to strengthen their hands in God.

On the other hand, this is a word for all who as Christian witnesses are called to be separate unto God. We may well be set down in lonely places in regard to family, neighborhood, or work; but it is no warrant to us to leave our place simply because there is no congenial Christian fellowship there: rather the opposite. The apostle Paul says, "Let each one remain in the same calling in which he was called" (1 Cor. 7:20), for this is God's purpose and strategy, to spread the witness as comprehensively as possible. How else is the law of the Lord to be made known, if not by us, just where we are?

This enshrines a basic principle of the spiritual life. Redemption for the world meant loneliness and deprivation for the Son of God, and it will hardly mean less for those who follow in His steps. If this be the price for spreading the message of grace throughout the land, should we not be prepared to pay it? This is surely a word of exhortation, for those who feel their isolation and loneliness in the service of the gospel, whether at home or abroad, to take heart and take courage, in the realization that their labor—including the loneliness and the isolation—is not in vain in the Lord (1 Cor. 15:58). It *will* tell for God, in the blessing of others: as poor, it will make many rich (2 Cor. 6:10).

The Cities of Refuge

> 35:9 Then the LORD spoke to Moses, saying,
> 10 "Speak to the children of Israel, and say to them: 'When you cross the Jordan into the land of Canaan,
> 11 'then you shall appoint cities to be cities of refuge for you, that the manslayer who kills any person accidentally may flee there.
> 12 'They shall be cities of refuge for you from the avenger, that the manslayer may not die until he stands before the congregation in judgment.
> 13 'And of the cities which you give, you shall have six cities of refuge.
> 14 'You shall appoint three cities on this side of the Jordan, and three cities you shall appoint in the land of Canaan, *which* will be cities of refuge.
> 15 'These six cities shall be for refuge for the children of Israel, for the stranger, and for the sojourner among them, that anyone who kills a person accidentally may flee there.'"
>
> *Num. 35:9–15*

From the Levitical cities, six were to be selected as asylums or places of refuge for those who had unwittingly committed manslaughter. The particular cities are not specified here, but are named in Joshua 20:1–9 as Kedesh, Shechem, and Kirjath Arba on the west of Jordan, and Bezer, Ramoth, and Golan on the east of Jordan (cf. also Deut. 4:41, 19:2, 9).

The appointment of these cities belonged to the general judicial system that was evolved among the Old Testament people of God. The concluding verses of the chapter (vv. 33–34) indicate the importance of this legislation: the concern was, as Wenham rightly points out, to preserve the purity of the land by dealing with blood guilt whenever it occurred.[20] It is important to note that the provision offered was for the manslayer, not the murderer (vv. 11, 12, 15), for the man who killed inadvertently or accidentally, not the man who deliberately took life. This distinction made here echoes Exodus 21:12ff., and is repeated in Deuteronomy 19:4ff.

In ancient times, not only in Israel but among other nations, the duty of avenging a killing lay upon the nearest kinsman (the *"avenger"* in v. 12); obviously, occasions would arise in which vengeance might well be wreaked on those who had not killed deliberately, and this merciful legislation was instituted to prevent excesses that might develop from blood-feuds. A man could flee to such a city of refuge for sanctuary (v. 12), pending an inquiry into the matter by the congregation, who would judge whether it was a deliberate murder or an inadvertent killing. If the latter, the killer could find refuge and sanctuary in the city and be free from the fear of retribution, so long as he remained within its walls. If he ventured outside its protection, it was his own responsibility: he could be slain with impunity then, with none but himself to blame.

Definition of Manslaughter

35:16 "'But if he strikes him with an iron implement, so that he dies, he *is* a murderer; the murderer shall surely be put to death.

17 'And if he strikes him with a stone in the hand, by which one could die, and he does die, he *is* a murderer; the murderer shall surely be put to death.

18 'Or *if* he strikes him with a wooden hand weapon, by which one could die, and he does die, he *is* a murderer; the murderer shall surely be put to death.

19 'The avenger of blood himself shall put the murderer to death; when he meets him, he shall put him to death.

20 'If he pushes him out of hatred or, while lying in wait, hurls something at him so that he dies,

21 'or in enmity he strikes him with his hand so that he dies, the one who struck *him* shall surely be put to death; he *is* a murderer. The avenger of blood shall put the murderer to death when he meets him.

22 'However if he pushes him suddenly without enmity, or throws anything at him without lying in wait,

23 'or uses a stone, by which a man could die, throwing *it* at him without seeing *him,* so that he dies, while he was not his enemy or seeking his harm,

24 'then the congregation shall judge between the manslayer and the avenger of blood according to these judgments.

25 'So the congregation shall deliver the manslayer from the hand of the avenger of blood, and the congregation shall return him to the city of refuge where he had fled, and he shall remain there until the death of the high priest who was anointed with the holy oil.'"

Num. 35:16–25

A number of examples defining both murder (vv. 16–21) and unwitting manslaughter (vv. 22–23) are now given, both to establish the distinction between the one and the other and to give guidance and direction to the congregation in the judgment they make concerning them (v. 24). The procedure to be followed where proof of guilt is established is made clear in verses 19 and 21b: the avenger of blood shall put the murderer to death. He is to be the executioner, but it is the congregation, not he, who makes the judgment after due process of examination, and that before at least two witnesses (v. 30; cf. Deut. 19:15).

The reference to the death of the high priest in verse 25 is particularly significant. Noth thinks that "in this respect the high priest . . . must have taken over the role formerly played by the king, and this must be a reference to the fact that a general amnesty was, or at least could be, bound up with a change in the occupancy of the throne."[21] Wenham, however, sees a deeper significance in this reference, maintaining that atonement for manslaughter came through the death of the high priest: only the death of another can atone for a killing, whether accidental or deliberate.[22]

VARIOUS PROVISIONS AND WARNINGS

35:26 "'But if the manslayer at any time goes outside the limits of the city of refuge where he fled,

27 'and the avenger of blood finds him outside the
limits of his city of refuge, and the avenger of blood
kills the manslayer, he shall not be guilty of blood,
28 'because he should have remained in his city of
refuge until the death of the high priest. But after the
death of the high priest the manslayer may return to
the land of his possession.
29 'And these *things* shall be a statute of judgment
to you throughout your generations in all your
dwellings.
30 'Whoever kills a person, the murderer shall be
put to death on the testimony of witnesses; but one
witness is not *sufficient* testimony against a person
for the death *penalty.*
31 'Moreover you shall take no ransom for the life
of a murderer who *is* guilty of death, but he shall
surely be put to death.
32 'And you shall take no ransom for him who has
fled to his city of refuge, that he may return to dwell
in the land before the death of the priest.
33 'So you shall not pollute the land where you
are; for blood defiles the land, and no atonement can
be made for the land, for the blood that is shed on it,
except by the blood of him who shed it.
34 'Therefore do not defile the land which you inhabit, in the midst of which I dwell; for I the LORD
dwell among the children of Israel.'"

Num. 35:26–34

Reference has already been made to the necessity for the fugitive to remain in the city of refuge for his own safety (27–28), and to the need for two or three witnesses before a death penalty could be imposed (v. 30). A further stipulation is made in verses 31 and 32: no ransom, either for the murderer or for the manslayer, was to be countenanced (in contrast to other ancient laws outside Israel, where the custom of paying compensation for murder was widespread). There could be no cheap way out of the seriousness of such a situation, and there was to be no other alternative than those laid down in this legislation. The statements with which the chapter concludes (vv. 33–34) underline the extreme seriousness of the issue, involving the pollution and defilement of the land. What is in fact emphasized is the importance of the Old Testament concept of the sanctity of human life. The idea of the sanctity and sacredness of life, expressed consistently throughout the Old Testament, is based on the fact that man is made in the image of God. We read in Genesis 9:5–6, "Surely for your lifeblood I will demand a reckoning; from the hand of every beast I will require it, and from the hand of man. From the hand of every man's brother I will require the life of man. Whoever sheds man's blood, by man his blood shall be shed; for in the image of God He made man."

These words contain foundational principles, perennially valid. They do not lose their relevance when we turn to the New Testament era, since they are built into the very structure of society as the way in which God intends that His world should operate in any age. Not only is the seminal, and in some senses embryonic, teaching, both in Genesis and in these verses, reasserted and brought to full flowering in the apostolic preaching about the powers that be and the ordinances of the state as an essential part of God's government of the world, but also the prohibition against violating the sanctity of human life is carried forward into the inner region of the heart, forbidding us to hate, and recognizing that this also violates the sacredness of life.

The cities of refuge have always been taken to afford a type of Christ, down the ages of the church history, and the various constituent parts of the type are remarkable in the way they point to, and illustrate, the spiritual realities of the gospel in the New Testament.

For one thing, the distinction between the murderer and the manslayer has its parallel in New Testament theology, although some little thought has to be given to it to understand it properly and to appreciate it fully. There was no mercy and no provision for the murderer in the Old Testament: he was to be put to death, for his crime was deliberate and premeditated. The question that therefore arises is what parallel there is in the New Testament when we think of man the sinner. For is not our sin also deliberate? Ah, yes: but human sin is rarely purely deliberate; most often it is admixed with something else—ignorance, weakness, or frailty.

One recalls what Jesus said of those who crucified Him: "Father, forgive them, for they do not know what they do" (Luke 23:34). They knew very well, in one sense; but in another, their deliberate malice and hatred were mixed with blindness and ignorance. What the apostle Paul says of himself to Timothy, "I obtained mercy because I did it ignorantly in unbelief" (1 Tim. 1:13), is another instance of the same thought. His sin in persecuting the church of God was deliberate enough, but it was also mixed with something else: he had been duped by the god of this world. And for this reason, mercy was possible for him. It is only when sin is purely deliberate—and therefore demonic—that there is no possibility of forgiveness. Then, the point of no return has been passed; it is the sin unto death, the "presumptuous sin" of the Old Testament, the "great transgression," which banishes a man from the presence of God forever.

This point is well and profoundly made by the little girl in a Sunday school class who asked her teacher, "Why can Satan not be converted?" This is why: Satan's sin is purely spiritual and therefore wholly deliberate, with no redeeming or redeemable feature of weakness or frailty or ignorance. It is essentially implacable and unchangeable, and therefore ultimate destruction must be his fate.

To take the type and analogy afforded by the cities of refuge further, we may say that they "speak" of Christ as the sinner's refuge in whom alone there is shelter and protection from the avenger of blood. As sinners, we are liable to the condemnation of the law; we are "wanted" men, guilty before God, and there is no other provision for our safety but in the sheltering mercy of the Savior. This gives a rich and wonderful meaning to the words in Proverbs 18:10, "The name of the Lord is a strong tower; the righteous run to it and are safe." Here, once more, is the Old Testament fulfilling its role as God's "picture book," giving a wonderful illustration of the way of salvation, and showing clearly that "coming to Christ" is not merely a mental assent to facts and doctrines, but a movement toward Him, a betaking of oneself to Him. The picture of a frightened child running to its mother, finding safety, reassurance, and protection in her unfolding arms, illustrates this "movement" graphically: this is salvation, and there is no condemnation to those who are thus in Christ Jesus and who have fled for refuge to Him. The great evangelical hymns that have so enriched the worship and experience of God's people are eloquent of this idea: Toplady's

Rock of ages, cleft for me,
Let me hide myself in Thee

and Wesley's

Jesus, Lover of my soul,
Let me to Thy bosom fly

and Bonar's

I heard the voice of Jesus say,
"Come unto Me and rest"

express it perfectly, and in reading these hymns one is conscious of never being far away from the picture provided here.

We should note particularly the significance of the fact that the cities of refuge were *Levite cities* (v. 13) and that the Levites were set apart especially to be ministers of the Lord, and teachers of His law to the people. The association of ideas in this is impressive and remarkable, for the function of these cities of refuge matched that of the Levites themselves. Happy is the man, separated unto the ministry of the Word of the Lord, who is recognized as constituting and creating a "place" to which the burdened and the heavy-laden can turn in time of need and find refuge and rest. We should not forget, in this connection, our Lord's words to the disciples, "You are the light of the world. A city that is set on a hill cannot be hidden" (Matt. 5:14). Here is the idea of a city of refuge as the calling and function of the church; we, too, may fulfill this calling by being like the Levites, separated unto God for the gospel's sake.

We may well take the apostle Paul as an example in this: he was a man who knew something of the loneliness of the calling to the ministry. What a record of privation and suffering was his! He also had no inheritance, in the sense of earthly possessions. "As having nothing . . ." (2 Cor. 6:10)—this was the simple truth about him: he counted all things lost for Christ's sake, and it was because of this that he could go on to say, ". . . yet possessing all things; . . . as poor, yet making many rich." The privation, the costly loneliness, the being cut off from so much that makes life humanly speaking pleasant and attractive—all this bore fruit in a life that told, wherever it went, for God. This is how to be a city set on a hill!

DAUGHTERS' RIGHTS OF INHERITANCE

36:1 Now the chief fathers of the families of the children of Gilead the son of Machir, the son of Manasseh, of the families of the sons of Joseph, came
near and spoke before Moses and before the leaders,
the chief fathers of the children of Israel.
2 And they said: "The LORD commanded my lord
Moses to give the land as an inheritance by lot to the
children of Israel, and my lord was commanded by
the LORD to give the inheritance of our brother
Zelophehad to his daughters.
3 "Now if they are married to any of the sons of
the *other* tribes of the children of Israel, then their
inheritance will be taken from the inheritance of our
fathers, and it will be added to the inheritance of the
tribe into which they marry; so it will be taken from
the lot of our inheritance.
4 "And when the Jubilee of the children of Israel
comes, then their inheritance will be added to the
inheritance of the tribe into which they marry; so
their inheritance will be taken away from the inheritance of the tribe of our fathers."
5 Then Moses commanded the children of Israel
according to the word of the LORD, saying: "What the
tribe of the sons of Joseph speaks is right.
6 "This *is* what the LORD commands concerning
the daughters of Zelophehad, saying, 'Let them marry
whom they think best, but they may marry only
within the family of their father's tribe.'
7 "So the inheritance of the children of Israel
shall not change hands from tribe to tribe, for every
one of the children of Israel shall keep the inheritance of the tribe of his fathers.
8 "And every daughter who possesses an inheritance in any tribe of the children of Israel shall be
the wife of one of the family of her father's tribe,
so that the children of Israel each may possess the
inheritance of his fathers.
9 "Thus no inheritance shall change hands from
one tribe to another, but every tribe of the children
of Israel shall keep its own inheritance."

10 Just as the LORD commanded Moses, so did the daughters of Zelophehad;
11 for Mahlah, Tirzah, Hoglah, Milcah, and Noah, the daughters of Zelophehad, were married to the sons of their father's brothers.
12 They were married into the families of the children of Manasseh the son of Joseph, and their inheritance remained in the tribe of their father's family.
13 These *are* the commandments and the judgments which the LORD commanded the children of Israel by the hand of Moses in the plains of Moab by the Jordan, *across from* Jericho.

Num. 36:1–13

The background for an understanding of this final chapter of the Book of Numbers is found in 27:1–11 where, as we saw, an unprotected, defenseless family of daughters, who seemed to have no provision made for them within the known and declared legislation concerning inheritance in the Promised Land, appealed to the justice and mercy of God for recognition and redress, and their appeal was upheld and honored. Legislation was instituted, and it became law that the inheritance of territory due to those who died could and should indeed pass to their daughters. But as the legislation was instituted, accepted, and examined, it began to be seen that it could raise certain problems. What would happen if and when the daughters of Zelophehad, having received their inheritance, should marry? Was there not the possibility that the inheritance could pass out of the tribe by marriage, if they should marry outside their own people? This, of course, was a possibility, and the heads of the family concerned with the issue brought the matter before Moses, and before the Lord, for a judgment. And the judgment was that the daughters of Zelophehad were to marry only within their own tribe, so that marriage could not jeopardize their inheritance or take it out of the tribe, thus altering the divine provision and pattern for the division of the land among the twelve tribes. This judgment was dutifully complied with by Zelophehad's daughters, as verses 10–12 show, where a note of the marriages contracted by them concludes the chapter. The measure of the importance of this legislation is seen both in the repeated insistence on it in verses 7 and 9, and also in the fact that the chapter stands as an appendix to the earlier passage in 27:1–11.

One almost finds oneself wishing that the final chapter of the Book of Numbers had been more in the nature of a climax to the book; this, however, is something less than spiritual, and perhaps unrealistic. For life does not consist of climaxes; a great deal of it is very ordinary for most of us, and it is the whole point about this Old Testament history that it typifies and illustrates the normal spiritual life and pilgrimage of believers in the Christian way. Consequently, more important than spectacular climaxes at the end of a series of studies is the knowledge that guidance is given to God's people in matters that are basic to the practical life of discipleship. It is in this direction that the final chapter of the book has value for us.

The question of inheritance as such is not a living issue with us today in any sense that was important for the Israelites, but the story does point out some significant lessons. For one thing, here is an instance of what might be called marriage by the will and guidance of God. Some marriages would be suitable and right in such a context; others would be unsuitable and wrong. The lesson for us as Christians, therefore, concerns what relationships are unwise, unsuitable, and harmful for the furtherance of the purposes of God in our lives and in His kingdom. This is a subject in which not a little is said in the Scriptures, particularly in the New Testament, and it is one which we do well to consider with particular care. One of the important lessons we are to learn in this connection is that the prime consideration for the believer should be the kingdom of God and His purposes in the gospel, just as in this case the primary concern was the preservation of the divine pattern for the division of the land in Canaan. Nothing was to be allowed to interfere with *that,* and the marriage of Zelophehad's daughters was to fit in and harmonize with it accordingly.

The modern temper of thought is not sympathetic to such a viewpoint, however. Human considerations are always considered paramount. We are so man-centered in all our thinking, and even in religion man tends to be the center of things. God is made our lackey, to cater to our every caprice. It is perhaps significant, however, that this is also the day when marriage is regarded as a lottery, and the divorce rate high and rocketing, and the incidence of unhappy marriages very great indeed. The fallacy, of course, in modern thinking is to suppose that it is hard on people to make the divine purposes so primary in human life and relationships.

The truth is, no one ever suffers for putting God and His will first in his life. God is no man's debtor: "Those who honor Me, I will honor" (1 Sam. 2:30), He says. "Seek first the kingdom of God and His righteousness, and all these things shall be added to you" (Matt. 6:33), says Jesus. Not only so: when God's will is put first, He does not ride roughshod over our human needs and desires, but caters to them in the most remarkable way. That is how much He is no man's debtor! Here, then, is the first lesson: marriage must be in the will of God, and be such that it preserves and enhances, rather than hinders, the purposes of God in His work and in our lives. And when it is, it will enrich, not impoverish, our lives.

But it is possible to go further than this. In what he says in 2 Corinthians 6:14 the apostle Paul is blunt and unequivocal: "Do not be unequally yoked together with unbelievers. For what fellowship has righteousness with lawlessness? And what communication has light with darkness?" Here is something that can certainly hinder and frustrate the purposes of God both in His work and in the lives of His people. It is in the highest degree tragic that believers should marry those who in the very nature of the case *cannot* share their deepest and most cherished experiences, and it is almost inevitable that in such a union the believer will be dragged down and lose the fine edge of his consecration and devotion to the Lord.

This kind of incompatibility is incompatibility indeed, and it will prove fatal to any chance of making a real success of marriage. For two such people will always necessarily be moving and pulling in opposite directions. And there is no warrant given in Scripture to make us suppose that the believer will win the unbeliever to Christ, although this is fondly and optimistically assumed. Experience proves otherwise (the promise in 2 Cor. 7:14 is made to a believer who has become a believer after marriage, and stands in an entirely different category).

Such a situation, however, does not properly find a foreshadowing in the story of the daughters of Zelophehad, for the men of other tribes whom they were forbidden to marry were also of Israel, and therefore within the fellowship of the faith. They were not unbelievers, but believers. The real lesson, therefore, is that even within the fold of the Christian church it does not inevitably follow that because the persons concerned are both believers it is therefore necessarily right for them to marry. There are other factors involved, and due consideration must be given to them.

A believer, for example, may wish to marry another believer; this is right in principle, but it is not necessarily right for him to marry that particular believer simply because she is a believer. The fact of her faith does not of itself "qualify" her and make her the right person. Perhaps the real application of this Old Testament story, in which Zelophehad's daughters were to marry only within their own tribe, is that believers should marry (in the faith) only within the limits of the kind of group in which they share a true, spiritual, cultural, and temperamental affinity.

Some idea of the importance of this kind of harmony may be gathered from the extreme care with which adoption societies seek to "match" the children who are to be adopted with the prospective adoptive parents. All this effort is to ensure, as far as is humanly possible, that the child gets the optimum chance to grow up in the kind of home in which in other happier circumstances it would have been brought up. It could be put this way: where two believers cannot, because of the conflict of cultural, spiritual, emotional, or temperamental interests, share in a common life in the things of God, these factors constitute a barrier to successful and advisable marriage. The phrase used in the Bible is "a helper comparable" (Gen. 2:18)—taken literally, that means the partner must be a help spiritually and otherwise, to enable one to be all one can be and is meant to be, in the full flowering of personality; the partner must be *comparable* (or suitable), that is, a match, not a mis-match.

Affinity of interest, however, is not the same as *identity* of interest, and it is not identity that is the norm so much as compatibility. For example, the fact that one partner loves music and the other is tone deaf would not necessarily, of itself, be an insurmountable barrier either to human happiness or to the furtherance of the interests of the kingdom—although one could perhaps imagine some rather trying situations because of this! But there can be insurmountable barriers when there is the constitutional impossibility of true understanding between two people. When this is so, the fact that they are both genuine and sincere believers can never make it right for them to marry. It would be inadvisable for them to do so. In situations like these, the value of the counsel of some wise and mature older Christian can be very great indeed. For there is a real blind spot here in most people: emotional involvement is a great distorting force for most of us, and few can see or think straight in such situations, without help. How wise, and far-seeing, is the teaching of Scripture in this realm, when properly understood!

NOTES

1. Gordon J. Wenham, *Numbers,* Tyndale Old Testament Commentaries (Leicester: Inter-Varsity Press, 1981), p. 213, maintains that throughout the story implicit allusions are found to the events some forty years earlier at Kadesh, and says, in an interesting footnote: "Outside verses 6–15 where the parallels with Nu. 13–14 are obvious, other terms in chapter 32 apparently alluding to the spy story include 'place' (1; cf. 14:40), 'smite' (4; cf. 14:45), 'pass over' (21, 27, 29, 30; cf. 13:32; 14:7, 41), 'little ones' (16, 17, 24, 26; cf. 14:3, 31), 'inhabitants of the land' (17; cf. 14:14), 'fortified cities' (17, 36; cf. 13:19), 'return' (18, 22; cf. 13:25; 14:36), 'drive out' (21, 39; cf. 14:12, 24), as well as more common terms such as 'land', 'congregation', etc."

2. L. Elliott Binns, *The Book of Numbers* (London: Methuen & Co., Ltd., 1927), p. 217.

3. Wenham, *Numbers,* p. 217.

4. For a detailed and valuable excursus on this and other geographical questions, see Wenham, *Numbers,* pp. 220–29, especially pp. 224–27.

5. Binns, *Numbers,* p. 218.

6. Wenham, *Numbers,* p. 286.

7. G. B. Gray, *A Critical and Exegetical Commentary on Numbers,* International Critical Commentary (Edinburgh: T. & T. Clark, 1903), p. 443.

8. Wenham, *Numbers,* p. 217.

9. F. B. Meyer, *Our Daily Homily* (London: Marshall, Morgan and Scott, 1951), 1:150.

10. Wenham, *Numbers,* p. 231.

11. Binns, *Numbers.*

12. Binns, *Numbers,* p. 226.
Gray, *Numbers,* p. 453.
Snaith, *Century Bible,* p. 340. See note 13 for full information.

13. N. H. Snaith, *The Century Bible, Leviticus and Numbers* (London: Thomas Nelson Printers, Ltd., 1967), p. 340, gives as an exception to this "a short period when Hezekiah revolted against the Babylonian supremacy and imprisoned Padi of Ekron in Jerusalem." This is nowhere mentioned in Scripture, but T. C. Mitchell, in an article on "Ekron" in *The New Bible*

Dictionary (IVF 1942), p. 355, identifies this information as being found in the Taylor Prism ii.69–iii.11; and the Chicago Prism ii.73–iii.17.

14. Binns, *Numbers,* p. 226.

15. Carl L. Keil and Franz Delitzsch, *Numbers,* Commentary on the Old Testament, vol. 3 (Grand Rapids: Wm. B. Eerdmans, repr. 1971), pp. 256–57.

16. Gray, *Numbers,* p. 461.

17. J. A. Thompson, *New Bible Commentary,* Revised (London: Inter-Varsity Press, 1970), p. 155.

18. Wenham, *Numbers,* p. 232.

19. Ibid., p. 234.

20. Ibid., p. 236.

21. Martin Noth, *Numbers: A Commentary,* Old Testament Library (London: SCM Press, 1970), p. 255.

22. Wenham, *Numbers,* p. 238. "That it was the high priest's death, not the exile of the manslaughterer, that atoned is confirmed by the mishnaic dictate, 'If after the slayer has been sentenced as an accidental homicide the high priest dies, he need not go into exile' and the talmudic comment thereon, 'But is it not the exile that expiates? It is not exile that expiates, but the death of the high priest.'"

EPILOGUE

"Written for Our Admonition"

10:1 Moreover, brethren, I do not want you to be unaware that all our fathers were under the cloud, all passed through the sea,

2 all were baptized into Moses in the cloud and in the sea,

3 all ate the same spiritual food,

4 and all drank the same spiritual drink. For they drank of that spiritual Rock that followed them, and that Rock was Christ.

5 But with most of them God was not well pleased, for *their bodies* were scattered in the wilderness.

6 Now these things became our examples to the intent that we should not lust after evil things as they also lusted.

7 And do not become idolaters as *were* some of them. As it is written, *"The people sat down to eat and drink, and rose up to play."*

8 Nor let us commit sexual immorality, as some of them did, and in one day twenty-three thousand fell;

9 nor let us tempt Christ, as some of them also tempted, and were destroyed by serpents;

10 nor complain, as some of them also complained, and were destroyed by the destroyer.

11 Now all these things happened to them as examples, and they were written for our admonition, upon whom the ends of the ages have come.

12 Therefore let him who thinks he stands take heed lest he fall.

13 No temptation has overtaken you except such as is common to man; but God *is* faithful, who will not allow you to be tempted beyond what you are

> able, but with the temptation will also make the way
> of escape, that you may be able to bear it.
>
> *1 Cor. 10:1–13*

We end our study of the Book of Numbers as we began, with a reference to the apostle Paul's words to the Corinthians, in one of the more important passages of the New Testament, in the definitive interpretation it puts upon the Old Testament history of the people of God and the kind of spiritual application that history has for the church. It is heightened and confirmed by the fact that it was written to a church—Corinth—in which the spiritual problems that beset the Israelites were evidently proving a hazard and a danger to its spiritual life. It is significant that the chapter is prefaced by a solemn word about the danger of becoming "disqualified" (1 Cor. 9:27)—this is what happened to that unfortunate generation of Israelites after Kadesh Barnea, and there is little doubt that this is why Paul speaks as he does in this chapter. The lesson is pointed out in verse 11—"*. . . these things were written for our admonition,*" and we have the best of all possible assurances in verse 13 about the faithfulness of God and His provision of a way of escape from temptation. Israel need not have failed in her calling, *nor need we!* His grace is sufficient to see us through and make us more than conquerors.

Bibliography

Binns, L. Elliott. *The Book of Numbers.* London: Methuen & Co., Ltd., 1927.
Bonar, Andrew A. *Commentary on Leviticus.* London: Nisbet & Co., 1861.
Brunner, Emil. *The Mediator.* London: Lutterworth Press, 1934.
———. *The Christian Doctrine of Creation and Redemption.* Dogmatics, vol. 2. London: Lutterworth Press, 1952.
Calvin, John. *Commentary on Harmony of Matthew, Mark and Luke, vol 2.* London: Calvin Translation Society, 1845.
———. *Harmony of the Pentateuch,* vol. 1.
Chadwick, Samuel. *Humanity and God.* The Expositor's Library. London: Hodder and Stoughton, n.d.
Denney, James. *The Way Everlasting.* London: Hodder and Stoughton, 1911.
Ellicott, C. J. *Leviticus.* An Old Testament Commentary for English Readers. London: Cassell & Co., Ltd., 1897.
Elliot, Elisabeth. *The Shadow of the Almighty.* London: S.T.L. Publications.
Gray, G. B. *A Critical and Exegetical Commentary on Numbers.* International Critical Commentary. Edinburgh: T. & T. Clark, 1903.
Henry, Matthew. *Genesis-Deuteronomy,* Commentary on the Whole Bible, vol 1. Old Tappan, N.J.: Fleming H. Revell.
Keil, Carl L. and Franz Delitzsch. *Numbers.* Commentary on the Old Testament, vol. 3. Grand Rapids: Wm. B. Eerdmans, 1971. Reprint.
Lewis, C. S. *The Lion, the Witch, and the Wardrobe.* London: Geoffrey Bles.
———. *Reflections on the Psalms.* London: Geoffrey Bles, 1958.
Maclaren, Alexander. *Exodus.* Expositions of Holy Scripture. London: Hodder and Stoughton, 1907.
MacRae, A. A. *New Bible Commentary.* London: Inter-Varsity Press, 1953.
Meyer, F. B. *Our Daily Homily.* London: Marshall, Morgan and Scott, 1951.
Noth, Martin. *Numbers: A Commentary.* Old Testament Library. London: SCM Press, 1968.
Philip, George. *Sandyford Henderson Congregational Record. Glasgow,* 1978.
Sayce, A. H. *The Early History of the Hebrews.* London: Rivingtons, 1891.
Snaith, N. H. *Leviticus and Numbers.* New Century Bible. London: Thomas Nelson Printers, Ltd., 1967.

Stewart, James S. *Heralds of God.* London: Hodder and Stoughton, 1946.

Sturdy, J. *Numbers.* The Cambridge Bible Commentary. Cambridge: Cambridge University Press, 1976.

Thompson, J. A. *New Bible Commentary.* Revised. London: Inter-Varsity Press, 1970.

Wenham, Gordon J. *Numbers.* Tyndale Old Testament Commentaries. Leicester: Inter-Varsity Press, 1981.

The Westminister Confession of Faith, 1647.

Young, E. J. *An Introduction to the Old Testament.* Wheaton, Ill.: Tyndale Press, 1949.